Using STEM-Focused Teacher Preparation Programs to Reimagine Elementary Education

Emily Cayton
Campbell University, USA

Miriam Sanders
Texas A&M University, USA

John A. Williams
Texas A&M University, USA

A volume in the Advances in Early Childhood and K-12 Education (AECKE) Book Series

Published in the United States of America by
IGI Global
Information Science Reference (an imprint of IGI Global)
701 E. Chocolate Avenue
Hershey PA, USA 17033
Tel: 717-533-8845
Fax: 717-533-8661
E-mail: cust@igi-global.com
Web site: http://www.igi-global.com

Copyright © 2024 by IGI Global. All rights reserved. No part of this publication may be reproduced, stored or distributed in any form or by any means, electronic or mechanical, including photocopying, without written permission from the publisher.
Product or company names used in this set are for identification purposes only. Inclusion of the names of the products or companies does not indicate a claim of ownership by IGI Global of the trademark or registered trademark.

Library of Congress Cataloging-in-Publication Data

Names: Cayton, Emily, editor. | Sanders, Miriam, editor. | Williams, John A., editor.
Title: Using STEM-focused teacher preparation programs to reimagine elementary education / Emily Cayton, Miriam Sanders, and John A. Williams, Editor.
Description: Hershey, PA : Information Science Reference, [2024] | Includes bibliographical references and index. | Summary: "There has been an increasing issue in STEM education as many lack the interest and knowledge in STEM disciplines and fields. It may be that exposure to STEM concepts and skills does not begin early enough. Indeed, most programs target older students. Given the high demand for STEM workers, and the projected growth of STEM fields (Washington, D.C., 2011), it is increasingly important to expose students to STEM education beginning as early as elementary school. Beginning in high school may be too late. If students are not exposed to STEM related activities and instruction in their early school years, they may never have the opportunity to gain skills and interest that allow them to be successful later. If teachers are able to expose students to STEM related curriculum, this exposure could potentially have the ability to spark a greater interest for math and science in students while also motivating them to continue to seek STEM-related opportunities. Clearly, part of the problem is in teacher education. Some K-6 programs are not preparing teacher candidates adequately for STEM content or skills, especially in the area of engineering (DiFrancesca, Lee & McIntyre 2014). Thus, while there is a noticeable disconnect between interest in STEM careers and early exposure to STEM education (Drew, 2015). Implementing these disciplines and practices throughout elementary education programs could result in more exposure for K-6 students. This book would seek to collect anecdotal stories of how elementary education programs have altered their content offerings, filed experiences, curriculum and the like to expand their teacher candidates' knowledge and exposure to STEM discplines and fields"-- Provided by publisher.
Identifiers: LCCN 2022039923 (print) | LCCN 2022039924 (ebook) | ISBN 9781668459393 (hardcover) | ISBN 9781668459430 (paperback) | ISBN 9781668459409 (ebook)
Subjects: LCSH: Elementary school teachers--Training of. | Science--Study and teaching (Elementary) | Technology--Study and teaching (Elementary) | Education, Elementary--Aims and objectives. | Educational change.
Classification: LCC LB1715 .U72 2023 (print) | LCC LB1715 (ebook) | DDC 372.11--dc23/eng/20220909
LC record available at https://lccn.loc.gov/2022039923
LC ebook record available at https://lccn.loc.gov/2022039924

This book is published in the IGI Global book series Advances in Early Childhood and K-12 Education (AECKE) (ISSN: 2329-5929; eISSN: 2329-5937)

British Cataloguing in Publication Data
A Cataloguing in Publication record for this book is available from the British Library.

All work contributed to this book is new, previously-unpublished material.
The views expressed in this book are those of the authors, but not necessarily of the publisher.

For electronic access to this publication, please contact: eresources@igi-global.com.

Advances in Early Childhood and K-12 Education (AECKE) Book Series

Jared Keengwe
University of North Dakota, USA

ISSN:2329-5929
EISSN:2329-5937

MISSION

Early childhood and K-12 education is always evolving as new methods and tools are developed through which to shape the minds of today's youth. Globally, educational approaches vary allowing for new discussions on the best methods to not only educate, but also measure and analyze the learning process as well as an individual's intellectual development. New research in these fields is necessary to improve the current state of education and ensure that future generations are presented with quality learning opportunities.

The **Advances in Early Childhood and K-12 Education (AECKE)** series aims to present the latest research on trends, pedagogies, tools, and methodologies regarding all facets of early childhood and K-12 education.

COVERAGE

- Pedagogy
- Urban K-12 Education
- Head Start and Pre-K Programs
- Poverty and Education
- Reading and Writing
- Curriculum Development
- STEM Education
- Early Childhood Education
- K-12 Education
- Special Education

IGI Global is currently accepting manuscripts for publication within this series. To submit a proposal for a volume in this series, please contact our Acquisition Editors at Acquisitions@igi-global.com or visit: http://www.igi-global.com/publish/.

The Advances in Early Childhood and K-12 Education (AECKE) Book Series (ISSN 2329-5929) is published by IGI Global, 701 E. Chocolate Avenue, Hershey, PA 17033-1240, USA, www.igi-global.com. This series is composed of titles available for purchase individually; each title is edited to be contextually exclusive from any other title within the series. For pricing and ordering information please visit http://www.igi-global.com/book-series/advances-early-childhood-education/76699. Postmaster: Send all address changes to above address. Copyright © 2024 IGI Global. All rights, including translation in other languages reserved by the publisher. No part of this series may be reproduced or used in any form or by any means – graphics, electronic, or mechanical, including photocopying, recording, taping, or information and retrieval systems – without written permission from the publisher, except for non commercial, educational use, including classroom teaching purposes. The views expressed in this series are those of the authors, but not necessarily of IGI Global.

Titles in this Series

For a list of additional titles in this series, please visit: http://www.igi-global.com/book-series/

Emergent Practices of Learning Analytics in K-12 Classrooms
Nurdan Kavaklı Ulutaş (Izmir Demokrasi University, Turkey) and Devrim Höl (Pamukkale University, Turkey)
Information Science Reference • © 2024 • 268pp • H/C (ISBN: 9798369300664) • US $235.00

PK-12 Professionals' Narratives of Working as Advocates Impacting Today's Schools
Patrick S. De Walt (California State University, Fresno, USA) and Dara N. Nix-Stevenson (Sincecombahee Educational Consulting, USA)
Information Science Reference • © 2024 • 220pp • H/C (ISBN: 9781668492369) • US $225.00

Perspectives on Empowering Intergenerational Relations in Educational Organizations
Soner Polat (Kocaeli University, Turkey) and Çağlar Çelik (Ministry of National Education, Turkey)
Information Science Reference • © 2023 • 388pp • H/C (ISBN: 9781668488881) • US $230.00

Mindful Listening Instruction in the Elementary Classroom Authentic Strategies Using Picturebooks
Donna Jessie Fortune (Virginia Tech, USA) and Mary Alice Barksdale (Independent Researcher, USA)
Information Science Reference • © 2023 • 287pp • H/C (ISBN: 9781668450772) • US $215.00

Meaningful and Active Family Engagement IEP, Transition and Technology Integration in Special Education
Millicent M. Musyoka (Lamar University, USA) and Guofeng Shen (University of Northern Colorado, USA)
Information Science Reference • © 2023 • 394pp • H/C (ISBN: 9798369313848) • US $230.00

701 East Chocolate Avenue, Hershey, PA 17033, USA
Tel: 717-533-8845 x100 • Fax: 717-533-8661
E-Mail: cust@igi-global.com • www.igi-global.com

Table of Contents

Preface xiv

Chapter 1
Preparing Elementary Pre-Service Teachers to Be Effective STEM Teachers 1
    Robert John Ceglie, Independent Researcher, USA

Chapter 2
"What Are We Missing?": Examining Culturally Relevant Teaching Practices
in STEM Educator Preparation Programs 25
    Miriam Sanders, Texas A&M University, USA
    Maiya Turner, Texas A&M University, USA
    John A. Williams, Texas A&M University, USA

Chapter 3
Enhancing Elementary Teacher Preparation: The Vital Role of STEM-
Integrated Experiences in Oman 50
    Mohamed A. Shahat, Sultan Qaboos University, Oman & Aswan
        University, Egypt
    Khalsa H. Al Bahri, Ministry of Education, Oman
    Sulaiman M. Al-Balushi, Sultan Qaboos University, Oman

Chapter 4
(Re)Imagining an Elementary Preservice Science Methods Course as
Inquiry-Based 68
    Sandy White Watson, University of Louisiana at Monroe, USA

Chapter 5
Supporting Beginning Teachers in STEM Content Areas Through Self-Directed Learning and Micro-Credentials 86
    Erin K. West, Appalachian State University, USA
    Rachel Nelson, Appalachian State University, USA
    Katherine Chesnutt, Appalachian State University, USA
    James Beeler, Appalachian State University, USA

Chapter 6
Finding Success in Adapting Repeated Microteaching Rehearsals (RMTR) for an Online Science Methods Course..111
    Franklin S. Allaire, University of Houston-Downtown, USA

Chapter 7
Promoting Conceptual Understanding Through Authentic Mathematics Instruction in Virtual Environments: More Than a Game 130
    Elizabeth Allison, Western Governors University, USA
    Megan Rzyski, Western Governors University, USA
    Jen Wallender, Western Governors University, USA
    Carol PeQueen, Western Governors University, USA
    Kristie Remaly, Western Governors University, USA
    M. Amanda Kain, Western Governors University, USA
    Adam Hiebel, Western Governors University, USA

Chapter 8
The Benefits of Wolfram Alpha Tool Applied to Interactive Learning Environments in STEM Education 158
    Vandeir Vioti dos Santos, Mackenzie Presbyterian University, Brazil
    Pollyana Notargiacomo, Universidade Presbiteriana Mackenzie, Brazil

Chapter 9
Smartphone and STEM...196
    Alessio Drivet, Geogebra Institute of Turin, Italy

Chapter 10
NSF-Funded Exploratory Study: Lessons Learned 231
    Eleanor Armour-Thomas, Queens College of the City University of New York, USA

Chapter 11
Integrating English Language Arts and Science: Promising Practices for
Undergraduate Elementary Teacher Licensure Candidates 251
    Kim Brown, University of North Carolina at Asheville, USA

Chapter 12
Fostering Inclusivity: Nurturing Diversity Within Elementary STEM Teacher
Preparation Programs 286
    Surjit Singha, Kristu Jayanti College (Autonomous), India

Compilation of References 312

About the Contributors 354

Index 360

Detailed Table of Contents

Preface xiv

Chapter 1
Preparing Elementary Pre-Service Teachers to Be Effective STEM Teachers 1
   Robert John Ceglie, Independent Researcher, USA

Nelson Mandela (1990) stated "[e]ducation is the most powerful weapon which you can use to change the world." This has never been truer as we live in a world in need of strong teachers. We live in a world that underappreciates teachers and their role in educating the next generation often goes unnoticed. Teaching children to become literate in math and science is a concern as these disciplines can lead to increased employment opportunities, higher pay, and a higher quality of life. Having a scientifically literate citizenship is critical to fostering innovation, improving the quality of life, and solving crises such as pandemics and climate change. Unfortunately, interest and motivation in STEM disciplines often decline after early grades which illustrates the important role that these teachers have in math and science education. This chapter combines research-based practices and activities that the author has used to promote STEM learning in preservice teachers. It combines these with narratives from former students who add evidence for their value.

Chapter 2
"What Are We Missing?": Examining Culturally Relevant Teaching Practices
in STEM Educator Preparation Programs 25
   Miriam Sanders, Texas A&M University, USA
   Maiya Turner, Texas A&M University, USA
   John A. Williams, Texas A&M University, USA

The STEM field now faces a two-fold crisis of students' waning interest and underrepresentation of marginalized populations such as People of Color and women contrary to the high demand for STEM-qualified professionals. STEM subjects such as mathematics have been viewed as a critical filter for high-status, high-salary careers. Thus, it is essential to examine EPP STEM methods curriculum as culturally relevant pedagogy that has been proven to enhance learning outcomes, pique and retain interest, and foster confidence in students from underrepresented groups and all students. Through a content analysis, we examine course descriptions from top-ranked teacher-training universities in the United States to determine the presence or lack of training that STEM PSTs receive in their respective EPPs regarding culturally responsive teaching.

Chapter 3
Enhancing Elementary Teacher Preparation: The Vital Role of STEM-
Integrated Experiences in Oman..50
    Mohamed A. Shahat, Sultan Qaboos University, Oman & Aswan
        University, Egypt
    Khalsa H. Al Bahri, Ministry of Education, Oman
    Sulaiman M. Al-Balushi, Sultan Qaboos University, Oman

This chapter highlights the importance of integrating STEM (science, technology, engineering, and mathematics) into teacher education to equip educators with the tools needed for effective teaching in contemporary STEM fields. The chapter strongly emphasizes the necessity of continuous professional development, innovative curriculum design, and the creation of supportive learning environments. Furthermore, it advocates for ongoing research to identify and implement effective STEM teaching strategies that engage students effectively. In conclusion, this chapter underscores Oman's commitment to STEM education as a cornerstone for preparing its citizens to face future challenges and seize opportunities. Oman's initiatives serve as an inspiring example for other nations seeking to enhance their own STEM educational frameworks and prepare their youth for the demands of tomorrow.

Chapter 4
(Re)Imagining an Elementary Preservice Science Methods Course as
Inquiry-Based..68
    Sandy White Watson, University of Louisiana at Monroe, USA

In response to research findings that elementary teachers are underprepared to teach science due to lack of both science content knowledge (SCK) and science pedagogical knowledge (SPK), the author restructured a teacher-centered, pedagogically focused elementary science methods course into one in which SCK and SPK were the primary foci of the class. SCK was provided via explanations that occurred after in-class and extended inquiry-based investigations, during active learning experiences, and after assigned readings and associated discussions, while SPK was provided through observations and analyses of practicing elementary science teachers teaching, modeling of strategies by the instructor, and development and delivery of two 5E lesson plans in area elementary school settings, all approaches deemed effective in increasing elementary preservice teachers' science pedagogical knowledge.

Chapter 5
Supporting Beginning Teachers in STEM Content Areas Through Self-Directed Learning and Micro-Credentials 86
    Erin K. West, Appalachian State University, USA
    Rachel Nelson, Appalachian State University, USA
    Katherine Chesnutt, Appalachian State University, USA
    James Beeler, Appalachian State University, USA

North Carolina teachers provide an important learning foundation for students. As teacher candidates complete their education requirements and begin working in schools, they are faced with many challenges. This discussion focuses on beginning teachers (BTs), or teachers with less than three years of teaching experience. After leaving their educator preparation programs (EPPs), BTs are required to complete onboarding programs and professional development plans while simultaneously learning to manage their daily workloads, plan and assess lessons, and manage their classroom. This can feel overwhelming for many BTs and may contribute to an early exit from the teaching profession. According to the North Carolina Department of Public Instruction (NCDPI) BTs in the state are much more likely to leave the classroom as compared to teachers that are not BTs, with the attrition rates for BTs and non BTs reported as 12.71% and 6.80%, respectively (NCDPI, 2023).

Chapter 6
Finding Success in Adapting Repeated Microteaching Rehearsals (RMTR) for an Online Science Methods Course... 111
    Franklin S. Allaire, University of Houston-Downtown, USA

In February/March 2020, postsecondary educators worldwide were required to suddenly shift from face-to-face to online instruction due to the COVID-19 pandemic. For teacher educators, this meant reimagining how to enact core pedagogical strategies, such as teaching rehearsals for online instruction. This chapter shares my experiences of integrating repeated microteaching rehearsals (RMTR) into my elementary science methods courses before the COVID-19 pandemic to disastrous results. Then, adapting RMTR for an online learning environment due to the rapid shift from face-to-face to online learning during the pandemic and its successful integration as an online practice teaching strategy. This chapter also shares how RMTR was and continues to be implemented in my post-pandemic science methods course and the lessons learned along the way.

Chapter 7
Promoting Conceptual Understanding Through Authentic Mathematics
Instruction in Virtual Environments: More Than a Game 130
    Elizabeth Allison, Western Governors University, USA
    Megan Rzyski, Western Governors University, USA
    Jen Wallender, Western Governors University, USA
    Carol PeQueen, Western Governors University, USA
    Kristie Remaly, Western Governors University, USA
    M. Amanda Kain, Western Governors University, USA
    Adam Hiebel, Western Governors University, USA

Delivering effective online instruction to preservice teacher candidates is important to ensure teachers are prepared for K–12 classrooms. Formal education has been reimagined several times throughout history, with both K–12 and higher education settings seeing significant changes in recent decades. Additionally, elementary teachers and preservice teacher candidates often view mathematics as only facts and procedures for memorization—a belief that infiltrates their instructional practices. Colleges that prepare teacher candidates must respond to this misconception. This chapter explores strategies one online university used to help preservice teacher candidates maximize student success by implementing live webinars called Put It into Practice (PiiP). During these sessions, preservice teachers explore online tools that can be used in the K–12 classroom to conceptualize math concepts. The webinars challenge preservice teachers to analyze how to teach math in today's classroom, while modeling the key prerequisite of establishing a safe psychological environment conducive to learning.

Chapter 8
The Benefits of Wolfram Alpha Tool Applied to Interactive Learning
Environments in STEM Education 158
    Vandeir Vioti dos Santos, Mackenzie Presbyterian University, Brazil
    Pollyana Notargiacomo, Universidade Presbiteriana Mackenzie, Brazil

The present chapter propose aims to show the benefits of using an interactive learning environment as a way of promoting greater engagement and consequently improving student performance. In this chapter, the benefits of using the Wolfram Alpha tool applied to interactive learning environments in STEM education will be shown. The quantitative and qualitative results obtained during the research showed the students' preference for classes in which the Wolfram Alpha tool was used allied to traditional teaching. Regarding performance, research has shown that these classes can increase students' academic performance by up to 35%. A tutorial about how to teach the students using the Wolfram Alpha tool will be shown.

Chapter 9
Smartphone and STEM 196
   Alessio Drivet, Geogebra Institute of Turin, Italy

Covid-19 has also had a significant impact on schools, the use of distance learning has raised questions already present, in particular with respect to the meaning of tools and technologies. Leaving aside the aspects related to the use of the network and those of communication, the authors want to provide a brief overview of the fundamental issues related to the use of a smartphone for STEM teaching. A theme that sees two opposing positions (pros and cons) colliding, often unavailable for discussion and dialogue. Without taking a position, the text tackles the problem from three points of view: the hardware, the apps, and some possible activities that can be associated with the main functions activated by the students.

Chapter 10
NSF-Funded Exploratory Study: Lessons Learned 231
   Eleanor Armour-Thomas, Queens College of the City University of New York, USA

In this NSF-funded exploratory study the author examined the impact of professional development on NGSS teaching of administrator-selected teachers in a large, urban, public school district in the United States. Currently, the research literature on professional development about NGSS in early grades about NGSS is sparce. Thus, the purpose of the study was to develop and implement a professional development program for Early Childhood and Elementary in-service teachers with the aim of understanding its impact on their knowledge for NGSS teaching and classroom practice. Findings from self-reports revealed improvement in teachers' knowledge for NGSS teaching particularly in the domains of lesson planning, classroom teaching, and classroom assessment. Lessons learned from the exploratory study for future professional development in professional development for NGSS teaching and learning are discussed.

Chapter 11
Integrating English Language Arts and Science: Promising Practices for
Undergraduate Elementary Teacher Licensure Candidates 251
   Kim Brown, University of North Carolina at Asheville, USA

The theory of Pragmatism naturally gives way to the concept of integrated and hands-on teaching methodologies. Teacher training programs grounded in the liberal arts are prime spaces for pre-service elementary teachers to learn about curricular integration. Pedagogy surrounding the integration of science and English language arts is particularly pertinent for today's classrooms. This chapter provides a description of how an elementary education science methods course was revised to include teaching methods for instructing teacher licensure candidates to teach their future students using an integrated and hands-on approach. Instructor lecture outlines and lab packets which include interactive class activities, instructions for teaching essential Science content, instructions for utilizing effective English Language Arts strategies for facilitating student comprehension and concept development, and inclusion of high-quality texts from the Common Core Exemplary Text list are provided.

Chapter 12
Fostering Inclusivity: Nurturing Diversity Within Elementary STEM Teacher Preparation Programs 286
    Surjit Singha, Kristu Jayanti College (Autonomous), India

This chapter examines the profound impact of inclusivity on STEM teacher preparation programs for elementary education, emphasizing its critical role in enhancing STEM instruction. Inclusivity underscores the importance of establishing thriving learning environments encompassing abilities, race, gender, and socioeconomic status. Practical recommendations, theoretical foundations, and a current landscape analysis underscore inclusivity's critical importance when equipping educators for diverse classrooms. The conclusion emphasizes the significance of diversity in moulding culturally competent and socially conscious STEM educators. While recognizing enduring obstacles, it foresees encouraging developments in technological integration and comprehensive diversity awareness. Continuous research is critical to assessing the effectiveness of inclusivity initiatives, ascertaining their enduring consequences, and enhancing pedagogical methodologies. To advance STEM education in the future, it is imperative to prioritize evidence-based practices, adaptability, and inclusivity.

Compilation of References 312

About the Contributors 354

Index 360

Preface

STEM education stands at the nexus of opportunity and necessity in our modern world. The growing demand for skilled professionals in science, technology, engineering, and mathematics (STEM) fields has underscored a critical gap in our education system. This book emerges as a response to this pressing need—to transform elementary education and better prepare our teachers for the challenges and opportunities of tomorrow.

Using STEM-Focused Teacher Preparation Programs to Reimagine Elementary Education encapsulates a collective effort by educators, scholars, and professionals deeply invested in reshaping the landscape of teacher preparation. Emily Cayton, Miriam Sanders, and John A. Williams, III, the editors of this volume, have meticulously curated a compendium of insights, anecdotes, and best practices that illuminate the path toward a more robust, integrated, effective, and inclusive STEM education.

The seeds of this endeavor were sown in recognition of a crucial issue: the dearth of interest and proficiency in STEM subjects among students, coupled with an inadequate preparation of educators in these disciplines. Traditional teacher preparation programs often fall short in equipping future educators with the requisite knowledge and skills to instill a passion for STEM among our youngest learners. This book aims to change that narrative and solidify approaches that sustain the current and next generation of learners.

Drawing from the experiences of pioneering elementary education programs, this volume is tailored for educator preparation professionals seeking to revolutionize their approach. It serves as a guiding beacon, offering a treasure trove of innovative strategies, success stories, and practical insights that can catalyze the transformation of elementary teacher education programs into robust hubs of STEM excellence.

From reimagining content offerings and integrating STEM experiences to forging vital partnerships with communities, businesses, and school districts, the chapters within this book traverse a rich terrain. They explore diverse avenues such as leveraging technology, enhancing clinical field experiences, fostering diversity, securing grant funding, and nurturing collaborative initiatives between university colleges.

Preface

Each chapter in this compendium encapsulates a distinct facet of the overarching endeavor to infuse STEM into elementary education preparation programs. Through these anecdotes, our aim is to inspire, guide, and empower fellow educators on the path to creating vibrant, impactful, and inclusive STEM-focused teacher education programs.

The journey toward a more adept and inspired cadre of educators primed to cultivate STEM curiosity and proficiency among elementary students is an ongoing pursuit. As editors, we aspire for this book to serve as a catalyst, sparking dialogue, innovation, and action in the realm of educator preparation.

We extend our deepest gratitude to the contributors whose experiences and wisdom enrich the pages of this volume. It is our sincere hope that *Using STEM-Focused Teacher Preparation Programs to Reimagine Elementary Education* ignites a transformative spark, illuminating the way forward in shaping a brighter, more STEM-enriched future for educators and students alike.

ORGANIZATION OF THE BOOK

Chapter 1: "Preparing Elementary Pre-Service Teachers to be Effective STEM Teachers" by Robert Ceglie In this chapter, Robert Ceglie draws inspiration from Nelson Mandela's assertion that education is a powerful tool for changing the world. Ceglie emphasizes the crucial role of elementary teachers in shaping the future by instilling scientific literacy in students. The chapter combines research-based practices and activities, providing insights into STEM learning for pre-service teachers. Personal narratives from former students add valuable evidence to the effectiveness of these practices.

Chapter 2: "What Are We Missing?": Examining Culturally Relevant Teaching Practices in STEM Educator Preparation Programs" by Miriam Sanders, Maiya Turner, and John A. Williams, III, address the dual challenge faced by the STEM field – waning student interest and underrepresentation of marginalized groups. The chapter explores the importance of culturally responsive teaching in STEM education, examining curriculum practices in teacher-training universities through content analysis. The authors advocate for culturally relevant pedagogy to enhance learning outcomes, retain interest, and boost confidence, particularly among underrepresented groups.

Chapter 3: "Enhancing Elementary Teacher Preparation: The Vital Role of STEM-Integrated Experiences in Oman" by Mohamed Shahat, Khalsa Al Bahri, Sulaiman Al-Balushi Mohamed Shahat, Khalsa Al Bahri, and Sulaiman Al-Balushi underscore the significance of integrating STEM into teacher education in Oman. The chapter emphasizes continuous professional development, innovative curriculum design, and supportive learning environments as essential elements. It positions Oman's commitment to STEM education as an exemplary model for other nations, fostering preparation for future challenges and opportunities.

Chapter 4: "(Re)Imagining an Elementary Preservice Science Methods Course as Inquiry-Based" by Sandy Watson Sandy Watson addresses the underpreparedness of elementary teachers in science education, focusing on both science content knowledge and pedagogical knowledge. The chapter describes the restructuring of a science methods course, placing emphasis on inquiry-based investigations and active learning experiences. The author employs effective strategies to enhance preservice teachers' science pedagogical knowledge.

Chapter 5: "Supporting Beginning Teachers in STEM Content Areas through Self-Directed Learning and Micro-Credentials" by Erin West, Rachel Nelson, Katherine Chesnutt, and James Beeler, focus on the challenges faced by beginning teachers in North Carolina, particularly in STEM content areas. The chapter discusses the importance of self-directed learning and micro-credentials to support these teachers during their initial years. The authors highlight the need for effective onboarding programs and professional development to prevent early exits from the teaching profession.

Chapter 6: "Finding Success in Adapting Repeated Microteaching Rehearsals (RMTR) for an Online Science Methods Course" by Franklin Allaire Franklin Allaire shares experiences of adapting repeated microteaching rehearsals for online instruction, particularly in response to the COVID-19 pandemic. The chapter outlines the challenges faced and lessons learned in integrating RMTR into elementary science methods courses, both during and post-pandemic.

Chapter 7: "Promoting Conceptual Understanding through Authentic Mathematics Instruction in Virtual Environments: More Than a Game" by Elizabeth Allison, Megan Rzyski, Jen Wallender, Carol PeQueen, Kristie Remaly, M. Kain, Adam Hiebel Elizabeth Allison and co-authors delve into the importance of delivering effective online instruction in mathematics to preservice teacher candidates. The chapter explores strategies employed by an online university, including live webinars called Put It into Practice (PiiP). The webinars challenge preservice teachers to analyze how to teach math in today's classroom, emphasizing the creation of a safe psychological environment conducive to learning.

Chapter 8: "The Benefits of Wolfram Alpha Tool Applied to Interactive Learning Environments in STEM Education" by Vandeir Santos, Pollyana Notargiacomo Vandeir Santos and Pollyana Notargiacomo focus on the benefits of using the Wolfram Alpha tool in interactive learning environments for STEM education. The chapter presents quantitative and qualitative results indicating students' preference for classes using Wolfram Alpha, along with improved academic performance. A tutorial is included to guide educators in teaching students to use the Wolfram Alpha tool effectively.

Preface

Chapter 9: "Smartphone and STEM" by Alessio Drivet Alessio Drivet explores the impact of using smartphones for STEM teaching, particularly in the context of the COVID-19 pandemic and distance learning. The chapter provides a balanced overview of the pros and cons, addressing hardware, apps, and possible activities associated with smartphone functions. Drivet encourages discussion and dialogue on the role of smartphones in STEM education.

Chapter 10: "NSF-Funded Exploratory Study: Lessons Learned" by Eleanor Armour-Thomas Eleanor Armour-Thomas presents findings from an NSF-funded exploratory study examining the impact of professional development on NGSS teaching in a large, urban school district. The chapter discusses the development and implementation of a professional development program for in-service teachers, revealing improvements in teachers' knowledge for NGSS teaching and classroom practice.

Chapter 11: "Integrating English Language Arts and Science: Promising Practices for Undergraduate Elementary Teacher Licensure Candidates" by Kim Brown Kim Brown emphasizes the importance of integrated and hands-on teaching methodologies in elementary education science methods courses. The chapter outlines how an elementary education science methods course was revised to include effective teaching methods that integrate Science and English Language Arts. It provides resources such as lecture outlines, lab packets, and instructions for facilitating student comprehension through an integrated approach.

Chapter 12: "Fostering Inclusivity: Nurturing Diversity within Elementary STEM Teacher Preparation Programs" by Surjit Singha Surjit Singha explores the impact of inclusivity on STEM teacher preparation programs for elementary education. The chapter highlights the critical role of inclusivity in enhancing STEM instruction and creating thriving learning environments. Practical recommendations, theoretical foundations, and a landscape analysis underscore the importance of diversity in molding culturally competent and socially conscious STEM educators. Continuous research and evidence-based practices are emphasized for advancing STEM education inclusively in the future.

IN SUMMARY

As we draw the curtains on this anthology, we reflect on the wealth of knowledge, experience, and innovation that has adorned its pages. *Using STEM-Focused Teacher Preparation Programs to Reimagine Elementary Education* has been a labor of passion and commitment—a tapestry woven from the collective efforts of educators, scholars, and visionaries dedicated to reshaping the landscape of teacher preparation.

Through the diverse narratives and insights shared within these chapters, a resounding message echoes: the imperative to infuse STEM into elementary education has never been more urgent. Our journey through these pages has unveiled a mosaic of strategies, best practices, and transformative initiatives that stand as testaments to the potential and promise of STEM-focused teacher preparation programs.

The anecdotes within these covers are not just accounts of change; they are beacons of inspiration, guiding lights illuminating a path toward a more vibrant, inclusive, and effective approach to elementary education. From the overhaul of content and methods courses to the integration of diverse disciplines and community outreach, each chapter represents a step forward in the evolution of teacher preparation.

As editors, we are humbled by the dedication of the contributors who have generously shared their experiences, successes, and challenges. Their stories serve as catalysts, sparking imagination, and guiding fellow educators toward the creation of dynamic STEM-centric programs that nurture curiosity, critical thinking, and innovation among our future generations.

This book stands not as a definitive end but as a commencement—a launching pad for dialogue, collaboration, and action. The seeds planted here are meant to germinate, fostering a culture of continuous improvement and innovation in educator preparation programs across the globe.

The vision encapsulated within these pages is a world where every aspiring educator is equipped with the tools, knowledge, and passion to ignite the spark of STEM curiosity within their students. We envision a future where elementary education becomes the fertile ground for budding scientists, engineers, mathematicians, and innovators—a future shaped by the transformative power of STEM-infused pedagogy.

As we bid farewell to this volume, we do so with gratitude for the shared dedication to reimagining elementary education. Our hope is that the conversations sparked and the ideas sown within these chapters will continue to flourish, creating ripples of change that resonate far beyond these pages.

Preface

May *Using STEM-Focused Teacher Preparation Programs to Reimagine Elementary Education* serve as both a testament to our collective resolve and an invitation to embark on a journey of transformation—one where the integration of STEM into elementary education becomes not just a goal but a reality that enriches the lives and minds of generations to come.

Warmest regards,

Emily Cayton
Campbell University, USA

Miriam Sanders
Texas A&M University, USA

John A. Williams
Texas A&M University, USA

Chapter 1
Preparing Elementary Pre-Service Teachers to Be Effective STEM Teachers

Robert John Ceglie
Independent Researcher, USA

ABSTRACT

Nelson Mandela (1990) stated "[e]ducation is the most powerful weapon which you can use to change the world." This has never been truer as we live in a world in need of strong teachers. We live in a world that underappreciates teachers and their role in educating the next generation often goes unnoticed. Teaching children to become literate in math and science is a concern as these disciplines can lead to increased employment opportunities, higher pay, and a higher quality of life. Having a scientifically literate citizenship is critical to fostering innovation, improving the quality of life, and solving crises such as pandemics and climate change. Unfortunately, interest and motivation in STEM disciplines often decline after early grades which illustrates the important role that these teachers have in math and science education. This chapter combines research-based practices and activities that the author has used to promote STEM learning in preservice teachers. It combines these with narratives from former students who add evidence for their value.

DOI: 10.4018/978-1-6684-5939-3.ch001

INTRODUCTION

Preparing teachers to be stewards in the creation of the next generation of science and math-literate citizens requires multiple partners. There is a wealth of research that examines the "leaky pipeline" of science and math students at the college level and beyond which then limits how many future mathematicians, engineers, doctors, and scientists (Blickenstaff, 2005). Other lines of research point to events that occur in middle and high school that trigger students to be turned off to math and science and thus never even consider futures in them and may harbor poor attitudes as a result (Sadler et al., 2012; Watkins & Mazur, 2013). One additional problem is that decades of research also illustrate that women and minority groups continue to be underrepresented in STEM careers (Seymour et al., 2019). This research is unfortunate as it illustrates that things are occurring within our educational system that is making these subjects uninviting and/or uninteresting to many of our bright students, despite the fact that secondary and college teachers have strong backgrounds in their fields and are typically enthusiastic about their areas of expertise. At the K-5 level, any observation of these children will reveal enthusiastic and curious minds that are often very excited about STEM subjects (Tippett & Milford, 2017). Unfortunately, problems also exist here and appears to focus on teachers that may be hesitant to teach STEM because they a) may lack confidence or self-efficacy in these topics (Kelley & Knowles, 2016), b) often are not as interested in these areas (Nadelson et al. 2013), and c) may be limited in their content preparation, particularly in science and engineering (Kang et al., 2018).

These issues leave STEM education in the position of making decisions on where to "best" intervene and some, including myself, argue that the most important place to begin is at the elementary education level. Research by DeJarnette (2018) demonstrates that not only can early STEM instruction build interest and enthusiasm in the children but can also support increased self-efficacy in the teachers. Even though elementary teachers typically have the lowest mastery of content knowledge in the K-16 pipeline, they often have superior teaching skills (Midgley et al., 1995). In addition, they work with children at such a fertile age where interest can be fostered and nurtured if the subjects are taught properly. The question remains, how do we instill confidence and pedagogical content knowledge in elementary teachers so that they can carry these into their teaching of the STEM disciplines?

At my former university, which is located in the 17th largest school district in the United States, we experienced a persistent need for STEM teachers. Every year that I can remember, the district has included STEM teachers on their list of high need teachers (http://cmshighimpact.com/high-need-subjects). In addition, I would receive dozens of personal emails requesting assistance with spotting graduates that will excel in these positions. Like many other school districts, finding skilled teachers in STEM disciplines has been a challenge. Although my institution is a small liberal arts college, we had a strong elementary education program, and our students typically have their choice of positions in the local schools upon graduation. Given my background in science education, and the persistent need in the area, our department made the decision to alter our elementary program to better meet the needs of our students and the community.

In my time at my former institution, that we will call STEM University (SU), I had primarily taught our instructional technology, math methods, and science methods courses for our elementary education students. Since these courses cover a range of STEM disciplines, I have been in a prime position to redesign our curriculum. This originated in a fundamental shift in the way that math and science methods had traditionally been taught. Changes were made in field placement experiences, course expectations, content focus, and five years ago an addition of a new course. After teaching the listed courses, I found that I was still not adequately reaching all the needed areas, particularly in content, thus I was fortunate to convince our department to add a STEM course which was taken following the technology and two methods courses. In this chapter, I will discuss in detail what these changes were and how they have allowed our program to reimagine elementary education to have a strong STEM focus. I will focus on the strategies used to build content knowledge, pedagogical content knowledge, and self-efficacy and confidence in our pre-service teachers. In addition, I will share comments from students who will describe their perspectives on their experiences becoming a competent and confident STEM teacher.

CONTEXT

When I first arrived at STEM University, the state had required that all potential elementary teachers pass both a science and a math content test in order to be licensed. This was reassuring that the state recognized that there must be some minimum level of content knowledge required for a teacher. This is not dissimilar to doctors, nurses, or lawyers, who must pass an exam to demonstrate that they have some minimal level of knowledge. The literature shows that there is a correlation between teacher content knowledge and achievement. For example, in a multiyear research study aimed at improving content knowledge in elementary teachers, Diamond and colleagues (2014) found that the largest significant predictor of student achievement was a teacher's score on the science content knowledge test that they administered. This is consistent in math as well and Campbell et al. (2014) found that in early career elementary teachers, their mathematical content knowledge had a statistically significant relationship with their students' achievement levels.

It is also important to remember that the level of knowledge that is "expected" of these teachers is rarely above the middle school level, and these teachers have all presumably taken several high school and college math and science courses. The fact that our state had required a minimum passing score on a state mandated test may impact how seriously an elementary teacher prepares in their STEM methods courses. My experience working with these students was evidence that, although they may not love math and science, they did take content acquisition serious in my courses.

What was unfortunate in my situation, was that shortly after I arrived, the state completely dropped the requirement of passing the science test and then a few years later, changed the math exam to an easier one because too many teachers were apparently failing the test, at least in this state (Helms, 2018). So much for a level of mastery, I thought. I immediately saw this in my students' attitudes, as I now had one less reason for them to brush up on their STEM content knowledge. Regardless of the laws governing licensing, my first experiences with my students were that they were underprepared to pass both tests, in general lacked anything other than surface level science content, and most struggled with math content starting at the 3rd grade level. Fortunately, my role was to teach them science methods in the fall of junior year, followed by math methods in that spring. I had one year, and two courses to work with them.

In both courses, I gave the students a pretest and posttest, not so much for my benefit, but to help them recognize where they started, and the progress that they made. In addition, I always started both classes the same way, with a story. The first day in science methods, we looked at NEAP test scores in science and then followed that with some reading and discussion regarding the lack of quality science teachers because of lack of content and pedagogical understanding of what promotes achievement in science. As a written reflection, I asked the students to reflect on their own experience in science. What things may have pushed them away from a potential career in science and what their current attitudes were toward the subject? Beth noted "I liked science when I was younger but then something changed in middle and high school. The classes got harder and my struggling left me looking at other areas such as writing." Cat explained "I think some of my worst teachers were science teachers … they never seemed to really want to help me. Thus, I did poorly, yet I was a good student in all my other courses." These two examples illustrate the commonalities that I have seen in my students and in sum, suggest that they experienced poor teaching or support which contributed to not pursuing science.

The following semester, I utilized the same activities in the math methods course, and I found that historically, this has usually instilled the initial perception of "I really better learn more science and math if I have any chance of teaching higher than kindergarten" as Alice once noted. In some years I have asked students to write a math autobiography, and unfortunately, heard so much about lack of success, that I stopped giving the assignment. Jodi explained "I hated math so much that I cried every night at the kitchen table. None of my teachers were supportive and eventually … I was so bad in math that it hurt my ability to take science courses." Unfortunately, the research literature is littered with similar stories of young student's problems with their ability to learn math (Brady & Bowd, 2005; Seymour & Hewitt, 1997).

These experiences with preparedness of the content matter suggests that there is much to be done at better preparing teachers. At my college, I recognized that fundamental changes were needed in our current curriculum if our students were to pass these tests, let alone be effective STEM teachers. In addition, our students had not been learning the fundamental inquiry, hands-on, relevant practices that are hallmarks of an effective science or math classroom. After ten years of teaching at SU, I feel that we reached a point where the vast majority of our graduates were fully prepared to teach the STEM disciplines. There is still room to improve and there are always some students that continue to resist math and science, but I believe the program has provided a strong model of some strategies and actions that can support positive outcomes in our elementary education graduates. What follows in this chapter are details of steps that our program took to make this happen.

CONTENT FOCUS

It is obvious that if teachers do not know the science and math content when they leave teacher education programs, they will encounter problems teaching these areas (Nadelson et al., 2013; Rinke et al., 2016). Since pre-tests and formative assessments that I used in these courses illustrated that most of our students were lacking the foundational content, I had to consider ways to add content to the methods courses. In addition, our university did not currently have a structure to support the acquisition of content knowledge through general education courses. The general education curriculum is an integrated curriculum which focuses on themes rather than content. And while many larger universities can offer courses such as math for elementary teachers, we could not, and thus our only place to support content knowledge was in the methods courses.

The science content needed for a well-prepared elementary teacher involves the mastery of content in biology, chemistry, and physical science. To review all that content in a 15-week methods course is quite a challenge but is made easier with an excellent tool produced by the National Science Teachers Association (NSTA). Several years ago, NSTA created a professional development tool for teachers called The Learning Center. This tool has been designed for both preservice and in-service teachers and offers a wealth of resources to promote science learning by supporting teachers. A user can create a personal professional development plan and use the site tools to improve their content knowledge, pedagogical content knowledge (PCK), and/or science skills. The resources range from text, articles, animations, simulations, videos, and other tools. Independent studies have demonstrated that this is an effective support for science teachers (Byers, & Mendez, 2016). In my own pilot study, I found that not only did pre-service teachers increase their content knowledge, but the experiences improved their self-efficacy for teaching science (Ceglie, 2014).

The use of the NSTA learning center was also accompanied by instruction and review in as many science content topics that I could fit throughout the semester. Unfortunately, time constraints are limited to a surface covering of about 50% of the K-5 science standards material. In math methods, content review was slightly different as the progressions of the course followed the typical math learning progressions for elementary and middle school math lessons (Fonger et al., 2018). Thus, we revisit areas such as number core and number sense which have been found to be crucial in early math learning (Jordan et al., 2010). Unfortunately, even a targeted effort to improve math content in elementary teachers can have mixed results. A study by Capraro and colleagues (2005) found that courses that focused on math content could contribute to pedagogical content knowledge, however the previous math ability was still the strongest predicator on the state-mandated math exam. Interestingly, in a follow-up study a decade later, they found that the lack of math content knowledge also impacted a teacher's ability to utilize problem solving (Lee et al., 2018). With the increased emphasis of problem solving in current math standards, this study illustrates that foundational content knowledge is crucial to address in these teachers.

Perhaps the most impactful action I was able to achieve at SU as related to content knowledge was the addition of a new course. At SU, we were in the process of a major credit conversion process, which followed an overhaul of the general education curriculum. These two processes offered an opportunity to make changes in our education course offerings and thus I was able to add a new course titled STEM teaching for elementary teachers. With this added course, I was able to cover more content and skills in both math and science, as well as address areas in engineering that I had been unable to get to. Throughout the first few years of adding the course, it was clear that this additional opportunity not only improved the student's content knowledge but built their pedagogical content knowledge and comfort level with the subjects. Danni noted "The STEM class has expanded when I know about science, and I have felt much more comfortable working with the students in my clinical placement." Although I do not have an empirical measure of pre vs post STEM course offering, one of the main areas where I have witnessed the difference was in our master's in arts in teaching program (MAT), where our adult students returning to school are not required to take the STEM course. Since I taught the different cohorts at the same time, I was able to witness the differences between the comfort and preparedness levels. It is a simplification to only suggest that adding one course can be a major benefit but having the students for a three-course sequence had undoubtedly benefited our students.

One final area that has been strengthened by the additional STEM course is the application of Technological Pedagogical Content Knowledge (TPACK). TPACK is a framework that integrates technological and content understandings with the appropriate ways to integrate technological tools to support instruction. Additionally, research suggests that these tools, knowledge, and understandings can, when appropriately integrated, improve learning outcomes (Koehler et al., 2014; Mishra, & Koehler, 2006). Researchers have studied the importance of TPACK acquisition in preservice teachers and a recent literature review found that most teacher education programs do not provide enough support in integrating technology into the different types of learning environments (Chai et al., 2013, Wang et al., 2018). The consequence of a lack of understanding of TPACK integration can lead to discouragement in technology use and in some cases can lead to ineffective, inefficient, and/or lack of technology utilization (Semiz & Ince, 2012; Wang et al., 2018).

The program at SU did provide one instructional technology related course at the beginning of the program. However, the placement of the course made it difficult for our students to understand the context and application of TPACK in the actual classroom. When students had more experience designing and instructing children, it is unlikely they recalled all the things that they previously learned, especially given the pace that technology has advanced. Our programmatic goal was to integrate technology applications throughout the methods courses, and while this was accomplished, the addition of the STEM course allowed additional opportunities for intentional design and instruction.

TARGETED INTENTIONAL CLINICAL EXPERIENCES

The preservice teachers who take math, science, and STEM methods courses are required to complete at least 10 hours of clinical work with a K-5 teacher, including teaching several lessons throughout the term. Research on clinical experiences has shown that some students experience a mismatch between their teacher preparation programs and the time spent in the field (Zeichner, 2010). Some of this is due to the challenge of matching theory and practice, other times placement may be hastily made with a teacher who themselves are still learning to teach. Unfortunately, there are times when preservice teachers see STEM lessons taught without enthusiasm and/or simply taught poorly (Varma & Hanuscin, 2008). While negative experiences do have their place in learning, this highlights the importance of debriefing, mentoring, and reflection as essential components of learning how to teach. Tarman's work (2012) demonstrates that self-perceptions and beliefs can be altered with positive clinical experience, but attention must be placed on areas such as placement location, type of school, mentor teachers and socioeconomic status. Active clinical experiences with positive mentors in supportive, reflective environments can be effective as new teachers build their skill and confidence (Giebelhaus & Bowman, 2002).

As preservice teachers advance in their coursework, they often have additional responsibilities in the clinical placement which ultimately leads to their student teaching experience. It is critical that students have experiences that match their college coursework. Leko and Brownell (2011) found that clinical experiences that include practical application to the content that has been learned in the classroom benefits both the teachers and students. In addition, Linda Darling-Hammond (2014) explained that clinical experiences can be strengthened when colleges and universities create partnerships with schools and districts. These partnerships provide opportunities for constructive feedback couched within supportive environments with staff and faculty that collaborate with each other, and novice teachers are able to apply what they are learning in their teacher preparation programs (Grossman et al., 2012).

Little research has been conducted that specifically focuses on math or science clinical experiences, however we do have studies that illustrate that many elementary teachers have initial apprehension in teaching science and math (Bekdemir, 2010; Kruse et al., 2022; Levitt, 2002). We know that elementary teachers have a higher likelihood of having negative past experiences in these fields, which often leads to lower self-efficacy and desire to teach these areas (Chen et al, 2021; Linder & Simpson, 2018). Decades of research has illustrated that math anxiety continues to be a problem, especially in females (Swars et al., 2006). However, with respect to clinical experiences, some new research has emerged that demonstrates that strong mentoring in clinical experiences can be positive influencers. Kruse and colleagues (2022) used a quasi-experimental study to investigate the value of a "highly supported field experience (HSET)" in preservice elementary teachers. Those in HSET experienced additional support in lesson planning and post lesson feedback, stronger connection between the university supervisor and mentor teacher, and additional opportunity for practice, modeling and feedback. They found that the HSET model "is effective in helping pre-service elementary teachers (PSETs) implement more effective science teaching" (p. 15). They also highlighted the added benefit that reflection and self-analysis had in building skill, even when the feedback was negative or critical as it helped the preservice teachers modify their practices and beliefs.

The clinical placement program at SU is unique to some universities in the course instructor finds schools and makes the placements in conjunction with an administrator at the local school. Since I am the instructor for the science, math, STEM methods course sequences, I hold the ability to locate supportive schools to place our students. Fortunately, our area holds several STEM and STEAM schools, many of which I have been able to place students. Because of the relationships with teachers in these schools, I have placed students with people who have been successful in STEM teaching and are strong in content and science skills. At SU we collect student feedback from the clinical placements and the ones in these courses have been overwhelmingly good. Emily noted "It was great working with Mr. M... He understands the content and he is great with the students. I have learned so much about how to be an effective science teacher." Emma added "My experiences have been so good at this school, that I want to do my student teaching here next year. I appreciate the use of math manipulatives and problem-solving approaches to their math instruction as this mirrors what Dr. C taught us." In addition to placing students for my clinicals, it has been consistent that many students remain in the same schools for multiple semesters. This adds continuity to the experience and both teachers and students have reported success in yearlong placements. Of course, not every placement is a perfect match, but there is little doubt that the vast majority of preservice teachers have had their STEM teaching abilities strengthened as a result of the intentional placement in these schools.

OUTSIDE OF SCHOOL ACTIVITIES

Non- STEM Related Activities

The in-class and clinical experiences make up the bulk of activities that preservice encounter during their teacher preparation programs. However, experiences that they have outside of the classroom can also contribute to their teacher training. These informal experiences can be led by individual faculty, may be a part of in course assignments like a museum visit, or they can be programmatic, such as a service-learning requirements. The value of these types of experiences has been studied extensively in high school and college-aged students.

Our teacher preparation program had a group of extracurricular activities that we believed contributed to the preservice teachers' preparation. Outside of the usual working with schools, all our students are asked to engage in extracurricular activities promoted withing their placements. There are a few experiences that students have shared that have been the most impactful. One such experience is the participation in parent nights or back-to-school nights that are held by schools. Like many teacher preparation programs, one of our consistent weaknesses is that students leave the program and still feel unprepared to work with parents (Epstein & Salinas, 2004). This is largely because it is difficult to create opportunities for our students to engage with parents, thus we have encouraged students to look for opportunities to do so. In addition, we systematically held seminars where we addressed various concerns, and this has been an area of focus for the past several years.

Since most of our placements are with Title One schools, our students often observe less parental involvement than they expected. Lee and Bowden (2006) share that lack of parental involvement in schooling is often observed in lower socioeconomic and majority-minority schools and this can leave teachers with the impression that they care less than other parents. This has been demonstrated in several other studies (Epstein, 2018; Wong et al., 2018), but building positive relationships with parents can build cultural capital and influence student achievement levels and thus we stress the importance of making connections with parents (D'Haem & Griswold, 2017; de Bruine et al., 2014). We have observed that students who have been able to attend parent teacher nights and other parent related events share that they learned a lot about how to communicate with parents as well as started to feel more comfortable in approaching them. In addition, since many of our students do not come from similar backgrounds as their future students, it is valuable for the, to have shared experiences with a child's family as this helps build relationships, build cultural competence, and apathy in our future teachers (Epstein, 2018).

STEM Related Activities

Some of the most important types of experiences which support science and math interest occur outside of the typical classroom environment. It is not surprising that research on informal education has a considerable impact on interest, motivation, and achievement in math and science (Bicer & Lee, 2019; Eshach, 2007). A recent policy report by scholars in Chicago, recommended that not only do we need to promote opportunities for informal STEM experiences but that educators must also find ways to create explicit connections and coherence between formal and informal science and math learning experiences, particularly in elementary schools (Hurst et al., 2019).

Given the value of these informal opportunities, it is critical for preservice teachers to acquire an understanding of how these may be leveraged in their own learning journey. One experience that I have created for my students has been the opportunity to work with children on science and math fair projects. Partnering with two Title One schools, we created opportunities where the students from my STEM courses would work with children outside of school hours on a science fair project. This started with our preservice teachers taking the child on an informal science experience after school. Some of the suggested experiences included a trip to a museum, a nature walk, a iNaturalist experience (https://www.inaturalist.org/), citizen science activity (https://www.citizenscience.gov/toolkit/howto/#) or a virtual trip (e.g. https://www.exploratorium.edu/education). Following this activity, the preservice teachers would work with the child on the process of designing and carrying out a science fair project.

In addition to participation in this experience, the students would then share these experiences in class to make explicit connections to what was learned. This included reflection and discussion to understand how this activity or similar ones contributed to relationship building and may have increased their cultural capital. Students reported that this activity has strengthened their understanding of home environments as well as uncovered how much natural curiosity these children have which is often not observed in the classroom. Finally, every year at least once school invites me and my classes to come and judge a science fair. This helps the teachers see the culmination of their work and allows the additional opportunities to work with peers, parents, teachers, and members of the local science community. In addition, this provides a novel opportunity for these teachers to feel like the science experts and thus build self-efficacy. Fran explained "I really enjoyed judging the science fair at MP and it was the first time that I saw myself as an expert in science, even if just for a day." This sentiment has been shared by others and contributes to the overall development of a growth mindset reading their science knowledge and ability and this has been demonstrated in similar studies (Cartwright & Hallar, 2018).

AUTHENTIC ASSIGNMENTS AND ACTIVITIES

Throughout the three course STEM courses, there are several individual activities and in-class experiences that contribute to the education of the preservice teachers. In many ways, these activities and assignments serve as much of the core pedagogy used to support these students as they become new teachers and build their science and math skills.

Science Fairs

In addition to the science fair that the preservice teachers foster with a local child, they are also tasked with designing and carrying out a science fair of their own as a part of the science methods course. This assignment is similar to the typical science fair project where the student finds a topic, designs a plan to "solve" the problem, collects data, and finally present this to the class. In my fifteen years of using this assignment, at least half of the students have never conducted a science fair, and the ones that have often reported that a family member helped (or in some cases, completed) with the assignment. This lack of personal experience where one uses one's curiosity to find an answer to a problem or interest is troubling, and students always report that they appreciated this opportunity and learned from it.

I have been fortunate to have studied and then reported growth in preservice teachers and how the assignment has benefited them (Ceglie, 2020; Ceglie, 2013). I found that three main themes have emerged. First, carrying out the science fair allowed the students an opportunity to practice and hone their scientific inquiry skills, something that we stress in class, but real application is critical (Cuevas et al., 2005; Haefner & Zembal-Saul, 2004). All too often, preservice teachers share that they have had little experience with scientific inquiry, and many were also prey to cookbook labs in schools which can lead to a loss of interest and motivation (Tobin, 1984). One of former student explained "conducting an experiment with tangible materials and using our own eyes and other senses to observe and evaluate variable changes, is also far more powerful to student learning than just reading about it or watching a video. This can help actually learn the concepts."

A second finding was that completing the activity increased preservice teacher's self-efficacy in doing science. In the last few years, more students have chosen projects that fall under the engineering umbrella which has strengthened the E component in STEM. I have witnessed that the ability to use the acquired knowledge and then apply it to a problem, in the way that an engineer does, builds confidence and skill and also makes it personal to each student (Kang et al., 2018). Finally, I discovered that students were building their science identity (Avraamidou, 2019; Settlage et al., 2009). For example, one preservice teacher explained "I feel like I was a scientist- at least in the context of our class… Presenting these to the class made me feel more like how scientists must share their work to others." In addition, to these findings, some studies on the use of science fairs have found they can have a positive impact on attitudes and motivation to teach science in their classrooms (Dionne et al., 2012; Schmidt, & Kelter, 2017). Given that preservice teachers often have a weakness in many of the aforementioned skills, it has been beneficial to observe the value of the science fair activity.

Data Analysis Project

One current trend within many universities is the promotion of data analytics programs which are intended to help our students become more knowledgeable, responsible, and productive with the use of the vast amount of data we are bombarded with (Parnell, 2022). SU is no exception to the advance in data analytics as they hired faculty for a new program, added a minor, and provided incentives for faculty to integrate it into their own courses. Four years ago, I took on this challenge with the addition of a

Data Analytics Project (DAP) in my STEM course. The main objective was to find a way to integrate science journal articles with math analysis and data visualization. The DAP required the students to pick a relevant current science issue (e.g., climate change, vaccination, fossil fuels) and research the background of the article and find corresponding research in other journal articles. Students were provided with the foundational article but needed to locate at least three related articles to support their background understanding. Next, the student pulled the relevant empirical data from any of the articles and reanalyzed a segment of this data and represented it using different visuals. Finally, each student presented and discussed their work to the class, similar to a conference presentation.

The DAP required a great deal of scaffolding and students have surprised me with their ability to carry out the project. Not only does it necessitate some level of expertise in the area of focus (science content), but the ability also to communicate their conclusions (science inquiry) and utilize data analytics and visualization skills (mathematical practices). I imagine this type of project may be something more common in a true science course and thus stretches the skills of the students in my course. In fact, I had a college faculty professor come up to me at a national conference and commend me for the activity. The two key contributions I have experienced from assigning the DAP is that it has allowed for the application of math skills which builds confidence, and that it is an application of science inquiry with some embedded content knowledge (Ceglie 2022). At its core, the DAP isn't about teaching, but the feedback from students has been strong and they often comment that this has contributed to their confidence to do science and math. The quotes that follow illustrate some of the thoughts that my students have shared with me in the past few years.

In a world where we are becoming reliant on data, it is important to be able to interpret it to help me better understand the science.

This project improved my data analysis skills and scientific literacy skills....I hope to apply this with my future students.

I better understand how research in science is done, this helps me better understand issues ... I have a better sense of the elements that make one scientifically literate ... and see this being helpful for my future teaching.

This assignment has been valuable in our program to better prepare teachers for STEM instruction. It can also be scaled down and modified to meet different needs in a math or science methods course.

Project/Problem Based Learning

Project or Problem Based Learning (PBL) is a teaching method often used in math and science classes where students are engaged in solving real-world problems through meaningful projects (pblworks.org, 2023). PBL is valued because it is a student-centered way of learning, it requires students to be active and engaged in the learning process, and it links the learner with the real work (Kubiatko & Vaculova, 2011). Research in science education has demonstrated that PBL can lead to higher achievement levels than traditional methods (Ergul & Kargin, 2014; Kokotsaki et al., 2016). In addition, since it is a more authentic way of learning, it is more aligned with scientific inquiry and is a more authentic approach to instruction. The challenge for some science teachers is that it requires a clear understanding of how PBL works which can compete with ones "teacher orientations" towards a more teacher centered approach (Boss & Krauss, 2022). In addition, implementation of PBL requires that teachers potentially change the curriculum, instruction, and assessment practices, some of these which can be hard to push against (Barron et al., 2014). Barron and colleagues (2014) influential work on PBL suggests that there are four key design principles that are important to effective use of PBL. These include

1) defining learning-appropriate goals that lead to deep understanding;
2) providing scaffolds such as "embedded teaching," "teaching tools," sets of "contrasting cases," and beginning with problem-based learning activities before initiating projects;
3) ensuring multiple opportunities for formative self-assessment and revision; and
4) developing social structures that promote participation and a sense of agency. (p 271)

Project Based Learning has long been advocated by reform-minded math educators (Myer et al., 1997). One doesn't need to look much further than the Harvard-Smithonian's *Private Universe Project in Mathematics* materials (2001) which began being implemented in New Jersey schools in 1988 and demonstrated increased achievement in these students. One of the key attributes of many PRL studies is that they have found that it often increases student interest and motivation in STEM fields. A study by Tseng et al. (2013) examined a STEM based PBL activity with students and found that their attitudes toward engineering and math changed significantly. A similar study by Sunyoung et al. (2016) reported improved scores on math content and problem-solving skills. One complaint that teachers sometimes have with student-centered approaches to learning is that the students must still pass a standardized assessment and fear approached like PBL will not prepare them. There is evidence to show that this isn't the case. Craig and Marshall (2019) report on their study which utilized PBL pedagogy with high school students and found that those using this approach significantly outscores their peers on the state mandated testing. Similar work was reported in a study that showed increased achievement levels in elementary aged students in math (Lazic et al., 2021).

What is even more interesting is that there are also studies that illustrate that PBL can be more effective in minority populations and traditionally low achieving students. In work in a minority serving middle school, Cervantes et al. (2015) found that a group of students who participated in PBL had higher achievement levels as compared to those who did not partake in this program. Finally, Han and colleagues (2015) studied the impact of PBL on high school students from three levels of achievement, high, middle, and low. While all three achievement groups outperformed the control group in this study, the low performing group showed statistically higher growth than both the middle and higher achievement groups. Unfortunately, the release of the student centered, and inquiry friendly Common Core Mathematics Standards has not made significant inroads into the use of project-based instruction despite studies showing positive outcomes in math education (McCarthy, 2019).

The integration of PBL in the courses at SU occurred in the STEM course. The assignment was to design an integrated math unit using PBL as a framework. The preservice teachers needed to use the common core math standards for the foundation and integrate science, technology, and ELA in a 2-week unit. Two key findings have led me to continue to use this assignment with my preservice teachers. One is that it provided one of the few opportunities for elementary preservice teachers to design an instructional unit. With so much of their curriculum being hand fed to them in schools and since our program tends to focus on writing and design of single lessons, this has been a positive experience. Students have explained that while this activity was a challenge "it has made me really think about longer term planning and how a project-based approach … can give an easy framework … as long as I can come up with a good issue to tie it to." Another student illuminated that "I have never seen any teacher I worked with design or even implement a whole unit, let alone a PBL one ... I show mine to her and she was so excited that she wanted to use it in her class next year."

The second takeaway for me has been that the assignment helped students see that it is not that difficult to integrate the various subjects and there are more benefits than they have perceived. Research conducted in Korea has shed light on this topic as they have recently shifted focus to a more integrated curricular design (Kim & Bolger, 2017). In a study which investigated the perceptions of STEM integrated lessons in preservice teachers, they found that using integrated curriculum has had a positive influence on their attitudes toward a STEM integrated model (Kim & Bolger, 2017). A similar study conducted in the United States explored integrating STEM lessons in in-service teachers and also found that following their use, teacher were more receptive to this model. In addition, it was uncovered that the newer teachers had a significantly higher receptivity in comparison to the veteran teachers. This suggests that starting the promotion of STEM integration with preservice teachers will yield higher utilization.

CONCLUSION

This chapter is intended to share my personal experiences and work to create a program that supports preservice teachers in STEM instructional practices, content, dispositions, and skills as they begin their journeys as future teachers. In addition, I utilized research that I have used as I have designed my courses and contributed to our program. Although the focus was primarily on those ready to enter the profession, most of these ideas also apply to those who are already in the profession and are seeking ways to become better STEM teachers. One limitation of my own work which I have been exploring is ways to make the E part of STEM a greater component. This year I presented my recent efforts at the National Science Teacher Association National Conference in the hope of getting feedback from teachers and other educators. I hope to add additional engineering components in my future work with teachers.

Not every idea presented in this chapter will work with every student or in every course, but my experiences have served my students well. They have been revised, scraped, reinvented during my career, and will undoubtedly be revised in future years. I recognize that teaching STEM disciplines, especially at the elementary level, is not an easy task. We are living in a world with increasing information, but we are also being bombarded with misinformation and attacks on science (West & Bergstrom, 2021). I am thankful for those former students who have embraced the challenge and hope that all that read this recognize the important role you play in the future education of children.

REFERENCES

Avraamidou, L. (2019). Stories we live, identities we build: How are elementary teachers' science identities shaped by their lived experiences? *Cultural Studies of Science Education, 14*(1), 33–59. doi:10.1007/s11422-017-9855-8

Barron, B. J., Schwartz, D. L., Vye, N. J., Moore, A., Petrosino, A., Zech, L., & Bransford, J. D. (2014). Doing with understanding: Lessons from research on problem-and project-based learning. In *Learning Through Problem Solving* (pp. 271–311). Psychology Press.

Bekdemir, M. (2010). The pre-service teachers' mathematics anxiety related to depth of negative experiences in mathematics classroom while they were students. *Educational Studies in Mathematics*, *75*(3), 311–328. doi:10.1007/s10649-010-9260-7

Bicer, A., & Lee, Y. (2019). Effect of STEM PBL embedded informal learning on student interest in STEM majors and careers. *Journal of Mathematics Education*, *12*(1), 57–73.

Blickenstaff, J. C. (2005). Women and science careers: Leaky pipeline or gender filter? *Gender and Education*, *17*(4), 369–386. doi:10.1080/09540250500145072

Boss, S., & Krauss, J. (2022). *Reinventing project-based learning: Your field guide to real-world projects in the digital age*. International Society for Technology in Education.

Brady, P., & Bowd, A. (2005). Mathematics anxiety, prior experience and confidence to teach mathematics among pre-service education students. *Teachers and Teaching*, *11*(1), 37–46. doi:10.1080/1354060042000337084

Byers, A., & Mendez, F. (2016). Blended professional learning for science educators: The NSTA Learning Center. Teacher learning in the digital age: Online professional development in STEM education. In C. Dede, A. Eisenkraft, K. Frumin & A. Hartley, A. (Eds.), Teacher learning in the digital age: Online professional development in STEM education. (167-198). Harvard Education Press.

Campbell, P. F., Nishio, M., Smith, T. M., Clark, L. M., Conant, D. L., Rust, A. H., DePiper, J. N., Frank, T. J., Griffin, M. J., & Choi, Y. (2014). The relationship between teachers' mathematical content and pedagogical knowledge, teachers' perceptions, and student achievement. *Journal for Research in Mathematics Education*, *45*(4), 419–459. doi:10.5951/jresematheduc.45.4.0419

Capraro, R. M., Capraro, M. M., Parker, D., Kulm, G., & Raulerson, T. (2005). The mathematics content knowledge role in developing preservice teachers' pedagogical content knowledge. *Journal of Research in Childhood Education*, *20*(2), 102–118. doi:10.1080/02568540509594555

Cartwright, T. J., & Hallar, B. (2018). Taking risks with a growth mindset: Long-term influence of an elementary pre-service after school science practicum. *International Journal of Science Education, 40*(3), 348–370. doi:10.1080/09500693.2017.1420269

Ceglie, R. (January, 2013). *Using science fairs to promote inquiry skills in an elementary science methods course.* Paper presented at the Association for Science Teacher Education annual international meeting, Charleston, SC.

Ceglie, R. (September, 2014). *Using NSTA's Learning Center to promote content knowledge in a preservice elementary methods course.* Paper presented at the Mid Atlantic Association for Science Teacher Education annual meeting, Blowing Rock, NC.

Ceglie, R. (October 9-10, 2020). *Building inquiry skill using science fairs.* Paper presented at the Mid Atlantic Association for Science Teacher Education annual meeting, Virtual (COVID-19).

Ceglie, R. (January 6-7, 2022). *Using data analytics to support school community scientific literacy: A Pilot study.* 2022 Association for Science Teacher Education Conference. Greenville, S.C.

Cervantes, B., Hemmer, L., & Kouzekanani, K. (2015). The impact of project-based learning on minority student achievement: Implications for school redesign. *Education Leadership Review of Doctoral Research, 2*(2), 50–66.

Chai, C. S., Koh, J. H. L., & Tsai, C. C. (2013). A review of technological pedagogical content knowledge. *Journal of Educational Technology & Society, 16*(2), 31–51.

Chen, Y. L., Huang, L. F., & Wu, P. C. (2021). Preservice preschool teachers' self-efficacy in and need for STEM education professional development: STEM pedagogical belief as a mediator. *Early Childhood Education Journal, 49*(2), 137–147. doi:10.1007/s10643-020-01055-3

Craig, T. T., & Marshall, J. (2019). Effect of project-based learning on high school students' state-mandated, standardized math and science exam performance. *Journal of Research in Science Teaching, 56*(10), 1461–1488. doi:10.1002/tea.21582

Cuevas, P., Lee, O., Hart, J., & Deaktor, R. (2005). Improving science inquiry with elementary students of diverse backgrounds. *Journal of Research in Science Teaching, 42*(3), 337–357. doi:10.1002/tea.20053

D'Haem, J., & Griswold, P. (2017). Teacher educators' and student teachers' beliefs about preparation for working with families including those from diverse socioeconomic and cultural backgrounds. *Education and Urban Society*, *49*(1), 81–109. doi:10.1177/0013124516630602

Darling-Hammond, L. (2014). Strengthening clinical preparation: The holy grail of teacher education. *Peabody Journal of Education*, *89*(4), 547–561. doi:10.1080/0161956X.2014.939009

de Bruïne, E. J., Willemse, T. M., D'Haem, J., Griswold, P., Vloeberghs, L., & Van Eynde, S. (2014). Preparing teacher candidates for family–school partnerships. *European Journal of Teacher Education*, *37*(4), 409–425. doi:10.1080/02619768.2014.912628

Dejarnette, N. K. (2018). Implementing STEAM in the Early Childhood Classroom. European. *Journal of STEM Education: Innovations and Research*, *3*(3), 18.

Diamond, B. S., Maerten-Rivera, J., Rohrer, R. E., & Lee, O. (2014). Effectiveness of a curricular and professional development intervention at improving elementary teachers' science content knowledge and student achievement outcomes: Year 1 results. *Journal of Research in Science Teaching*, *51*(5), 635–658. doi:10.1002/tea.21148

Dionne, L., Reis, G., Trudel, L., Guillet, G., Kleine, L., & Hancianu, C. (2012). Students' sources of motivation for participation in science fairs: An exploratory study within the Canada-wide science fair 2008. *International Journal of Science and Mathematics Education*, *10*(3), 669–693. doi:10.1007/s10763-011-9318-8

Epstein, J. L. (2018). *School, family, and community partnerships: Preparing educators and improving schools*. Routledge.

Epstein, J. L., & Salinas, K. C. (2004). Partnering with families and communities. *Educational Leadership*, *61*(8), 12–19.

Ergül, N. R., & Kargın, E. K. (2014). The effect of project based learning on students' science success. *Procedia: Social and Behavioral Sciences*, *136*, 537–541. doi:10.1016/j.sbspro.2014.05.371

Eshach, H. (2007). Bridging in-school and out-of-school learning: Formal, non-formal, and informal education. *Journal of Science Education and Technology*, *16*(2), 171–190. doi:10.1007/s10956-006-9027-1

Fonger, N. L., Stephens, A., Blanton, M., Isler, I., Knuth, E., & Gardiner, A. M. (2018). Developing a learning progression for curriculum, instruction, and student learning: An example from mathematics education. *Cognition and Instruction*, *36*(1), 30–55. doi:10.1080/07370008.2017.1392965

Giebelhaus, C. R., & Bowman, C. L. (2002). Teaching mentors: Is it worth the effort? *The Journal of Educational Research*, *95*(4), 246–254. doi:10.1080/00220670209596597

Grossman, P., Ronfeldt, M., & Cohen, J. J. (2012). *The power of setting: The role of field experience in learning to teach.*

Haefner, L., & Zembal-Saul, C. (2004). Learning by doing? Prospective elementary teachers' developing understandings of scientific inquiry and science teaching and learning. *International Journal of Science Education*, *26*(13), 1653–1674. doi:10.1080/0950069042000230709

Han, S., Capraro, R., & Capraro, M. M. (2015). How science, technology, engineering, and mathematics (STEM) project-based learning (PBL) affects high, middle, and low achievers differently: The impact of student factors on achievement. *International Journal of Science and Mathematics Education*, *13*(5), 1089–1113. doi:10.1007/s10763-014-9526-0

Harvard-Smithsonian Center for Astrophysics (2001). *Private Universe Project in Mathematics.* Harvard.

Helms, A. (2018, August 2). Hundreds of NC teachers are flunking math exams. It may not be their fault. *The Charlotte Observer.* https://www.charlotteobserver.com/news/local/education/article215848065.html

Hurst, M. A., Polinsky, N., Haden, C. A., Levine, S. C., & Uttal, D. H. (2019). Leveraging research on informal learning to inform policy on promoting early STEM. *Social Policy Report*, *32*(3), 1–33. doi:10.1002/sop2.5

Jordan, N. C., Glutting, J., & Ramineni, C. (2010). The importance of number sense to mathematics achievement in first and third grades. *Learning and Individual Differences*, *20*(2), 82–88. doi:10.1016/j.lindif.2009.07.004 PMID:20401327

Kang, E. J., Donovan, C., & McCarthy, M. J. (2018). Exploring elementary teachers' pedagogical content knowledge and confidence in implementing the NGSS science and engineering practices. *Journal of Science Teacher Education*, *29*(1), 9–29. doi:10.1080/1046560X.2017.1415616

Kelley, T. R., & Knowles, J. G. (2016). A conceptual framework for integrated STEM education. *International Journal of STEM Education*, *3*(1), 1–11. doi:10.1186/s40594-016-0046-z

Kim, D., & Bolger, M. (2017). Analysis of Korean Elementary Pre-Service Teachers' Changing Attitudes About Integrated STEAM Pedagogy Through Developing Lesson Plans. *International Journal of Science and Mathematics Education*, *15*(4), 587–605. doi:10.1007/s10763-015-9709-3

Koehler, M. J., Mishra, P., Kereluik, K., Shin, T. S., & Graham, C. R. (2014). The Technological Pedagogical Content Knowledge Framework. In J. M. Spector (Eds.), *Handbook of Research on Educational Communications and Technology* (pp. 101–111). Springer. doi:10.1007/978-1-4614-3185-5_9

Kokotsaki, D., Menzies, V., & Wiggins, A. (2016). Project-based learning: A review of the literature. *Improving Schools*, *19*(3), 267–277. doi:10.1177/1365480216659733

Kruse, J., Wilcox, J., Patel, N., Borzo, S., Seebach, C., & Henning, J. (2022). The Power of Practicum Support: A Quasi-experimental Investigation of Elementary Preservice Teachers' Science Instruction in A Highly Supported Field Experience. *Journal of Science Teacher Education*, *33*(4), 392–412. doi:10.1080/1046560X.2021.1949099

Kubiatko, M., & Vaculová, I. (2011). Project-based learning: Characteristic and the experiences with application in the science subjects. *Energy Education Science and Technology, Part B. Social and Educational Studies*, *3*(1), 65–74.

Lazic, B., Knežević, J., & Maričić, S. (2021). The influence of project-based learning on student achievement in elementary mathematics education. *South African Journal of Education*, *41*(3), 1909. doi:10.15700/saje.v41n3a1909

Lee, Y., Capraro, R. M., & Capraro, M. M. (2018). Mathematics teachers' subject matter knowledge and pedagogical content knowledge in problem posing. *International Electronic Journal of Mathematics Education*, *13*(2), 75–90. doi:10.12973/iejme/2698

Leko, M. M., & Brownell, M. T. (2011). Special education preservice teachers' appropriation of pedagogical tools for teaching reading. *Exceptional Children*, *77*(2), 229–251. doi:10.1177/001440291107700205

Levitt, K. E. (2002). An analysis of elementary teachers' beliefs regarding the teaching and learning of science. *Science Education*, *86*(1), 1–22. doi:10.1002/sce.1042

Linder, S. M., & Simpson, A. (2018). Towards an understanding of early childhood mathematics education: A systematic review of the literature focusing on practicing and prospective teachers. *Contemporary Issues in Early Childhood*, *19*(3), 274–296. doi:10.1177/1463949117719553

Margot, K. C., & Kettler, T. (2019). Teachers' perception of STEM integration and education: A systematic literature review. *International Journal of STEM Education*, *6*(1), 1–16. doi:10.1186/s40594-018-0151-2

McCarthy, J. (2019, October 23). 3 common PBL problems- and solutions. *Edutopia*. https://www.edutopia.org/article/3-common-pbl-problems-and-solutions/

Meyer, D. K., Turner, J. C., & Spencer, C. A. (1997). Challenge in a mathematics classroom: Students' motivation and strategies in project-based learning. *The Elementary School Journal*, *97*(5), 501–521. doi:10.1086/461878

Midgley, C., Anderman, E., & Hicks, L. (1995). Differences between elementary and middle school teachers and students: A goal theory approach. *The Journal of Early Adolescence*, *15*(1), 90–113. doi:10.1177/0272431695015001006

Mishra, P., & Koehler, M. J. (2006). Technological Pedagogical Content Knowledge: A Framework for Integrating Technology in Teacher Knowledge. *Teachers College Record*, *108*, 1017–1054. doi:10.1111/j.1467-9620.2006.00684.x

Nadelson, L. S., Callahan, J., Pyke, P., Hay, A., Dance, M., & Pfiester, J. (2013). Teacher STEM perception and preparation: Inquiry-based STEM professional development for elementary teachers. *The Journal of Educational Research*, *106*(2), 157–168. doi:10.1080/00220671.2012.667014

Parnell, A. (2022, February 6). You are a data person. *Inside Higher Education*. https://www.insidehighered.com/news/2022/02/07/why-everyone-higher-education-data-person

Rinke, C. R., Gladstone-Brown, W., Kinlaw, C. R., & Cappiello, J. (2016). Characterizing STEM teacher education: Affordances and constraints of explicit STEM preparation for elementary teachers. *School Science and Mathematics*, *116*(6), 300–309. doi:10.1111/ssm.12185

Sadler, P. M., Sonnert, G., Hazari, Z., & Tai, R. (2012). Stability and volatility of STEM career interest in high school: A gender study. *Science Education*, *96*(3), 411–427. doi:10.1002/sce.21007

Schmidt, K. M., & Kelter, P. (2017). Science fairs: A qualitative study of their impact on student science inquiry learning and attitudes toward STEM. *Science Educator, 25*(2), 126–132.

Semiz, K., & Ince, M. L. (2012). Preservice physical education teachers' technological pedagogical content knowledge, technology integration self-efficacy and instructional technology outcome expectations. *Australasian Journal of Educational Technology, 28*(7). doi:10.14742/ajet.800

Settlage, J., Southerland, S. A., Smith, L. K., & Ceglie, R. (2009). Constructing a doubt-free teaching self: Self-efficacy, teacher identity, and science instruction within diverse settings. *Journal of Research in Science Teaching, 46*(1), 102–125. doi:10.1002/tea.20268

Seymour, E., & Hewitt, N. M. (1997). *Talking about leaving*. Westview Press.

Seymour, E., Hunter, A. B., Harper, R. P., & Holland, D. G. (2019). *Talking about leaving revisited. Talking About Leaving Revisited: Persistence*. Relocation, and Loss in Undergraduate STEM Education. doi:10.1007/978-3-030-25304-2

Sunyoung, H. A. N., Rosli, R., Capraro, M. M., & Capraro, R. M. (2016). The effect of science, technology, engineering and mathematics (STEM) project-based learning (PBL) on students' achievement in four mathematics topics. *Journal of Turkish Science Education, 13*(special), 3.

Swars, S. L., Daane, C. J., & Giesen, J. (2006). Mathematics anxiety and mathematics teacher efficacy: What is the relationship in elementary preservice teachers? *School Science and Mathematics, 106*(7), 306–315. doi:10.1111/j.1949-8594.2006.tb17921.x

Tarman, B. (2012). Prospective Teachers' Beliefs and Perceptions about Teaching as a Profession. *Educational Sciences: Theory & Practice, 12*(3), 1964–1973.

Tippett, C. D., & Milford, T. M. (2017). Findings from a pre-kindergarten classroom: Making the case for STEM in early childhood education. *International Journal of Science and Mathematics Education, 15*(1), 67–86. doi:10.1007/s10763-017-9812-8

Tseng, K. H., Chang, C. C., Lou, S. J., & Chen, W. P. (2013). Attitudes towards science, technology, engineering and mathematics (STEM) in a project-based learning (PjBL) environment. *International Journal of Technology and Design Education, 23*(1), 87–102. doi:10.1007/s10798-011-9160-x

Varma, T., & Hanuscin, D. L. (2008). Pre-service elementary teachers' field experiences in classrooms led by science specialists. *Journal of Science Teacher Education, 19*(6), 593–614. doi:10.1007/s10972-008-9110-y

Wang, W., Schmidt-Crawford, D., & Jin, Y. (2018). Preservice teachers' TPACK development: A review of literature. *Journal of Digital Learning in Teacher Education*, *34*(4), 234–258. doi:10.1080/21532974.2018.1498039

Watkins, J., & Mazur, E. (2013). Retaining students in science, technology, engineering, and mathematics (STEM) majors. *Journal of College Science Teaching*, *42*(5), 36–41.

West, J. D., & Bergstrom, C. T. (2021). Misinformation in and about science. *Proceedings of the National Academy of Sciences of the United States of America*, *118*(15), e1912444117. doi:10.1073/pnas.1912444117 PMID:33837146

Wong, R. S. M., Ho, F. K. W., Wong, W. H. S., Tung, K. T. S., Chow, C. B., Rao, N., Chn, K. L., & Ip, P. (2018). Parental involvement in primary school education: Its relationship with children's academic performance and psychosocial competence through engaging children with school. *Journal of Child and Family Studies*, *27*(5), 1544–1555. doi:10.1007/s10826-017-1011-2

Zeichner, K. (2010). Rethinking the connections between campus courses and field experiences in college-and university-based teacher education. *Journal of Teacher Education*, *61*(1–2), 89–99. doi:10.1177/0022487109347671

Chapter 2
"What Are We Missing?":
Examining Culturally Relevant Teaching Practices in STEM Educator Preparation Programs

Miriam Sanders
https://orcid.org/0000-0002-7625-6841
Texas A&M University, USA

Maiya Turner
Texas A&M University, USA

John A. Williams
Texas A&M University, USA

ABSTRACT

The STEM field now faces a two-fold crisis of students' waning interest and underrepresentation of marginalized populations such as People of Color and women contrary to the high demand for STEM-qualified professionals. STEM subjects such as mathematics have been viewed as a critical filter for high-status, high-salary careers. Thus, it is essential to examine EPP STEM methods curriculum as culturally relevant pedagogy that has been proven to enhance learning outcomes, pique and retain interest, and foster confidence in students from underrepresented groups and all students. Through a content analysis, we examine course descriptions from top-ranked teacher-training universities in the United States to determine the presence or lack of training that STEM PSTs receive in their respective EPPs regarding culturally responsive teaching.

DOI: 10.4018/978-1-6684-5939-3.ch002

INTRODUCTION

Despite efforts to bolster the STEM (science, technology, engineering, and mathematics) career pipeline, underrepresentation of marginalized groups such as women and People of Color persists (National Science Board, 2016). For instance, in 2018, a disproportionate percentage of bachelor's degrees in science and engineering were earned by students of Hispanic or Latino descent (15.1%), by Black students (8.5%), and by students of Indigenous group origin (0.4%) (Bock, 2022). In 2019, although women made up 48% of the workforce, women made up only 27% of the STEM workforce in the U.S., and the percentage of women of color in the STEM workforce was even lower (Martinez & Christnacht, 2021). Moreover, there is an overall drop in STEM career interests in adolescents (Henry, 2018), and this disinterest is only exacerbated by inequitably dispensed opportunities for historically marginalized students to take STEM courses in their P-12 journey (Crabtree et al., 2019; Casto & Williams, 2020). The large-scale change in student dispositions towards STEM threatens to widen the gap between STEM labor demand and qualified STEM workers (Vilorio, 2014). Thus, it is imperative to reinvigorate and improve educational practices in STEM fields (Litzler et al., 2014). To this end, providing high-quality instruction and hands-on experiences with research-based practices to elementary pre-service teachers (PSTs) in Educator Preparation Programs (EPPs) is essential (McClure et al., 2017). Furthermore, providing PSTs' with a strong foundation in culturally relevant pedagogy in their STEM methods courses allows an avenue to mitigate the leaky STEM pipeline and make STEM learning accessible and engaging for all students. Currently, EPPs seek to bridge gaps in PSTs' STEM knowledge and skills by immersing students in interdisciplinary learning activities using models such as inquiry learning, engineering design, problem-based learning, and project-based learning. Participation in epistemic activities provides PSTs with firsthand experiences with contextualized-applied learning. Moreover, the STEM curriculum grounded in constructivism and social cognitive theory has positive effects on students' STEM sense of belonging and persistence (Bell et al., 2017; Maiorca et al., 2021; Young et al., 2017). As the sociopolitical climate changes and the intersection of social justice and education becomes more pronounced, EPPs have a role to assist pre-service teachers in developing the knowledge and training necessary to work with students of color. To shift the trajectory of marginalized students' involvement in STEM, EPPs must enrich their programs and courses with approaches that align with the lived experiences of students that teacher candidates are seeking to instruct. One such approach is culturally relevant pedagogy (CRP, Ladson-Billings, 1995).

While this framework has evolved over the last few decades, seeping into certain aspects of K-12 instruction (Paris, 2012), its presence in institutions of higher education and into EPPs remains barely visible (Schmid et al., 2016; Williams & Lewis, 2020). Research demonstrates the importance and effectiveness of CRP in K-12 classrooms (Abiola-Farinde et al., 2017; Herrera, 2017), which raises the question; are EPPs immersing pre-service teachers in methods course that blend national standards and CRP authentically? Thus, this study has two aims; to analyze nationally ranked EPPs offering of STEM methods courses to ascertain what STEM content is provided through course description; and determine to what extent these courses explicitly or implicitly insert aspects of CRP in these artifacts. Next, is a cogent literature review of EPPs responsibilities when offering method courses to pre-service teachers, followed by the conceptual framework which guides this study, CRP. We conclude with implications and recommendations of how EPPs can insert CRP into their STEM methods course with fidelity.

LITERATURE REVIEW

EPPs' Role in Preparing Teacher Candidates to Apply Pedagogical Content Knowledge

Yearly, thousands of pre-service teachers undertake what are known as methods courses. These courses are typically offered during the third year of coursework after pre-service teachers have completed general education courses and content-specific courses. What sets method courses apart from general education courses is that university faculty are responsible for facilitating pre-service teachers' acquisition of pedagogical and content knowledge. Schulman indicates that PCK is knowledge used to reconfigure subject matter content into more manageable forms so students are able to recognize, organize, and apply content beyond strictly memorization (Schulman, 1986, 1987). There are two knowledge bases for which teachers draw on and each base influences the other. Grossman (1990) notes, subject matter knowledge requires that teachers have a firm understanding of syntactic knowledge and substantive knowledge. However, this knowledge alone is mute without teachers acquiring the pedagogical knowledge of their students' learning styles, the ability of teachers to manage their classroom by utilizing the curriculum to offer engaging instruction, and teachers conducting and analyzing formative and summative assessments to usher students towards their educational goals (1990). The last element that is often ignored in PCK is the incorporation of context (social, emotional, economic, etc.) and how that context influences students' ability to understand how teachers deliver content and apply pedagogy. PCK is recognized as a fundamental capability that teachers must have and understand how to refine prior to entering the classroom (American Association for the Advancement of Science,1993). While the origination of PCK attempted to bridge the distance between theoretical and conceptual underpinnings in content areas and pedagogical approaches that teachers utilize to best instruct students, other iterations of PCK have emerged to include things such as the importance of technology (TPACK) in instruction (Koehler & Mishra, 2009). PCK as a framework continues to evolve as more refined standards emerge but also as the learners who sit in classrooms continue to require more robust offering content that is relevant to their lives.

EPPs' STEM Methods Courses and Guiding Standards

Around 2018, the Council for the Accreditation of Education Preparation (CAEP) emerged to proffer standards to guide how EPPs prepared elementary teachers in the U.S. These standards were built on several previous standards constructed by the National Council for Accreditation of Teacher Education (NCATE) and the Teacher Education Accreditation Council (TEAC). These governing bodies previously oversaw the accreditation of most EPPs in the U.S.; however, based on a report on the status of accreditation of EPPs in the U.S., NCATE and TEAC agreed to the formation of a new governing body known as CAEP (CAEP, n.d.a). According to CAEP's website, "CAEP advances equity and excellence in educator preparation through evidence-based accreditation that assures quality and supports continuous improvement to strengthen P-12 student learning," (CAEP, n.d.b.). CAEP provides six strategic goals which are continuous improvement; quality assurance; credibility; diversity, equity and inclusion; strong foundation; and innovation. While each of the strategic goals are important, for the purposes of this study we lean on the goals of diversity, equity, and inclusion, and a strong foundation. Goal 4 indicates that "CAEP will ensure the consistent application of the principles of diversity, equity, and inclusion in its evaluation of providers,"; and Goal 5 states that CAPE will continuously monitor and improve internal policies, processes, and procedures to assure transparency, accountability, fiscal efficiency, and high-quality service and support, to serve as a model of equity and attention to diversity and inclusion," (CAEP, n.d.b). Applying goal Goal 4 and 5 specifically, CAEP will assess EPPs' ability to intertwine five standards as it relates to diversity, equity, and inclusion in STEM methods courses.

Further, CAEPs indicate that EPPs must ensure that teachers enter the field showcasing proficiency among five standards; 1) understanding and addressing each child's developmental and learning needs; 2) understanding and applying content and curricular knowledge for teaching; 3) assessing, planning, designing contexts for learning, 4) supporting each child's learning using effective instruction; 5) and showcase the ability to develop as a profession. Figure 1 provides a more detailed explanation of the standards.

Figure 1. CAEP standards for K-6 elementary teacher preparation standards

Standard 1	Candidates use their understanding of child growth and development, individual differences, and diverse families, cultures and communities to plan and implement inclusive learning environments that provide each child with equitable access to high quality learning experiences that engage and create learning opportunities for them to meet high standards. They work collaboratively with families to gain a holistic perspective on children's strengths and needs and how to motivate their learning
Standard 2	Candidates demonstrate and apply understandings of major concepts, skills, and practices, as they interpret disciplinary curricular standards and related expectations within and across literacy, mathematics, science, and social studies.
Standard 3	Candidates assess students, plan instruction and design classroom contexts for learning. Candidates use formative and summative assessment to monitor students' learning and guide instruction. Candidates plan learning activities to promote a full range of competencies for each student. They differentiate instructional materials and activities to address learners' diversity. Candidates foster engagement in learning by establishing and maintaining social norms for classrooms. They build interpersonal relationships with students that generate motivation, and promote students social and emotional development.
Standard 4	Candidates make informed decisions about instruction guided by knowledge of children and assessment of children's learning that result in the use of a variety of effective instructional practices that employ print, and digital appropriate resources. Instruction is delivered using a cohesive sequence of lessons and employing effective instructional practices. Candidates use explicit instruction and effective feedback as appropriate, and use whole class discussions to support and enhance children's learning. Candidates use flexible grouping arrangements, including small group and individual instruction to support effective instruction and improved learning for every child
Standard 5	Candidates promote learning and development of every child through participation in collaborative learning environments, reflective self-study and professional learning, and involvement in their professional community.

Note. Retrieved from CAEP 2018, K-6 Elementary Teacher Preparation Standards, Updated 2021

While each of these standards is critical to the development of preservice teachers, there is a clear connection between standards 1-4 to Schulman's request for EPPs to better support teachers' ability to master PCK. With regard to STEM pre-service teachers, Standard 2, specifically 2.b and 2.c, requires that "candidates not only demonstrate and apply understanding of major mathematical concepts (algorithms, procedures, and practices)" but also, "demonstrate and apply understands and integration of the three dimensions of science and engineering practices, crosscutting concepts, and major disciplinary core ideas, within the major content areas of science" (CAEP, p. 10). Typically, pre-service teachers can come to enroll in one or multiple methods courses, with sequenced courses offering pre-service teachers immersive opportunities to utilize what they learned in the classroom alongside a mentor teacher. The explicitness of Standard 2 allows EPPs to construct rubrics that gauge what aspects are covered in university methods courses, and which aspects pre-service teachers display in the classroom. However, what remains elusive for EPPs, as evident throughout the literature (Sleeter, 2017; Williams & Glass, 2019), is the ability of PSTs to adhere to aspects of diversity, individual differences among students, students' culture, and cultivating interpersonal relationships with students (i.e., Standards 1 and 3).

Extant literature on EPPs denote that the majority of teachers struggle to develop the pedagogical capabilities to incorporate students' diversity, individual differences, and culture (Ladson-Billings, 2014, 2021a). Furthermore, research underscore the difficulty that teachers have with ensuring that the content provided is relevant to the lives of students, especially students from culturally, linguistically, economically, and ethnically diverse backgrounds (CLEED) (Sleeter, 2008). Although this reality existed prior to CAEP developing their standards, the lack of cultural relevance/responsiveness by educators is alarming, given statistical evidence that over half of the K-6 student population is CLEED. Scholars indicate that cultural relevance, as context, is just as vital to PCK (Aguirre et al., 2012) as subject matter knowledge and pedagogical knowledge (Ladson-Billings, 1995). While CAEP appears to value diversity, equity, and inclusion, their language in the standards appears to, in a roundabout way, indicate that PCK is not sufficient enough with teachers' having the capability to be culturally relevant.

CONCEPTUAL FRAMEWORK: CULTURALLY RELEVANT PEDAGOGY

The guiding framework for this study is culturally relevant pedagogy (CRP, Ladson-Billings, 1995, 2006). Leading up to Ladson-Billings' (1995) conceptualization of CRP, scholars examined methods of improving educational experiences and outcomes for students of color through analyses of differences between school learning and cultural learning outside of school (Au & Jordan, 1981; Jensen, 1969; Macias, 1987); cultural patterns of teacher behaviors and the effects on students (Mohatt & Erickson, 1981); and the racial aspects of culture in education (Irvine, 1990). Building on prior scholarship and analyzing exemplary teachers of Black students, Ladson-Billings (1995) utilized grounded theory to develop CRP, a pedagogical theory that recognizes the cultural assets that students bring into the classroom.

Ladson-Billings (1995) identified three broad propositions regarding common characteristics that exemplary teachers of Black students possessed to outline the practical basis of CRP. The first proposition is the commitment of teachers to the conceptions of themselves as community members, giving back to the community through teaching and asset perspective of students' knowledge and capabilities (Ladson-Billings, 1995). This proposition highlights not only the teachers' commitment to promoting high expectations for academic achievement but also their belief in the potential for value added to the curriculum by incorporating community events and students' backgrounds. Ladson-Billings's (1995) second proposition, the importance of social relations, describes the value of creating a community of learners through encouraging classroom interactions that foster collaboration and equitable/reciprocal teacher-student relationships. Student-centered learning through constructive interactions with teachers and peers supports student growth through affirming social relationships. The last proposition pertains to teachers' conceptions of knowledge. Exemplary teachers view knowledge as a dynamic, multifaceted product that is "shared, recycled, and constructed" (Ladson-Billings, 1995, p. 481) and subjected to critical analysis. Further, Ladson-Billings (1995) posits that multiple assessment strategies of students' knowledge support student learning and success. Although the propositions of CRP may seem straightforward or obvious characteristics of "good teaching", Ladson-Billings (1995) highlights the absence of the application of the strategies in classrooms populated with Black students. Further, Ladson-Billings (1995) emphasizes the importance of providing PSTs with both practical and theoretical examples of culturally relevant teaching to support the learning of all of their future students.

Our analysis of STEM methods course descriptions is guided by the three tenets of CRP: *academic achievement* (student learning), *sociopolitical conciousness*, and *cultural competence*. The CRP tenet of *academic achievement* refers to students' knowledge and skills developed "as a result of pedagogical interactions with skilled teachers" (Ladson-Billings, 2006, p. 34). Evidence of students' learning and academic achievement may include outcomes such as high standardized exam scores, however, this is only a mechanism that allows students to suceed academically (Milner, 2011). The next tenet, *sociopolitcal consciousness* describes teachers developing students' abilities to think critically about their own social position within their environment (e.g., school, city, state) and how students' daily lives and education are impacted by political and social factors (Ladson-Billings, 2006). The final tenet of CRP is *cultural competence*. Through this tenet, teachers affirm and support students' cultural backgrounds by "helping students recognize and honor their own cultural beliefs" (Ladson-Billings, 2006, p. 36), and teachers expand students' awareness of other cultures. Developing students' cultural competence is providing students with knowledge of cultures in *addition* to their own in order to prepare them for succeeding in a multicultural society. Thus in order for teachers to infuse CRP into their practice, teachers must first have exposure and experience.

Furthermore, research underscores the critical role that CRP has had on teachers ability to authentically engage students, but also how CRP has served as a approach to improve students academic progress in K-12 classrooms (Christianakis, 2011; Ensign, 2003; Rodriguez et al., 2004; Tate, 1995). Throughout the past decade CRP has grown to encompass other frameworks such as culturally sustaining pedagogy (Paris, 2012), CRP the Remix 2.0 (Ladson-Billings, 2014, 2021a), and culturally relevant education (Aaronson & Laughter, 2016) which encourage teachers to extend past their nuanced – often deficit based – understanding of culture, and embrace and sustain students' entire cultural identity (race, ethnicity, language, nationality, ability, etc.) in the classroom. What is concerning is that although this framework has aided numerous educators and improved the educational opportunities for historically marginalized students and White students alike, there is a considerable amount of distrust – particularly among K12 educators in the U.S. (Flory, 2016). Literature on CRP and STEM has grown considerably over the years, yet more work is still needed to bridge theory into practice.

CRP Integrated Into STEM

The research on CRP and its use in K-5 classrooms as it relates to STEM is burgeoning, and its impact continues to be revealed through small-scale studies (Adams & Laughter, 2012; Brown et al., 2019; Dimmick, 2012; Howard, 2011). Still, Brown et al. (2019) denotes that much of what STEM teachers are gaining in regard to CRP is through professional development; which informs teachers how to provide STEM content through an extremely narrow lens; one where students are indoctrinated through limited content without having the content tied back to the "culture of the students' lived lives as valuable areas of inquiry," (p. 778). The cultural evasiveness of teachers, and in this case, teachers in STEM fields, is derived from preconceived notions of what is and what is not CRP in the classroom (Brown & Krippen, 2017; Lee & Buxton, 2010; Parker et al., 2017; Patchen & Cox-Petersen, 2008). Much of the resistance by teachers in the field is from their lack of understanding of this framework, with many feeling that by being relevant, they must "dumb" down the content. CRP is not simply slapping on media sensationalized elements such as popular song or movie or reorganizing one's dress to mirror what students wear – unauthentically (Ladson-Billings, 2000). Additionally, some teachers expressed that this framework pushes them to have lower expectations: which is in stark contrast to the core tenet Ladson-Billings put forth. These misconceptions and the misapplication of CRP highlight a longstanding disconnect between the use of the framework and EPPs incorporation of CRP throughout the courses that pre-services are mandated to enroll in (Williams & Lewis, 2022). If teachers are not entering the field with a firm understanding of CRP and how to deploy it authentically in the classroom, then how can they bridge CRP and STEM to get K-5 students to engage in STEM activities in the classroom and beyond? Drawing back to Brown et al. (2019) and CAEP Standards 1-3, the capability of a teacher to understand mathematical concepts and applications, apply the concepts and applications toward students learning opportunities, and buttress the aforementioned items through culture, diversity, and equity is directly connected to content offered in their methods courses.

METHOD

The present study utilized a content analysis of EPP's STEM methods course descriptions to evaluate the types of STEM methods courses offered as well as to what extent course descriptions offer aspects of CRP. Content analysis is the systematic review of texts and artifacts, which are then coded into categories to describe explicit messages and inferences (Weber, 1990). Moreover, researchers have conducted content analyses of course syllabi in recent years to elucidate the presence or lack of specific content such as group work, social justice, and ethics (Griffith et al., 2014; Mehrotra et al., 2017; Sweifach, 2015). The initial intention of this study was to utilize STEM methods course syllabi for the content analysis; however, due to the absence of publicly available syllabi, the research utilized course descriptions. Thus, in employing a content analysis, we aimed to glean if EPPs inserted specific words and phrases in their course descriptions that aligned with CRP. This study was driven by two research questions:

1. What types of methods courses (science, technology, engineering, and mathematics) are offered to K-5 pre-service teachers EPPs?

2. To what extent are course descriptions offering some or all aspects of culturally relevant pedagogy, and how are they for K-5 STEM pre-service teachers specifically?

Data Collection

Using the most recent data from the National Center for Education Statistics (NCES, 2021), the research team analyzed the top teacher-producing EPPs graduating during the 2019-2020 academic year (based on the number of graduates produced per year whose major was education). The majority of institutions were located in New York, Texas, California, Texas, Illinois, and Florida. The research team sought to determine if these EPPs held elementary education programs, resulting in a sample of n = 25 institutions (see Table 1). Out of the n = 25 institutions, 76% were public universities, while 24% were private. All of the universities in the sample were face-to-face.

Table 1. Frequency count of EPPs by institution type (n = 25)

Factor	Total	%
Type	25	
Public	19	76
Private	6	24
Location		
Campus-based	25	100
Web-based	0	

This study sought after publicly available information, as CAEP indicates that transparency of programs is vital to ensuring diversity, equity, and inclusion during the accreditation process (CAEP, n.d.c). To extract information on STEM methods courses, the research team visited each institution's website to gather course descriptions from course catalogs and course offerings in the last 2 years. Data was then inserted into an Excel document, separated out by the EPP, the course identification number, the course name, and whether or not the course had a description.

Data Analysis

For the content analysis, the research team developed a rubric using CRP (Ladson-Billings, 1995, 2006), which allowed all the researchers to assess each EPP (see Table 2). The researchers adapted the rubric to an online Google Form and included questions regarding the institution name, type (i.e., public, private), course name, discipline (e.g., engineering), and *explicit/implicit* mention of aspects of CRP (see Table 2). If a course description *explicitly* mentioned CRP, it verbatim included keywords such as relationship or high expectations. Further, the identified keywords must also follow the definitions included in Table 2. If a course description included an *implicit* mention of CRP, it included a description of an aspect of a CRP element from Table 2 without mentioning it verbatim. Pseudonyms were assigned to the universities. The research team coded a sample of n = 3 course descriptions to establish an inter-rater agreement of 80% (Gisev et al., 2013).

Table 2. Course description rubric

Aspect	Definition
Student choice	Student participation in the selection and discussion of curriculum (Morrison et al., 2008)
Student collaboration	Encourage students to teach each other, learn from peers, and be accountable for each others' learning (Ladson-Billings, 1995)
Curriculum towards collective action	Development of democratic citizenship through applying content knowledge (e.g., mathematics and science) and processes (Tate, 1995)
Meeting the needs of individual students	Equitable treatment of the diverse social emotional, cultural, and/or academic needs of students (Gay, 2002; Jagers et al., 2019)
Instructional conversation	Student-driven discussions of content (Ladson-Billings, 1995)
Language development	Additive academic language development that places value on students' language learning and processes in-side and out-side of school (Godley & Minnici, 2008; Ortiz & Ruwe, 2022)
High expectations	Belief that all students are capable of achieving high standards and providing appropriate scaffolds (Ladson-Billings, 1995)
Multiple means of demonstrating understanding	Variety of ways of assessing students' mastery of material such as written or verbal prompts (Ladson-Billings, 1995)
Relationships/trust	Establishing positive teacher-student and student-student relationships to create a community of learners (Ladson-Billings, 1995)
Connections to other disciplines and world outside of school	Multiple disciplines are used to understand the problem accounting for the sociopolitical context (Gunckel & Tolbert, 2018)
None	None of the aforementioned aspects were explicitly or implicity included

FINDINGS

The findings from this study are truncated into the two respective research questions: *what courses (science, technology, engineering, and mathematics) are offered to K-5 pre-service teachers in high-ranked EPPs; and to what extent are course descriptions offering some or all aspects of culturally relevant pedagogy for K-5 STEM pre-service teachers?*

STEM Methods Courses Offered

Across the n = 25 EPPs examined, there were n = 73 STEM methods courses publicly available online. These courses were specifically offered for elementary education PSTs. There was a higher percentage of mathematics (47.95%) and science (39.73%) methods courses. Further, less than 10% of the STEM methods courses were interdisciplinary (i.e., mathematics and science, STEM), and less than 5% of the STEM methods courses were pertaining to technology. This illuminates a heavy emphasis on separately focusing on mathematics and science methods in EPPs.

Content Analysis of Course Descriptions

Out of the n = 73 STEM methods courses from the EPPs, n = 21 (28.77%) did not include course descriptions. After analyzing the n = 52 course descriptions, only n = 34 (65.38%) included aspects of CRP. Table 3 shows the frequency of CRP aspects across STEM methods courses. The aspects of CRP *connections to other disciplines*, *meeting the needs of individual students*, and *multiple means of demonstrating understanding* had the highest frequencies (see Table 3), while there was an absence of *language development, relationships/trust,* and *curriculum towards action*. Table 4 includes coding samples from the content analysis.

Table 3. Frequency of CRP Aspects Across STEM Methods Courses

	Overall	Mathematics	Science	Mathematics & Science	STEM	Technology
Connections to Other Disciplines	13	3	7	0	3	0
Meeting the Needs of Individual Students	14	6	7	0	1	0
Student Collaboration	2	1	1	0	0	0
Multiple Means of Demonstrating Understanding	15	12	0	0	2	0
Instructional Conversations	4	3	1	0	0	0
High Expectations	1	1	0	0	0	0
Language development	0	0	0	0	0	0
Relationships/trust	0	0	0	0	0	0
Curriculum towards collective action	0	0	0	0	0	0

Connections to Other Disciplines and the World Outside of School

Approximately a quarter of the STEM methods courses contained an explicit or implicit reference to integrating multiple disciplines and accounting for the sociopolitical contexts of problems (see Figure 2). Specifically, course descriptions that included this aspect mentioned examples such as incorporating students' personal and social understandings, culture, and setting (e.g., urban) (see Table 4). Furthermore, course descriptions that included interdisciplinary and real-world connections placed an emphasis on making connections from the main discipline (e.g., science) to other disciplines.

"What Are We Missing?"

Figure 2. Percentage of CRP Aspects Across STEM Methods Course Descriptions

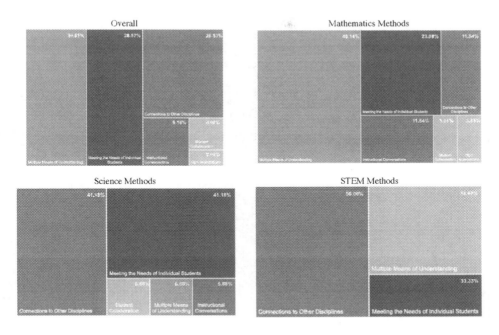

Table 4. Content Analysis Sample Coding

CRP Aspect	College/University (pseudonym)	Discipline(s)	Example
Connections to other disciplines and world outside of school	Huerta University	STEM	Analysis, application and evaluation of strategies for transformative teaching of STEM education in a diverse linguistic, socioeconomic, and cultural milieu.
	Huerta University	Science	Analysis, application, evaluation of strategies for transformative teaching of elementary school science in urban classrooms.
	Tourney University	Science	Build student understanding of personal and social applications, to convey the nature of science, and student development for the practice of skills that contribute to good health.
Meeting the Individual Needs of Students	Cardinal University	Mathematics	Intentional planning for instruction, the interrelated nature of assessment and instruction, and the diverse needs of learners (including a focus on modifications, accommodations, and students with exceptionalities) are addressed through class discussions, activities, and assignments.
	Fred University	Mathematics	Meeting the needs of culturally and academically diverse learners
	Finnigan University	Mathematics	Articulate the responsibilities of teachers of mathematics to teach in ways that are culturally responsive, promote equity in mathematics education, and support elementary students develop positive mathematical identities

continues on following page

Table 4. Continued

CRP Aspect	College/University (pseudonym)	Discipline(s)	Example
Student Collaboration	Chelsea University	Mathematics	Problem solve, communicate with others about mathematics, and make mathematical connections while working within groups to complete activities and assignments.
	Finnigan University	Science	Model professional skills required in elementary science including: reading, writing, listening, speaking, problem solving, teaching and learning in diverse settings, and cooperative group work.
Multiple means of demonstrating understanding	Pine University	Mathematics	Emphasis will be placed on using multiple representations in mathematics
	Steven University	Mathematics	Informal and formal assessments of student thinking
	Cardinal University	Mathematics	Intentional planning for instruction, the interrelated nature of assessment and instruction, and the diverse needs of learners (including a focus on modifications, accommodations, and students with exceptionalities) are addressed through class discussions, activities and assignments.
	Williams State University	Science	Explores scientific inquiry by examining science as a way of knowing and by experiencing scientific inquiry in the elementary classroom.
High Expectations	Joseph University	Mathematics	Establish mathematics goals that accommodate students' varied mathematical trajectories and align appropriately with state content and practice standards as well as informal and formal assessments of student thinking.
Instructional Conversations	Joseph University	Mathematics	Create high levels of mathematical interaction by planning for discussion, questioning
	Cardinal University	Mathematics	Developmentally appropriate/effective instructional delivery, facilitation, and methodologies are outlined in regard to the content of the course

Meeting the Needs of Individual Students

Course descriptions that contained explicit or implicit mention of meeting the needs of individual students provide explicit or implicit evidence of providing instruction for PSTs that aims to promote the equitable treatment of students with diverse needs (e.g., academic, cultural). A little over a quarter of the course descriptions (26.92%) included meeting the needs of individual students. The majority of course descriptions included meeting the needs of individual students regarding academic needs (i.e., modifications and accommodations) followed by cultural considerations. Furthermore, a mathematics course description from Finnigan University, was the only description with mention of supporting the development of positive student identities (i.e., mathematics identities).

Multiple Means of Demonstrating Understanding

The most frequently incorporated aspect of CRP in STEM methods course descriptions was multiple means of demonstrating understanding. These course descriptions provided explicit or implicit explanations that PSTs would learn multiple ways to assess students' content mastery. Mathematics methods courses had an emphasis on multiple representations, while science methods courses encouraged multiple ways of demonstrating understanding through inquiry learning. Course descriptions also included reference to PSTs learning to use formative assessment or observations of student conversations and work to gauge content mastery.

Instructional Conversations

In CRP, Ladson-Billings (1995) encourages educators to promote instructional conversations that are student-centered and discussion-based. The teacher acts as a facilitator to elicit classroom conversations on problem solving processes and solutions. In the sample of n = 52 STEM methods courses, only n = 4 course descriptions incorporated training PSTs to utilize instructional conversations. These descriptions included examples such as planning discussion questions for student interaction (see Table 4).

Student Collaborations

Few STEM methods course descriptions included references to student collaboration (see Table 3). However, the n = 2 course descriptions from a mathematics and science methods course included explicit mention of promoting students to work collaboratively through cooperative group work.

High Expectations

An interesting result was that only one STEM methods course included setting high expectations for students (see Tables 3 & 4). The mathematics methods course description from Joseph University discusses teaching PSTs to set expectations for students through establishing individualized mathematics goals. These high expectations are based on student growth and are scaffolded for the student based on prior performance and state standards. Furthermore, the course description includes that goals are measured through multiple means of assessment (i.e., formal and informal).

Distribution of CRP Aspects

Out of the n = 52 STEM methods course descriptions, n = 18 did not include aspects of CRP (i.e., n = 7 mathematics, n = 10 science, n = 1 technology). However, n = 34 of the STEM methods course descriptions included at least one aspect of CRP. Figure 2 illustrates the percentage of CRP aspects across the n = 34 STEM methods courses that included CRP. The distribution of CRP aspects varies across methods course disciplines. Mathematics methods courses not only included the highest frequency of CRP aspects (see Table 3) but also included the widest variety of aspects included (see Figure 2).

DISCUSSION

As teacher educators seek to refine and reinvigorate EPPs, attending to the cultural underpinnings of STEM is essential to provide PSTs with strong pedagogical content knowledge and a strong foundation in culturally relevant pedagogies. Our two research questions focused on the type of STEM methods courses offered by EPP known to graduate the largest number of teachers in the U.S. and explicating through course descriptions if culturally relevant pedagogical content was present. Following a cogent discussion of our findings in connection with the larger literature base, this section will conclude with limitations, implications, and recommendations for EPPs to improve the quality and quantity of STEM methods courses with CRP as a foundational element.

So Much Math and Science, So Little of Everything Else

As per the findings, mathematics and science courses were prevalent among elementary education programs. However, as the acronym suggests, STEM also includes engineering and technology. The meager representation of technology or interdisciplinary courses warrants the question of if methods for interdisciplinary STEM instruction are incorporated into the main methods courses, mathematics, and science. Moreover, since 2013, STEM EPPs have worked to prepare curricula that integrate engineering design into science methods courses (Capobianco & Radloff, 2021; NGSS Lead States, 2013). *Next Generation Science Standards* place heavy emphasis on the design element of engineering as the "iterative development of an object, process, or system to meet human needs and wants" (Wendell, 2014). Furthermore, due to the absence of engineering methods courses for pre-service elementary teachers, it is critical in science methods courses to develop PSTs conceptual and procedural knowledge of engineering design so that they can not only replicate examples from faculty and mentor teachers but so that they can adapt and adjust their lessons to meet the unique needs of their learners (Anderson & Stillman, 2013; Braten, 2019; Stein et al., 2002).

Culturally Relevant Pedagogy: What is Missing and Where

Our findings coincide with other findings which denote missing aspects of CRP in STEM educator preparation courses (Brown et al., 2019). Our findings support the discrepancy of CRP applications across STEM disciplines. Furthermore, the findings also illuminate a disconnect between the realities in the classroom and the theoretical underpinnings present in STEM methods courses. Returning to Schulman's concept of inserting context from students' lives into instruction, the findings highlight the following question: How can teachers begin to construct the lessons necessary to engage elementary students in STEM if they do not know how to build relationships that bring forth the cultural context required to employ PCK? Johnson and colleagues (2011) constructed a transformative professional framework to aid EPPs and university faculty in assessing and evaluating how culturally relevant education is offered to pre-service teachers. Their framework emphasizes the value of providing pre-service teachers the capability to see instruction as bound to the context within and outside of the classroom. Additionally, the framework strives to immerse pre-service teachers in the idea that the lives of students must play an active role in the development of science and mathematics lessons (Johnson et al., 2011).

STEM is a meta-discipline grounded in learning standards where content is discussed and explored as a dynamic, fluid study through the integration of engineering and engineering design practices (Merrill, 2009; Moore et al., 2015). Educators aim to situate STEM in meaningful, authentic contexts through a comprehensive approach (Capraro & Han, 2014). However, as educators seek to promote students' curiosity, problem-solving, creativity, and understanding, attending to the cultural relevance of the lesson is essential. Critical consciousness is necessary to encourage all students to persist, persevere, and succeed in STEM to counter the belief that the meta-discipline is objective and unrelated to race or cultural issues (Ladson-Billings, 2021). Adding a lens of cultural relevance to instruction design, delivery, and assessment can bolster students' interests, self-beliefs, and achievement through a transformative and emancipatory epistemology (Browne, 2017).

RECOMMENDATIONS AND IMPLICATIONS

As colleges and universities aim to produce STEM educators equipped to utilize culturally relevant pedagogical practices, it is important that required methods courses provide students with the tools necessary to teach content and intertwine students' culture and curriculum effectively. To this point, we proffer the following recommendations to ensure that STEM educators are not taught in isolation and are exposed to culturally relevant pedagogy tenets. First, EPPs must reexamine their methods and general education courses to ensure that aspects of CRP are enmeshed throughout. As per CAEP standards, teachers must enter the field ready to engage in equity-based work that values the diversity that their students bring into the classroom. CRP should not exist solely in one course, however, by the time pre-service teachers enter their methods courses (typically junior year), they should have acquired a foundational understanding of CRP. This will allow preservice teachers to employ CRP in conjunction with their newly acquired PCK during their field experiences in the classroom. Secondly, we assert that CRP in methods courses must be accompanied by field experiences with mentor teachers whose practices directly align with the content in the course and CRP. Many pre-service teachers abandon CRP while teaching due to their misunderstanding, the lack of tangible practices provided to them in university coursework, and their inability to witness actual CRP by mentor teachers. To this end, it is imperative that university faculty develop mutually beneficial partnerships with mentor teachers. This partnership can allow mentor teachers to shape the content provided in methods courses and aid in the realignment of course syllabi/descriptions. For university faculty, this partnership will provide them with data on pre-service teachers from mentor teachers as to what elements (PCK, CRP) pre-service teachers are performing well at or need additional support.

CONCLUSIONS AND LIMITATIONS

To expand the STEM pipeline, it is imperative that the teacher workforce is supplied with pre-service teachers equipped to educate a vastly diverse student population. The sample from this study found that pre-service teachers are not provided with methods courses that address pedagogical and content knowledge with CRP as a core component. While we attempted to examine syllabi, one of the limitations of the study was the inability to access syllabi that were not publicly accessible. Furthermore, the course descriptions were from 2019-2020, and it is possible that these descriptions could have changed. Future studies attempting to gauge the extent to which CRP has permeated STEM methods courses should conduct curriculum audits with permission from deans of EPPs. This would provide a more comprehensive examination of the activities, assessments, objectives, and goals within syllabi, which could reveal more language around CRP. These recommendations necessitate additional support for university faculty who instruct STEM teachers to obtain training in CRP at the post-secondary level. Without such training, university faculty in STEM courses could be replicating false concepts of CRP, which would further prevent pre-service teachers from authentically connecting this framework to STEM content. As EPPs attempt to bolster the effectiveness and impact methods courses have on pre-service teachers' acquisition of PCK, the insertion of CRP would assist in that endeavor and offer new elementary teachers approaches that improve culturally diverse students engagement in and mastery of STEM content.

REFERENCES

Adams, A., & Laughter, J. (2012). Making space for space traders. *Multicultural Learning and Teaching*, *7*(2). doi:10.1515/2161-2412.1121

Aguirre, J. M., Zavala, M. D. R., & Katanyoutanant, T. (2012). Developing robust forms of pre-service teachers' pedagogical content knowledge through culturally responsive mathematics teaching analysis. *Mathematics Teacher Education and Development*, *14*(2), 113–136.

American Association for the Advancement of Science (AAAS). (1993). *Benchmarks for scientific literacy*. AAAS.

Anderson, L. M., & Stillman, J. A. (2013). Student teaching's contribution to preservice teacher development: A review of research focused on the preparation of teachers for urban and high-needs contexts. *Review of Educational Research*, *83*(1), 3–69. doi:10.3102/0034654312468619

Aronson, B., & Laughter, J. (2016). The theory and practice of culturally relevant education: A synthesis of research across content areas. *Review of Educational Research*, *86*(1), 163–206. doi:10.3102/0034654315582066

Au, K., & Jordan, C. (1981). Teaching reasoning to Hawaiian children: Finding a culturally appropriate solution. In H. Trueba, G. Guthrie, & K. Au (Eds.), *Culture and the bilingual classroom: Studies in classroom ethnography* (pp. 139–152). Newbury House.

Bell, P., Van Horne, K., & Cheng, B. H. (2017). Special issue: Designing learning environments for equitable disciplinary identification. *Journal of the Learning Sciences*, *26*(3), 367–375. doi:10.1080/10508406.2017.1336021

Bock, C. (2022). Diversity, equality, and inclusion in our professions: A thin and leaky pipeline. *The Electrochemical Society Interface*, *31*(41), 41–44. doi:10.1149/2.F08221IF

Brown, B. A., Boda, P., Lemmi, C., & Monroe, X. (2019). Moving culturally relevant pedagogy from theory to practice: Exploring teachers' application of culturally relevant education in science and mathematics. *Urban Education, 54*(6), 775–803. doi:10.1177/0042085918794802

Brown, J. C. (2017). A metasynthesis of the complementarity of culturally responsive and inquiry-based science education in K-12 settings: Implications for advancing equitable science teaching and learning. *Journal of Research in Science Teaching, 54*(9), 1143–1173. doi:10.1002/tea.21401

Capobianco, B. M., & Radloff, J. (2021). Elementary preservice teachers' trajectories for appropriating engineering design–based science teaching. *Research in Science Education*. Advance online publication. doi:10.1007/s11165-021-10020-y

Capraro, R. M., & Han, S. (2014). STEM: The education frontier to meet 21st-century challenges. *Middle Grades Research Journal, 9*(3), xv.

Casto, A. R., & Williams, J. A. (2020). Seeking proportionality in the North Carolina STEM pipeline. *High School Journal, 103*(2), 77–98. doi:10.1353/hsj.2020.0004

Christianakis, M. (2011). Hybrid texts: Fifth graders, rap music, and writing. *Urban Education, 46*(5), 1131–1168. doi:10.1177/0042085911400326

Council for the Accreditation of Educator Preparation. (n.d.a). *History of CAEP.* CAEP. https://caepnet.org/about/history

Council for the Accreditation of Educator Preparation. (n.d.b.). *Vision, mission, & goals.* CAEP. https://caepnet.org/about/vision-mission-goals

Council for the Accreditation of Educator Preparation. (n.d.c). [Elementary Teacher Preparation Standards: Updated Resources.]. *CAEP, 2018*, K-6.

Crabtree, L. M., Richardson, S. C., & Lewis, C. W. (2019). The gifted gap, STEM education, and economic immobility. *Journal of Advanced Academics, 30*(2), 203–231. doi:10.1177/1932202X19829749

Dimmick, A. (2012). Student empowerment in an environmental science classroom: Toward a framework for social justice education. *Science Education, 96*(6), 990–1012. doi:10.1002/sce.21035

Ensign, J. (2003). Including culturally relevant math in an urban school. *Educational Studies, 34*(4), 414–423.

Flory, S. B. (2016). Culturally responsive pedagogy and teacher socialization. In *Teacher socialization in physical education* (pp. 178–191). Routledge.

Gay, G. (2002). Preparing for culturally responsive teaching. *Journal of Teacher Education*, *53*(2), 106–116. doi:10.1177/0022487102053002003

Gisev, N., Bell, J. S., & Chen, T. F. (2013). Interrater agreement and interrater reliability: Key concepts, approaches, and applications. *Research in Social & Administrative Pharmacy*, *9*(3), 330–338. doi:10.1016/j.sapharm.2012.04.004 PMID:22695215

Godley, A. J., & Minnici, A. (2008). Critical language pedagogy in an urban high school English class. *Urban Education*, *43*(3), 319–346. doi:10.1177/0042085907311801

Griffith, S. M., Domenech Rodríguez, M., & Anderson, A. J. (2014). Graduate ethics education: A content analysis of syllabi. *Training and Education in Professional Psychology*, *8*(4), 248–252. doi:10.1037/tep0000036

Grossman, P. L. (1990). *The making of a teacher: Teacher knowledge and teacher education*. Teachers College Press.

Gunckel, K. L., & Tolbert, S. (2018). The imperative to move toward a dimension of care in engineering education. *Journal of Research in Science Teaching*, *55*(7), 938–961. doi:10.1002/tea.21458

Henry, H. (2018, July 10). *Research reveals boys' interest In STEM careers declining; Girls' interest unchanged*. Junior Achievement of Southern Massachusetts. https://somass.ja.org/news/blog/research-reveals-boys-interest-in-stem-careers-declining-girls-interest-unchanged

Herrera, S. G., Holmes, M. A., & Kavimandan, S. K. (2012). Bringing theory to life: Strategies that make culturally responsive pedagogy a reality in diverse secondary classrooms. *International Journal of Multicultural Education*, *14*(3), 1–19. doi:10.18251/ijme.v14i3.608

Howard, T. C. (2011). Culturally responsive pedagogy. In J. A. Banks (Ed.), *Transforming multicultural education, policy, & practice: Expanding educational opportunity* (pp. 137–163). Teachers College Press.

Irvine, J. J. (1990). *Black students and school failure: Personnel, practices, and prescriptions*. Greenwood.

Jagers, R. J., Rivas-Drake, D., & Williams, B. (2019). Transformative social and emotional learning (SEL): Toward SEL in service of educational equity and excellence. *Educational Psychologist*, *54*(3), 162–184. doi:10.1080/00461520.2019.1623032

Jensen, A. R. (1969). How much can we boost IQ and scholastic achievement? *Harvard Educational Review*, *19*(1), 1–123. doi:10.17763/haer.39.1.13u15956627424k7

Johnson, A., Brown, J., Carlone, H., & Cuevas, A. K. (2011). Authoring identity amidst the treacherous terrain of science: A multiracial feminist examination of the journeys of three women of color in science. *Journal of Research in Science Teaching, 48*(4), 339–366. doi:10.1002/tea.20411

Koehler, M., & Mishra, P. (2009). What is technological pedagogical content knowledge (TPACK)? *Contemporary Issues in Technology & Teacher Education, 9*(1), 60–70.

Ladson-Billings, G. (1995). Toward a theory of culturally relevant pedagogy. *American Educational Research Journal, 32*(3), 465–491. doi:10.3102/00028312032003465

Ladson-Billings, G. (2006). Yes, but how do we do it? Practicing culturally relevant pedagogy. In J. Landsman & C. W. Lewis (Eds.), *White teachers/diverse classrooms: A guide to building inclusive schools, promoting high expectations and eliminating racism* (pp. 29–42). Stylus Publishers.

Ladson-Billings, G. (2014). Culturally relevant pedagogy 2.0: Aka the remix. *Harvard Educational Review, 84*(1), 74–84. doi:10.17763/haer.84.1.p2rj131485484751

Ladson-Billings, G. (2021a). *Culturally relevant pedagogy: Asking a different question*. Teachers College Press.

Ladson-Billings, G. (2021b). Does that count? How mathematics education can support justice-focused anti-racist teaching and learning. *Journal of Urban Mathematics Education, 14*(1B, 1b), 1–5. doi:10.21423/jume-v14i1Ba444

Lee, O., & Buxton, C. A. (2010). *Diversity and equity in science education: Research, policy, and practice*. Teachers College Press.

Macias, J. (1987). The hidden curriculum of Papago teachers: American Indian strategies for mitigating cultural discontinuity in early schooling. In G. Spindler & L. Spindler (Eds.), *Interpretive ethnography at home and abroad* (pp. 363–380). Lawrence Erlbaum Associates.

Maiorca, C., Roberts, T., Jackson, C., Bush, S., Delaney, A., Mohr-Schroeder, M. J., & Soledad, Y. S. (2021). Informal learning environments and impact on interest in STEM careers. *International Journal of Science and Mathematics Education, 19*(1), 45–64. doi:10.1007/s10763-019-10038-9

Martinez, A., & Christnacht, C. (2021, January 26). *Women are nearly half of U.S. workforce but only 27% of STEM workers*. United States Census Bureau. https://www.census.gov/library/stories/2021/01/women-making-gains-in-stem-occupations-but-still-underrepresented.html

McClure, E., Guernsey, L., Clements, D., Bales, S., Nichols, J., Kendall-Taylor, N., & Levine, M. (2017). Guest editorial: How to integrate STEM into early childhood education. *Science and Children*, *55*(2), 8–10. doi:10.2505/4/sc17_055_02_8

Mehrotra, G. R., Hudson, K. D., & Self, J. M. (2017). What Are We Teaching in Diversity and Social Justice Courses? A Qualitative Content Analysis of MSW Syllabi. *Journal of Teaching in Social Work*, *37*(3), 218–233. doi:10.1080/08841233.2017.1316342

Milner, R. IV. (2011). Culturally relevant pedagogy in a diverse urban classroom. *The Urban Review*, *43*(1), 66–89. doi:10.1007/s11256-009-0143-0

Moore, T. J., Johnson, C. C., Peters-Burton, E. E., & Guzey, S. S. (2015). The need for a STEM road map. In C. C. Johnson, E. E. Peters-Burton, & T. J. Moore (Eds.), *STEM road map: a framework for integrated STEM education*. Routledge. doi:10.4324/9781315753157-1

Morrison, K. A., Robbins, H. H., & Rose, D. G. (2008). Operationalizing culturally relevant pedagogy: A synthesis of classroom-based research. *Equity & Excellence in Education*, *41*(4), 433–452. doi:10.1080/10665680802400006

National Science Board (NSB). (2016). *Science and engineering indicators*. National Science Foundation.

NGSS Lead States. (2013). *Next generation science standards: For states, by states*. The National Academies Press., doi:10.17226/18290

Ortiz, N. A., & Ruwe, D. (2022). Black English and mathematics education: A critical look at culturally sustaining pedagogy. *Teachers College Record*, *123*(10), 185–212. doi:10.1177/01614681211058978

Paris, D. (2012). Culturally sustaining pedagogy: A needed change in stance, terminology, and practice. *Educational Researcher*, *41*(3), 93–97. doi:10.3102/0013189X12441244

Parker, F., Bartell, T. G., & Novak, J. D. (2017). Developing culturally responsive mathematics teachers' evolving conceptions of knowing students. *Journal of Mathematics Teacher Education*, *20*, 385–407. doi:10.1007/s10857-015-9328-5

Patchen, T., & Cox-Petersen, A. (2008). Constructing cultural relevance in science: A case study of two elementary teachers. *Science Education*, *92*(6), 994–1014. doi:10.1002/sce.20282

Rodriguez, J. L., Jones, E. B., Pang, V. O., & Park, C. D. (2004). Promoting academic achievement and identity development among diverse high school students. *High School Journal*, *87*(3), 44–53. doi:10.1353/hsj.2004.0002

Schmid, M. E., Gillian-Daniel, D. L., Kraemer, S., & Kueppers, M. (2016). Promoting student academic achievement through faculty development about inclusive teaching. *Change*, *48*(5), 16–25. doi:10.1080/00091383.2016.1227672

Shulman, L. (1986). Those who understand: Knowledge growth in teaching. *Educational Researcher*, *15*(1), 4–14. doi:10.2307/1175860

Shulman, L. (1987). Knowledge and teaching: Foundations of the new reform. *Harvard Educational Review*, *57*(1), 1–22. doi:10.17763/haer.57.1.j463w79r56455411

Sleeter, C. E. (2008), Preparing white teachers for diverse students, in Cochran-Smith, M., FeimanNemser, S., McIntyre, D.J. and Demers, K.E. (Eds), Handbook of Research on Teacher Education: Enduring Questions in Changing Contexts. Routledge.

Sleeter, C. E. (2017). Critical race theory and the whiteness of teacher education. *Urban Education*, *52*(2), 155–169. doi:10.1177/0042085916668957

Sweifach, J. S. (2015). Has group work education lost its social group work essence? A content analysis of MSW course syllabi in search of mutual aid and group conflict content. *Journal of Teaching in Social Work*, *35*(3), 279–295. doi:10.1080/08841 233.2015.1031928

Tate, W. F. (1995). Returning to the root: A culturally relevant approach to mathematics pedagogy. *Theory into Practice*, *34*(3), 166–173. doi:10.1080/00405849509543676

Vilorio, D. (2014). STEM 101: Intro to tomorrow's jobs. *Occupational Outlook Quarterly*, 2–12. http://www.bls.gov/caree routlook/

Weber, R. P. (1990). Basic content analysis. Springer. doi:10.4135/9781412983488

Wendell, K. B. (2014). Design practices of preservice elementary teachers in an integrated engineering and literature experience. *Journal of Pre-College Engineering Education Research*, *4*(2), 4. doi:10.7771/2157-9288.1085

Williams, J. A. III, & Glass, T. S. (2019). Teacher education and multicultural courses in North Carolina. *Journal for Multicultural Education*, *13*(2), 155–168. doi:10.1108/JME-05-2018-0028

Williams, J. A. III, & Lewis, C. W. (2020). Enriching their potential: Supporting Black male teacher candidates in the age of edTPA. *Peabody Journal of Education*, *95*(5), 472–483. doi:10.1080/0161956X.2020.1828685

Young, J. R., Ortiz, N., & Young, J. L. (2017). STEMulating interest: A meta-analysis of the effects of out-of-school time on student STEM interest. *International Journal of Education in Mathematics. Science and Technology*, *5*(1), 62–74. doi:10.18404/ijemst.61149

Chapter 3
Enhancing Elementary Teacher Preparation:
The Vital Role of STEM-Integrated Experiences in Oman

Mohamed A. Shahat
https://orcid.org/0000-0002-9637-8192
Sultan Qaboos University, Oman & Aswan University, Egypt

Khalsa H. Al Bahri
Ministry of Education, Oman

Sulaiman M. Al-Balushi
Sultan Qaboos University, Oman

ABSTRACT

This chapter highlights the importance of integrating STEM (science, technology, engineering, and mathematics) into teacher education to equip educators with the tools needed for effective teaching in contemporary STEM fields. The chapter strongly emphasizes the necessity of continuous professional development, innovative curriculum design, and the creation of supportive learning environments. Furthermore, it advocates for ongoing research to identify and implement effective STEM teaching strategies that engage students effectively. In conclusion, this chapter underscores Oman's commitment to STEM education as a cornerstone for preparing its citizens to face future challenges and seize opportunities. Oman's initiatives serve as an inspiring example for other nations seeking to enhance their own STEM educational frameworks and prepare their youth for the demands of tomorrow.

DOI: 10.4018/978-1-6684-5939-3.ch003

Copyright © 2024, IGI Global. Copying or distributing in print or electronic forms without written permission of IGI Global is prohibited.

INTRODUCTION

The integration of STEM into educational systems, particularly in teacher preparation programs, is a critical undertaking in our rapidly evolving world. STEM covers a broad spectrum of knowledge and skills that are vital to contemporary society. The Next Generation Science Standards (NGSS) underscore the importance of these competencies in addressing societal challenges. By integrating STEM principles into teacher education, future educators are equipped with essential skills to effectively impart this knowledge to their students. The primary goal of incorporating STEM into teacher education is to develop students who are not only knowledgeable in STEM fields but also capable of applying this knowledge innovatively (NGSS Lead States, 2013).

According to Shahat et al. (2023a), ensuring teachers graduate training programs with STEM proficiency is crucial for fostering global competitiveness and innovation, and for preparing students for significant contributions to scientific and technological advancements. The integration of STEM in teacher preparation is deeply anchored in constructivist learning theories. These theories posit that learners construct their own understanding and knowledge through active engagement and reflection on experiences. In STEM-focused educational settings, teacher trainees are not mere recipients of information but active participants in problem-solving and critical thinking, leading to a deeper understanding of the subject matter and its real-world applications (Al-Balushi et al., 2023).

Experiential learning is a fundamental aspect of STEM education, emphasizing hands-on, inquiry-based experiences that prompt learners to explore, experiment, and question. Such engagement helps future teachers gain both a deeper grasp of STEM concepts and the ability to innovatively apply these ideas in their teaching practices. This not only enhances their subject matter expertise but also arms them with the pedagogical skills necessary to facilitate a similar learning experience for their students (Shahat et al., 2023b).

Moreover, this immersive learning approach in STEM education aligns with the contemporary educational shift towards competence-based learning. This paradigm shift focuses on the development of specific skills and competencies, such as problem-solving, critical thinking, and collaboration, rather than solely on rote memorization of facts. By weaving STEM principles into teacher preparation, educators are better positioned to develop these competencies in their students, equipping them for the complexities of the modern world (Al-Balushi et al., 2022).

Furthermore, the constructivist approach in STEM education fosters a culture of continuous learning and adaptability. If future teachers develop a genuine interest in STEM concepts, they will become lifelong learners who strive to continually update their knowledge and skills in response to new scientific and technological discoveries. This adaptability is essential in an ever-evolving educational landscape that requires teachers to stay abreast with the latest developments in their field in order to provide relevant and updated instruction (Shahat et al., 2023a).

In summary, due to it being grounded in constructivist learning theories, integrating STEM into teacher education extends learning beyond mere knowledge transfer. It involves shaping a new generation of educators adept at creating dynamic, interactive, and pertinent learning environments. These environments not only deepen students' understanding of STEM but also prepare them to be innovative, critical thinkers capable of addressing future challenges. Thus, STEM has a crucial role in evolving educational practices, and it has never been more important to prepare teachers who can lead this transformative journey.

INSIGHTS FROM STEM TEACHER PREPARATION INITIATIVES IN DIFFERENT COUNTRIES

Teacher self-efficacy regarding STEM is critical in shaping educational outcomes. Essentially this relates to a teacher's confidence in their ability to effectively impart knowledge and positively impact student learning in STEM subjects. When teacher preparation programs incorporate STEM education, they significantly enhance teacher self-efficacy. This enhancement comes from a combination of direct experience and mastery of STEM content, which bolsters educators' confidence in their teaching abilities. This improved self-assurance in educators not only leads to better teaching practices but also elevates student performance and interest in STEM fields (Ambusaidi et al., 2022).

Though fully integrating STEM education into teacher training programs not only provides future educators with a comprehensive understanding of STEM subject matter but also the necessary pedagogical techniques to teach these subjects effectively. This dual focus on content mastery and teaching methods equips teachers to create enriching and impactful STEM learning experiences for their students. The interdisciplinary nature of STEM education, which requires the application of knowledge and skills across various domains to tackle complex problems, is a key component of this approach. Teachers trained in programs with a strong emphasis on STEM are more adept at nurturing critical problem-solving abilities and fostering innovative thinking in their students, thus preparing them for the challenges of a rapidly evolving global job market (Shahat et al., 2023a).

Moreover, the inclusion of STEM in teacher training programs is instrumental in promoting equitable access to STEM education. By preparing a diverse group of educators proficient in STEM, these programs ensure that students from all backgrounds have the opportunity to receive high-quality STEM education and the benefits it offers. This approach is vital in bridging the educational divide and ensuring that all students, regardless of their socio-economic or cultural background, have access to the skills and knowledge necessary to thrive in STEM fields (Shahat & Al-Balushi., 2023).

This focus on diversity and inclusivity in STEM teacher training is not just beneficial for underrepresented student groups; it is essential for the development of a robust and diverse workforce employed in STEM fields. As the demand for skilled professionals in these areas increases, the need for educators who can inspire and prepare a wider range of students becomes increasingly important. Teachers equipped with strong STEM skills and an inclusive teaching approach are better positioned to unlock the potential in every student, contributing to a more diverse and innovative STEM workforce (Shahat & Al-Amri., 2023).

Specific issues related to diversity and inclusivity are the gender gap and the underrepresentation of certain minorities in STEM fields. Integrating STEM into teacher preparation programs helps to address these challenges. By empowering a diverse group of teachers with the tools and knowledge to provide effective STEM education, these programs play a pivotal role in inspiring a new generation of students from various backgrounds to pursue careers in STEM (Shahat et al., 2023b).

Taking the above into consideration, we present insights from three different contexts around the world in preparing STEM teachers - Finland, Singapore and Australia - and compare these insights to current practices in Oman.

Finland's Experience in Preparing STEM Teachers

Teacher preparation in Finland is overseen by universities, with approximately 10 departments across the country dedicated to this endeavor. Finnish universities base their teacher preparation programs on the National Curriculum standards. Additionally, several centers and online resources support teacher training (Wiksten, 2019) including:

The BioPop Website: This platform promotes biology education and encourages the study of biology at all grade levels. It collaborates with the University of Helsinki and schools, organizing courses, workshops and biology clubs for students.

Laboratory 2F: Focusing on physics and technology, this initiative seeks to enhance understanding and interest in these subjects among Finns. It provides in-service training through workshops and summer courses for physics teachers and classroom teachers. To promote awareness of contemporary physics research, it also organizes science clubs and summer camps for students aged 8 to 14 where they can conduct practical experiments.

Geopiste: As a national resource for geography education, Geopiste serves geography and biology teachers and classroom teachers. It consolidates educational materials and shares information about innovative teaching ideas and methods in geography.

Kemma: This resource center's main objectives are to support in-service and pre-service chemistry teachers, facilitate improved learning and competence in chemistry, and advance chemistry education and research.

Summamutikka: Functioning as a resource center for mathematics education, Summamutikka operates under the National LUMA Center and the Department of Mathematics and Statistics. It provides guidance on teaching activity-based mathematics, supports mathematics teaching, and fosters interest in mathematics across all age groups.

The LUMA Center further supports formal STEM education in schools by facilitating opportunities for teachers to bring their students to authentic STEM laboratories and classrooms located at nearby universities, free of charge. These laboratories include the Gadolin Chemistry Lab, the Linkki Computing Lab, MATLAB Origo, MathLab, the Physics F2k PhysicsLab at the University of Helsinki, the Teknokas Chemistry Laboratory at Chydenius University Centre, the LUMARTS Laboratory at Aalto University, the Physics and Robotics Laboratory at the University of Eastern Finland, a Physics Laboratory at Lappeenranta University of Technology, and the Gadolin Chemistry Laboratory. The Gadolin Chemistry Laboratory, established in 2008, is an active learning environment designed to enhance chemistry-related teaching and learning.

Due to the development of multiple support initiatives, Finland's comprehensive approach to teacher preparation serves as an exemplary model for the effective integration of STEM disciplines in education.

Singapore's Experience in Preparing STEM Teachers

Singapore has a well-structured approach to preparing primary and secondary school teachers that involves three main institutions:

1. The National Institute of Education (NIE): The NIE is the primary provider of courses and programs aimed at equipping novice teachers with postgraduate qualifications in education. These programs also cover educational leadership for senior teachers, heads of departments, deputy principals, and principals.
2. **The Singapore Academy of Teachers (SAT)**: The AST serves as the second provider contributing to the development of educators in Singapore.
3. **Centers** of Excellence: The Ministry of Education in Singapore established six centers of excellence in 2010 to enhance teacher preparation.

Singapore's 21st-century model for teacher education is based around producing 'thinking teachers' and strongly emphasizes collaboration with key stakeholders and schools (Koh & Tan, 2021). Simultaneously, it aims to provide a foundation for general education. This model was developed to bolster essential aspects of teacher education and closely aligns with a STEM-based educational approach. Three key values underpin this model:

- **Learner-Centric Focus:** The model places the learner at the center of the educational process, recognizing the importance of tailoring education to individual needs and fostering student engagement.
- **Teacher's Identity:** The model recognizes the significance of shaping a teacher's identity, which involves instilling a sense of purpose, commitment, and professional growth among educators.
- **Service to the Profession and Society:** In addition to the learner and teacher focus, the model emphasizes the role of educators in serving both the teaching profession and society at large. This includes a commitment to continuous improvement and the sharing of best practices.

Furthermore, the model places a strong emphasis on equipping teachers with the necessary knowledge and skills to respond effectively to the latest global trends. It places great emphasis on the principles and foundations of STEM-based education, and recognizes the significance of science, technology, engineering, and mathematics in modern education. Singapore's approach to preparing STEM teachers is notable for its comprehensive and forward-thinking perspective, emphasizing collaboration, adaptability, and a commitment to the evolving needs of education in the 21st century (Koh & Tan, 2021).

Australian STEM Teacher Preparation

Australia has made significant strides in supporting the professional development of STEM teachers through various projects aimed at enhancing science and mathematics teacher training (Fraser et al., 2019). These initiatives include the following five projects:

1. **Project to Inspire the Numbers of Science and Mathematics Teachers**: Led by the University of Queensland in collaboration with partners such as James Cook University, The University of Newcastle, The University of Sydney, The University of Tasmania, and The University of Wollongong, this project focuses on promoting interdisciplinary approaches to pre-service science and mathematics teacher preparation. It aims to foster sustainable collaboration

among mathematics, science, and education scholars, and develop innovative methods of integrating content and pedagogical experiences to enhance teacher preparation and ongoing professional learning.

2. **A Project That Is Part of My Life**: Led by Southern Cross University and partnered with institutions including CQ University Australia, the University of Ballarat, the University of New England, the University of Southern Queensland, and the University of the Sunshine Coast, this project connects pre-service teachers with science and mathematics in everyday life in regional Australian communities. It seeks to establish collaboration between university science and mathematics researchers, school education professionals, and community representatives to enhance pre-service science and mathematics education.

3. **Real Science Project: Teaching Real Science and Mathematics in Australia:** Led by Macquarie University and involving partners such as the Australian Catholic University, Charles Sturt University, Edith Cowan University, and others, this project aims to improve the quality and outcomes of science and mathematics education in Australia. It accomplishes this by engaging pre- and in-service teachers in real-world science experiences. The project encourages collaboration between teacher leaders, scientists, and mathematicians and provides creative resources for school teachers to inspire students through inquiry-based learning.

4. **Project to Reconceptualize Science and Mathematics Teacher Preparation Programs**: Led by the University of Melbourne in conjunction with partners like Deakin University, La Trobe University, Monash University, and the Victorian Department of Education and Early Childhood Development, this project focuses on the development of new teacher preparation practices. It places an emphasis on contemporary practices in science and mathematics education, emphasizing the importance of teaching practices over mere content delivery.

5. **Step Up Project: Transforming the Preparation of Pre-Service Secondary Science and Mathematics Teachers in Queensland**: Led by the Queensland University of Technology and in collaboration with the Australian Catholic University, Griffith University, James Cook University, the University of Queensland, and the Department of Employment, Training and Education, this project aims to reshape curricula, partnerships, and academic practices to better prepare students for pre-service secondary science and mathematics teacher roles in Queensland.

Australia's commitment to enhancing STEM teacher preparation through these projects reflects a dedication to nurturing a highly skilled and motivated teaching workforce that can improve STEM education across the country. These initiatives promote collaboration, innovation, and the development of effective teaching practices within the STEM disciplines.

In conclusion, this selection of examples from different parts of the world demonstrates the significant investment into teacher preparation and professional development in STEM education. By investing in teachers and providing them with the necessary knowledge, resources, and support, these countries are actively shaping the future of STEM learning and fostering the skills and talents needed to address the complex challenges of the 21st century. These insights from Finland, Singapore, and Australia offer valuable lessons and inspiration for other nations seeking to elevate STEM education on a global scale.

STEM EDUCATION IN OMAN: STRATEGIC INITIATIVES AND IMPACT

The STEM OMAN program, initiated by Oman's Ministry of Education, epitomizes the country's commitment to elevating its educational standards to meet global benchmarks and future demands. This comprehensive initiative spans multiple educational levels, from primary school through to higher education, aiming to imbue students with high-caliber STEM learning experiences (Shahat & Al Amri, 2023).

A cornerstone of this program is the development and refinement of curricula deeply ingrained with STEM principles. It involves both the integration of STEM elements into existing curricula and the creation of innovative educational materials. This approach ensures that students gain foundational knowledge in science, technology, engineering, and mathematics and an understanding of how these disciplines intertwine and relate to real-world contexts (Shahat & Al Amri, 2023).

Recognizing the pivotal role of educators in successful STEM education, the STEM OMAN program heavily invests in professional development for teachers. This investment manifests in various forms, including workshops, training sessions, and continual support to equip teachers with the necessary expertise to teach STEM subjects proficiently. This initiative also fosters an educational atmosphere conducive to inquiry, problem-solving, and critical thinking (Shahat & Al Amri, 2023).

Through this program, the Omani government is also channeling resources into creating state-of-the-art STEM learning environments. These include modern facilities and advanced technology that provide hands-on, experiential learning opportunities. Access to such resources ensures that STEM education transcends theoretical knowledge and deeply engages students in practical applications (Shahat & Al-Balushi, 2023).

Another key objective of the STEM OMAN program is to spark and sustain student interest in STEM fields. This goal is pursued through various initiatives such as STEM clubs, competitions, and events that highlight STEM's dynamic and exciting aspects. Such initiatives encourage students to explore STEM topics outside conventional classroom settings, nurturing a lasting interest in these fields and potentially steering them towards STEM-related careers (Al-Balushi et al., 2022)

The program also emphasizes establishing partnerships with industry, higher education institutions, and international STEM education networks. These collaborations aim to enhance the quality of STEM education, expose students to real-world applications, and align educational content with industry needs and global standards.

A critical aspect of the STEM OMAN program is its commitment to continual assessment and improvement. An effective monitoring and evaluation system is in place to gauge the program's impact, gather stakeholder feedback, and inform future enhancements. This dynamic approach ensures that the program adapts to changing societal and student needs, driving ongoing advancement in STEM education in Oman (Shahat & Al-Balushi, 2023).

In summary, the STEM OMAN program represents a comprehensive, strategic effort to transform STEM education in Oman. It lays a solid foundation for a future where Omani students are well-prepared with the skills, knowledge, and mindset essential for success in the 21st century. Through initiatives in curriculum development, teacher professional development, state-of-the-art learning environments, student engagement programs, collaborative partnerships, and a commitment to continuous improvement, the program is setting the stage for a more innovative and prosperous future for Oman and its citizens.

Oman Vision 2040 and STEM Education

Oman Vision 2040 represents a strategic blueprint reflecting the nation's commitment to advancing STEM education as a cornerstone of its future development. This vision underscores the country's aspirations to foster an inclusive educational system, promote lifelong learning, and support scientific research, with a particular focus on cultivating local talent in STEM disciplines. A key component of this vision is the previously discussed STEM OMAN program, which was designed and launched by the Ministry of Education to elevate the nation's prowess in STEM education across all educational tiers (Ministry of Education, 2021).

The impact of these efforts to enhance STEM education in Oman is becoming increasingly apparent. There is a notable shift towards inquiry-based learning and problem-solving approaches in both school and higher education settings. This evolution in the educational landscape not only benefits Oman but also serves as an instructive model for other countries aiming to strengthen their STEM educational infrastructure. Results from Oman demonstrate the effectiveness of strategic planning and government backing in integrating STEM principles into educational systems, particularly in the realm of teacher training (Shahat & Al-Balushi, 2023).

Oman Vision 2040's focus on STEM education is not merely about enhancing academic performance but also about preparing the Omani youth for the challenges and opportunities of the 21st century. By investing in STEM education, Oman is laying the groundwork for economic diversification, technological advancement, and sustainable development. This approach aligns with global trends and requirements, and positions Oman as a forward-thinking nation ready to contribute significantly to the global knowledge economy (Ministry of Education, 2021). Oman Vision 2040, with its strong emphasis on STEM education, represents a visionary and holistic strategy. Its overarching goal is to elevate Oman into a hub of knowledge, innovation, and excellence within STEM disciplines, ensuring a prosperous and sustainable future for the nation and its people. This vision serves as a benchmark for educational reform and development, demonstrating the transformative potential of strategic planning and government support in shaping a nation's future through education.

Furthermore, the Vision 2040 initiative recognizes the critical role of STEM education in addressing contemporary global challenges, such as climate change, health crises, and technological innovation. By nurturing a generation of skilled problem solvers and innovators, Oman is investing in a future where its citizens are not just participants but leaders in finding solutions to these challenges (Ministry of Education, 2021).

The integration of STEM into teacher education programs carries profound implications for educational practices and policies. Equipping future educators with essential STEM skills lays the foundation for a future where students not only master STEM subjects but also possess the capacity to drive innovation and global competitiveness. Policymakers and educational leaders play a pivotal role in this process, as their support and guidance are essential to aligning teacher training with the latest principles and advancements in STEM education.

Looking forward, it remains imperative to sustain and enhance the integration of STEM into teacher education. This commitment should manifest in the continual evolution of curricula, the provision of ongoing professional development for educators, and the implementation of strategic initiatives similar to Oman's STEM OMAN program. Such endeavors are critical to ensuring that future educators, and subsequently their students, are well-prepared to comprehend and contribute to the dynamic and complex world of STEM.

In summary, the incorporation of STEM principles into teacher preparation extends beyond mere necessity; it represents a fundamental investment in the future of education. Through well-crafted educational initiatives, comprehensive teacher training programs, and unwavering dedication to fostering innovation and inclusivity, we can pave the way for a future where every student is empowered to excel in STEM fields. This approach not only fosters individual academic success but also propels societal progress and innovation for generations to come.

National Initiatives and Experiences in Oman Regarding STEM Education

Oman has been proactively fostering STEM education and aligning it with its broader educational and economic development objectives. This commitment is particularly evident in the realm of elementary education as evidenced by the following initiatives (Shahat & Al-Amri, 2023):

1. Integration of STEM in School Curricula: The Omani education system is progressively integrating STEM subjects into school curricula. This process involves updating and modernizing both content and teaching methods to make STEM education more engaging and relevant. Grants are offered to elementary schools to develop and enhance STEM programs which has enabled the purchase of new technology, laboratory equipment and educational materials designed for young learners.
2. STEM Outreach Programs: A variety of outreach programs have been established to spark student interest in STEM. These include science fairs, robotics clubs, and STEM-focused competitions, aiming to stimulate curiosity and innovation.
3. Scholarships for STEM Studies: The government provides scholarships for students to pursue higher education in STEM fields, both domestically and internationally. This initiative is aimed at cultivating a skilled workforce for critical economic sectors.
4. Collaboration with International Institutions: Oman collaborates with global universities and research institutions to enhance STEM education through exchange programs, joint research, and access to advanced scientific resources.
5. Investment in STEM Infrastructure: Significant investments have been made in developing state-of-the-art STEM education facilities, including modern laboratories, research centers, and technologically equipped classrooms. Grants are also provided for setting up innovation labs or 'maker spaces' in elementary schools, equipped with 3D printers, robotics kits, and computers.

6. Teacher Training and Development: Oman places high importance on the professional development of teachers in STEM and training programs are focusing on new teaching methodologies and technologies. Additionally, funds are allocated for the training of elementary school teachers in STEM subjects through workshops, courses, and certifications.
7. Promotion of STEM Careers: Efforts are underway to raise awareness about the diversity of career opportunities in STEM fields, with career counseling and guidance programs underscoring STEM's relevance across various sectors.
8. National Innovation Strategy: Oman's innovation strategy emphasizes the preparation of students for economic and technological contributions by fostering creativity and problem-solving skills through STEM education.
9. Digital Literacy Programs: Digital literacy and computer science are increasingly emphasized alongside traditional STEM subjects in order to prepare students for a technology-driven future.
10. Research and Development Initiatives: A key focus is encouraging STEM field research in universities, including funding projects, establishing research partnerships, and promoting innovation and entrepreneurship.

These initiatives aim to establish a robust STEM education framework in Oman, nurturing a generation capable of contributing to the nation's economic diversification and technological advancement. The impact on students includes a more holistic and practical STEM learning approach, enhanced academic performance, and increasing interest in STEM careers. This hands-on, contextual approach helps students appreciate the practical applications of STEM in daily life. Additionally, by integrating STEM principles into the curriculum and shifting towards more inventive and analytical thinking, these initiatives have cultivated a culture of innovation in schools. A dynamic environment for ongoing improvement and creativity is fostered by having students and teachers engage in collaborative projects, tackle complex problems, and participate in innovation contests.

The success stories from Oman's national STEM initiatives offer insights into the efficacy of targeted funding at the elementary level. They underscore the transformative power of strategic investments in STEM education and the pivotal role of teachers in this journey. As Oman continues its pursuit of excellence in STEM, these experiences serve as valuable guides for future policies and strategies, promoting further integration of STEM in teacher preparation and classroom teaching. The journey thus far points to a future brimming with opportunities for sustained innovation, impactful learning experiences, and progressive developments in Oman's STEM education.

Special Focus: Enhancing STEM Education for Elementary Teachers in Oman

The crucial role that elementary teachers play in laying the groundwork for a child's educational journey underscores the need for a well-rounded and thoughtful approach to integrating STEM into their professional development. In Oman, this pivotal stage of education has received special attention, with a suite of targeted initiatives and programs designed to empower elementary teachers with the necessary skills and knowledge to deliver effective STEM education (Al-Balushi et al., 2022).

Recognizing the distinct challenges and possibilities inherent in elementary education, the Omani government has launched bespoke professional development programs for teachers at this level. These programs are carefully tailored to meet the unique needs of elementary educators, offering them practical training, resources, and support to incorporate STEM principles fluidly into their teaching. A fundamental component of these programs is the focus on developing a strong base of content knowledge in STEM disciplines; to achieve this, Omani elementary teachers are helped to gain in-depth understanding of basic scientific concepts, mathematical principles, and technological applications. This comprehensive knowledge base ensures that they are well-equipped to introduce these subjects to their young learners in an engaging and accessible manner (Shahat & Al-Amri, 2023).

Beyond content mastery, these programs also emphasize innovative pedagogical approaches specifically suited to elementary education. Teachers receive training in methods including inquiry-based learning and problem-solving techniques, which are central to effective STEM education. These methodologies create a classroom environment that nurtures student curiosity, encourages critical thinking, and fosters a love for learning (Shahat & Al-Amri, 2023).

Another vital aspect of these initiatives is the establishment of supportive STEM learning environments within elementary schools. With the aid of funded grants, schools have been able to acquire the necessary resources and equipment to set up dedicated STEM laboratories and interactive learning spaces. These settings act as innovation incubators, offering students hands-on experiences and the chance to engage actively in their learning (Shahat & Al-Balushi, 2023).

To guarantee the ongoing effectiveness and sustainability of these programs, robust assessment and evaluation frameworks are in place. These systems provide critical feedback on the impact of the programs and facilitate continual improvements in teaching methods and curriculum design. Through this ongoing refinement process, Oman is committed to ensuring that its investment in early STEM education translates into enduring and meaningful educational outcomes (Shahat & Al-Balushi, 2023).

The focused initiatives targeting elementary teachers in Oman are representative of the significant strides Oman has made towards realizing the national goal of a society proficient in STEM. By prioritizing the professional development of educators at this foundational level, Oman is setting a solid base for its STEM education, preparing even its youngest learners to succeed in a rapidly changing global landscape. The success of these programs not only creates a solid foundation for future STEM education efforts but also highlights the indispensable role of elementary teachers in shaping a nation's future in the realm of STEM (Al-Balushi et al., 2023).

Funded Research Programs targeting STEM Education for Elementary Teachers

In recognition of the critical need for a society proficient in STEM, Oman has initiated a range of funded research programs focused specifically on enhancing STEM education at the elementary level. These initiatives are vital for advancing our understanding of effective STEM teaching methodologies, curriculum development, and student engagement in these key fields (Shahat & Al-Balushi, 2023).

A central objective of these research programs is to explore and identify optimal teaching methods for delivering STEM education to young learners. This includes funding research into innovative pedagogical techniques, the effective use of technology in education, and the cultivation of critical thinking and problem-solving abilities in students. In addition to investigating teaching strategies, these programs also concentrate on the curricular aspects of STEM education. This involves assessing existing curricular frameworks, suggesting improvements, and formulating new curriculum models that align more closely with the tenets of STEM education. The aim here is to create curricula that are not only intellectually stimulating but also captivating for elementary students, thereby nurturing an early interest in STEM disciplines (Shahat & Al-Amri, 2023).

Another focal point of these funded research programs is understanding how elementary students interact with STEM subject material and the outcomes of such interactions. These research initiatives aim to identify factors that drive student interest in STEM, assess the influence of STEM education on student achievement, and evaluate the long-term effects of early STEM exposure on career paths and skills development.

In collaboration with educational and research institutions, the Omani government provides extensive grant opportunities for researchers focusing on STEM education. These grants are intended to offer substantial financial backing, covering expenses related to research activities, resources, and any necessary training or professional development for researchers (Shahat & Al-Amri, 2023).

Beyond financial support, these programs also aim to foster a community of collaboration and knowledge exchange among researchers, educators, and policymakers. This is achieved through regularly organizing conferences, workshops, and seminars which serve as platforms for sharing insights, resources, and best practices in STEM education (Shahat & Al-Amri, 2023).

The contributions of these funded research programs in Oman are integral to the national vision for educational excellence. By generating research-based insights into effective STEM teaching methodologies and curriculum design, these programs are shaping policies and initiatives that are pivotal to enhancing STEM education nationwide (Shahat & Al-Balushi, 2023).

The outcomes of these research programs are invaluable in informing and enhancing teacher preparation and ongoing professional development programs. By anchoring these educational initiatives in empirical research, Oman is ensuring that its elementary teachers are equipped with the latest and most effective STEM teaching strategies (Shahat & Al-Amri, 2023). This approach is not only beneficial for the nation's current student population but also instrumental in preparing a future workforce that is adept in STEM, thereby contributing significantly to the nation's development and prosperity.

CONCLUSION AND FUTURE DIRECTION

This chapter has comprehensively explored the significance of STEM education within teacher preparation, offering international perspectives from various countries, with a particular focus on Oman's national strategies and development agendas. The analysis has highlighted the pivotal role of government-led initiatives, such as STEM OMAN, in enhancing the skills and competencies of educators at different educational levels. Notably, the chapter has emphasized the importance of elementary educators, recognizing their pivotal role in laying a strong foundation for STEM proficiency from an early age.

The chapter established that STEM education is a key pillar in Oman's national development and is in line with the objectives of Oman Vision 2040. This vision aims to cultivate a knowledge-driven society and develop competitive national talent pools. The incorporation of STEM principles into teacher education not only enhances the training of future teachers but also ensures that subsequent generations are adept in essential STEM concepts. This proficiency is crucial for fostering innovation and sustaining a competitive position in the increasingly interconnected global landscape.

The special focus on enhancing STEM education for elementary teachers in Oman is a testament to the nation's commitment to fostering a thriving and capable generation adept in science, technology, engineering, and mathematics. By recognizing the pivotal role of elementary educators and implementing tailored professional development programs, Oman has taken proactive steps to empower teachers with the skills and knowledge essential for effective STEM integration. The comprehensive approach, encompassing content mastery, innovative pedagogical methods, and the creation of supportive learning environments, reflects the government's dedication to providing a holistic educational experience. As Oman continues to assess and refine these initiatives, the nation not only ensures the sustainability of its investment in early STEM education but also lays the groundwork for future success in an increasingly complex global landscape. The accomplishments achieved through these programs underscore the vital contribution of elementary teachers in shaping the trajectory of STEM education and, consequently, the nation's future prosperity.

To maintain and augment the progress of STEM integration in education, a continued emphasis must be placed on ongoing professional development for teachers, the creation of innovative curricular frameworks, and the establishment of supportive educational environments. Furthermore, this chapter has stressed the importance of continued investment in research programs focused on identifying effective teaching methodologies and understanding student engagement in STEM. Such research is vital for continually refining and advancing STEM education practices.

Oman's dedication to improving STEM education reflects the nation's vision and commitment to preparing its citizens for the evolving challenges and opportunities of the 21st century. The initiatives and strategies discussed in this chapter lay a solid groundwork for a future where educators are adept at imparting essential STEM skills, and students are both proficient and passionate about their involvement in STEM disciplines. This educational foundation is beneficial for the individual growth of students and teachers and crucial for the nation's overall prosperity and international standing. The comprehensive approach taken by Oman serves as a model for other countries looking to strengthen their educational systems and prepare their citizens for a future driven by STEM advancements.

REFERENCES

Al-Balushi, S. M., Al-Harthi, A. S., & Shahat, M. A. (2022). Teacher education in Oman: Retrospectives and prospects. In: Khine, M.S. (Eds.), Handbook of research on teacher education. Springer (WOS & Scopus indexed). doi:10.1007/978-981-19-2400-2_6

Al-Balushi, S. M., Martin-Hansen, L., & Song, Y. (Eds.). (2023). *Reforming Science Teacher Education Programs in the STEM Era. Palgrave Studies on Leadership and Learning in Teacher Education*. Palgrave Macmillan. doi:10.1007/978-3-031-27334-6

Ambusaidi, A. K., Shahat, M. A., & Al Musawi, A. S. (2022). Science education in Oman. In R. Huang, B. Xin, A. Tlili, F. Yang, X. Zhang, L. Zhu, & M. Jemni (Eds.), *Science education in countries along the belt & road: Future insights and new requirements* (pp. 113–127). Springer Nature Singapore. doi:10.1007/978-981-16-6955-2_8

Fraser, S., Beswick, K., & Crowley, S. (2019). Responding to the Demands of the STEM Education Agenda: The Experiences of Primary and Secondary Teachers from Rural, Regional and Remote Australia. *Journal of Research in STEM Education*, 5(1), 40–59. doi:10.51355/jstem.2019.62

Koh, D., & Tan, A. L. (2021). Singaporean Pre-service Teachers' Perceptions of STEM Epistemic Practices and Education. *Journal of STEM Teacher Education*, 56(2). doi:10.30707/JSTE56.2.1649165366.257139

Ministry of Education. (2021). STEM Oman Overview of external undergraduate scholarships. *Ministry of Education Ministry of Higher Education, Research and Innovation*. MoE. https://heac.gov.om/media/doc/DE001_2021.pd

NGSS Lead States. (2013). *Next generation science standards: For states, by states*. National Academies Press.

Shahat, M. A., & Al Amri, M. (2023). Science Teacher Preparation in Oman: Strengths and Shortcomings Related to STEM Education. In S. M. Al-Balushi, L. Martin-Hansen, & Y. Song (Eds.), *Reforming Science Teacher Education Programs in the STEM Era*. Palgrave Studies on Leadership and Learning in Teacher Education. Palgrave Macmillan. doi:10.1007/978-3-031-27334-6_10

Shahat, M. A., & Al-Balushi, S. M. (2023). The development of STEM education in the Sultanate of Oman. In *STEM Education Approaches and Challenges in the MENA Region* (pp. 56–73). IGI Global. doi:10.4018/978-1-6684-6883-8.ch003

Shahat, M. A., Al-Balushi, S. M., Abdullah, S., & Al-Amri, M. (2023b). *Pre- and In-service STEM Teachers' Skills in Preparing Engineering Design-based Activities: A Systematic Literature Review*. [Submitted for publication]

Shahat, M. A., Al-Balushi, S. M., & Al-Amri, M. (2022). Investigating pre-service science teachers' self-efficacy beliefs for teaching science through engineering design processes. *Interdisciplinary Journal of Environmental and Science Education*, 18(4), 2291. doi:10.21601/ijese/12121

Shahat, M. A., Al-Balushi, S. M., & Al-Amri, M. (2023a). Measuring preservice science teachers' performance on engineering design process tasks: Implications for fostering STEM education. *Arab Gulf Journal of Scientific Research*. doi:10.1108/AGJSR-12-2022-0277

Wiksten, S. (2019). Talking About Sustainability in Teacher Preparation in Finland and the United States. [NJCIE]. *Nordic Journal of Comparative and International Education*, *3*(1), 69–87. doi:10.7577/njcie.3302

Chapter 4
(Re)Imagining an Elementary Preservice Science Methods Course as Inquiry-Based

Sandy White Watson
https://orcid.org/0000-0002-8885-6203
University of Louisiana at Monroe, USA

ABSTRACT

In response to research findings that elementary teachers are underprepared to teach science due to lack of both science content knowledge (SCK) and science pedagogical knowledge (SPK), the author restructured a teacher-centered, pedagogically focused elementary science methods course into one in which SCK and SPK were the primary foci of the class. SCK was provided via explanations that occurred after in-class and extended inquiry-based investigations, during active learning experiences, and after assigned readings and associated discussions, while SPK was provided through observations and analyses of practicing elementary science teachers teaching, modeling of strategies by the instructor, and development and delivery of two 5E lesson plans in area elementary school settings, all approaches deemed effective in increasing elementary preservice teachers' science pedagogical knowledge.

BACKGROUND

Shulman's 1986 seminal work stressed the criticality of providing three interconnected knowledge types for preservice teachers to ensure their success as future teachers: content knowledge (CK), pedagogical knowledge (PK), and pedagogical content knowledge (PCK). CK is usually obtained in preservice teachers' general education

DOI: 10.4018/978-1-6684-5939-3.ch004

coursework, PK is garnered in generic education courses such as classroom management and curriculum while PCK will often be gained in specific methods courses. PCK addresses teaching strategies specific to content areas. All three types of knowledge are usually equally addressed in teacher education programs, but for the purposes of this book chapter, the focus will be on science content knowledge (SCK) and pedagogical content knowledge (PCK).

SCIENCE CONTENT KNOWLEDGE

Elementary level teachers are considered generalists who must be prepared to teach multiple subjects to include reading, mathematics, social studies, science, and more but are often woefully underprepared to teach science primarily due to a lack of a command of science content knowledge, science pedagogical skills/knowledge, and/or a lack of interest in science (Cervato & Kerton, 2017; Kind, 2009; Kisiel, 2013; Santau et al., 2014). Further, when elementary teachers lack proficient science content and science pedagogical knowledge, their confidence, competence and comfort levels for teaching science fall (Kind, 2009) and their science teaching self-efficacy also dips (Al Sutton et al., 2019). In fact, a 2013 study revealed that only 40% of elementary school teachers felt prepared and confident to teach science (Trygstad, 2013).

When elementary teachers lack science content understanding, they are more likely to develop science misconceptions (often in the physical sciences) which can be transferred to their students (Aydeniz & Brown, 2010; Bursal, 2012). While leading science class discussions, underprepared elementary teachers are also more likely to ask lower-level questions of students, are less likely to demand higher levels of student participation in science (Carlsen, 1987), are more likely to deliver low-quality science teaching (Santau et al., 2014), and are less likely to provide inquiry investigation opportunities for their students, instead often choosing to impart science facts (Newton & Newton, 2001) and rely on science textbooks and lecture-based pedagogy (Abell, 2007).

When elementary teachers are provided opportunities to improve their science content understandings, they are more apt to lead class discussions that involve critical thinking that are connected to real-world scenarios/experiences (Davis, 2004). Additionally, when preservice teachers participate in inquiry-based science investigations in their content or methods courses and are involved in active learning in science, they are more likely to gain conceptual science understandings and duplicate the inquiry-based methodology in the classes they currently or will teach (Nowicki et al., 2012) and their future students will be more likely to experience greater science learning gains (Krall et al., 2009).

The lack of science content knowledge among elementary in-service and preservice teachers is also reflective of science teaching methods utilized in US schools as compared to those utilized in other countries, from elementary to collegiate levels. For example, the Trends in International Mathematics and Science Study (TIMSS, 2019) found that 66% of science content taught in US K-12 schools emphasized factual memorization compared to only 28% in Japan. And, even though the literature is rife with science reform research suggesting the success of hands-on, authentic, inquiry-based learning experiences, most teacher education programs utilize traditional lecture-based instructional methods with minimal to no inquiry based or active learning opportunities (Nowicki et al., 2012). Moreover, these programs usually stress SPK over SCK, when the research tells us that to effectively teach science, one must first understand it, thus SPK and SCK should be equally emphasized in science methods courses (McConnell et al., 2013).

Most U.S. elementary teacher education programs require candidates to take 3 or fewer science courses (Cobern et al., 2914; Sackes, 2014) while some states such as Missouri and Michigan, require only one science course (Bleicher, 2009; Sindel, 2010). Of the courses required, the emphasis is usually on life science, often with no chemistry or physics course requirements (Trygstad, 2013), even though as practicing teachers, they are to teach all science subjects. After obtaining a teaching position, most of these teachers will not seek science-related professional development for at least three years, if at all (Dorph et al., 2011).

The lack of science content knowledge among elementary teachers may explain why they report spending less time teaching it (Marx & Harris, 2006; Trygstad, 2013), often believing students will make up for lost science instruction at the elementary level in middle and high school (Milner et al., 2011). Also, when elementary teachers do teach science, it is often through traditional teacher-centered methods (Blank, 2012) such as lectures, worksheets, and textbook assignments (Banilower et al., 2013). However, research indicates that during students' elementary school years is when they demonstrate high science interest, and when they should be developing strong science foundational understandings (Eshach & Fried, 2005), thus the elementary level is a critical time for students to experience active and inquiry-based learning in science.

Moreover, when the primary subjects receiving emphasis in US elementary schools are literacy and math, science may not be taught at all or may be given only cursory attention. However, because most states have adopted the Next Generation Science Standards (NGSS), science as an elementary level subject may begin to receive more attention. Additionally, since the NGSS standards stress teaching science through inquiry investigations, it is expected that more elementary schools will require their teachers to be knowledgeable about and capable of implementing this type of science instruction.

SCIENCE PEDAGOGICAL KNOWLEDGE

Linked with science content knowledge is science pedagogical knowledge, knowledge related to effectively teaching science in ways that garner high learning gains among students. An elementary teacher who lacks confidence in science content knowledge will often also be weak in science pedagogy (Bencze, 2010). Planning for, implementing, and evaluating inquiry- based science learning requires a specialized science teacher skill set that when utilized, often results in greater levels of scientific understandings among students (Blanchard et al., 2009). The combination of low SCK and low SPK can result in science teaching anxiety, which may have roots in past science education experiences that were perceived as negative (Welder & Champion, 2011). Further, many elementary teachers report having received no inquiry-based instruction (IBI) training in their teacher preparation programs and none since employment as teachers via professional development or other means.

Science Methods Courses

The elementary science methods course is taken by all pre-service generalist elementary teachers and while its goals and content differ across institutions (Yager, 2005), all science methods courses have the potential to positively impact candidate beliefs, confidence levels, and attitudes toward science and science teaching, all of which can lead to more effective instructional practices (Bhattacharyya et al., 2013). Unfortunately, many science methods courses are not taught with active or inquiry-based methods, but instead are offered via traditional teaching strategies such as lecture with cook-book lab experiences, if labs are even offered (Bhattacharyya et al., 2013; Darling-Hammond et al., 2008; DeHaan, 2005; Ozdemir & Isik, 2015; Nowicki et al., 2012). Students exposed to science content through lecture are 1.5 times more likely to fail than those who received science content through active learning (Freeman et al., 2014). Thus, it behooves us to teach science methods courses from an active learning perspective that encourages students' involvement in their own learning (DeHaan, 2005), and that leads them to examine their science misconceptions, assumptions, and biases (Bhattacharyya et al., 2013).

INQUIRY-BASED INVESTIGATION/INSTRUCTION KNOWLEDGE BACKGROUND

Inquiry-based instruction refers to any instruction that involves students utilizing strategies of practicing scientists to better understand scientific knowledge (NRC, 2012) and encourages to think critically about science concepts (Llewellyn, 2002).

The roots of inquiry-based instruction (IBI) can be traced back to Dewey (1938), who believed authentic inquiry involves using previously acquired knowledge to solve a problem in a process where students collaborate with peers while engaged in various tasks to solve the problem, all the while reflecting on the process.

The learning theories most often associated with inquiry-based learning (IBL) are constructivism and social constructivism. Constructivism posits that individuals construct their own knowledge from experiences they are engaged in (Tamim & Grant, 2013). Thus, according to constructivism, knowledge is not delivered by teachers. The social constructivism learning theory (Vygotsky, 1978) maintained that students learn best when they are interacting with others while thinking critically, two conditions present in true IBI.

Definitions of and strategies associated with science IBI have changed over the decades, contributing to teachers' confusions surrounding what is and what is not IBI. In fact, many elementary science teachers believe any hands-on activity or experiment is considered IBI, thus falsely believing they are utilizing IBI in their classrooms (Llewellyn, 2002; Flick & Lederman, 2006). Despite the multiple descriptions and definitions of IBI, most science education scholars agree that IBI is both a "student-centered and teacher-guided approach to learning that places the responsibility of learning upon the student" (Colclasure et al., 2020, p. 4). When the learning responsibility shifts to students coupled with their active engagement in the learning process, they will be more likely to gain new concept knowledge (Easterly & Myers, 2011). Additionally, IBI instruction typically engages students in examining authentic, real-world problems and finding solutions for those problems through a process of data collection and analysis, while building on prior knowledge (Minner et al., 2010).

The National Research Council (NRC, 2012) released the following statement regarding inquiry-based learning:

Inquiry is a multifaceted activity that involves making observations; posing questions; examining books and other sources of information to see what is already known in light of experimental evidence; using tools to gather, analyze, and interpret data; proposing answers, explanations, and predictions and communicating the results. Inquiry requires identification of assumptions, use of critical and logical thinking, and consideration of alternative explanations. (p. 23)

Mackenzie (2016) indicated that there are four types of inquiry students experience in schools:

(1) Structured: the teacher leads one large inquiry with whole-class participation
(2) Controlled: students are engaged in inquiry surrounding a teacher-selected topic and teacher-selected questions/problems
(3) Guided: students are engaged in inquiry surrounding a teacher-selected topic and teacher selected questions/problems, but students have the freedom to devise the product or solution
(4) Free: students choose topic/question/problem and devise procedures to investigate it with no restrictions.

Marshall (2013) explored each of these inquiry types and concluded that in structured and controlled inquiry, students engage in little critical thinking, while in guided and free inquiry, "learning is rich and challenging to students of all ability levels" (p. 17).

Gyllenpalm et al. (2010) devised a taxonomy of instructional approaches based on question/problem, method, and answer/result as well as degrees of freedom provided by each method. Gyllenpalm et al.'s table is reproduced here (Table 1) with the addition of descriptions for each approach.

Multiple studies have shown that inquiry-based investigations have positive impacts for learning as well as teaching (Marshall & Horton, 2011; Powell-Moman & Brown-Schild, 2011; Walker et. al., 2008) and it is well known in the literature that preservice teachers who themselves experienced interactive science opportunities (field trips, science competitions, professional scientist mentors, etc.) and hands-on experimentation (investigating, creating, problem-solving, etc.) in elementary school, are more confident in teaching science, have more positive attitudes toward teaching science, and are more likely to teach it in the ways they were taught in elementary school (Docherty-Skippen et al., 2020; Riegle-Crumb et al., 2015; Santau et al., 2014). Hence, all the more reason for the preparation of elementary teachers who embrace science, are confident in their science knowledge and pedagogy, and know how to teach science to children with inquiry-based, hands-on methods.

There are other equally compelling reasons for utilizing inquiry-based instruction across K-12 and in teacher education programs: (1) students are more apt to develop problem-solving skills that are conducive to developing an initiative for science exploration that often leads to problem answers, an ability that is transferable to other subjects and contexts (Wang, et al., 2015); (2) students who are engaged in science through inquiry-based instruction experience gains in science literacy (Xie & Shauman, 2003); (3) students are more likely to experience gains in curiosity for discovery (Docherty-Skippen et al., 2020); (4) and, long-term economic benefits can be realized in terms of better prepared students who are motivated to consider and pursue science-related careers, filling many of the anticipated vacancies in these career fields (Docherty-Skippen et al., 2020). Moreover, IBI puts students at the center of their own learning, giving them a high level of ownership in the learning process (Caswell & LaBrie, 2017), a process that is student-directed (Spronken & Walker, 2010). In addition to these benefits, Goldston et al. (2010) found that IBL improves communication skills and Gu et al. (2015) determined that students engaged in IBL were better at conflict resolution, were more willing to take risks, try new avenues of exploration, and report increased academic self-efficacy. Finally, Marks (2013) posited that students engaged in IBL are more likely to possess habits of mind. From the literature we can conclude that all students in all grade levels should participate in scientific inquiry, using the skills and processes scientists use, including their ways of thinking (Flick & Lederman, 2006) for optimal learning gains.

Because research has consistently indicated that the most effective science pedagogical methods are inquiry or discovery based, these methods can serve as interventions for preservice teachers with minimal science content knowledge and interest (Avery & Meyer, 2012). Thus, university teacher education programs should adopt the same methods for science methods courses, especially for preservice elementary teachers.

Obstacles to Inquiry-Based Instruction

The literature is rife with studies that report the benefits of inquiry-based learning to students, as previously mentioned in this chapter. However, it also provides evidence of many obstacles to IBL for both teachers and students. Anderson (2002) studied barriers to IBL and placed them in three dimensions: technical, political, and cultural. Anderson's (2002) dimensions and their barriers are listed in table 2, along with additional barriers identified by Martin (2010) Songer et al. (2002), and Gejda and LaRocco (2006).

Of all of these barriers, the literature identifies time constraints as the one barrier most often mentioned by teachers (Anderson, 2002; Gejda & LaRocco, 2006: Songer et al., 2002; Tairab & Al-Naqbi (2017).

K-12 Teachers as IBL Lesson Developers

What has not been addressed with great depth in the literature is how to facilitate the development of inquiry-based lessons and materials appropriate for K-12, by K-12 practicing teachers, not educational researchers and university science methods instructors (Keys & Byron, 2001). To address this gap in secondary schools, Gyllenpalm et al. (2010), conducted a study in which they asked 12 secondary teachers to submit samples of lessons that they thought were representative of IBI and then sit for interviews regarding how the submitted lessons were utilized in their classes. Results revealed that the 12 participants submitted the following types of instruction:

expository (4), discovery (4), problem-based (2), guided inquiry (6), inquiry (1), and open inquiry (1). Thus, only two lessons submitted represented true inquiry.

True inquiry-based learning/instruction involves students performing an investigation to reveal scientific knowledge. That investigation includes asking questions, conducting a test/experiment, making observations, collecting data, and drawing conclusions (Pedaste et al., 2015), all steps undertaken by practicing scientists. Ideally, the investigation should surround real-world concepts authentic to the students (Dolenc & Kazanis (2020).

5E Lesson Plan as Inquiry-Based Instruction Framework

A search of the literature will reveal several inquiry-based learning models, most represented by procedures (Pedaste et al., 2015) such as Marshall's (2013) phases of Engage, Explore, Explain, and Extend with formative assessments and reflection opportunities or Bybee et al.'s (2006) phases of Engage, Explore, Explain, Elaborate, and Evaluate. These models typically lend themselves quite well to IBL. For the purposes of the author's elementary science methods courses, Bybee's (2006) model was utilized. A summary of each step is noted in Table 2.

The instructor of the course that is the focus of this chapter models effective pedagogical strategies, walking students through each phase of a 5E lesson. This 5E lesson will be similar to the one they will teach in a K-12 classroom as a requirement of the course. After watching the instructor model the lesson, students work in small groups conducting investigations (Explore and Elaborate) related to the modeled lesson's topic. They are then asked to teach the Explore they have been working on in class to their classmates in small groups while the instructor moves from one group to another to observe and coach. This allows the pre-service teacher to become confident in the content and pedagogical knowledge before teaching this same lesson to students in a local K-5 setting the following week. For the actual teaching of the lesson in a local K-5 public school, one pair of students conducts the Engage. After the Engage, students enter the Explore phase set up as a rotation lab, where each elementary student moves from one Explore to another in small groups, all operated by the pre-service teachers. Due to time constraints, the students cannot present an entire 5E lesson. Instead, after each mini-Explore, the pre-service teachers Explain the content.

Modified Elementary Science Methods Course

The author of this chapter taught the elementary science methods course upon which this chapter is based. This course is a two-credit-hour course with a one-credit-hour lab and is offered during the second block of pre-service teachers' educational coursework just prior to entering a year-long residency program. The students met once a week for 16 weeks for 3.5 hours for this course with some of the course meetings occurring in area elementary schools for observations and practice teaching experiences (with some shifts to video observations during COVID surges). The teacher candidates were preparing to teach grades 3-5. The course was designed to address science content knowledge and science pedagogical knowledge (approximately 50% of class time devoted to each). Science content topics were selected based on weak areas of the science portion of PRAXIS tests taken by current and past students in the program. Weak areas were chemistry and physics, so these topics were heavily emphasized. Pedagogical strategies stressed included inquiry-based instruction, problem/project-based learning, and developing lesson plans based on the 5E Instructional Model (Bybee, 1997).

    The author of this chapter reconfigured the elementary science methods course after having moved to a new university and being assigned this course that had previously not been taught with IBI by the former instructor, as evidenced by past syllabi and conversations with the department chair. In fact, there was no evidence of any forms of active learning or inquiry-based instruction in the course. Instead, the emphasis was on lesson planning and unit construction. The author designed the new version of the course with inquiry-based instruction within the 5E lesson plan framework as one of its central foci. Early in the semester, students were introduced to the 5E lesson plan when the author modeled each phase during a lesson on physical and chemical properties and changes. The following week, the author discussed with the students the concept of inquiry-based instruction/learning, being sure to identify each of the instructional methods often associated with IBI (see table 1). To be sure students understood the differences, they participated in a rotation lab, in which they moved through six investigations, expository, discovery, problem-based, guided inquiry, inquiry, and open inquiry. Afterwards, the students discussed with peers the dimensions of each method as outlined in table 1 in terms of (1) question/problem, (2) method, and (3) answer/result and determined the degrees of freedom for each. For example, one of the stations presented a mixture of sand and iron filings where students were asked to devise a method by which the mixture might be separated (teacher determined problem, but student determined solution procedure). If correctly analyzed, students will identify this investigation as inquiry with two degrees of freedom. Later in the semester, students received much needed teaching practice by duplicating the rotation lab in a local 3rd grade classroom.

    For full understanding of open inquiry, students developed a project or problem-based cycle of instruction that might be utilized in their future classes, first completing it themselves once it was developed. For this assignment, students decided the topic and the process for investigation. For example, one student elected to investigate how her future elementary school class might develop a plan for planting a school vegetable garden whose produce would be served during lunches and send home with lower-income students.

To provide students a more comprehensive science investigation experience, students were tasked with building bottle rocket cars in class from 16 oz water bottles (car body), four bottle caps of the same size (wheels), bamboo skewers (axels), balloons (pressure source to move the cars), straws, and tape. Once the cars were constructed, students took them out in the hall and tested them with their peers, and then made adjustments as needed to make the cars travel faster and farther. Once the cars were constructed and the control model had been tested, students selected a variable to modify to make the car either travel faster or further, crafted a research question based on the selected variable, and devised a hypothesis. Official testing of the control versus the experimental car versions then proceeded, with data collection. Students were to write their investigation up and submit it as the signature assessment for the lab portion of the science methods class. Their papers were to be divided into the following components:

1. Introduction and Research: In this section, students discussed the appropriate scientific concepts and principals explored in the investigation that addressed all three of Newton's Laws.
2. Rationale for the Study: Here, the students stated their research question, described how it was developed, and stated an associated hypothesis.
3. Materials/Methods: In this section, students were to fully describe the methods and materials used for building the car and the procedures that were followed to test the control and experimental models (data collection plans), being sure to describe types of data collected and identify the controlled, manipulated and responding variables. Finally, the differences between the control and experimental set-ups were to be disclosed.
4. Results: Here, the students were to provide a data table and a graph that presented the full results of the investigation.
5. Analysis and Conclusions: In this final section, students were to thoroughly describe the specifics and evidence from the investigation, along with what they learned. They were to also state what they learned about their manipulated variable and link it to research, pose additional questions, reflect on the process, discuss how they might use a version of this assignment in their future classes, link it to an appropriate state standard (stating why it fits with the standard), and explain any error sources.

The author also elected to include science content knowledge as a second consistent focus in the methods course, hoping that a focus on science content would increase students' science content knowledge self-efficacy and confidence. For every inquiry-based learning activity that occurred in class, students collaborated by sharing their findings, which was confirmed through the Explain portion of the lesson when the instructor shared vocabulary, definitions and content.

CONCLUSION

In conclusion, the author examined the literature about the under-preparation of elementary teachers for teaching science due to their lack of both science content knowledge and science pedagogical knowledge that often leads to their reluctance to teach science (Marx & Harris, 2006; Trygstad, 2013). Further, the author discussed findings from the literature that indicate that when students receive science content through active learning, they are more likely to pass their science courses (Freeman et al., 2014). Because of the problems elementary teachers have understanding both SCK and SPK, the author restructured an elementary science methods course from one with only traditionally taught methods to a more inquiry-based teaching approach with many active learning opportunities. In doing so, the author provided the procedures followed, adhering to recommended strategies for positively impacting science learning and teaching (Marshall & Horton, 2011; Powell-Moman & Brown-Schild, 2011; Walker et al., 2008).

REFERENCES

Abell, S. K. (2007). Research on science teacher knowledge. In S. K. Abell & N. G. Lederman (Eds.), *Handbook of Research on Science Education* (pp. 1105–1149). Erlbaum.

Al Sultan, A., Henson, H. J., & Fadde, P. J. (2018). Pre-service elementary teachers' scientific literacy and self-efficacy in teaching science. *IAFOR Journal of Education, 6*(1), 15 – 41. doi:10.22492/ije.6.1.02

Anderson, R. D. (2002). Reforming science teaching: What research says about inquiry. *Journal of Science Teacher Education, 13*(1), 1–12. doi:10.1023/A:1015171124982

Avery, L. M., & Meyer, D. Z. (2012). Teaching science as science is practiced: Opportunities and limits for enhancing preservice elementary teachers' self-efficacy for science and science teaching. *School Science and Mathematics, 112*(7), 395–409. doi:10.1111/j.1949-8594.2012.00159.x

Aydeniz, M., & Brown, C. L. (2010). Enhancing pre-service elementary school teachers' understanding of essential science concepts through a reflective conceptual change model. *International Electronic Journal of Elementary Education, 2*(2). doi:10.1007/s10763-005-9016-5

Banilower, E. R., Smith, P. S., Weiss, I. R., Malzahn, K. A., & Weiss, A. M. (2013). *Report of the 2012 National Survey of Science and Mathematics Education.* Horizon Research, Inc., doi:10.1119/1.4795387

Bencze, J. L. (2010). Promoting student-led science and technology projects in elementary teacher education: Entry into core pedagogical practices through technological design. *International Journal of Technology and Design Education, 20*(1), 43–62. doi:10.1007/s10798-008-9063-7

Bhattacharyya, S., Mead, T. P., Junot, M., & Welch, A. (2013). Effectiveness of science method teaching in teacher education: A longitudinal case study. *The Electronic Journal of Science Education, 17*(2).

Blanchard, M., Southerland, S. A., & Granger, D. E. (2009). No silver bullet for inquiry: Making sense of teacher change following inquiry-based research experiences for teachers. *Science Education, 93*(2), 322–360. doi:10.1002/sce.20298

Blank, R. K. (2012). *What is the impact of decline in science instructional time in elementary school?* Paper prepared for the Noyce Foundation. www.csss-science.org/downloads/NAEPElemScienceData.pdf

Bleicher, R. E. (2009). Variable relationships among different science learners in elementary science-methods courses. *International Journal of Science and Mathematics Education, 7*(2), 293–313. doi:10.1007/s10763-007-9121-8

Bursal, M. (2012). Changes in American preservice elementary teachers' efficacy beliefs and anxieties during a science methods course. *Science Education International, 23*(1), 40–55.

Bybee, R. W. (1997). *Achieving scientific literacy: From purposes to practices.* Heinemann.

Bybee, R. W., Taylor, J. A., Gardner, A., Van Scotter, P. Carlson Powell, J., Westbroook, J. & Landes, N. (2006). *BSCS 5E instructional model: Origins and effectiveness*. A report prepared for the Office of Science Education, National Institutes of Health. BSCS.

Carlsen, W. S. (1987). Why do you ask? The effects of science teacher subject-matter knowledge on teacher questioning and classroom discourse. *Paper presented at the annual meeting of the American Educational Research Association*. ERIC Document Reproduction Service no. ED 293 181.

Caswell, C. J., & LaBrie, D. J. (2017). Inquiry-based learning from the learner's point of view: A teacher candidate's success story. *Journal of Humanistic Mathematics*, *7*(2), 161–186. doi:10.5642/jhummath.201702.08

Cervato, C., & Kerton, C. (2017). Improving the science teaching self-efficacy of preservice elementary teachers: A multiyear study of a hybrid geoscience course. *Journal of College Science Teaching*, *47*(2), 83–91. doi:10.2505/4/jcst17_047_02_83

Cobern, W. W., Schuster, D., Adams, B., Skjold, B. A., Mugaloglu, E. Z., Bentz, A., & Sparks, K. (2014). Pedagogy of science teaching tests: Formative assessments of science teaching orientations. *International Journal of Science Education*, *36*(3), 2265–2288. doi:10.1080/09500693.2014.918672

Colclasure, B. C., Thoron, A. C., Osborne, E. W., Roberts, T. G., & Pringle, R. M. (2020). Comparing the 5E method of inquiry-based instruction and the four-stage model of direct instruction on students' content knowledge achievement in an ENR curriculum. *Journal of Agricultural Education*, *61*(3), 1–21. doi:10.5032/jae.2020.03001

Darling-Hammond, L., Barron, B., Pearson, P. D., Schoenfeld, A. H., Stage, E. K., Zimmerman, T. D., Cervetti, G. N., & Tilson, J. (2008). *Powerful learning: What we know about teaching for understanding*. John Wiley & Sons, Inc.

Davis, E. A. (2004). Knowledge integration in science teaching: Analyzing teachers' knowledge development. *Research in Science Education*, *34*(1), 21–53. doi:10.1023/B:RISE.0000021034.01508.b8

DeHaan, R. L. (2005). The impending revolution in undergraduate science education. *Journal of Science Education and Technology*, *14*(2), 253–269. doi:10.1007/s10956-005-4425-3

Dewey, J. (1938). Education and democracy in the world of today. *Schools: Studies in Education, 9*(1), 96–100. doi:10.1086/665026

Docherty-Skippen, S. M., Karrow, D., & Ahmend, G. (2020). Doing science: Preservice teachers' attitudes and confidence teaching elementary science and technology. *Brock Education Journal, 29*(1), 24 – 34. https://journals.library.brocku.ca/brocked

Dolenc, N. R., & Kazanis, W. H. (2020). A potential for interest driven learning to enhance the inquiry-based learning process. *Science Education, 27*(2), 121–128.

Dorph, R., Shields, P., Tiffany-Morales, J., Hartry, A., & McCaffrey, T. (2011). *High hopes-few opportunities: The status of elementary science education in California.* The Center for the Future of Teaching and Learning at WestEd.

Easterly, R. G. III, & Myers, B. E. (2011). Inquiry-based instruction for students with special needs in school based agricultural education. *Journal of Agricultural Education, 52*(2), 36–46. doi:10.5032/jae.2011.02036

Eshach, H., & Fried, M. N. (2005). Should science be taught in early childhood? *Journal of Science Education and Technology, 14*(3), 313–336. doi:10.1007/s10956-005-7198-9

Flick, L. B., & Lederman, N. G. (Eds.). (2006). *Scientific inquiry and nature of science: Implications for teaching, learning, and teacher education.* Springer.

Freeman, S., Eddy, S. L., McDonough, M., Smith, M. K., Okoroafor, N., Jordt, H., & Wenderoth, M. P. (2014). Active learning increases student performance in science, engineering, and mathematics. *Proceedings of the National Academy of Sciences of the United States of America, 111*(23), 8410–8415. doi:10.1073/pnas.1319030111 PMID:24821756

Gejda, L., & LaRocco, M. (2006). *Inquiry-based instruction in secondary science classrooms: A survey of teacher practice.* Paper presented at the 37th Annual Northeast Educational Research Association Conference, Kerhonkson, NY.

Goldston, M. J., Day, J. B., Sundberg, C., & Dantzler, J. (2010). Psychometric analysis of a 5E learning cycle lesson plan assessment instrument. *International Journal of Science and Mathematics Education, 8*(4), 633–648. doi:10.1007/s10763-009-9178-7

Gu, X., Chen, S., Zhu, W., & Lin, L. (2015). An intervention framework designed to develop the collaborative problem-solving skills of primary school students. *Educational Technology Research and Development, 63*(1), 143–159. doi:10.1007/s11423-014-9365-2

Gyllenpalm, J., Wickman, P., & Holmgren, S. (2010). Secondary science teachers' selective traditions and examples of inquiry-oriented approaches. *NorDiNa*, *6*(1), 44–60. doi:10.5617/nordina.269

Keys, C. W., & Bryan, L. A. (2001). Co-constructing inquiry-based science with teachers: Essential research for lasting reform. *Journal of Research in Science Teaching*, *38*(6), 631–645. doi:10.1002/tea.1023

Kind, V. (2009). A conflict in your head: An exploration of trainee science teachers' subject matter knowledge development and its impact on teacher self-confidence. *International Journal of Science Education*, *31*(11), 1529–1562. doi:10.1080/09500690802226062

Kisiel, J. (2013). Introducing future teachers to science beyond the classroom. *Journal of Science Teacher Education*, *24*(1), 67–91. doi:10.1007/s10972-012-9288-x

Krall, R., Lott, K. H., & Wymer, C. L. (2009). Inservice elementary and middle school teachers' conceptions of photosynthesis and respiration. *Journal of Science Teacher Education*, *20*(1), 41–55. doi:10.1007/s10972-008-9117-4

Llewellyn, D. (2002). *Inquire within: Implementing inquiry-based science standards*. Corwin Press, Inc.

Mackenzie, T. (2016). *Dive into inquiry: Amplify learning and empower student voice*. Ed Tech Team Press.

Marks, D. B. (2013). Inquiry-based learning: What's your question? *National Teacher Education Journal*, *6*(2), 21–25.

Marshall, J. C. (2013). *Succeeding with inquiry in science and math classrooms*. ASCD., doi:10.2505/9781416616085

Marshall, J. C., & Horton, R. M. (2011). The relationship of teacher-facilitated, inquiry-based instruction to student higher-order thinking. *School Science and Mathematics*, *111*(3), 93–101. doi:10.1111/j.1949-8594.2010.00066.x

Martin, L. (2010). *Relationship between teacher preparedness and inquiry-based instructional practices to students' science achievement. Evidence from TIMSS 2007* [Unpublished doctoral dissertation, Indiana University of Pennsylvania].

Marx, R. W., & Harris, C. J. (2006). No Child Left Behind and science education: Opportunities, challenges, and risks. *The Elementary School Journal*, *106*(5), 455–466. doi:10.1086/505441

McConnell, T. J., Parker, J. M., & Eberhardt, J. (2017). Assessing teachers' science content knowledge: A strategy for assessing depth of understanding. *Journal of Science Teacher Education, 24*(4), 717–743. doi:10.1007/s10972-013-9342-3

Milner, A. R., Sondergeld, T. A., Demir, A., Johnson, C. C., & Czerniak, C. M. (2011). Elementary teachers' beliefs about teaching science and classroom practice: An examination of pre/post NCLB testing in science. *Journal of Science Teacher Education, 23*(2), 111–132. doi:10.1007/s10972-011-9230-7

Minner, D. D., Levy, A. J., & Century, J. (2010). Inquiry-based science instruction – what is it and does it matter? Results from a research synthesis years 1984 – 2002. *Journal of Research in Science Teaching, 47*(4), 474–496. doi:10.1002/tea.20347

National Research Council (NRC). (2012). *A framework for K-12 science education: Practices, crosscutting concepts, and core ideas.* National Academies Press. doi:10.17226/13165

Newton, D. P., & Newton, L. D. (2001). Subject content knowledge and teacher talk in the primary science classroom. *European Journal of Teacher Education, 24*(3), 369–379. doi:10.1080/02619760220128914

Nowicki, B. L., Sullivan-Watts, B., Shim, M. K., Young, B., & Pockalny, R. (2012). Factors influencing science content accuracy in elementary inquiry science lessons. *Research in Science Education, 43*(3), 1135–1154. doi:10.1007/s11165-012-9303-4

Ozdemir, O., & Isik, H. (2015). Effect of inquiry-based activities on prospective elementary teachers' use of science process skills and inquiry strategies. *Journal of Turkish Science Education, 12*(1), 43–56. doi:10.12973/tused.10132a

Pedaste, M., Maeots, M., Siiman, L. A., De Jong, T., Van Reisen, S. A., Kamp, E. T., Manoli, C. C., Zacharia, Z. C., & Tsourlidaki, E. (2015). Phases of inquiry-based learning: Definitions and the inquiry cycle. *Educational Research Review, 14*, 47–61. doi:10.1016/j.edurev.2015.02.003

Powell-Moman, A. D., & Brown-Schild, V. B. (2011). The influence of a two-year professional development institute on teacher self-efficacy and use of inquiry-based instruction. *Science Educator, 20*(2), 47–53.

Riegle-Crumb, C., Morton, K., Moore, C., Chimonidou, A., Labrake, C., & Kopps, S. (2015). Do inquiring minds have positive attitudes? The science education of preservice elementary teachers. *Science Education, 99*(5)m 819 – 836. https://doi.otg/10.1002/sce.21177

Sackes, M. (2014). How often do early childhood teachers teach science concepts? Determinants of the frequency of science teaching in kindergarten. *European Early Childhood Education Research Journal*, *22*(2), 169–184. doi:10.1080/1350 293X.2012.704305

Santau, A. O., Maerten-Rivera, J. L., Bovis, S., & Orend, J. (2014). A mile wide or an inch deep? Improving elementary preservice teachers' science content knowledge within the context of a science methods course. *Journal of Science Teacher Education*, *25*(8), 953–976. doi:10.1007/s10972-014-9402-3

Shulman, L. S. (1986). Paradigms and research programs in the study of teaching: A contemporary perspective. In M. C. Wittrock (Ed.), *Handbook of research on teaching* (3rd ed., pp. 3–36). McMillan Publishing Company.

Sindel, K. D. (2010). *Can experiential education strategies improve elementary science teachers' perceptions of and practices in science teaching?* [Doctoral dissertation].

Songer, N. B., Lee, H.-S., & Kam, R. (2002). Technology-rich inquiry science in urban classrooms: What are the barriers to inquiry pedagogy? *Journal of Research in Science Education*, *39*(2), 128–150. doi:10.1002/tea/10013

Spronken-Smith, R., & Walker, R. (2010). Can inquiry-based learning strengthen the links between teaching and disciplinary research? *Studies in Higher Education*, *35*(6), 723–740. doi:10.1080/03075070903315502

Tairab, H., & Al-Naqbi, A. (2017). Provision of inquiry instruction and actual level of practice as perceived by science teachers and their students. *Eurasia Journal of Mathematics, Science and Technology Education*, *14*(1). doi:10.12973/ejmste/80320

Tamim, S. R., & Grant, M. M. (2013). Definitions and uses: Case study of teachers implementing project-based learning. *The Interdisciplinary Journal of Problem-Based Learning*, *7*(2), 3. doi:10.7771/1541-5015.1323

Trygstad, P. J. (2013). *National survey of science and mathematics education: Status of elementary school science.* Horizon Research. http://www.horizon-research.com/2012ns-sme/wp-content/uploads/2013/09/2012-NS-SME-The-Status-of-Elementary-Science.pdf

Vygotsky, L. S. (1978). *Mind in society: The development of higher psychological processes*. Harvard University Press.

Walker, C. L., McGill, M. T., Buikema, A. L., & Stevens, A. M. (2008). Implementing inquiry-based learning in teaching serial dilutions. *Journal of College Science Teaching, 37*(6), 56–61.

Wang, P., Wu, P., Yu, K., & Lin, Y. (2015). Influence of implementing inquiry-based instruction on science learning motivation and interest: A perspective of comparison. *Procedia: Social and Behavioral Sciences, 174*(12), 1292–1299. doi:10.1016/j.sbspro.2015.01.750

Welder, R. M., & Champion, J. (2011). Toward an understanding of graduate preservice elementary teachers as adult learners of mathematics. *Adults Learning Mathematics, 6*(1), 20–40.

Xie, Y., & Shauman, K. A. (2003). *Women in science: Career processes and outcomes*. Harvard University Press.

Yager, R. E. (2005). Achieving the staff development model advocated in the national standards. *Science Educator, 14*, 16–24.

Chapter 5
Supporting Beginning Teachers in STEM Content Areas Through Self-Directed Learning and Micro-Credentials

Erin K. West
https://orcid.org/0000-0002-4331-2333
Appalachian State University, USA

Rachel Nelson
https://orcid.org/0000-0001-7335-7914
Appalachian State University, USA

Katherine Chesnutt
Appalachian State University, USA

James Beeler
Appalachian State University, USA

ABSTRACT

North Carolina teachers provide an important learning foundation for students. As teacher candidates complete their education requirements and begin working in schools, they are faced with many challenges. This discussion focuses on beginning teachers (BTs), or teachers with less than three years of teaching experience. After leaving their educator preparation programs (EPPs), BTs are required to complete onboarding programs and professional development plans while simultaneously learning to manage their daily workloads, plan and assess lessons, and manage

DOI: 10.4018/978-1-6684-5939-3.ch005

Copyright © 2024, IGI Global. Copying or distributing in print or electronic forms without written permission of IGI Global is prohibited.

their classroom. This can feel overwhelming for many BTs and may contribute to an early exit from the teaching profession. According to the North Carolina Department of Public Instruction (NCDPI) BTs in the state are much more likely to leave the classroom as compared to teachers that are not BTs, with the attrition rates for BTs and non BTs reported as 12.71% and 6.80%, respectively (NCDPI, 2023).

INTRODUCTION

North Carolina teachers provide an important learning foundation for students. As teacher candidates complete their education requirements and begin working in schools, they are faced with many challenges. Our discussion focuses on K-12 beginning teachers (BTs), or teachers with less than three years of teaching experience. After leaving their educator preparation programs (EPPs), BTs are required to complete onboarding programs and professional development plans while simultaneously learning to handle their daily workloads, plan and assess lessons, and manage their classroom. This can feel overwhelming for many BTs and may contribute to an early exit from the teaching profession. According to the North Carolina Department of Public Instruction (NCDPI), BTs in the state are much more likely to leave the classroom as compared to teachers who are not BTs, with the attrition rates for BTs and non-BTs reported as 12.71% and 6.80%, respectively (NCDPI, 2023). This rate has remained the same (12.6% in 2023) despite calls to action (Fox et al., 2023) and efforts across the state to support BTs (NCDPI, 2023). With higher attrition rates, the need for additional support for all North Carolina teachers in their first three years is clear. STEM teachers in their first three years face additional challenges (Faulkner & Cook, 2006; McConnell, 2017), which we discuss in the next section. To support BTs, we discuss offering teacher-directed professional learning opportunities (TDPL) through the use of micro-credentials. In this chapter, we share the experiences of a group of K-12 BTs teaching STEM subjects in Western North Carolina as they embark on a self-directed professional learning journey with TDPL and micro-credentials.

REFORM IN PROFESSIONAL LEARNING FOR BEGINNING TEACHERS IN STEM

The need for reform and research in STEM teacher education is a decades-old problem (Cochran-Smith et al., 2005; Darling-Hammond, 2005; Milner-Bolotin, 2018; National Research Council, 1996), with the American Association for the

Advancement of Science (1998) and National Research Council (1996; 2010) both recommending changes at all stages of teacher preparation, including learning opportunities for beginning teachers (BTs). While there is a need for shifting preparation for teachers in all content areas, BTs in STEM content areas bear a particular societal burden when it comes to preparing the next generation of citizens who will need the knowledge and skills to navigate the 21st century. Elementary and middle-grade teachers are considered generalists, sometimes lacking degrees (majors or minors) in STEM content areas (Goodnough et al., 2014; Heck et al., 2019). This lack of preparation in STEM manifests itself in a high reliance on textbooks and outside resources, traditional (i.e., not student-centered) science and mathematics pedagogies, and, as has been observed in some instances in elementary science, by nearly removing it entirely from the curriculum (Davis, 2006; Holroyd & Harlen, 1996; Murphy & Mancini-Samuelson, 2012; Trumper 2006; Zembal-Saul et al., 2000). Thus, it is paramount that BTs in STEM have access to resources that can support their individual growth in STEM education.

Coupled with a lack of adequate preparation in STEM, BTs are often burdened with tasks that require additional time outside of the traditional school day while also learning how to implement and fine-tune pedagogy all for a beginning teacher salary. BTs are often required to participate in tasks such as orientation and onboarding sessions, meetings with mentors, and a greater number of supervisor observations in addition to the regularly scheduled professional development required by the school and district (North Carolina Department of Public Instruction, 2018). These additional requirements for BTs are meant to serve as added support but can often become overwhelming and may lead to increased attrition rates (Kang, 2020, VanLone et al., 2022).

One potential solution to meet BTs' professional learning needs could be using a self-directed learning framework that allows for Teacher-Directed Professional Learning (TDPL). The following sections outline the experiences of a group of beginning teachers as they embark on a self-directed professional learning journey that leverages competency-based micro-credentials and a strong, collaborative support network. A discussion around implications for research, policy, and educator preparation programs follows.

Self-Directed Learning as a Framework for TDPL

With teacher resignations at an all-time high and job satisfaction at an all-time low (Merrimack College, 2022) it is time for the field of education to explore new options for professional learning. One option is the adoption of a Self-directed Learning (SDL) model grounded in adult learning theories developed by Knowles (1975) and Mezirow (1985). Generally, SDL includes assessing one's own learning needs, setting goals or objectives, planning and conducting the learning process, and evaluating the learning outcomes (Mezirow, 1985). This process allows learners to engage in a learner-centered environment that incorporates freedom, autonomy, independence, and reflection (Brookfield, 1985; Mezirow, 1985). Notably, SDL does not occur in isolation and often employs group collaboration in which the learner has a large degree of autonomy over the topics, resources, strategies, and evaluation involved with the learning, allowing for increased motivation (Garrison, 1997).

Leveraging the andragogical success of SDL, TDPL scaffolds the self-directed learning process for teachers as they assess their professional learning needs, set goals for professional growth, seek out professional learning opportunities, and continually consider their pedagogical practice through self-reflection and collaboration. TDPL increases teacher choice and provides a flexible environment for professional learning focused on the teacher's needs (Artman et al., 2020). To support TDPL learning needs, we employ the use of micro-credentials (MCs).

Using Micro-Credentials to support TDPL

Micro-credentials (MCs) are a "verification of proficiency in a job-embedded discrete skill or competency that an educator has demonstrated through the submission of evidence assessed via defined evaluation criteria'' (McDiarmid, Berry, & Barringer, 2023, p. 9). Micro-credentials support the work of TDPL because they are self-selected based on professional goals. They are self-paced, allowing teachers to actively investigate and experience a particular instructional or pedagogical strategy. Teachers are more invested in this process because they are personalized to their needs. MCs are, according to Sawchuk (2016), "bite-sized competencies that, via samples of student work, videos, and other artifacts, teachers show that they've mastered to students' or colleagues' benefit." (p. 2). Teachers review MC information by reading through the key method, method components, current research, and resources related to the topic, and then begin working to implement the strategy in their classroom practice. As they complete the strategy, they document their work, reflect on their findings, and provide supporting evidence.

After teachers complete their documentation for each self-selected micro-credential, they submit their work to external assessors. If assessors rate the documentation as passing, teachers are awarded a micro-credential badge. Badges, like certificates, demonstrate that a new skill or strategy has been accomplished. Jones et al (2018) argue that "Digital badges can provide transparent credentials for teachers who have completed professional development learning activities" (p. 428). The badges can be copied and pasted into digital forums such as emails, discussion boards, and other online learning management systems. The popularity of digital badges is growing. Hurst (2015) asserts: "Badges could provide important verifiable information to employers about an individual's varying skills, backed by evidence. Badges can present a well-rounded picture of knowledge and competencies that resumes and degrees do not reflect" (p. 186).

Therefore, MCs provide opportunities for teachers to direct their learning around skills they are most interested in, and then demonstrate these skills in practice. The badges provide validation from external assessors of teachers' new learning and competencies. This model of SDL allows teachers to be more invested in their learning and provides autonomy and agency. While the majority of work in K-12 education MCs has been with in-service teachers, there is a growing movement to incorporate more competency-based credentialing into the teacher preparation landscape (Clausen, 2022).

Micro-Credential Use in K-12 Professional Development Programs

School and district administrators and educational researchers need to understand teachers' experiences with micro-credentials to improve professional development programs. When these stakeholders understand teachers' experiences with MCs, they can provide better support and time for professional development opportunities for staff members. TDPL opportunities that align with teachers' needs and interests help teachers achieve personal and school-wide professional goals. Further, MCs offer targeted pedagogical and instructional skill development. Reviewing and participating in MC offerings helps teachers reflect and improve their classroom teaching practices. Learning from MCs, therefore, helps teachers address gaps in their professional understanding and practice, which leads to improved teaching quality and in turn, better student outcomes.

As dedicated professionals, teachers are required to continue their education and professional growth. MCs promote continuous professional growth because the offerings are chosen based on teacher interests and reflections. Schools and districts using TDPL and MCs can foster a culture of ongoing learning among teachers, which ultimately benefits students through reflective and innovative teaching practices. The use of MCs also helps to build a supportive school community, because teachers are encouraged to share ideas, collaborate, and support each other through their professional learning.

PARTICIPANTS AND STUDY CONTEXT

Teachers (n=7) in this TDPL cohort were part of a larger study, called the Empowering Teacher Learning Project (described in more detail below), and received continuing education units (CEUs) and stipends for completing various project-related milestones, including earning online, competency-based micro-credentials (discussed in more detail below). The Empowering Teacher Learning Project (ETL), is a 5-year research study examining the impacts of using MCs for teacher-directed professional learning. The four components of the ETL TDPL process include: 1) assessment of professional learning needs, 2) setting learning goals through the completion of a self-directed learning plan (SDLP), 3) accomplishing goals by earning micro-credentials, and 4) reflecting and collaborating on the process through one-on-one coaching support.

The four components of the ETL project are supported through an online learning management system and the involvement of coaches. Coaches provide feedback, suggestions, and support throughout the process and help teachers navigate the process of self-directed professional learning. Teachers select micro-credentials from an online platform, review and research the requirements for the micro-credential, and implement the strategy in their teaching practice. They submit their reflections and work samples to external assessors linked to the online micro-credential platform.

After passing each micro-credential, teachers then complete reflection activities in the learning management system through scheduled online modules. When all requirements for each module are complete, teachers receive program-funded stipend payments. They also receive certificates for continuing education units (CEUs), which are required for license renewal in the state of North Carolina. This model provides support and pays teachers for their time and effort through self-directed professional learning. To demonstrate the use of MCs and TDPL in practice, we provide ETL teacher participants' experiences in the next section. We describe each component of TDPL through the experiences of seven BTs in STEM content areas from rural, high-need K-12 schools in western North Carolina as they participated in each part of the TDPL process.

TEACHERS' EXPERIENCES

Now that we have briefly outlined the Empowering Teaching Learning Project, we examine each element of the TDPL process through the lens of a BT. The following sections include reflections from participants as they experienced each element of the TDPL process.

Assessment of Professional Learning Needs

To address opportunities for professional growth in their classrooms, teachers must first have the time and skills to identify their professional learning needs and direct their learning to meet those needs. The TDPL process for this cohort of teachers began with a self-assessment and reflection of practice as the teachers completed a needs assessment aligned to their state teaching standards. This instrument, the Teachers' Professional Learning Assessment of Needs (T-PLAN), included the five North Carolina state standards for teacher professional growth: 1) Teacher Leadership, 2) Diversity, 3) Content Knowledge, 4) Facilitating Learning, and 5) Content Knowledge (North Carolina Department of Public Instruction, 2018). Teachers in North Carolina are asked to do a self-evaluation of their strengths and areas for growth each year using the standards mentioned above; however, they are not necessarily provided with officially sanctioned space (i.e., paid time) for reflection. Additionally, they are not provided with potential pathways for growth that directly align with the standards.

To address these challenges, teacher participants in the Empowering Teacher Learning Project were provided the time and space to reflect, assess, and collaborate on their professional learning needs. Teachers completed the T-PLAN during an in-person summer convening event before the start of the school year during which time, teachers were provided with ample time to discuss and reflect on their self-perceived needs for professional learning for the upcoming school year alongside a cohort of teachers from a variety of backgrounds in experience (BTs, mid-career, and veteran). While teachers were encouraged to have conversations with colleagues from their school or district, some teachers collaborated with teachers in similar content areas, like STEM.

As teachers completed their T-PLAN instrument, they were provided a digital or paper summary of their self-reported data which they used as a tool for reflection and discussion with their colleagues. BTs appreciated the personalization that came from examining their data as noted by one BT who reported that the assessment (T-PLAN): "showed me what I needed to work on as an educator" and another explained, "I really enjoyed being able to analyze my scores… This was a way to identify needs based on where I believe I am, personally." Another teacher stated that they "loved how personalized this program was." Others noted that this report provided them with much-needed information, with one teacher stating "[l]ast year was my first year in the classroom, the only data I have had to reflect upon my practice as an educator have been peer and administrator evaluations," and another explaining "I will be able to express my strengths and weaknesses with administration and gain support in the needed areas because I will know where I need support."

While several teacher participants noted their experience in using data related to student test scores (e.g., End-of-Grade, iReady benchmarks) none stated that they had experience in using a teacher-led self-assessment to reflect on their pedagogy. Teachers contrasted this report to other professional development requirements and noted how this experience has been different, explaining "this process has been different from any practice I have been involved with in the past. The self-direction aspect helps identify needs and learn to address weakness in a productive way." Another teacher explained that previous "trainings or resources did not directly relate to what I teach."

One teacher also provided support for the need to scaffold the process of collecting and analyzing data that could be used as a self-assessment for BTs, stating that "[a]s a beginning teacher I do not have experience in reviewing data for reflection regarding my practice as an educator," and another teacher explained that this experience with self-assessment will help to remove the guesswork in determining where to focus their professional learning efforts, stating "[t]he assessment showed areas of weakness and exactly what to specifically target." Overall, teachers acknowledged that this experience in self-assessment was beneficial to them as educators and recognized a need to embrace more comprehensive and varied data sources to inform teaching strategies, personalize instruction, and identify areas in their pedagogy that may need improvement.

Self-Directed Learning Plan

Following the self-assessment and reflection on their individual T-PLAN reports teachers were asked to use their data to create a Self-Directed Learning Plan (SDLP) in which the teachers analyzed their reports from the needs assessment and used the data to create professional learning goals for the coming year. First, teachers identified areas for growth and areas of strength by utilizing their personalized reports. After reflection, they then began to create goals for the year based on their needs assessment results. Their goals are ultimately rooted in the professional learning domains utilized for teacher evaluation, providing a clear connection to quality teaching and learning in their classrooms.

Upon completing their learning goals for the year teachers reflected on the process. One BT described how their needs assessment impacted their individualized goals for the year: "In the past, my goals as an educator have been more student driven. I did not stop to think about how bettering myself as a teacher will help the students in the long run." Another BT reflected on how the creation of the SDLP differed from her goal creation in the past:

When creating my PDP last year I had sat down with my BT mentor and we decided on the goals together based on her experiences. I think that working through the self-directed learning plan will impact my practice as a professional this year by giving me the tools to focus on the specific areas I need help with, rather than guessing.

By allowing BTs to reflect on their individualized results and personalized their goals based on results, the teachers reported feeling more connected to their goals:

The self-directed nature of this plan, in my opinion, is much better than how goals have previously been assigned in prior years. Often we would have a choice in a goal or two, but there was typically a school or district-wide goal(s) that were required as well. By being personalized to my needs, I feel as though they will specifically benefit me and my students more.

The traditional goal-creation process is intended to promote teacher autonomy, but often their goals are set for them by their administrators. Allowing teachers to connect with their goals, they also felt empowered to address potential shortcomings in their instruction. Yet another BT reflected on how the results motivated them to address their own needs:

The self direction aspect [of this plan] is helpful in identifying needs and learning to address weakness in a productive way. In the coming year this process will impact the way I assess myself and impact the way I choose to develop as a professional.

Providing space and time for teachers to reflect on their plans is in stark contrast to how they would normally create a professional development plan. Oftentimes their learning plans are due after the school year begins and the demands of their students begin to set in. No time is taken to reflect on their goals or how they will impact their learning. The BTs continued to reflect on how the T-PLAN data and reflection process bolstered the creation of their goals for the school year:

I feel as though I am often the type to naturally self-reflect anyways, but writing it all out and seeing the needs assessment data has really helped me key in on what's most needed to improve on.

Lastly, BTs reported that having the opportunity to not only see individualized data but also spend time focusing on strengths and areas for growth helped them focus on what topics may be beneficial to them as professionals. One teacher stated, "I think that working through the self-directed learning plan will impact my practice as a professional this year by giving me the tools to focus on the specific areas I need help with, rather than guessing." Providing BTs with personalized data and time for self-reflection was beneficial to their experiences in creating meaningful and obtainable learning goals.

Coaching

One asset of this model of TDPL is that each teacher is provided with a coach to help guide them through the process of reflection and also the selection of MCs. If teachers are searching for a particular MC that bolsters a specific skill, they have direct access to an individual to help. This coach also serves as an external thought partner for the teachers, and a safe space to reflect and be vulnerable about their practice. Coaches help teachers throughout the process by providing positive feedback, support, and guidance. They help teachers select micro-credentials based on their needs assessments, and meet with teachers regularly as they complete each micro-credential. This model is non-evaluative and helps teachers truly reflect on their practice without fear of judgment.

While the idea of completing a MC was new to these teachers, they shared how they were supported by their coaches through the process of completing their MCs: "My coach was very helpful along the way. She helped me look at the requirements for the MC in a different perspective". Coaches provide feedback for improvement on drafts of teachers' MCs and often have discussions about the learning goals and implementation of MCs in the classroom. "The meetings I had with my coach supported me in completing my MC and to better understand the learning objectives". Participants also mentioned how their coaches helped them navigate the digital platform that our project utilizes for the assessment of MCs: "My coach gave me pointers on how to get started with my MC and also where to go [online] to complete it". Other BTs shared that their coaches were "helpful and encouraging" throughout the process.

Teachers often worked with their colleagues to complete micro-credentials as well. The use of self-selected micro-credentials allows teachers to collaborate with their colleagues in meaningful ways. One teacher shared that for their goal of: "incorporating other disciplines into my content, I could reach out to my fellow 7th grade team and ask for their input and ideas on really fun or interesting ways I can pull their content into my class". Thus, coaches and colleagues can work collaboratively to support learning and instruction throughout this process.

Reflective Practice Using Video

Teachers created their SDLPs during the summer, before the start of the school year. Within the first twelve weeks of school, each of the teacher participants was video recorded during classroom instruction and were asked to watch and reflect on the video of their teaching. Once teachers watched and reflected on their video, each teacher met with their micro-credential coach to discuss the reflective experience and watch the video together. In addition to providing insight into teachers' classroom practices, the video served as a supplemental data source (in addition to their T-PLAN data) to further guide teachers' self-directed learning journey and make final decisions as to which micro-credentials they could select to best support their professional learning needs.

The use of reflective practice using video has demonstrated positive outcomes in previous studies, such as providing a space for self-analyzing strengths and weaknesses as captured on video and adapting instruction to improve future instruction (Fatimah et al., 2021). Calandra et al (2009) found that using reflective practice through video allows teachers to "restructure prior understanding and define pedagogical thinking," (p. 73). Grounded in a framework of noticing (Sherin & van Es, 2005), teachers were encouraged as they watched the video to observe in a non-judgemental way, viewing the video with an open, curious mind. This approach allowed teachers to notice aspects of their teaching practice that were surprising, observe previously unknown strengths, and identify areas for potential improvement. Reviewing these videos in a non-evaluative fashion allowed the teachers to truly reflect on their practice and consider ways in which it could inform and support their professional growth. Though many teachers were hesitant to embrace video recording their instruction, all of the BTs reported the exercise as useful, and most agreed it would inform their instructional practice moving forward. One teacher explained, " I found the video reflection process and the completion of my reflection document to be extremely valuable in the reflection process to determine what I was doing in my class." Another teacher noted the utility value of the video, stating "[w]atching the video and completing the reflection was very useful to me. I was able to see what worked in that class and what didn't," and another noted "I found the whole process very useful. The video gave me new perspectives and the chance to really reflect on my practice and interactions with students, and the document asked great questions about those interactions."

Reviewing and reflecting on videotaped lessons allows BTs the ability to see multiple components and perspectives of their practice. This practice enables teachers, according to Trent and Gurvitch (2015), "to view their teaching in a different light beyond their limited memory capabilities" (p. 20). In a non-evaluative setting, this viewpoint allows teachers to grow safely and sustainably. This non-evaluative setting coupled with a scaffolded, structured framework in self-directed learning can empower teachers, even BTs, to drive the decision-making process around their professional learning needs with self-compassion and confidence.

Meeting State Professional Development Goals Through Micro-Credentials

Informed by their T-PLAN data, classroom video, and reflective practice, teachers used the goals outlined in their SDLPs to select micro-credentials (MCs) that they could earn to help meet their identified professional learning needs. Teachers were provided a list of MCs that have been aligned with the state teacher evaluation (NCEES) standards (North Carolina Department of Public Instruction, 2018). Having clear and concise results from their needs assessment along with a curated list of MCs is especially helpful for BTs to see the alignment between their self-assessment, their required NCEES standards, and the creation of their self-directed learning plan. This plan not only facilitates the selection of their MCs, it also provides space for the teachers to reflect on what learning topics they want to focus on for the school year. It also asks them to reflect on their practice of teaching and how developing their own learning goals can potentially impact student learning in their classroom.

My needs assessment results did play a role in my goal creation for section 3. I looked at the sections in which I scored myself the lowest and picked micro-credentials that I believe can assist me in filling those gaps for myself and becoming a better teacher.

I am much more engaged in micro-credentials that directly relate to my subject area and grade area.

Teachers select micro-credentials based on their needs and interests. Having micro-credentials organized by NCEES standards helps teachers provide evidence and documentation to their school administrators for their end-of-year evaluations. The NCEES standards include five categories: leadership, promoting a positive classroom environment, content knowledge, facilitating instruction, and reflection (North Carolina Department of Public Instruction, 2018). Teachers shared that the alignment of the micro-credentials to their evaluations:

Allow me to have a much more solid idea of what I want to accomplish this year and be able to present this idea to my admins. As such, I feel as though my admins can help me foster and grow on these goals during my evaluations and additional meetings with them throughout the year.

The creation of the SDLP for our model differs from state-mandated professional development plans, called PDPs because it is non-evaluative. One teacher shared: "I have enjoyed creating this learning plan. It feels like a more thorough and in-depth version of our Professional Development Plans (PDPs) in NCEES." Thus, teachers can select and try different pedagogical approaches based on their own needs and interests. Teachers feel a greater sense of independence and efficacy through this model. Our team provides support to teachers as they complete this model. After teachers complete their self-directed learning plans, they begin working through self-selected micro-credentials. Overall, teachers shared positive feedback about their experiences with micro-credentials as aligned to the NCEES standards and PDP requirements:

I really enjoyed using the micro-credentials to complete my PDP. I liked the self-assessment portion of the ETL project at the beginning because that helped me pick an appropriate micro-credential. I was easily able to see the results of my learning. I also didn't have to come up with an idea on my own to fulfill my PDP requirement. The micro-credential also matched what I do as an EC teacher because I was able to choose.

I believe that using the micro-credentials is a great idea! It allows teachers to choose what they want to work on and specifically target their areas of weakness. I was able to work on something that directly related to my field.

I believe that the use of micro-credentials as a means for teachers to maintain licensure is an excellent idea. This program seems to be a good method in order to achieve professional learning.

After working through micro-credentials, reflecting on their practice, and meeting with coaches, teachers had the opportunity to provide end-of-year feedback. Overall, teachers shared positive feedback about their experiences with teacher-directed professional learning and the micro-credentialing process:

I have enjoyed the self-directed learning and micro-credentials within the ETL project over my experience with other professional learning opportunities because I was able to choose what I wanted to work on.

I loved the aspect of being able to complete these micro-credentials at my own pace. I really appreciated being given options and choosing these PDs, so I could align it to things I really wanted to work on this year.

This feedback supports using teacher-directed professional learning with beginning teachers in the future.

Teachers' Experiences with SDL Using Micro-credentials

BTs that have engaged in SDL that uses MCs have reported that the experience allowed them to focus on their specific needs as educators, with some noting the impact it had on teaching and learning in their classrooms. When asked about their experience with MCs over one year of teaching, nearly all the BTs expressed a view that the MCs gave them autonomy in determining their professional learning needs.

By having choice, I was allowed to work on what would best benefit me... It allowed my students to get a better education and version of myself.

I am choosing to work on areas in which I need to strengthen my abilities in the classroom. My experience with self-directed learning impacted student learning in my classroom by allowing me the opportunity to learn firsthand how my students were progressing in their self-directed learning paths.

I believe that using the micro-credentials is a great idea! It allows teachers to choose what they want to work on and specifically target their areas of weakness. I was able to work on something that directly related to my field.

Others noted the structure of the SDL model, referencing the components such as self-assessment, goal setting, and reflection and how it impacted teaching and learning in their classrooms:

I was able to see exactly what I needed to work on with the self-assessment and choose appropriately based on the micro-credentials provided. I had [a] say in exactly what I was going to do... I was able to reflect on how I handled situations and adjust as needed based on what I learned from the micro-credential. I was able to come up with new ideas to manage my classroom.

Another teacher noted that going through the MC selection process broadened their knowledge of areas of professional learning.

As a BT I have not had much Professional Development, but overall the micro credentials have been helpful in giving me insight into concepts that I hadn't considered before. Being able to choose the topics that I am not as familiar or confident in has been beneficial as I am still learning and developing my teaching pedagogy.

It was more beneficial than PD offered in the past. It's allowed me to broaden learning options that otherwise would have been pinpointed on a certain subject.

Teachers' end-of-year reflections demonstrate the benefits of the TDPL model for this cohort of North Carolina beginning teachers. While the results do not indicate specific benefits for STEM content, all participants in the Empowering Teacher Learning Project were STEM teachers. We discuss potential benefits specific to STEM teachers in the next section.

TDPL would help to meet the varying degrees of STEM expertise within BT cohorts and could help to establish skills around SDL that have the potential to translate into self-directed professional learning as teachers continue in their professional lives. A self-directed learning model for educator preparation programs (EPPs) would provide pre-service teachers the skills to be more self-aware of their individual learning needs and the empowerment to seek out resources that could support their learning. TDPL experiences can also potentially translate into fostering self-directed learning for their students. When implemented using a structured, SDL framework that is supported through coaching and collaboration, micro-credentials can serve as a tool for implementing SDL in pre-service STEM teacher preparation programs.

DISCUSSION AND CONCLUSION

Teachers' experiences with the ETL program have demonstrated promising outcomes in promoting TDPL among a cohort of seven BTs in STEM content areas by providing teachers with an opportunity to engage with professional learning in a new way during each of the four stages of the TDPL process. The value of this self-assessment process was underscored by BTs, who expressed appreciation for the focus on individualized data, emphasizing its benefits in informing teaching strategies and facilitating targeted professional development. The creation of a SDLP, further empowered BTs by allowing them to set meaningful and personalized goals based on their needs assessment results. This departure from traditional goal-setting processes, often influenced by administrators, provided BTs with a stronger sense of autonomy and efficacy in addressing their unique challenges.

As previously stated, North Carolina beginning teachers have a higher attrition rate than their more experienced colleagues (NCDPI, 2023). BTs in STEM fields have additional burdens, which increases attrition rates for this population. STEM teacher attrition is linked to factors like the rise in high-stakes testing in STEM subjects. This leads to a decrease in autonomy as teachers shift focus toward test-taking strategies and content memorization, contributing to their departure from the profession (Faulkner & Cook, 2006; McConnell, 2017). Therefore, providing STEM teachers with additional support, voice, and agency will help improve teacher retention and improve teacher morale.

The use of reflective practice, particularly through video analysis of classroom instruction, offered BTs a valuable perspective on their teaching practices. The non-evaluative setting, grounded in a framework of noticing (Sherin & van Es, 2005), facilitated a deeper understanding of instructional strengths and areas for improvement. The positive feedback from BTs on this aspect of the TDPL model highlights its effectiveness in promoting self-reflection and sustainable professional growth. Coaches played a pivotal role in helping BTs select MCs aligned with their needs assessment, creating a non-evaluative space for reflection, and fostering collaboration among teachers. This model, distinct in its external thought partnership, offered BTs a safe and supportive environment for navigating the complexities of self-directed professional learning. The alignment of MCs with the North Carolina state teacher evaluation standards provided BTs with a clear pathway to meet their professional development goals. The deliberate connection between the needs assessment, SDLP, and MC selection process scaffolded BTs in their approach to professional learning, enhancing their ability to present a comprehensive plan to administrators. The positive responses from BTs regarding the impact on their evaluation process further validate the efficacy of this approach and have implications for supporting teacher growth and retention.

The autonomy provided to teachers experiencing SDL can potentially combat the deprofessionalization of teaching (de Saxe et al., 2020) by allowing them to reflect on their interests and needs as a professional instead of prescribing a one-size-fits-all learning experience. Using MCs helps teachers with possible career advancement opportunities and helps to build a community of continuous learning. By earning micro-credentials, teachers can demonstrate their commitment to professional growth. These credentials may lead to career advancement opportunities, promotions, or increased responsibilities, countering the stagnation that contributes to deprofessionalization. MCs promote a culture of continuous learning among educators. Emphasizing ongoing professional development helps teachers stay updated with innovative teaching practices, technologies, and methodologies, reinforcing their professional status.

Using self-directed learning and micro-credentials such as reflective practice using video helps BTs feel a stronger sense of self-efficacy. Self-efficacy helps teachers have more confidence: "People who have strong beliefs about their competencies of success and efficacy tend to perform better and work on more challenging tasks" (Bandura, 1994; Eccles & Wigfield, 2002). BTs need our support to remain in the profession. With increasing attrition rates, North Carolina would benefit from empowering both beginning and pre-service teachers with this model of self-directed learning and reflective practice. Establishing a teacher-centered PL program in STEM that celebrates teacher success as they demonstrate competencies in research-based instructional skills, places value on teachers' time and efforts in a way that traditional teacher professional development has failed to do. Highlighting teacher accomplishments in this way can lead to a sense of belonging and is a research-based DEI practice that can support teachers from all backgrounds (Creary & Locke, 2021). While recognizing that this approach to teacher professional learning is unconventional, this program could offer a solution to support elementary teachers as they grow professionally.

Limitations

Despite the positive impact observed in a limited sample, the transition to TDPL demands thoughtful preparation, and consistent support, and faces challenges in under-resourced schools. Strategies to address these challenges include flexible learning opportunities, affordability considerations, and integrating MCs into career advancement structures. We see from the responses of participants that utilizing micro-credentials and a self-directed learning framework can positively impact teacher morale and motivation. However, our sample is limited to a small sample size (n=7) and geographic area. Further, shifting teacher professional development to a self-directed learning model requires thoughtful preparation and consistent support. This is essential for teachers during their micro-credentialing process, but it does require additional support from well-trained teachers and administrators.

Having this level of support is difficult, especially when schools are historically under-staffed and under-resourced. Thorsteinson (2018) argues, "The kind of work involved with teaching through SDL is less prescriptive and didactic, but more improvisational and dynamic. Thus, teachers must shift their pedagogical methods, skill-sets, and expectations" (p. 45). Partnering with universities and postsecondary institutions can provide the additional support teachers need to complete their MCs through self-directed learning.

Teachers may worry about the sustainability of the learning gained through micro-credential programs if there is no opportunity to consistently apply or reinforce those skills in their day-to-day teaching practices. The expectation for continuous learning to maintain or update MCs could lead to burnout if not managed effectively alongside other professional and personal commitments.

Addressing these limitations involves developing strategies to support teachers, such as providing flexible learning opportunities, addressing affordability concerns, integrating micro-credentials into career advancement structures, ensuring accessibility to quality programs, and offering adequate support and recognition for teachers pursuing these credentials.

Implications for Future Research

While this exploratory examination focuses on a small sample of BTs, we believe that future research could address teacher self-efficacy and classroom teaching quality. Future studies regarding teacher motivation and student engagement related to self-directed learning would enhance research and practitioner understanding of the micro-credentialing process. Using coaches and mentor support through professional development programs and professional learning communities could contribute to the completion and application of micro-credential topics schoolwide. Last, future research could address the assessment of micro-credentials to ensure the validity and reliability of the content. Researchers could address issues of equity and inclusion within micro-credential content and implementation. These suggestions are not an exhaustive list of potential research projects about micro-credentials and self-directed learning, but they do provide a starting point for educational researchers and interested stakeholders.

Potential Impact on Policy

Shifting the landscape of teacher professional development from a time-based model to a competency-based one requires intentional efforts and changes in how educational leaders design, implement, and assess professional development programs. Using personalized learning plans such as TDPL allows teachers to create personalized professional development plans tailored to their needs and goals and may offer a variety of learning pathways, including micro-credentials, workshops, mentoring, online courses, and collaborative projects. A policy consideration for this work is to explore the potential for policy frameworks that encourage a more flexible and personalized approach to professional development.

Micro-credentials offer teachers the autonomy to choose their professional development paths. Empowering educators to direct their learning can boost morale and restore a sense of control over their professional growth. Earning micro-credentials can lead to career advancement opportunities or increased recognition within the educational community. When teachers feel their efforts are acknowledged and rewarded, they are more inclined to stay within the profession. Further offering autonomy in selecting learning pathways empowers teachers. Feeling in control of their professional growth can positively impact job satisfaction and decrease the likelihood of seeking opportunities elsewhere. Micro-credentials have the potential to counteract the deprofessionalization of teaching by validating teachers' expertise, supporting their continuous professional growth, enhancing teaching quality, and empowering educators within the educational landscape. They contribute to reshaping the narrative around teaching as a dynamic and respected profession.

Micro-Credential Application in Diverse Industries

Micro-credentials have gained popularity across various professions as a means to enhance and validate specific skills or competencies. They offer a flexible, targeted approach to professional development, allowing individuals from diverse fields to acquire new knowledge and validate their expertise in specialized areas. Of course, teachers use MCs to enhance their teaching pedagogy and instructional and classroom management practices. Nurses and healthcare professionals use MCs to stay updated on the latest medical practices and gain expertise in specific procedures and new technologies. Managers and business professionals use MCs to acquire new leadership skills and learn about project management and data analysis. Members of creative and design fields use MCs to learn new software tools such as the Adobe suite of products and learn about business and digital marketing. Skilled tradespeople use MCs to gain expertise in their specific trades and learn about safety protocols, new technologies, and specialized techniques.

Micro-credentials cater to a wide range of professions, providing professionals with the opportunity to continuously learn, specialize, and validate their expertise in specific areas crucial to their respective fields. These credentials play a vital role in improving professional practice by offering targeted, flexible, and relevant learning experiences aligned with the evolving demands of various industries.

Potential for Micro-Credentialing in Educator Preparation Programs

Within this chapter, BTs serve as a proxy for understanding how pre-service teachers might engage with SDL using MCs. As in-service BTs are still learning the craft of teaching, focusing on beginning teachers (BTs) provides insight into how utilizing MCs could potentially shape pedagogical and content knowledge. Workplace learning through an SDL framework could strengthen BT preparation and allow them to focus on specific, research-backed skills that apply to their classroom. Bal, et al. (2022) posit that micro-credentialing could provide a way to incorporate specific content into pre-service teacher curriculum.

Based on our program data and research shared above, we believe that earning micro-credentials during pre-service education can provide a head start in building a strong foundation for continued professional growth once they enter the teaching workforce. Few EPPs use MCs for teacher preparation, though similar competency-based programs exist (e.g., EdTPA). Having additional credentials beyond a degree can make pre-service teachers more competitive in the job market, demonstrating their commitment to ongoing learning and professional development. Given the need for improvement in STEM teacher education, MCs could serve as a pathway to fostering skills around SDL that could be transferred to STEM classrooms, engaging STEM education students in a way that empowers and retains them as education majors, and acknowledges their accomplishments so that they feel recognized for their work in learning new skills around STEM teaching and learning.

While there is little research on the efficacy of MCs as a means of supporting pre-service teacher growth and subsequent student outcomes, anecdotal responses from BTs about their experiences with MCs show promise in the ability of MCs to have a meaningful impact on STEM teaching and learning. More research is needed to understand in- and pre-service teachers' experiences with MCs so that they can be implemented in a way that recognizes teachers' accomplishments and supports them with coaching and collaboration throughout their self-directed learning journey.

In our experience with BTs, they have a myriad of responsibilities and duties in addition to learning and mastering instructional strategies and developing their classroom pedagogy. At present, those who are still categorized as BTs have had the unique experience of becoming a BT during and immediately after a global pandemic. These individuals may need additional support for their continuing professional learning (Kang, 2020, VanLone et al., 2022). This unique cohort of teachers could potentially benefit from a self-directed learning model that provides them with support and guidance in the development and attainment of their professional learning goals.

REFERENCES

Alliance for Excellent Education. (2013). Expanding education and workforce opportunities through digital badges. https://all4ed.org/wp-content/uploads/2013/09/DigitalBadges.pdf

American Association for the Advancement of Science. (1998). *Blueprints for reform: Science, mathematics, and technology education. American Association for the Advancement of Science & Project 2061*. Oxford University Press.

Artman, B., Danner, N., & Crow, S. R. (2020). Teacher-directed professional development: An alternative to conventional professional development. *International Journal of Self-Directed Learning*, *17*(1), 39–50.

Bal, I. A., Alvarado–Albertorio, F., Marcelle, P., & Oaks-Garcia, C. T. (2022). Pre–service Teachers Computational Thinking (CT) and Pedagogical Growth in a Micro–credential: A Mixed Methods Study. *TechTrends*, *66*(3), 468–482. doi:10.1007/s11528-022-00732-x PMID:35499060

Bandura, A. (1994). Regulative function of perceived self-efficacy. In M. G. Rumsey, C. B. Walker, & J. H. Harris (Eds.), *Personnel selection and classification* (pp. 261–271). Lawrence Erlbaum Associates, Inc. https://psycnet-apa-org.proxy006.nclive.org/record/1994-98076-013

Calandra, B., Gurvitch, R., & Lund, J. (2008). An exploratory study of digital video editing as a tool for teacher preparation. *Journal of Technology and Teacher Education, 16*, 137–153.

Clausen, J. M. (2022). Learning to Fly: Development and Design of a Micro-Credentialing System for an Educator Preparation Program in the Absence of a Required Educational Technology Course. *TechTrends, 66*(2), 276–286. https://doi-org.proxy006.nclive.org/10.1007/s11528-021-00673-x. doi:10.1007/s11528-021-00673-x PMID:34664042

Cochran-Smith, M., Banks, J., Moll, L., Richert, A., Zeichner, K., LePage, P., Darling-Hammond, L., Duffy, H., & McDonald, M. (2005). Teaching Diverse Learners. In L. Darling-Hammond & J. Bransford (Eds.), *Preparing teachers for a changing world: What teachers should learn and be able to do* (pp. 232–274). Jossey-Bass.

Creary, S. J., & Locke, K. (2021). To reduce the strain of overwork, learn to listen to your body. Harvard Business Review Digital Articles, 1–7. https://hbr.org/2021/11/to-reduce-the-strain-of-overwork-learn-to-listen-to-your-body

Darling-Hammond, L. (2005). Teaching as a profession: Lessons in teacher preparation and professional development. *Phi Delta Kappan, 87*(3), 237–240. https://journals-sagepub-com.proxy006.nclive.org/doi/pdf/10.1177/003172170508700318

Darling-Hammond, L., & Bransford, J. (2007). *Preparing teachers for a changing world (Report of the Committee on Teacher Education of the National Academy of Education)*. Jossey Bass.

Davis, E. A. (2006). Preservice elementary teachers' critique of instructional materials for science. *Science Education, 90*(2), 348–375. https://doi-org.proxy006.nclive.org/10.1002/sce.20110

de Saxe, J. G., Bucknovitz, S., & Mahoney-Mosedale, F. (2020). The Deprofessionalization of Educators: An Intersectional Analysis of Neoliberalism and Education "Reform.". *Education and Urban Society, 52*(1), 51–69. doi:10.1177/0013124518786398

Eccles, J. S., & Wigfield, A. (2002). Motivational beliefs, values, and goals. *Annual Review of Psychology, 53*(1), 109. https://doi-org.proxy006.nclive.org/10.1146/annurev.psych.53.100901.135153

Fatimah, S., Tiarina, Y., Fitrawati, F., & Mira, A. S. (2021). English teachers' and lecturers' perceptions of reflective practice through video recording at the teacher certification program. *Studies in English Language and Education, 8*(2), 670–689. https://doi-org.proxy006.nclive.org/10.24815/siele.v8i2.18931. doi:10.24815/siele.v8i2.18931

Faulkner, S. A., & Cook, C. M. (2006). Testing vs. teaching: The perceived impact of assessment demands on middle grades instructional practices. *Research in Middle Level Education Online, 29*(7), 1–13. https://doi-org.proxy006.nclive.org/10.1080/19404476.2006.11462030

Fox, L., Howell, S., Kazouh, A., Paul, E., & Peacock, J. (2023). *Teacher recruitment and retention trends across North Carolina and the impact of the COVID-19 pandemic*. Public School Forum of North Carolina. https://www.ncforum.org/2023/teacher-recruitment-and-retention-trends-across-north-carolina-and-the-impact-of-the-covid-19-pandemic/

Garrison, D. R. (1997). Self-directed learning: Toward a comprehensive model. *Adult Education Quarterly, 48*(1), 18–33. https://doi-org.proxy006.nclive.org/10.1177/074171369704800103

Gibson, D., Ostashewski, N., Flintoff, K., Grant, S., & Knight, E. (2015). Digital badges in education. *Education and Information Technologies, 20*(2), 403–410. https://doi-org.proxy006.nclive.org/10.1007/s10639-013-9291-7. doi:10.1007/s10639-013-9291-7

Goodnough, K., Pelech, S., & Stordy, M. (2014). Effective professional development in STEM education: The perceptions of primary/elementary teachers. *Teacher Education and Practice, 27*(2/3), 402–423. https://www.researchgate.net/publication/281121613_Effective_Professional_Development_in_STEM_Education_The_Perceptions_of_PrimaryElementary_Teachers

Heck, D. J., Plumley, C. L., Stylianou, D. A., Smith, A. A., & Moffett, G. (2019). Scaling up innovative learning in mathematics: Exploring the effect of different professional development approaches on teacher knowledge, beliefs, and instructional practice. *Educational Studies in Mathematics, 102*(3), 319–342. https://doi-org.proxy006.nclive.org/10.1007/s10649-019-09895-6

Holroyd, C., & Harlen, W. (1996). Primary teachers' confidence about teaching science and technology. *Research Papers in Education: Policy and Practice, 11*(3), 323–335.

Hurst, E. J. (2015). Digital badges: Beyond learning incentives. *Journal of Electronic Resources in Medical Libraries*, *12*(3), 182–189. https://doi-org.proxy006.nclive.org/10.1080/15424065.2015.1065661

Jones, W. M., Hope, S., & Adams, B. (2018). Teachers' perceptions of digital badges as recognition of professional development. *British Journal of Educational Technology*, *49*(3), 427–438. https://doi-org.proxy006.nclive.org/10.1111/bjet.12557

Kang, R. L. (2020, July). Struggles and strengths of being preservice in a pandemic. *Educator's Update*, 2–3.

Knowles, M. S. (1975). *Self-directed learning: A guide for learners and teachers*. Follett.

McConnell, J. (2017). A model for understanding teachers' intentions to remain in STEM education. *International Journal of STEM Education*, *4*(1), 1–21. https://doi-org.proxy006.nclive.org/10.1186/s40594-017-0061-8

Merrimack College. (2022). *Merrimack College Teacher Survey*. Merrimack College. https://www.merrimack.edu/academics/education-and-social-policy/merrimack-college-teacher-survey

Mezirow, J. (1985). A critical theory of self-directed learning. *New Directions for Continuing Education*, *25*, 17–30.

Milner-Bolotin, M. (2018). Evidence-based research in STEM teacher education: From theory to practice. *Frontiers in Education*, *3*, 389767. https://doi.org/10.3389/feduc.2018.00092

Murphy, T. P., & Mancini-Samuelson, G. J. (2012). Graduating STEM competent and confident teachers: The creation of a STEM certificate for elementary education majors. *Journal of College Science Teaching*, *42*(2), 18–23. https://login.proxy006.nclive.org/login?url=https://www-proquest-com.proxy006.nclive.org/scholarly-journals/graduating-stem-competent-confident-teachers/docview/1151391363/se-2

National Research Council. (1996). *National Science Education Standards*. National Academy Press.

North Carolina Department of Public Instruction. (2018). *North Carolina teacher evaluation process. Public Schools of North Carolina. State Board of Education. Department of Public Instruction.* https://ncchildcare.ncdhhs.gov/Portals/0/documents/pdf/2/2018_NCTeacherEvaluation_NCEES_Teacher_Manual.pdf?ver=O2SejpORRPS0nwdqgzDeNw%3d%3d

Public Schools of North Carolina. (2022). *Report to the North Carolina General Assembly 2020-2021 State of the Teaching Profession in North Carolina.* Public Schools of North Carolina. https://www.google.com/url?client=internal-element-cse&cx=007953340131544038496:b3cb1hux6m4&q=https://www.dpi.nc.gov/documents/advancedlearning/cihs/2022-ccp-cihs-annual-report/download%3Fattachment&sa=U&ved=2ahUKEwirqtiW0pmDAxWuFlkFHcbdBUcQFnoECAMQAQ&usg=AOvVaw0zX-u7iuOuSV6gPiLE5-Os

Public Schools of North Carolina (2023). Report to the North Carolina General Assembly: 2021-2022 state of the teaching profession in North Carolina. https://www.google.com/url?client=internal-element-cse&cx=007953340131544038496:b3cb1hux6m4&q=https://www.dpi.nc.gov/districts-schools/districts-schools-support/district-human-capital/surveys-and-reports&sa=U&ved=2ahUKEwirqtiW0pmDAxWuFlkFHcbdBUcQFnoECAEQAQ&usg=AOvVaw3tHYhHWw5zOewmQf97KyWN

Sawchuk, S. (2016, March 30). Can "micro-credentialing" salvage teacher PD? *Education Week, 35*(26).

Sherin, M. G., & Van Es, E. A. (2005). Using Video to Support Teachers' Ability to Notice Classroom Interactions. *Journal of Technology and Teacher Education, 13*(3), 475–491.

Spangler, D. (2019). Micro Approach, Major Impact: With Microcredentials, Educators Can Tailor Learning to Their Specific Needs. *Learning Professional, 40*(4), 60–64.

Thorsteinson, K. (2018). Anarchy in the classroom: The efficacy of self-directed learning for critical whiteness pedagogy. Transformations. *The Journal of Inclusive Scholarship & Pedagogy, 28*(1), 38–60. https://doi-org.proxy006.nclive.org/10.1353/tnf.2018.0003

Tooley, M., & Hood, J. (2021, January 13) *Harnessing micro-credentials for teacher growth: a model state policy guide.* Washington, DC: New America, p. 9. https://www.newamerica.org/education-policy/reports/harnessing-micro-credentials-for-teacher-growth-a-model-state-policy-guide/

Trent, M., & Gurvitch, R. (2015). Fostering Teacher Candidates' Reflective Practice through Video Editing. *Journal of Physical Education, Recreation & Dance, 86*(5), 5, 14–20. doi:10.1080/07303084.2015.1022674

Trumper, R. (2006). Factors affecting junior high school students' interest in physics. *Journal of Science Education and Technology, 15*(1), 47–58. https://doi-org.proxy006.nclive.org/10.1007/s10956-006-0355-6

VanLone, J., Pansé-Barone, C., & Long, K. (2022). Teacher preparation and the COVID-19 disruption: Understanding the impact and implications for novice teachers. *International Journal of Educational Research Open, 3*, 100120. doi:10.1016/j.ijedro.2021.100120 PMID:35059675

Zembal-Saul, C., Blumenfeld, P., & Krajcik, J. (2000). Influence of guided cycles of planning, teaching, and reflection on prospective elementary teachers' science content representations. *Journal of Research in Science Teaching, 37*(4), 318–339.

Chapter 6

Finding Success in Adapting Repeated Microteaching Rehearsals (RMTR) for an Online Science Methods Course

Franklin S. Allaire
https://orcid.org/0000-0003-1053-0462
University of Houston-Downtown, USA

ABSTRACT

In February/March 2020, postsecondary educators worldwide were required to suddenly shift from face-to-face to online instruction due to the COVID-19 pandemic. For teacher educators, this meant reimagining how to enact core pedagogical strategies, such as teaching rehearsals for online instruction. This chapter shares my experiences of integrating repeated microteaching rehearsals (RMTR) into my elementary science methods courses before the COVID-19 pandemic to disastrous results. Then, adapting RMTR for an online learning environment due to the rapid shift from face-to-face to online learning during the pandemic and its successful integration as an online practice teaching strategy. This chapter also shares how RMTR was and continues to be implemented in my post-pandemic science methods course and the lessons learned along the way.

DOI: 10.4018/978-1-6684-5939-3.ch006

INTRODUCTION

In February and March 2020, K-12 and postsecondary institutions became the epicenters of rapidly expanding curricular and service disruptions as local and state government leaders took dramatic steps to "flatten the curve" and reduce the number of new COVID-19 cases. The COVID-19 pandemic was a pedagogical reckoning in education due to the dramatic shift from face-to-face to online learning (Allaire & Killham, 2022, 2023; Hartlep et al., 2021). This shift was accomplished with varying degrees of preparedness and technological competency.

Besides finding ways to "do science" virtually, science teacher educators searched for ways to address core instructional pedagogy – such as teaching rehearsals (practice teaching) – in online learning environments. This chapter shares my experience adapting repeated microteaching rehearsals (RMTR) for an online undergraduate elementary science methods course. This course is part of the teacher preparation program for elementary teacher candidates (ETC) enrolled the University of Houston-Downtown - a four-year federally-recognized Hispanic/Minority-serving institution – during the COVID-19 pandemic. Furthermore, this chapter also explores online RMTR's successful integration as an online teaching rehearsal strategy in my post-pandemic course and the lessons learned along the way.

THE UNIVERSITY, COURSE, AND STUDENTS

The University of Houston-Downtown (UHD) is a four-year federally designated Minority and Hispanic-serving institution located in an urban metropolitan area of the southern United States. Many undergraduates at UHD are the first in their families to attend college, come from a lower socioeconomic status, work full-time, and balance family, professional, and academic lives while attending college. Approximately 54% (7,106) of all undergraduates self-identify as Hispanic, and over 56% of Hispanic undergraduates are female, with an average undergraduate age of 26.5 years. Hispanic females are also the student demographic with the highest graduation rate (23%). Within UHD's teacher preparation program, 92% of undergraduates were/are female, with 73% self-identifying as Hispanic/Latinx and an average age of 28.51 years (Data USA, 2022; University, 2022). ETCs participating in RMTR mirror the overall university demographics. The majority of the ETCs participating in this study self-identified as female (94.6%) and Hispanic/Latinx (78.7%), with Spanish being their first/home language (60.2%).

Elementary Science Methods (ESM) is a required one-semester course taken by undergraduate ETCs in the third semester of their teacher preparation program, the semester before student teaching. ESM engages teacher candidates through their coursework in age/grade-appropriate hands-on and virtual inquiry-based activities, learning/practicing strategies to integrate science with other disciplines, and preparing, teaching, and reflecting on science lessons. Like other teacher preparation programs, UHD's teacher candidates must conduct four field-based teaching rehearsals, two per semester, before their student teaching semester. However, for reasons that will be explored later, ESM courses are likely the only opportunity for teacher candidates to plan and teach science within their teacher preparation program.

ON THE IMPORTANCE OF SCIENCE TEACHING REHEARSALS

It is widely recognized that teaching rehearsals are essential in developing elementary teacher candidates' (ETC) confidence and expertise. Teaching rehearsals (e.g., Cinici, 2016; d'Alessio, 2018; Long et al., 2019; Pauline, 1993) prepare "beginning teachers to be able to do teaching when they get into classrooms and prepar[e] them to do teaching that is more socially and intellectually ambitious than the current norm" (Lampert et al., 2013, p. 240). Strategies for implementing rehearsals and their specifics vary. Versions of rehearsals can involve ETCs reteaching a lesson that has been modeled by their mentor or instructor (Kazemi et al., 2016; Lotter et al., 2009) or planning and teaching new lessons within a methods course in the field, or both (Hanuscin, 2004; Javeed, 2019; Long et al., 2019; Masters, 2020). Regardless, teaching rehearsals, as a teacher education pedagogy, create a situation that approximates the work of teaching (Kazemi et al., 2016; Lampert et al., 2013; Pauline, 1993) are used within courses and in the field to "illustrate real classroom environments to the trainee teacher in a simplified classroom situation, in terms of class size, lesson length, and focus on teaching tasks" (Cinici, 2016, p. 229). Whether in the classroom or the field, real or virtual, teaching rehearsals offer ETCs an opportunity to hone their teaching skills, improve their content knowledge, and develop confidence in their teaching abilities under the guidance of an expert teacher or teacher educator (Cheong, 2010; Ghousseini, 2017; Hanuscin & Zangori, 2016; Kazemi et al., 2016). In general, teaching rehearsals can have a powerful influence on the development and maintenance of ETCs' sense of self-efficacy and, therefore, impact both the time ETCs spend in the teaching profession and student achievement (Hoy & Spero, 2005; Riggs & Enochs, 1990).

Teaching rehearsals are especially critical for developing ETCs' ability to plan and teach science effectively. Elementary teachers' low science teaching self-efficacy (Brígido et al., 2013; Enochs & Riggs, 1990; McCall, 2017; Morris et al., 2017) and lack of science content knowledge (Banilower et al., 2018; Hanuscin et al., 2011; Hume & Berry, 2011) are frustratingly persistent issues. Complicating matters is the reality that many elementary classrooms are self-contained. As a result, elementary teachers are typically responsible for planning and teaching multiple disciplines, including science, mathematics, reading/language arts, and social studies. Additionally, emphasizing standardized testing has forced elementary teachers to spend more time on reading, writing, and mathematics to the detriment of science and social studies instruction.

Despite improvements in teacher preparation programs, increases in professional development opportunities for teachers. The 2018 National Survey of Science and Mathematics Education (NSSME+) (Banilower et al., 2018; Plumley, 2019) made it clear that "elementary school teachers do not feel equally well prepared to teach all academic subjects" (Plumley, 2019, p. 5). Only 31% of self-contained elementary teachers reported feeling "very well prepared" to teach science, compared to 77% and 73% for reading/language arts and mathematics, respectively. In this same vein, elementary teachers needed more preparation to teach all sciences. Only 13% feel "very well prepared" to teach physical science compared to 24% and 20% for life science and earth/space science, respectively. The percentage of elementary teachers who felt "very well prepared" for science teaching-related tasks is even more worrisome. While 31% felt very well prepared to encourage [K-6] student participation in science or engineering, only 23% felt prepared to develop students' conceptual understanding, 19% felt prepared to differentiate science instruction for diverse learners, and 17% felt prepared to develop students' abilities to do science (e.g., develop scientific questions, design and conduct experiments, analyze data) (Banilower et al., 2018; Plumley, 2019).

In order to build and maintain high levels of science teaching self-efficacy and support science content knowledge acquisition, ETCs need as many opportunities as possible to rehearse teaching science and reflect upon their experience. More importantly, candidates need to be able to teach and reflect under the guidance of a mentor teacher or teacher educator with expertise in science. Recognizing that ETCs in UHD's teacher preparation program have limited opportunities for science teaching rehearsals in the field, even fewer opportunities to reflect, revise, and reteach their lessons, and based on recommendations by Chval (2004) and Hanuscin and Zangori (2016), repeated microteaching rehearsals (RMTR) were adapted and integrated into an online elementary science methods course from Spring 2020 to the Spring 2023 semester.

THE CHALLENGE...

There were, and continue to be, three significant challenges to meeting the field-based practice science teaching needs of ETCs. First and foremost, science methods course instructors in the University of Houston-Downtown's teacher preparation program do not determine the type of lessons an ETC teaches in the field. The type and timing of lessons in determined by a collaboration between the ETC, the mentor teacher, and the clinical coach – an individual representing the institution who observes and provides guidance to the ETC in the field.

Secondly, the emphasis on standardized testing means field-based lessons tend to focus on reading, writing, and mathematics. Therefore, the odds of ETCs teaching a science lesson in the field are not in their favor. The NSSME+ (Banilower et al., 2018; Plumley, 2019) reported that 39% of self-contained elementary classes receive science some weeks but not every week and that "primary grades classes spend an average of 17 minutes per day on science, compared to 89 minutes on reading/language arts and 55 minutes on mathematics" (Plumley, 2019, p. 15).

Finally, ETCs may have little to no control over the mentor teachers they receive. As a result, ETCs may work with classroom teachers who are relatively inexperienced and feel uncomfortable teaching science, which could hinder ETCs' professional growth. For example, Brown (1999) explains that ETCs may be less likely to try new methods or strategies and "decide in favor of the 'safe' path of emulating the cooperating teacher" (p. 307) even if those methods are without merit.

MEETING CANDIDATES' NEEDS IN CLASS

To meet ETCs' needs, in terms of science teaching experience, I sought to create low-stakes, high-impact teaching rehearsal opportunities as part of my elementary science methods course. Pre-pandemic, I became interested in merging three strategies – course-based rehearsals, microteaching, and repeated teaching – and integrating them into my courses (see Figure 1). I felt that merging some of the best aspects of each of these strategies would be key to creating opportunities for candidates to practice teaching science.

Course-Based Rehearsals

Course-based rehearsals were chosen due to general and institutionally specific challenges related to the field-based model. Course-based rehearsals mirror, to a certain extent, what occurs in the field in that ETCs are assigned a topic, create a lesson plan, and teach the lesson. The difference is that ETCs teach their lesson to their peers and course instructors instead of teaching them to school-aged children. There are variations within the broad spectrum of course-based rehearsals with options to have ETCs work alone or in a small group (Ghousseini, 2017; Kazemi et al., 2016; Lampert et al., 2013), observe each other teach the same lesson to different students (e.g., lesson study) (Marble, 2007; Zhou et al., 2016), or rehearse their lesson to their instructor and peers before teaching it in the field (e.g., Masters, 2020).

Figure 1. Theoretical framework merging three strategies: Course-based rehearsals, microteaching, and repeated teaching

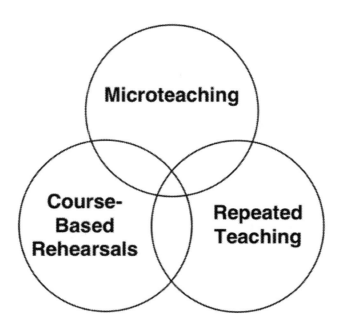

Course-based rehearsals may not be as accurate a representation of classroom teaching as field-based rehearsals – particularly in terms of elementary classroom teaching. However, course-based rehearsals offer several benefits. Firstly, course-based rehearsals guarantee that ETCs will have opportunities to teach science. Secondly, course-based rehearsals ensure that ETCs practice teaching science and receive feedback from a mentor with experience and expertise in science. They can be a safe space to "experiment" with different teaching styles, techniques, and strategies. Finally, course-based rehearsals offer instructors a level of control they may not have in the field. For example, course-based teaching rehearsals could be done in one more modality (online, in-person, hybrid) to create different types of experiences for ETCs. Additionally, rehearsals can be tailored to specific science disciplines (i.e., physical science) (Long et al., 2019) or strategies (i.e., integrating technology) (Zhou et al., 2016).

Microteaching

Microteaching is a technique that involves breaking down planning and teaching into smaller, more manageable components. The purpose of this is for teachers, or teacher candidates, to concentrate on practicing or refining specific aspects of their teaching, such as delivery, classroom management, questioning techniques, technology integration, or use of instructional aids without the pressure of managing a full-scale classroom (Allen & Eve, 1968; Cavanaugh, 2022; Cooper & Allen, 1970; Remesh, 2013). It is a time-efficient technique that effectively improves teaching skills (Pauline, 1993; Remesh, 2013).

During a microteaching rehearsal, a teacher candidate presents a short lesson to a small group of students or peers focusing on a specific topic or skill. After delivering the lesson, the teacher receives individualized feedback from their instructor, peers, or students, identifying strengths and areas of improvement. Multiple studies have shown microteaching to be an effective method for teacher preparation (Göçer, 2016; Pauline, 1993). These studies provide evidence that microteaching can improve teacher candidates' teaching effectiveness by developing their instructional skills (Bakır, 2014; Zhou et al., 2016), supporting their pedagogical content knowledge (Basturk, 2016; Kartal et al., 2012; Long et al., 2019), developing and maintaining their teaching self-efficacy (Cinici, 2016; d'Alessio, 2018; Mergler & Tangen, 2010), and refining teaching methods and strategies (Akkuş & Sinem, 2017).

In my case, the prefix "micro" had a double meaning. It referred to the length of the lesson (only 15 – 20 minutes) rather than a 60- or 90-minute field-based lesson traditionally taught by the candidates. Secondly, "micro" also referenced focusing on a particular "teaching skill" for the lesson. Like Long et al. (2019), the "teaching skill" was science – a discipline many ETCs have little to no experience teaching.

Repeated Teaching

Repeated teaching rehearsal refers to practice teaching sessions conducted multiple times so teachers can prepare/refine their lesson plans, teaching methods and strategies, materials, interactions with learners, and delivery. Course- and field-based rehearsals are traditionally "one shot." Teacher candidates are assigned a topic and proceed to plan, teach, reflect on a lesson, and receive peer/mentor feedback (see Figure 2). Due to the curricular constraints of field observation classes and time constraints of science methods course structures, this method has become the norm for rehearsals in teacher preparation programs.

Figure 2. In traditional course- and field-based rehearsals, ETCs have "one shot" to teach and reflect on a lesson

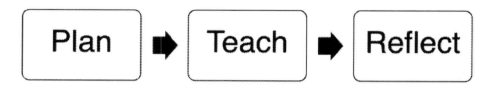

Repeated teaching moves beyond the traditional "one shot" lesson through an iterative cycle that includes at least one opportunity to reflect, revise, and reteach a lesson (see Figure 3). Research like Hanuscin (2004), Hanuscin and Zangori (2016), and Marble (2006) show that this iterative cycle helps teacher candidates familiarize themselves with the content, refine content and instructional strategies, enhance delivery and communication skills, practice pacing and managing time, and address potential challenges. However, this same research accomplishes these cycles of practice under very specific conditions – which science methods instructors may not be able to replicate.

Figure 3. In the iterative repeated teaching sequence, teachers can reflect and revise their lesson before reteaching it to a new group of students

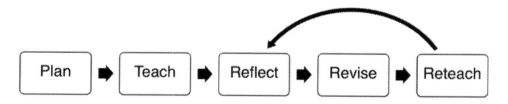

PRE-PANDEMIC IMPLEMENTATION OF RMTR

RMTR was implemented before the COVID-19 pandemic during the Spring and Fall 2019 semesters as part of an in-person ESM course. The RMTR was a 15-minute team-taught lesson (content, reinforcing demonstration/activity, and assessment). The assignment required a small group of ETCs (chosen randomly and no more than three in a group) to plan and teach a science lesson based on an assigned science teaching competency – a state-approved educator standard for beginning teachers. To support candidates' content knowledge acquisition and create a more cohesive experience, assigned competencies for each RMTR session focused on a particular science area (e.g., physical science).

The choice to focus RMTR on science teaching competencies rather than state standards for EC-6 students was strategic. First, focusing on the science teaching competencies eliminated the need to assign ETCs to a particular grade level (i.e., 3rd grade) for their lesson. Secondly, the science teaching competencies form the basis for part of the state certification exam. Thus, the RMTR served as both a teaching practice and a review session with a lesson that helps the "teachers" and "students" prepare for their certification exam by focusing on specific core science content. Topics and due dates were assigned several weeks ahead of lessons to allow groups time to plan and for the instructor to meet with groups individually, preview the lesson, and guide them if necessary.

The RMTR was facilitated as a "round-robin" with ETCs assigned the role of "teachers" (those who were teaching) and "students" (those who were watching/participating in the lesson) depending on when they were assigned to teach their lesson. RMTR lessons took place during consecutive class meetings with a predetermined teaching order. During the first RMTR session, approximately half of the candidates were "teachers," and the other half were "students." For the second RMTR session, the following week, the roles were reversed.

The "teachers" were assigned to a specific space and stayed in place for the entire rehearsal exercise. The "students" rotated around to each lesson at 15-minute intervals. In between lessons, "students" returned to a central space for a 7-minute break. During each break, "teachers" reflected on and revised their lesson while the "students" provided peer feedback using an instructor-generated form. The round-robin method ensured that the "teachers" had multiple opportunities to teach the same lesson to different groups of "students."

The Result...

From both instructor and student perspectives, the in-person RMTR experience fell somewhere between "challenging" and "train wreck." Multiple logistical challenges prevented in-person RMTR from being an effective strategy. Firstly, when multiple lessons were held within the same classroom, the noise level prevented "students" from fully engaging with the "teachers." Secondly, when I attempted to assign "teachers" to individual classrooms, we encountered a lack of available classroom space. Managing "student" movement to different lessons with multiple simultaneous lessons was another challenge. The multiple simultaneous lessons also raised an important question that struck at the heart of the strategy – how do I watch, comment, and grade individual lessons being taught simultaneously without recording equipment or ideal recording conditions?

The ETCs that participated in the in-person iterations of RMTR were brutally honest in that it was an overwhelmingly negative experience for both the "students" and "teachers." While they appreciated the strategy's intent, the logistical challenges got in the way. I was very disheartened, and honestly, had it not been for the pandemic and the shift from in-person to online learning, I probably would have abandoned the strategy in favor of the traditional "one-shot" model for in-class teaching rehearsals.

IMPLEMENTATION OF RMTR DURING THE COVID-19 PANDEMIC

The pandemic and rapid shift from in-person to online teaching and learning forced educators at all levels to be pedagogically inventive and adaptive. RMTR was no different, and an online iteration of this strategy was first implemented during the Fall 2020 semester. Like the in-person iterations, online RMTR was facilitated as a "round-robin." However, the round-robin was accomplished using the breakout room feature in Zoom. "Teachers" were assigned and placed in a specific breakout room and stayed in place for the entire rehearsal exercise. "Students" were grouped, assigned, and rotated around to each lesson at 15- or 20-minute intervals.

In between lessons, "students" returned to the main Zoom session for a 7-minute break. During each break, "teachers" reflected on and revised their lesson while the "students" provided peer feedback using a link to an online instructor-generated form. Figure 4 demonstrates how the round-robin online RMTR was organized for four teaching groups. The final iteration of each group's lesson was recorded in Zoom and later uploaded to be viewed and graded. My role throughout the online RMTR was to act as timekeeper and I.T. support – helping "students" get to the breakout rooms, assisting in breakout rooms when necessary, and getting ETCs back to the breakout rooms if/when they were booted from the Zoom class due to technical difficulties.

Immediately following the final iteration of the rehearsals, the "students" and "teachers" came back together in the main Zoom session and discussed the lessons. The "students" were invited to share some feedback they provided between the lessons. The "teachers" primarily reflected on the repeated teaching experience. While this conversation was organic and free-flowing, it was helpful to have questions ready to guide the discussion (e.g., What can we 'Glow' about (aspect(s) of the lessons that were done well)?; What can we 'Grow' on (aspect(s) of a lessons that could be improved)?; What questions do we have?).

Finding Success in Adapting RMTR for an Online Science Methods Course

Figure 4. An example of online RMTR facilitated through four breakout rooms on Zoom

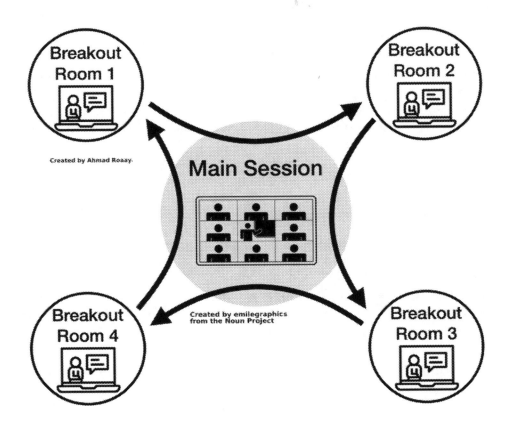

The Result...

Interestingly, RMTR worked better as an online strategy than in-person. There were no volume or space issues because "teachers" were assigned to specific Zoom breakout rooms. It was easier to manage students moving from room to room and facilitate reflective breaks during online RMTR. I could also send messages and updates to all breakout rooms simultaneously, ensuring that time for lessons (15 or 20 minutes) was consistent and equitable for all teaching groups. Additionally, the built-in record feature enabled all groups to record their lesson so that they could be uploaded and watched/scored later.

STUDENT FEEDBACK ON ONLINE RMTR

To determine the effectiveness of this strategy, I collected data via lesson reflections and an optional anonymous survey as part of the ETC's coursework. Survey results (93.2% response rate) and lesson reflections showed that ETCs were initially uncertain about the online RMTR procedure and the impact of repeated teaching experiences. Survey responses and reflections noted that previous class- and field-based lesson rehearsals were taught only once. Thus, repeatedly teaching a lesson with an opportunity to reflect and revise was a new experience. The iterative process was appreciated, with ETCs noting on the same survey and reflection that they felt their lessons improved during the iterative process and had a positive experience with online RMTR.

Teachers' Perspectives of Online RMTR

Survey responses point to ETCs having a positive experience with online RMTR, with 97.1%, 94.1%, and 100% liking the structure of online RMTR, being able to teach the same lesson multiple times to different students, and being able to revise and reteach their lesson, respectively. 94.11% of respondents strongly agreed that their lessons improved as they gained more experience teaching the topic. One ETC commented that as they taught, they "were able to understand more about the topic, the delivery, and about my students and their reactions." Similarly, 87.7% of respondents strongly agreed that they felt more confident teaching similar science topics. In a lesson reflection, an ETC wrote, "At first, I was very nervous, but it got better when I repeated the lesson. My body language got less awkward, and I felt more confident." Another student echoed this sentiment in their reflection, writing, "I took the errors that I did in the other lessons, and the things that the students were having a bit of trouble understanding, I explained better, as well as fixed my errors."

Students' Perspectives of Online RMTR

Overall, "students" liked the structure of the online RMTR (90.6%), with 50% reporting that it was more engaging than other course- or field-based lessons. Despite the challenges mentioned by the "teachers," the "students" felt the lessons were well-prepared and thorough, with an average rating of 3.75 out of 4 points. Open-ended responses showed that "students" felt the short lesson format focused the lessons and "forced the 'teachers' to get straight to the point." Additionally, 59.4% of survey respondents felt multiple micro lessons were more engaging than a single, longer lesson. The shorter lessons enabled "students" to receive more content and "see the different ways each group taught."

Critiques of Online RMTR

While candidates generally enjoyed participating in online RMTR, they had a few critiques of the strategy and experience. While 76.5% of "teachers" felt the experience of teaching their lesson multiple times was better than other course-/field-based rehearsals, only 35.3% found the experience more engaging. Open-ended feedback revealed that one of the most challenging aspects of the online RMTR was the physical and mental act of teaching the same lesson multiple times. Several respondents said they felt like they "had no voice after teaching the same lesson four times in a row." Others noted that they got "tired," "bored," and that "the energy wasn't there anymore" by the final iteration of their lesson.

A second theme was related to the 15-minute time limit. Having grown accustomed to teaching rehearsals that were 60- or 90 minutes in length, ETCs reacted negatively to the lesson/reflection time constraints, with one ETC stating that they "did not like the amount of time we had for our lessons because with more time we can give a more thorough lesson." Some ETCs noted that they would have liked more reflection time between iterations. Conversely, some felt the "rapid fire reflection" (as one ETC called it) forced them to be strategic and focus on minor changes to improve the lesson. Finally, technical difficulties were another common theme from "teachers" in both the survey and reflections. Despite having used Zoom for multiple courses, due to the COVID-19 pandemic, during their lessons, some ETCs struggled with their WIFI connection, sharing screens, and recording their lessons.

Like the "teachers," "students" felt that technical difficulties impacted their ability to participate in the lessons with one ETC, noting that "it was really hard trying to work Zoom" but also acknowledging "this was a good practice and will eventually come in handy later on." Some ETCs lamented the 15-minute time limit on lessons, feeling that it was not enough time. They also felt three or four lessons in one class meeting were "a lot of information to take in." As such, several "students" wrote that they had difficulty processing and absorbing the information like they would with a single, longer, more "traditional" 60- or 90-minute lesson rehearsal. Finally, "students" critiqued "teachers" who tried to "cram too much information into their lesson." The "information overload" led, according to some "students," to "monotone presentations" that relied too heavily on lectures and lacked student-teacher interaction.

Amusingly, and just a bit ironically, especially from an instructor perspective, "teacher" reflections noted the lack of participation by some groups of "students" and the impact they felt that had on the quality of their lessons. Similarly, "teachers" criticized "students" for not having their cameras on. They also noted in their surveys and reflections the challenges of teaching online when they could not see students' faces and reactions to the lesson.

LESSONS LEARNED AND POST-PANDEMIC USE OF ONLINE RMTR

Just as RMTR is an iterative teaching process for ETCs, the development and implementation of online RMTR was also an iterative process for me. In an early iteration, I visited the breakout rooms to observe lessons with the "students" during the online RMTR exercise. During these iterations, I attempted to take notes on the lesson while acting as timekeeper and tech support for all the groups.

Not only was this degree of multitasking too much, but it also raised a critical equity issue for the teaching groups. As the instructor, I rotated around to different lessons and saw different iterations for each group – meaning I saw the first rehearsal iteration of the first group I visited and the fourth iteration of the last group. Thus, the groups were not being scored and receiving feedback based on the same iteration of their lessons.

Therefore, I determined that I would stay in the main Zoom session, and my role would be to keep time for each rehearsal iteration and the reflective break and provide support ETCs when needed. To ensure that all teaching groups were judged as equitably as possible, the "teachers" were required to record and submit the final iteration of their rehearsal to their instructor. After the online RMTR, I provided a link to a cloud-based folder in which ETCs could upload the video of their lesson.

Post-Pandemic Use of Online RMTR

Unfortunately, the issues cited at the start of this chapter that prevent most ETCs from teaching science lessons as part of the field experience – lack of control over the type of lesson, emphasis on testing, and inexperience of mentors in science teaching – have not be resolved since the return to in-person teaching. As a result, online RMTR continues to be an integral part of my hybrid elementary science methods courses and over 350 candidates have participated. In the current iteration of my courses, ETCs teach two lessons – one online and one in-person. The online lesson uses RMTR to provide the iterative process for ETCs to teach, reflect, revise, and reteach their lessons. The in-person lesson is, therefore, an opportunity for candidates to take lessons learned from RMTR peer/instructor feedback and apply it to a "one shot" in-person microteaching lesson.

Online RMTR continues to be introduced as an exercise in iterative teaching – a process that, sadly, continues to be underutilized in elementary teacher preparation. However, I also frame online RMTR as vital to ETCs' futures as teachers where knowledge and experience teaching in online learning environments is a marketable skill and an expectation for K-12 teachers (Digital Learning Collaborative, 2020; Molnar et al., 2021; Taie & Goldring, 2019).

The opportunity to plan, teach, reflect, revise, and reteach their lesson helps ETCs to be more confident in their teaching abilities because they can see their improvement in real-time. The "students" enjoyed participating in multiple short lessons connected to a common theme and benefitted from seeing a variety of methods and strategies used. Admittedly, online RMTR does not accurately represent the reality of teaching a classroom full of school-aged students. However, as instructors search for new ways to engage ETCs in the science teaching practice, particularly as online teacher preparation courses continue to be offered, online RMTR is an efficient and innovative way to provide science teaching rehearsals and reflection opportunities.

REFERENCES

Akkuş, H., & Sinem, Ü. N. E. R. (2017). The effect of microteaching on pre-service chemistry teachers' teaching experiences. *Cukurova University Faculty of Education Journal*, *46*(1), 202–230. doi:10.14812/cuefd.309459

Allaire, F. S., & Killham, J. E. (2022). Introduction. In F. S. Allaire & J. E. Killham (Eds.), *Teaching and Learning Online: Scinece for Elementary Grade Levels* (pp. ix–ixv). Information Age Publishing.

Allaire, F. S., & Killham, J. E. (2023). Introduction. In F. S. Allaire & J. E. Killham (Eds.), *Teaching and Learning Online: Scinece for Secondary Grade Levels* (pp. ix–xv). Information Age Publishing.

Allen, D. W., & Eve, A. W. (1968). Microteaching. *Theory into Practice*, *7*(5), 181–185. doi:10.1080/00405846809542153

Bakır, S. (2014). The effect of microteaching on the teaching skills of pre-service science teachers. *Journal of Baltic Science Education*, *13*(6), 789–801. doi:10.33225/jbse/14.13.789

Banilower, E., Smith, P., Malzahn, K., Plumley, C., Gordon, E., & Hayes, M. (2018). *Report of the 2018 NSSME+*. Horizon Research. https://horizon-research.com/NSSME/wp-content/uploads/2020/04/Report_of_the_2018_NSSME.pdf

Basturk, S. (2016). Investigating the Effectiveness of Microteaching in Mathematics of Primary Pre-Service Teachers. *Journal of Education and Training Studies*, *4*(5), 239–249. doi:10.11114/jets.v4i5.1509

Brígido, M., Borrachero, A., Bermejo, M., & Mellado, V. (2013). Prospective primary teachers' self-efficacy and emotions in science teaching. *European Journal of Teacher Education*, *36*(2), 200–217. doi:10.1080/02619768.2012.686993

Brown, A. H. (1999). Simulated classrooms and artificial students: The potential effects of new technologies on teacher education. *Journal of Research on Computing in Education*, *32*(2), 307–318. doi:10.1080/08886504.1999.10782281

Cavanaugh, S. (2022). Microteaching: Theoretical Origins and Practice. *Educational Practice and Theory*, *44*(1), 23–40. doi:10.7459/ept/44.1.03

Cheong, D. (2010). The effects of practice teaching sessions in second life on the change in pre-service teachers' teaching efficacy. *Computers & Education*, *55*(2), 868–880. doi:10.1016/j.compedu.2010.03.018

Chval, K. B. (2004). Making the complexities of teaching visible for prospective teachers. *Teaching Children Mathematics*, *11*(2), 91–96. doi:10.5951/TCM.11.2.0091

Cinici, A. (2016). Pre-service Teachers' Science Teaching Self-efficacy Beliefs: The Influence of a Collaborative Peer Microteaching Program. *Mentoring & Tutoring*, *24*(3), 228–249. doi:10.1080/13611267.2016.1222812

Cooper, J. M., & Allen, D. W. (1970). *Microteaching: History and Present Status*. W. ERIC Clearinghouse on Teacher Education.

d'Alessio, M. A. (2018). The effect of microteaching on science teaching self-efficacy beliefs in preservice elementary teachers. *Journal of Science Teacher Education*, *29*(6), 441–467. doi:10.1080/1046560X.2018.1456883

Data U.S.A. (2022). *University of Houston-Downtown*. Data USA. https://datausa.io/profile/university/university-of-houston-downtown

Digital Learning Collaborative. (2020). *Snapshot 2020: A review of K-12 online, blended, and digital learning*. Digital Learning Collaborative. https://www.digitallearningcollab.com

Enochs, L., & Riggs, I. (1990). Further development of an elementary science teaching efficacy belief instrument: A preservice elementary scale. *School Science and Mathematics*, *90*(8), 694–706. doi:10.1111/j.1949-8594.1990.tb12048.x

Ghousseini, H. (2017). Rehearsals of Teaching and Opportunities to Learn Mathematical Knowledge for Teaching. *Cognition and Instruction*, *35*(3), 188–211. doi:10.1080/07370008.2017.1323903

Göçer, A. (2016). Assessment of the Opinions and Practices of Student Teachers on Micro-Teaching as a Teaching Strategy. *Acta Didactica Napocensia*, *9*(2), 33–46.

Hanuscin, D. L. (2004). A workshop approach: Instructional strategies for working within the constraints of field experiences in elementary science. *Journal of Elementary Science Education*, *16*(1), 1–8. doi:10.1007/BF03174746

Hanuscin, D. L., Lee, M. H., & Akerson, V. L. (2011). Elementary Teachers' Pedagogical Content Knowledge for Teaching the Nature of Science. *Science Education*, *95*(1), 145–167. doi:10.1002/sce.20404

Hanuscin, D. L., & Zangori, L. (2016). Developing practical knowledge of the next generation science standards in elementary science teacher education. *Journal of Science Teacher Education*, *27*(8), 799–818. doi:10.1007/s10972-016-9489-9

Hartlep, N. D., Stuchell, C. V., Whitt, N. E., & Hensley, B. O. (2021). *Critical Storytelling During the COVID-19 Pandemic* (N. D. Hartlep, C. V. Stuchell, N. E. Whitt, & B. O. Hensley, Eds.). Information Age Publishing.

Hoy, W. K., & Spero, R. B. (2005). Changes in teacher efficacy during the early years of teaching: A comparison of four measures. *Teaching and Teacher Education*, *21*(4), 343–356. doi:10.1016/j.tate.2005.01.007

Hume, A., & Berry, A. (2011). Constructing CoRes - A strategy for building PCK in pre-service science teacher education. *Research in Science Education*, *41*(3), 341–355. doi:10.1007/s11165-010-9168-3

Javeed, L. (2019). Supporting clinical practice through rehearsals. *Northwest Journal of Teaching Education*, *14*(1). https://doi.org/https://doi.org/10.15760/nwjte.2019.14.1.2

Kartal, T., Ozturk, N., & Ekici, G. (2012). Developing pedagogical content knowledge in preservice science teachers through microteaching lesson study. *Procedia: Social and Behavioral Sciences*, *46*, 2753–2758. doi:10.1016/j.sbspro.2012.05.560

Kazemi, E., Ghousseini, H., Cunard, A., & Turrou, A. C. (2016). Getting inside rehearsals: Insights from teacher educators to support work on complex practice. *Journal of Teacher Education*, *67*(1), 18–31. doi:10.1177/0022487115615191

Lampert, M., Franke, M. L., Kazemi, E., Ghousseini, H., Turrou, A. C., Beasley, H., Cunard, A., & Crowe, K. (2013). Keeping it complex: Using rehearsals to support novice teacher learning of ambitious teaching. *Journal of Teacher Education*, *64*(3), 226–243. doi:10.1177/0022487112473837

Long, C. S., Harrell, P. E., Subramaniam, K., & Pope, E. (2019). Using microteaching to improve preservice elementary teachers' physical science content knowledge. *The Electronic Journal for Research in Science & Mathematics Education, 23*(4).

Lotter, C., Singer, J., & Godley, J. (2009). The influence of repeated teaching and reflection on preservice teachers' views of inquiry and nature of science. *Journal of Science Teacher Education, 20*(6), 553–582. doi:10.1007/s10972-009-9144-9

Marble, S. (2006). Learning to teach through lesson study. *Action in Teacher Education, 28*(3), 86–96. doi:10.1080/01626620.2006.10463422

Marble, S. (2007). Inquiring into teaching: Lesson study in elementary science methods. *Journal of Science Teacher Education, 18*(6), 935–953. doi:10.1007/s10972-007-9071-6

Masters, H. (2020). Using Teaching Rehearsals to Prepare Preservice Teachers for Explanation-Driven Science Instruction. *Journal of Science Teacher Education, 31*(4), 414–434. doi:10.1080/1046560X.2020.1712047

McCall, M. (2017). Elementary Pre-Service Science Teaching Efficacy and Attitude Toward Science: Can A College Science Course Make A Difference? *The Electronic Journal of Science Education, 21*(6).

Mergler, A. G., & Tangen, D. (2010). Using microteaching to enhance teacher efficacy in pre-service teachers. *Teaching Education, 21*(2), 199–210. doi:10.1080/10476210902998466

Molnar, A., Miron, G., Barbour, M. K., Huerta, L., Shafer, S. R., Rice, J. K., Glover, A., Browning, N., Hagle, S., & Boninger, F. (2021). *Virtual Schools in the U.S. 2021.* National Education Policy Center. https://nepc.colorado.edu/publication/virtual-schools-annual-2021

Morris, D., Usher, E., & Chen, J. (2017). Reconceptualizing the sources of teaching self-efficacy: A critical review of emerging literature. *Educational Psychology Review, 29*(4), 795–833. doi:10.1007/s10648-016-9378-y

Pauline, R. F. (1993). Microteaching: An integral part of a science methods class. *Journal of Science Teacher Education, 4*(1), 9–17. doi:10.1007/BF02628852

Plumley, C. L. (2019). *2018 NSSME+: Status of elementary school science.* Horizon Research.

Remesh, A. (2013). Microteaching, an efficient technique for learning effective teaching. *Journal of Research in Medical Sciences, 18*(2), 158–163. PMID:23914219

Riggs, I., & Enochs, L. (1990). Toward the development of an elementary teacher's science teaching efficacy belief instrument. *Science Education, 74*(6), 625–637. doi:10.1002/sce.3730740605

Taie, S., & Goldring, R. (2019). *Characteristics of Public and Private Elementary and Secondary Schools in the United States: Results From the 2017–18 National Teacher and Principal Survey First Look (NCES 2019-140)*. U. S. D. o. Education. htttps://nces.ed.gov/pubsearch/pubsinfo.asp?pubid=2019140

Zhou, G., Xu, J., & Martinovic, D. (2016). Developing pre-service teachers' capacity in teaching science with technology through microteaching lesson study approach. *Eurasia Journal of Mathematics, Science and Technology Education, 13*(1), 85–103. doi:10.12973/eurasia.2017.00605a

Chapter 7
Promoting Conceptual Understanding Through Authentic Mathematics Instruction in Virtual Environments:
More Than a Game

Elizabeth Allison
Western Governors University, USA

Carol PeQueen
Western Governors University, USA

Megan Rzyski
Western Governors University, USA

Kristie Remaly
Western Governors University, USA

Jen Wallender
Western Governors University, USA

M. Amanda Kain
Western Governors University, USA

Adam Hiebel
Western Governors University, USA

ABSTRACT

Delivering effective online instruction to preservice teacher candidates is important to ensure teachers are prepared for K–12 classrooms. Formal education has been reimagined several times throughout history, with both K–12 and higher education settings seeing significant changes in recent decades. Additionally, elementary teachers and preservice teacher candidates often view mathematics as only facts and

DOI: 10.4018/978-1-6684-5939-3.ch007

Copyright © 2024, IGI Global. Copying or distributing in print or electronic forms without written permission of IGI Global is prohibited.

procedures for memorization—a belief that infiltrates their instructional practices. Colleges that prepare teacher candidates must respond to this misconception. This chapter explores strategies one online university used to help preservice teacher candidates maximize student success by implementing live webinars called Put It into Practice (PiiP). During these sessions, preservice teachers explore online tools that can be used in the K–12 classroom to conceptualize math concepts. The webinars challenge preservice teachers to analyze how to teach math in today's classroom, while modeling the key prerequisite of establishing a safe psychological environment conducive to learning.

INTRODUCTION

The teaching and learning process has been revitalized and changed in the wake of the pandemic caused by the novel coronavirus (COVID-19). As such, colleges and universities across the nation have been encouraged, or even required, to rethink the way they deliver effective instruction to teacher candidates. Additionally, the pandemic has significantly affected K–12 education, with many of the changes forecasted to be permanent. Therefore, it is imperative that teacher preparation programs across the nation evaluate their core goals and programming options to prepare teacher candidates for the application within the K–12 setting (Black et al., 2021). As such, Patrick (2021) argued that college administrators and policymakers should explore a competency-based model of instruction along with effective and best practices for preparing teacher candidates to work and deliver instruction through virtual platforms, including the effective use of mathematical tools to build conceptual understanding.

Policymakers and university officials who are serious about preparing students for success should fully embrace a whole-system transformation that leads to a more student-centered approach to education (Patrick, 2021). At the college level, policymakers must explore the power of the competency-based model that focuses more on mastering skills rather than seat time or hours on [a] task. "A competency-based structure is built upon personalized learning experiences tailored to each student's strengths, needs, and interests and requires student voice and choice in what, how, when, and where they learn" (Patrick, 2021, p. 23).

The process of creating a positive educational experience must be a conscious effort in which an atmosphere of learning is active. Education is not separate from learning, and it is important to remember and plan with a purpose. Mathematics is a basic science and, as a subject, studied at various levels. It also provides a tool to guide thinking and enhance problem-solving abilities. Therefore, it is essential that online mathematics methods courses provide an authentic experience for teacher candidates that includes the combination of active modeling and appropriate andragogical applications. Andragogy refers to methods and principles used in adult education, and Fayne (2014) noted regardless of whether courses are delivered face-to-face or online, there are approaches that are considered best practices. Online methods courses that prepare teacher candidates for the K–12 setting should include interactive learning experiences. For example, online teaching programs can make learning more interactive by embedding theories such as the constructivist, social-cultural, and cognitive approaches. Regardless of the emphasized learning theory, teacher preparation programs have an obligation to find effective ways to meet the demands of learners and better prepare them for the complexity of the classroom.

This chapter will explore effective methods to assist preservice teachers and educators that combine active modeling and appropriate andragogical applications within the context of an elementary mathematics methods course. Online teacher preparation programs should provide an authentic and interactive learning experience for teacher candidates. The *Put It into Practice* (PiiP) sessions, discussed later in this chapter, offer a unique opportunity for teacher candidates to interact within a social-cultural learning environment through an online platform. By attending these sessions, teacher candidates learn how to interact and effectively use virtual tools to help conceptualize mathematics concepts. These *Put It into Practice* sessions combine proactive and effective andragogical strategies and experiential learning experiences for adult students.

BACKGROUND

Online teacher preparation programs should embrace and enact ways to help teacher candidates increase student retention and conceptualize math concepts. This chapter will explore how one online university embraces adult learning principles to effectively engage preservice teachers in online learning strategies that help students in the K–12 classroom conceptualize math, compared to the more traditional approach. The teaching and learning process is dynamic, and delivering effective online instruction to preservice teacher candidates is important to ensure that teachers are prepared to enter the K–12 classroom.

Adult Learning

With recent developments in educational systems, there is a growing need to improve the skills and competencies of teacher candidates along with the continued need to find effective ways to engage students in the K–12 classroom. The educational system, including K–12 and higher education settings, has seen significant changes in recent decades, and formal education has been redesigned several times throughout history. For example, scholars have pointed out in recent studies that the main tenets of andragogy as developed by Malcolm Knowles did not adequately incorporate the diverse ways of learning and knowing represented in today's populations of adult learners (Dantus, 2021). Additionally, future classrooms are expected to further progress along a path of increased inquiry-based learning, where instruction shifts away from direct, prescriptive approaches and moves more toward learners making and doing, critical thinking, and solving problems (Skilbeck & Connell, 2004). As such, colleges that help prepare teacher candidates must adjust and become more responsive to the needs of the moment (Mohammed & Kinyo, 2020).

Adult education is a well-established educational sub-discipline, and despite the rising number of educational institutions, there is still a gap and skill deficit within many online teacher preparation programs. Adult learning is highly affected by social and cultural environments, and as such, is best understood within a social context. Foundationally, social learning theory focuses on creating a community where learning and thinking are grounded in social processes (Mohammed & Kinyo, 2020). Therefore, the context for these learning opportunities is significant, and the methods for gathering information are an important construct when developing effective learning opportunities. Furthermore, collaborative learning sessions in the online environment are an important element of universal learning design, whereby participant discussion and interaction help support and promote independence and concept mastery in the learners (Finn, 2022). The PiiP webinars and live sessions referenced in this chapter support the development of a much-needed social learning environment with experiential learning for adult students in virtual settings.

Online Mathematics Methods

The population and enrollment in online or virtual universities are rising, and university policymakers, administrators, and faculty are embracing these changes. In a world of growing technology, there are numerous benefits to exposing teacher candidates to an online math methods course. Flexibility and accessibility are important benefits of any online program, especially those that offer asynchronous courses. Students can typically log on from any location at any time, on a wide variety of devices. The personalization of learning experiences afforded by such technology can be maximized at a programmatic and course level. For example, online courses often have a built-in system to track participation to ensure that all students are engaged (Gedeborg, 2016). If participation is lacking, or a student is not performing well, an instructor could easily reach out to offer support to individual students. In addition to structural benefits, an online mathematics methods course encourages teacher candidates to explore virtual resources and tools that can benefit students in a 21st century technology-rich classroom. In teacher preparation, online experiences provide another benefit: modeling effective virtual instruction. While many teacher candidates are comfortable with the online learning environment, they often need support in learning how to *teach* in an online environment (Nazerian, 2020). Teacher preparation programs must spend a deliberate amount of time modeling how to teach in a virtual setting.

While necessary, social interaction can be a prevalent challenge in any virtual course. "The social opportunity is not organic to online courses; therefore, to have this social interaction as part of online classes requires purposeful design" (Gedeborg, 2016, p. 273). Offering webinars and other live sessions, such as the PiiP webinars, can be effective solutions for increasing communication and social interaction within the virtual platform. Additionally, these PiiP sessions demonstrate the connection between and interrelationship with conceptual understanding and procedural fluency.

Math Games for Procedural Fluency

Procedural fluency is a critical component of mathematical proficiency that includes both procedural and conceptual knowledge (Van de Walle et al, 2019). Procedural fluency is the ability to apply procedures accurately, efficiently, and flexibly; to transfer procedures to different problems and contexts; to build or modify procedures from other procedures; and to recognize when one strategy or procedure is more appropriate to apply than another (Van de Walle et al., 2019). To develop procedural fluency, students need experience integrating concepts and building on familiar strategies as they create their own informal strategies and procedures.

Bay-Williams (2019) encourages the use of games to provide enjoyable practice that is interactive to build procedural fluency. Math games can be an effective way to motivate students; however, they should be introduced after students have had the opportunity to explore and build their conceptual understanding of a math concept. A carefully selected game can provide a "meaningful mathematics experience" while providing a teacher with critical information about a student's progress (Bay-Williams, p. 11). Though they are familiar with implementing online mathematics games to increase procedural fluency, teachers and teacher candidates may be less familiar with using virtual manipulatives to develop the prerequisite conceptual understanding of mathematics. In an educational landscape where virtual instruction is becoming a permanent and comprehensive modality, online mathematics instruction must expand to include teaching for conceptual understanding.

Virtual Manipulatives for Conceptual Understanding

Implementing manipulatives in the classroom to enhance mathematical understanding is not a novel instructional strategy. In fact, research has repeatedly affirmed that using manipulatives increases students' motivation and understanding of mathematical concepts (Bolyard & Moyer-Packenham, 2006, 2012; Gersten et al., 2009; Hunt et al., 2011; Jimenez & Besaw, 2020; Reimer & Moyer, 2005; Suh et al., 2005; Suh & Moyer, 2007). Even though the benefits of implementing manipulatives are well-documented, creating a mathematics lesson with manipulatives may not be easy or obvious for teachers (Moyer, 2001; Temel Dogan & Ozgeldi, 2018). Thus, mathematical lessons that appropriately implement manipulatives to develop conceptual understanding require considerable teacher preparation.

By mere exposure to manipulatives in a mathematics lesson, students will not fully grasp mathematics concepts; teachers and teacher candidates need explicit instruction on how to effectively implement manipulatives in their lessons, including the justifications and advantages for using them. For example, the more traditional physical manipulatives may be accompanied by issues of feasibility, such as high purchase costs, a lack of at-home use, more off-task behaviors, and increased transition time. Without proper training, these barriers may be enough to turn teachers away from using manipulatives because they will not fully recognize or appreciate the benefits (Moyer, 2001).

Mathematical manipulatives need not be limited to tangible objects to counteract potential barriers. As digital counterparts, virtual manipulatives are becoming more commonplace in today's classrooms. A virtual manipulative is defined as "an interactive, technology-enabled visual representation of a dynamic mathematical object, including all of the programmable features that allow it to be manipulated, that presents opportunities for constructing mathematical knowledge" (Moyer-Packenham & Bolyard, 2016, p. 13). Virtual manipulatives offer a wide range of distinct advantages (Bouck et al., 2014; Steen et al., 2006; Van de Walle et al., 2019). For example, many feasibility barriers stemming from physical manipulatives are mostly eliminated when implementing virtual manipulatives (Center for Technology Implementation, 2014; Moyer et al., 2002).

Also, virtual manipulatives facilitate the development of conceptual understanding during hybrid or virtual mathematics lessons due to their availability and accessibility beyond the classroom walls. In fact, Van de Walle et al. (2019) pointed out that virtual manipulatives can be accessed quickly and when physical tools are not available. In addition, virtual manipulatives can provide a natural segue from concrete to abstract understanding (Hunt et al., 2011). Lastly, many virtual manipulative websites include the ability to check the correctness of a response, so students—

including those with disabilities or low motivation—may enjoy and thrive while using this immediate self-assessment option (Drickey, 2000; Reimer, 2005; Shin et al., 2021). Virtual manipulatives offer myriad advantages and are vital to expanding mathematical conceptual understanding and access to all students. However, without a teacher's belief that manipulatives are effective, as well as the knowledge of how to effectively implement them, manipulatives are just another online tool (Moyer, 2001). Cultivating that belief and knowledge was a key motivation for developing the *Put It into Practice* webinars.

MAIN FOCUS OF THE CHAPTER

Providing some additional context about the challenges in teacher preparation work, particularly in math instruction, will be helpful at this point to better understand the design decisions that went into *Put It into Practice*. These challenges fall into three main categories: 1) challenges that pertain to teacher preparation programs generally, 2) challenges specific to the online learning environment, and 3) challenges unique to the teaching and learning of mathematics.

Challenges Experienced by Teacher Preparation Programs

While COVID-19 created a sense of urgency for many school districts and teacher preparation programs regarding online pedagogy, the call for teacher preparation programs to prepare their candidates to facilitate online learning is not new. Prior to the pandemic, many states offered either fully online or hybrid K–12 programs; this practice will likely continue to expand as school districts consider how they might leverage hybrid learning to address acute events, such as weather-related school closures.

Though there is an ongoing identified need for online learning within the K–12 educational system, few teacher preparation programs include online education as a part of their curriculum, with one estimate being as low as 1.3% of programs (Barbour et al., 2014). However, the United States Department of Education (2017) states,

Teachers need to leave their teacher preparation programs with a solid understanding of how to use technology to support learning. Effective use of technology is not an optional add-on or a skill that we simply can expect teachers to pick up once they get into the classroom. Teachers need to know how to use technology to realize each state's learning standards from day one. (p. 35)

Teachers must leave their preparation programs with the skills and competency to meaningfully integrate technology into their lessons, both in-person and online, from their first day in the classroom. Yet teacher preparation programs struggle to rise to the challenge of ensuring their graduates are prepared for the issues they will face in today's classrooms. Incorporation of relevant learning activities and meaningful teaching practices into methods courses is critical. However, these courses often include too many inauthentic tasks, as well as lesson planning with no implementation and little resemblance to the more curriculum guide-based, collaborative planning teachers do in the classroom (Beck et al., 2020). Additionally, it is universally accepted in the teacher preparation community that university programs desperately need to form more K–12 partnerships and work much more closely with school districts to better understand and help meet district needs (Doran, 2020).

Teacher candidates tend to thrive when working closely with in-service teachers as mentors, and at least some evidence suggests lack of mentoring contributes to new teachers not persisting in the profession (Beck et al., 2020). When quality host teachers with adequate experience are in short supply even for clinicals and internships, how can preparation programs facilitate this mentor-like experience and modeling of authentic instructional practice within methods courses? While not a substitute for being in a real classroom either physically or virtually, the interactive webinar experience discussed here may provide much of the benefit that working alongside a partnering classroom teacher would allow. The experience also allows instructors to demonstrate a wider variety of instructional approaches and how to form connections within the mathematical curriculum. This advantage could positively affect the quality of instruction exhibited by teacher candidates when they reach their own classrooms.

Challenges with Online Platforms

K-12 online teaching—design and delivery—requires an additional set of skills that must be taught, modeled, and evaluated within teacher preparation programs (Barbour et al., 2014). Additionally, the need for preservice teachers to complete clinical and internship experiences as virtual field experiences further supports the importance of gaining some level of mastery in online teaching and learning (Luo et al., 2017). While it may seem that pedagogical skills transfer cleanly from the classroom to the online environment, that simply is not the case. One study from Smith & Schlaack (2021) noted the following:

When it came to feedback and formative assessment, TCs (Teacher Candidates) relied on strategies learned in methods coursework that worked in the face-to-face setting (i.e., praise). However, when teaching synchronously at a distance, TCs noticed that they could not monitor students' work. TCs missed opportunities to provide "struggling" students with feedback because students were silent, not working, had their cameras off, or the TC did not notice the student was experiencing difficulty. TCs began to consider technological tools that could help them monitor student work (i.e., Jamboard) and use explicit feedback to promote students' cognitive engagement. Findings from this research reiterate the need for TPPs (Teacher Preparation Programs) to reconceptualize teacher competency. Teacher competency should include a teacher's ability to teach at a distance. (p. 18)

These challenges can be further exacerbated by the ineffective use of the online platform as a learning environment in teacher preparation coursework. The computer systems and software powering online courses do not always keep up with what instructors want to do in terms of optimal learning activities. Additionally, teacher preparation instructors may hold dated perceptions and incorrect assumptions about online learning. Such ideas lead to relying on older, more traditional higher-ed teaching strategies, such as readings and lecturing, that are moved online, rather than more interactive strategies.

Simply put, many face-to-face classroom methods do not transfer seamlessly to the online environment. Teachers must use technology thoughtfully to teach new content rather than simply reinforce skills. The onus is on teacher preparation programs to empower teacher candidates with the skills and competencies to effectively facilitate interactive lessons and activities that promote the construction of conceptual knowledge.

Challenges Specific to Math Knowledge and Skills

Conceptual Understanding versus Algorithmic Approach

Elementary teachers and preservice teacher candidates alike often view mathematics as a set of facts and procedures to be memorized, and this frame of reference deeply infiltrates their instructional practices. Unfortunately, many college mathematics courses tend to reinforce rather than deconstruct this understanding (National Research Council, 2001). Additionally, when teacher candidates enter their new classrooms retaining only singular and largely algorithmic procedures to solve math problems, they are unlikely to successfully facilitate discussions about multiple problem-solving strategies with their students. Rather than taking time to connect the learning to students' prior knowledge, for example, or model different approaches through think-alouds, candidates will often be laser focused on elementary students correctly applying a procedure to get a problem "right." This mindset and approach reinforce mathematics understanding at a procedural, superficial level. However, today's focus is no longer on merely a correct or incorrect answer to a problem. While the ability to calculate the correct answer is important, the process used by students to solve problems provides teachers with much more valuable information about a student's conceptual understanding of a math concept.

When students do not arrive at a correct answer, a "teacher must have a sense of the mathematical territory involved and be curious about the student's thinking" (Shaughnessy et al., 2021, p. 336). Asking questions and eliciting student thinking informs the teacher of the intricacies of the student's content knowledge and thought processes (Shaughnessy et al., 2021). Developing a teacher candidate's ability to elicit student thinking can be exciting yet challenging. Candidates must learn to establish a classroom environment where explaining their thinking is not only encouraged but also expected of students daily. Furthermore, developing this ability in a virtual environment requires an extra level of consideration.

SOLUTIONS AND RECOMMENDATIONS

Interactive Webinars

To support the teacher candidates' conceptual understandings of mathematics and their ability to teach conceptually, instructors have implemented a collection of live webinars called *Put It into Practice* (PiiP). During these sessions, teacher candidates engage with virtual math tools, solve math problems using conceptual strategies, and discuss how to implement them in the classroom to build deeper mathematical understanding. Each session focuses on a different math concept, such as understanding fractions or integer operations or telling time.

Put It into Practice (PiiP) webinars are facilitated by a pair of faculty members and delivered completely online. During each session, teacher candidates can explore virtual math tools that can be used to develop a conceptual understanding of the session's topic. After allowing learners time to explore the tools, the instructor supports learning by modeling how to use the tool to assist students in making connections between abstract concepts and concrete or semi-concrete representations. In addition, the instructor provides sample problems for teacher candidates to solve using their math tools while also posing questions to support critical thinking. As a part of the discussion, the instructor provides potential misconceptions or sample student work to allow teacher candidates time to problem solve ways to support conceptual understanding based on student misconceptions or errors. Candidates are also encouraged to reflect on the benefits and challenges of the virtual tools and whether they lend themselves to effective student exploration and conceptualization.

Teacher candidates are strongly encouraged (but at this time, not required) to attend the PiiP webinars. A live session is offered monthly and listed on the course Cohort Offerings page. In addition, email invitations with session specifics are sent to enrolled students two weeks prior to the date of the session, with an additional reminder email sent a few days prior. Candidates who are unable to attend the live webinar have access to a small library of previously held webinars on a variety of math concepts; thus, they are still able to access and benefit from the sessions asynchronously.

Because participation is optional, no formal assessment of candidate knowledge occurs during the PiiP session itself; candidate competencies with mathematical tools and manipulatives are assessed later in the course. However, session objectives still allow attendees to walk away with a more concrete conception of how virtual tools are incorporated into instruction, and to better visualize use of such tools when instruction must temporarily become fully virtual (such as inclement weather days that force school closures). Despite the absence of formal assessment, instructors are still able to formatively assess learning and progress of participants through real time feedback during the PiiP sessions. A recent suggestion under consideration is allowing candidates themselves to try facilitating, perhaps by partnering with an instructor or a peer. A more formal assessment of learning progress and level of competency could then be layered into the webinars as well, if desired.

Planning

The instructors carefully plan each webinar to create a meaningful learning experience for teacher candidates. Preparing for each webinar includes identifying a topic, determining appropriate tools, and creating practice problems. Instructors also predetermine relevant crosscutting concepts for the webinar. Each of these will be discussed in detail.

Topic Selection. The instructor team selects and discusses potential math topics for the webinars based on areas of need gleaned through conversations and learning sessions with teacher candidates. The team also looks at historical patterns from summative course assessments and teacher licensure exams. Once the team chooses a topic, the presenting instructors meet to plan the details of the live session.

The live session serves as a deep dive into the given math topic. The instructors focus on one math topic per session to allow teacher candidates ample time to explore the concept in detail. For example, rather than planning a session about geometry concepts, the instructors will focus particularly on area and perimeter or 2D versus 3D shapes. A narrower focus allows teacher candidates to gain specific teaching ideas, activities, and tools they could implement in the classroom rather than broad strategies that lack specific, actionable practices.

Tools and Platform Needs. While meeting to plan the session, the instructors brainstorm potential virtual tools that can be used, misconceptions about the topic, challenges to teaching the topic or using the tool, and sample problems to model that are related to the math topic. The instructors locate specific virtual math tools that can be used to teach the concept. Examples of corresponding concepts and virtual tools are shared in Table 1. For example, during the session on telling time, a virtual geared clock was used. In the session on 2D and 3D shapes, virtual shape pieces, as well as websites with representations of 3D shapes and their 2D nets, were employed. Instructors select virtual tools and websites that are accessible to students without needing to log in, download, or subscribe. This ensures that the students can quickly and easily access the tools and interact with them during the live session.

The live sessions are presented in a Webex (Cisco, 2022) conference room, though any platform with screen sharing and chat capabilities would suffice. The sessions typically start with a PowerPoint presentation prepared by the instructors to facilitate discussion about the background of the topic, challenges to teaching the topic, and tools that can be used with the topic.

Crosscutting Concepts. During the planning phase, the instructors will also look for opportunities to showcase connections between the math topic and other areas of focus including diversity and inclusion, literature, geography, and real-world connections. Leveraging these crosscutting concepts helps learners make connections to prior knowledge, and also to content covered in their previous coursework. For example, during the session on telling time, the instructors discussed the phrases used to tell time in various cultures. Similarly, during the session on currency, the instructors shared a variety of children's books that can be incorporated into lessons on money. The instructors also highlighted how utilizing currency from various countries may present opportunities to explore other facets of the math topic of study. For instance, when using coins to teach skip counting, it can be helpful to introduce currency that comes in denominations different from the United States currency so that students can practice skip counting by additional values. These examples nicely illustrate explicitly incorporating crosscutting concepts into instruction; in this case, that the use of symbols and mathematical notation may differ significantly by region and nationality – a concept which applies to telling time, working with currency, and even performing basic mathematical operations.

Table 1. List of mathematics concepts and corresponding online manipulative that can be utilized to support instruction

Mathematics Concept	Potential Online Tool or Manipulative	Representation
Telling time	Virtual geared clock	*Figure 1. Virtual geared clock used to teach telling time.*
2D shapes	Virtual shape pieces	*Figure 2. Virtual shape pieces used to explore 2-D shapes.*

continues on following page

Table 1. Continued

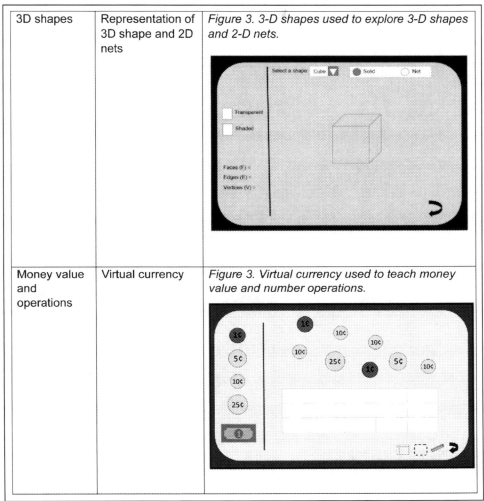

3D shapes	Representation of 3D shape and 2D nets	*Figure 3. 3-D shapes used to explore 3-D shapes and 2-D nets.*
Money value and operations	Virtual currency	*Figure 3. Virtual currency used to teach money value and number operations.*

continues on following page

Implementation

After preparing for the sessions by determining a topic, tools, and crosscutting concepts, the PiiP sessions are developed; however, implementation of these live webinars presents potential barriers for the instructors to consider. For example, many teacher education candidates are uncomfortable because they are "challenged to learn math in a different way than they were initially taught as they replace procedural knowledge with conceptual understanding" (Soltis, 2016, p. 73). Furthermore, candidates sometimes bring ingrained notions of ineffective models

Table 1. Continued

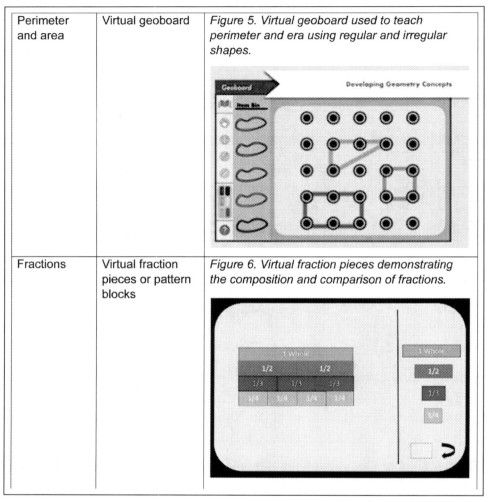

continues on following page

of instruction due to unfavorable math classroom experiences they endured as elementary students themselves. The live webinars challenge students to think outside the box when considering how to teach math in today's classroom, while also modeling the key prerequisite of establishing a safe psychological environment conducive to learning and exploring. As stated by a teacher candidate, instructors challenge teacher candidates to "think as constructivists." Thus, an important goal of the constructed experiences is to extend candidates' understanding of virtual mathematics instruction beyond the use of online games, which are commonly used to simply increase procedural fluency. This objective is accomplished by providing an experience in which teacher candidates participate firsthand in online instruction aligned to conceptual development.

Table 1. Continued

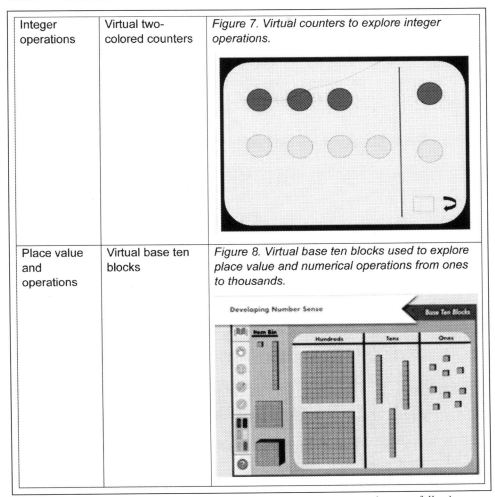

continues on following page

After considering potential barriers, the following steps are recommended to implement a PiiP webinar:

Step 1: Set expectations. The webinars are interactive sessions open for discussion and idea sharing. The instructors start the sessions by inviting students to actively participate, share, and ask questions.

Step 2: Introduce the topic. Then the instructors begin with a discussion about the math topic, inviting teacher candidates to share their own reflections and experiences with learning the topic.

Conceptual Understanding Through Authentic Mathematics Instruction

Table 1. Continued

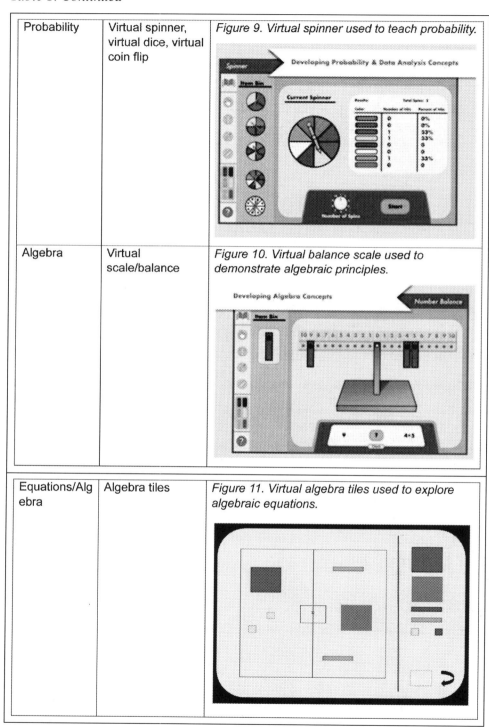

Note: Virtual manipulative images retrieved from Western Governors University, 2022.

Conceptual Understanding Through Authentic Mathematics Instruction

Step 3: Open exploration of virtual tools. Following the introduction, the instructors share the websites for the virtual tools and allow teacher candidates time to interact and explore the functionality of the tools.

Step 4: Discuss tools. After the exploration period, the instructors and teacher candidates discuss potential avenues for using the tool to teach the specified concept, helpful features of the tool, and limitations of the tool.

Step 5: Solve math problems. Next, the instructors lead the teacher candidates through a variety of math problems and activities using the virtual tools. During this time, instructors share their screens while using the virtual tool. Teacher candidates often walk the instructors through their ideas for problem-solving and modeling, and sometimes the teacher candidates even take control of the screen to model the problem themselves. For instance, during the webinar on understanding fractions, the instructor presented students with a problem called "Playground Fractions" from Van de Walle et al. (2019, p.342). In this math problem, a pattern block outline of a playground is provided, as shown in Figure 12, and teacher candidates are asked to use pattern blocks to determine exactly half of the playground.

Figure 1. Sample mathematics problem: "Playground Fractions"
(Adapted from J. Van de Walle et al., 2019, p. 342).

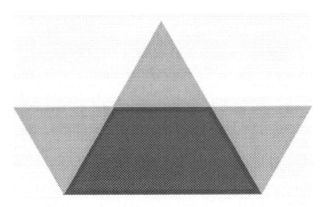

To support critical thinking, the instructor asked questions such as, "What strategies did you use to determine what constitutes half of the playground?" and "Is there more than one way to represent half of the playground with pattern block pieces?" The instructor also displayed the image in Figure 13 and asked teacher candidates to consider how this version of the playground outline would change students' approach to the problem.

147

Figure 2. Sample image to elicit mathematical critical thinking in students (Adapted from "Pattern Shapes," Math Learning Center, 2022).

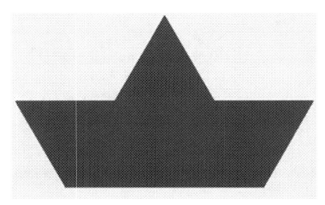

The instructor invites multiple approaches to problem-solving and often compares multiple strategies.

Step 6: Discuss potential misconceptions. Then, the instructors present questions to teacher candidates based on possible misconceptions. To illustrate this, during the session on telling time, the instructor displayed the math problem, "Show 2:45 on a clock." While exploring with virtual geared clocks, the teacher candidates represented the time. Then, the instructor asked the teacher candidates how they would use the virtual geared clock to support a student who believes the hour hand should be placed directly over the number two and the minute hand on the number nine, when the hour hand *should* be closer to three. Teacher candidates analyzed and shared strategies and representations that could be used to support this student's rethinking of this misconception.

Step 7: Reflect and close. Each webinar concludes with a brief review of the concepts, tools, and discussion shared by participants. This is a time to provide positive feedback for the learners on their participation in the discussion, as well as encouragement to explore additional virtual tools throughout the course, their program, and as a classroom teacher when developing a conceptual understanding of mathematics.

Planning and Implementation Framework

Throughout the planning and implementation processes, instructors consider various questions, potential barriers, and content connections. An outline of these important factors is provided below in Table 2.

Conceptual Understanding Through Authentic Mathematics Instruction

Table 2. Framework of mathematics webinar planning and implementation

	Key Questions and Considerations
Planning	
Topic Selection	● Based on historical patterns of assessment results or current student interests/needs *Where, in course or licensure assessments, have learners struggled in the past?* ● Focused on a singular topic to allow for deep exploration and learning *Is this topic singular enough to explore and discuss in detail in the allotted amount of time?*
Tools and Platform	● Tools must directly align to the related math topic *Does the tool provide the opportunity for learners to explore the topic, misconceptions, and math problems?* ● Must be easily accessible *Does the tool need to be downloaded or require a subscription?*
Crosscutting Concepts	● Explore opportunities to align the math topic with other content areas and concepts ● *Are there opportunities to explicitly include a crosscutting concept? (Potential connections: literature, geography, history, diversity, inclusion, visual and performing arts)*
Implementation	
Set Expectations	● Discuss norms and expectations for asking questions and interacting ● Encourage active participation, sharing, and asking questions
Introduce the Topic	● Share the mathematics topic or concept ● Encourage learners to reflect on previous experiences *How have the learners engaged with this concept in the past?* *What are the learners' initial reactions to the topic?*
Open Exploration	● Introduce how to access the tool ● Allow time for learners to openly explore the virtual tool without explicit instructions *Can learners fully experience the tool?* *Are there any initial functionality questions that need to be addressed before moving forward?*
Discuss Tools	● Lead a discussion on the tool *What are potential applications?* *What are some helpful features?* *What are some limitations?* ● Discuss crosscutting concepts
Solve Math Problems	● Model how to use the tools when solving math problems ● Encourage learners to share their ideas on solving problems and modeling ● Ask guiding questions *What strategies did you use?* *Are there other ways to solve the problem?* ● Alter the math problems to extend learner thinking *How does changing this factor affect the strategy?*
Discuss Misconceptions	● Ask learners to explore potential student misconceptions ● Lead a discussion on how to address misconceptions through using the virtual tool
Reflect and Close	● Review concepts and virtual tool *Did the strategies and tools shared enhance or broaden understanding?* *Are learners visualizing the application of the tool in a real classroom?* ● Share additional resources ● Provide positive feedback and encouragement ● Invite attendees to complete a post-session survey to reflect on the usefulness and relevancy of the webinar and share any other comments or suggestions

Student Discussion and Feedback

In addition to the mathematical and pedagogical information shared, candidates enjoy the ability to interact with each other as learners, an opportunity that can be rare in online coursework if instructors are not intentionally constructing such experiences. Students can build on each other's examples and math representations, respond to each other's ideas, and more. Sharing experiences can boost higher-order thinking and accelerate the transfer of new knowledge in adult learners (Roumell, 2019). It is one thing to read about the many benefits of collaborative learning; it is quite another to experience those benefits firsthand with other learners. As one teacher candidate said, "I loved hearing all the different ideas that were shared and how 'math talk' was open and inviting."

Based on the feedback from attendees, the teacher candidates leave the PiiP sessions with a better understanding of how to use the math tools in their classroom to develop their students' conceptual understanding. One teacher candidate noted that attending this session "helps [them] with feeling more comfortable with planning lessons and seeing them come alive." Another candidate said, "Fantastic webinar! I can see myself putting all of this into practice in the classroom." Many attendees have noted the value and relevancy of the sessions that they have asked to continue attending future sessions even after completing the Math Methods course.

FUTURE RESEARCH DIRECTIONS

The importance of developing a solid mathematics foundation early in a student's educational journey cannot be overstated. In elementary school, the building blocks of mathematics are forged through experiences interwoven with exploration, discourse, and teacher guidance. Teacher preparation programs shoulder the responsibility of providing the theoretical foundation in methodology courses and the need to model effective instructional practices so that candidates can experience, internalize, and practice mathematics. Traditionally, this included the implementation of hands-on, inquiry-based activities utilizing manipulatives and tools to reinforce mathematics concepts. As higher education and K–12 schools have transitioned more frequently to the virtual space, methods instructors are compelled to reimagine how their courses are structured, as well as how their courses prepare elementary education candidates for the multimodal K–12 landscape. Just as the use of physical manipulatives to teach mathematics has been modeled in methods courses, so too must instructors model the appropriate use of *virtual* manipulatives. This need reveals the first area in which further research is needed: What are the most effective methods in teaching conceptual understanding in online mathematics courses? While this chapter outlines the use of interactive webinars in the virtual space, more exploration is needed on the specific impact on learning in virtual mathematics methods courses. Furthermore, researchers should target the more pointed need of how to use virtual manipulatives in both the K–12 and university settings to develop a conceptual understanding of mathematics.

As candidates progress through their program and ultimately transition to classroom teachers, further research can be done to better understand the transferability of knowledge, skills, and dispositions in a virtual mathematics methods course to the elementary classroom. For example, how easily can a novice teacher adapt to various teaching modalities in mathematics? What support and professional development is most impactful in improving teachers' abilities to fluidly modify one's pedagogy in and out of the virtual space? And, with the growing need for flexible next-generation teachers, how do preservice experiences such as *Put It into Practice* better prepare teacher candidates for success, and ultimately retention, in the K–12 classroom? A logical first step in the examination of these questions is to explore opportunities within the math methods course for candidates to practice facilitating webinars relating to mathematics conceptual understanding. Can the candidates, in a low-stakes environment, transfer what was learned after participating in a PiiP webinar into instruction within the teacher preparation course, perhaps with a peer audience?

Additional studies would help answer these critical questions, especially when focused on whether engaging in instructional practices in the virtual environment with virtual tools alongside instructors provides adequate experience for teacher candidates soon to be in their own classrooms. While there is no perfect substitute for true field experience working with real K–12 students, utilizing virtual tools is an online setting is a burgeoning area of interest with the potential to positively impact teacher preparedness. Additional evidence would support the exploration of expanding such interactive virtual practice to other elementary content areas, such as science and social studies. Additionally, these interactive webinars could serve as a convenient and effective vehicle for institutions to continue to support graduates during their first few years in the classroom, as is increasingly being required for maintaining status with state departments of education as an approved teacher preparation program.

CONCLUSION

As policymakers, educators, and school administrators look to the future of education, it will be important to prioritize and forecast the needs of the K–12 classroom setting. First, policymakers and school administrations must consider a competency-based approach to higher education where learning is more personalized and unique to each student's needs. Next, online teacher preparation programs should provide teacher candidates with authentic learning experiences that propel students to express a passion for education by combining an active modeling and appropriate andragogy applications within the context of the course.

As noted in this chapter, exposing teacher candidates to virtual tools such as virtual Cuisenaire rods when learning about fractions or virtual base ten blocks when exploring place value can alleviate the assumption that math is a set of facts and procedures to be memorized. This puts more focus on the conceptualization and deeper understanding of mathematics. The framework shared in this chapter outlines the development and implementation of webinars used to engage teacher candidates in the practice of using virtual manipulatives to teach conceptual understanding in mathematics. After all, authentic mathematics methods instruction using virtual manipulatives is a game where everyone is a winner.

This research received no specific grant from any funding agency in the public, commercial, or not-for-profit sectors.

REFERENCES

Barbour, M. K., Siko, J., Gross, E., & Waddell, K. (2014). Virtually unprepared: Examining the preparation of K–12 online teachers. In R. Hartshorne, T. L. Heafner, & T. M. Petty (Eds.), *Teacher education programs and online learning tools* (pp. 187–208). IGI Global.

Bay-Williams, J., & King, G. (2019). *Math fact fluency: 60+ games and assessment tools to support learning and retention*. ASCD.

Beck, J., Lunsmann, C., & Garza, T. (2020). "We need to be in the classroom more": Veteran teachers' views on teacher preparation and retention. *Professional Educator*, *43*(1), 91–99.

Black, E., Ferdig, R., & Thompson, L. A. (2021). K–12 Virtual Schooling, COVID-19, and Student Success. *JAMA Pediatrics*, *175*(2), 119–120. doi:10.1001/jamapediatrics.2020.3800 PMID:32780093

Bolyard, J., & Moyer-Packenham, P. (2012). Making sense of integer arithmetic: The effect of using virtual manipulatives on students' representational fluency. *Journal of Computers in Mathematics and Science Teaching*, *31*(2), 93–113.

Bolyard, J. J., & Moyer-Packenham, P. S. (2006, November). *The impact of virtual manipulatives on student achievement in integer addition and subtraction.* Paper presented at the annual meeting of the North American Chapter of the International Group for the Psychology of Mathematics Education, Mérida, Yucatán, Mexico.

Bouck, E. C., Satsangi, R., Doughty, T. T., & Courtney, W. T. (2014). Virtual and concrete manipulatives: A comparison of approaches for solving mathematics problems for students with autism spectrum disorder. *Journal of Autism and Developmental Disorders, 44*(1), 180–193. doi:10.1007/s10803-013-1863-2 PMID:23743958

Center for Technology Implementation. (2014). *Using virtual manipulatives to teach mathematics. American Institutes for Research.* American Institutes for Research.

Cisco. (2022). *Cisco Webex Meetings* [Computer software]. Cisco. https://www.webex.com/

Dantus, S. J. (2021). *A triadic worldview? The misconception and bias of universality in Knowles' andragogy.* Commission for International Adult Education.

Doran, P. (2020). What they didn't teach us: New teachers reflect on their preparation experiences. *Professional Educator, 43*(1), 59–69.

Drickey, N. A. (2000). A comparison of virtual and physical manipulatives in teaching visualization and spatial reasoning to middle school mathematics students. (Doctoral dissertation, Utah State University, 2000). *Dissertation Abstracts International, 62*(02), 499A. (UMI No. 3004011).

Fayne, H. R. (2014). Preparing preservice teachers in a virtual space: A case study of a literacy methods course. *Teacher Educator, 49*(4), 305–316. doi:10.1080/08878730.2014.934081

Finn, D. (2022). Online Learning and Universal Design: Practical Applications for Reaching Adult Learners. *COABE Journal: The Resource for Adult Education, 11*(1), 101–109.

Gedeborg, S. (2016). Designing social online math activities. *Mathematics Teacher, 110*(4), 272–278. doi:10.5951/mathteacher.110.4.0272

Gersten, R., Chard, D., Jayanthi, M., Baker, S., Morphy, P., & Flojo, J. (2009). *A Meta-analysis of mathematics instructional interventions for students with learning disabilities: A technical report.* Instructional Research Group.

Hunt, A. W., Nipper, K. L., & Nash, L. E. (2011). Virtual vs. concrete manipulatives in mathematics teacher education: Is one type more effective than the other? *Current Issues in Middle Level Education*, *16*(2), 16.

Jimenez, B. A., & Besaw, J. (2020). Building early numeracy through virtual manipulatives for students with intellectual disability and autism. *Education and Training in Autism and Developmental Disabilities*, *55*(1), 28–44.

Luo, T., Hibbard, L., Franklin, T., & Moore, D. R. (2017). Preparing teacher candidates for virtual field placements via an exposure to K–12 online teaching. *Journal of Information Technology Education*, *16*(1), 1–14. doi:10.28945/3626

Math Learning Center. (2022). *Pattern Shapes*. MLC. https://apps.mathlearningcenter.org/pattern-shapes/

Mohammed, S., & Kinyo, L. (2020). Constructivist Theory as a Foundation for the Utilization of Digital Technology in the Lifelong Learning Process. *Turkish Online Journal of Distance Education*, *21*(4), 90–109. doi:10.17718/tojde.803364

Moyer, P. S. (2001). Are we having fun yet? How teachers use manipulatives to teach mathematics. *Educational Studies in Mathematics*, *47*(2), 175–197. doi:10.1023/A:1014596316942

National Research Council. (2001). *Adding It Up: Helping Children Learn Mathematics*. The National Academies Press., doi:10.17226/9822

Nazerian, T. (2020). Looking ahead: Four ways 2020 might share the future of teacher prep. *Literacy Today*, *38*(3), 26–29.

Patrick, S. (2021). Transforming Learning through Competency-Based Education. *State Education Standard*, *21*(2), 23–29.

Reimer, K., & Moyer, P. S. (2005). Third-graders learn about fractions using virtual manipulatives: A classroom study. *Journal of Computers in Mathematics and Science Teaching*, *24*(1), 5–25.

Roumell, E. A. (2019). Priming adult learners for learning transfer: Beyond content and delivery. *Adult Learning*, *30*(1), 15–22. doi:10.1177/1045159518791281

Shaughnessy, M., DeFino, R., Pfaff, E., & Blunk, M. (2021). I think I made a mistake: How do prospective teachers elicit the thinking of a student who has made a mistake? *Journal of Mathematics Teacher Education*, *24*(4), 335–359. doi:10.1007/s10857-020-09461-5

Shin, M., Park, J., Grimes, R., & Bryant, D. P. (2021). Effects of using virtual manipulatives for students with disabilities: Three-level multilevel modeling for single-case data. *Exceptional Children*, *87*(4), 418437. doi:10.1177/00144029211007150

Skilbeck, M., & Connell, H. (2004). Teachers for the Future: The Changing Nature of Society and Related Issues for the Teaching Workforce. *Ministerial Council on Education, Employment, Training and Youth Affairs (NJ1)*.

Smith, M. G., & Schlaack, N. (2021). Teaching during a pandemic: Elementary candidates' experiences with engagement in distance education. *I*, *9*(4), 7–22. doi:10.22492/ije.9.4.01

Soltis, L. (2016). Do mathematics courses for elementary teachers contribute to the development of mathematical knowledge needed for teaching of preservice elementary teachers? *National Teacher Education Journal*, *9*(1), 71–76.

Steen, K., Brooks, D., & Lyon, T. (2006). The impact of virtual manipulatives on first grade geometry instruction and learning. *Journal of Computers in Mathematics and Science Teaching*, *25*(4), 373–391.

Suh, J., & Moyer, P. S. (2007). Developing students' representation fluency using virtual and physical algebra balances. *Journal of Computers in Mathematics and Science Teaching*, *26*(2), 155–173.

Suh, J., Moyer, P. S., & Heo, H. (2005). Examining technology uses in the classroom: Developing fraction sense using virtual manipulative concept tutorials. *Journal of Interactive Online Learning*, *3*(4), 1–21.

Temel Dogan, D., & Ozgeldi, M. (2018). How do preservice mathematics teachers use virtual manipulatives to teach algebra through lesson study? *Necatibey Faculty of Education Electronic Journal of Science and Mathematics Education*, *12*(1), 152–179.

United States Department of Education. (2017). Reimagining the role of technology in education: 2017. *National education technology plan update*. US DoE. https://tech.ed.gov/files/2017/01/NETP17.pdf

Van de Walle, J. A., Karp, K. S., & Bay-Williams, J. M. (2019). *Elementary and middle school mathematics: Teaching developmentally* (10th ed.). Pearson.

Western Governors University. (2022). *Elementary math methods: Unit 7*. Tools for Mathematics. [WGU Learning Resource, Elementary Math Methods]

ADDITIONAL READING

Bay-Williams, J. M., & SanGiovanni, J. J. (2021). *Figuring out fluency in mathematics teaching and learning, grades K-8: Moving beyond basic facts and memorization.* Corwin Mathematics.

Reiten, L. (2018). Teaching with (not near) technology. *Mathematics Teacher, 112*(3), 208–214. doi:10.5951/mathteacher.112.3.0208

Shagiakhmetova, M. N., Bystritskaya, E. V., Demir, S., Stepanov, R. A., Grishnova, E. E., & Kryukova, N. I. (2022). Primary teachers difficulties related to compulsory distance education during COVID-19. *Contemporary Educational Technology, 14*(2), 1–9. doi:10.30935/cedtech/11589

Urbina, A., & Polly, D. (2017). Examining elementary school teachers' integration of technology and enactment of TPACK in mathematics. *The International Journal of Information and Learning Technology, 34*(5), 439–451. doi:10.1108/IJILT-06-2017-0054

Utah State University. (2022). *National Library of Virtual Manipulatives.* NLVM. http://nlvm.usu.edu/en/nav/vlibrary.html

Van de Walle, J., Lovin, L., Karp, K., & Bay-Williams, J. (2017). *Teaching student-centered mathematics: Developmentally appropriate instruction for grades pre-K–2* (3rd ed.). Pearson.

Van de Walle, J., Lovin, L., Karp, K., & Bay-Williams, J. (2017). *Teaching student-centered mathematics: Developmentally appropriate instruction for grades 3–5* (3rd ed.). Pearson.

Van de Walle, J., Lovin, L., Karp, K., & Bay-Williams, J. (2017). *Teaching student-centered mathematics: Developmentally appropriate instruction for grades 6–8* (3rd ed.). Pearson.

Widjaja, W., Groves, S., & Ersozlu, Z. (2021). Designing and delivering an online lesson study unit in mathematics to preservice primary teachers: Opportunities and challenges. *International Journal for Lesson & Learning Studies, 10*(2), 230–242. doi:10.1108/IJLLS-10-2020-0080

KEY TERMS AND DEFINITIONS

Conceptual Understanding: Conceptual understanding occurs when there is a relational understanding of mathematical concepts that is a fluid network of links and interconnections of ideas, interpretations, and pictures of mathematical concepts are formed (Van de Walle et al., 2019).

Constructivism: Constructivism is the concept that learners are not blank slates but rather producers or architects of their own. People adapt their previous schemas to integrate new concepts through reflective cognition, which is the endeavor to link existing ideas to new information (Van de Walle et al., 2019).

Crosscutting Concepts: Ideas that appear across multiple domains within the math curriculum, helping to connect and interrelate mathematical knowledge

Mathematical Representation: Students can use representations to organize, record, and explain mathematical concepts. Furthermore, representation enables students to choose, apply, and translate between different mathematical representations in order to solve issues. Students can model and comprehend physical, social, and mathematical processes by using representations (Van de Walle et al., 2019).

Mathematics Methods: Math methods help prepare teacher candidates to enter the K–12 school system and introduce teacher candidates to the constructivist and social-cultural learning theories. Additionally, math methods provide the structure to support teacher candidates with best practices and strong pedagogical strategies to support math acquisition in the K–12 setting.

Procedural Fluency: Procedural fluency is sometimes mistaken with the ability to perform basic algorithms properly and rapidly, but it is much more. Efficiency, accuracy, flexibility, and appropriate strategy selection are the four components of fluency (Van de Walle et al., 2019).

Virtual Environments: A virtual learning environment in educational technology is a web-based platform for the digital aspects of courses of study, usually within educational institutions. In this context, virtual learning may take place through an online platform to reinforce a social-cultural learning environment.

Virtual Manipulative: A virtual manipulative is an interactive, technology-enabled visual representation of a dynamic mathematical item that includes all of the programmable elements. A virtual manipulative allows students to manipulate the object to help with the construction of mathematical knowledge (Van de Walle et al., 2019).

Chapter 8
The Benefits of Wolfram Alpha Tool Applied to Interactive Learning Environments in STEM Education

Vandeir Vioti dos Santos
Mackenzie Presbyterian University, Brazil

Pollyana Notargiacomo
https://orcid.org/0000-0001-8292-1644
Universidade Presbiteriana Mackenzie, Brazil

ABSTRACT

The present chapter propose aims to show the benefits of using an interactive learning environment as a way of promoting greater engagement and consequently improving student performance. In this chapter, the benefits of using the Wolfram Alpha tool applied to interactive learning environments in STEM education will be shown. The quantitative and qualitative results obtained during the research showed the students' preference for classes in which the Wolfram Alpha tool was used allied to traditional teaching. Regarding performance, research has shown that these classes can increase students' academic performance by up to 35%. A tutorial about how to teach the students using the Wolfram Alpha tool will be shown.

DOI: 10.4018/978-1-6684-5939-3.ch008

INTRODUCTION

The object of this chapter aims to show the benefits of using an interactive learning environment as a way of promoting greater engagement and consequently improving student performance. In this chapter, the benefits of using the Wolfram Alpha tool applied to interactive learning environments in STEM education will be shown. The quantitative and qualitative results obtained during the research showed the students' preference for classes in which the Wolfram Alpha tool was used allied to traditional teaching. Regarding performance, research has shown that these classes can increase students' academic performance by up to 35%. A tutorial about how to teach the students to use the Wolfram Alpha tool will be also shown.

The study of the tools and methods focused on the improvement of the academic performance and the engagement of the students can bring relevant information to the development of new technologies and research. According to PISA 2018 (Programme for International Student Assessment - 2018) BRASIL (2020), Brazilian students have shown low levels of learning since 2003 and still haven't presented relevant improvements. The PISA report evaluates the abilities of 15 years old students in solving problems related to daily life. The difference in the score of the students who took the test in 2003 (356 points) and 2018 (384 points) was 28 points. Despite the enhancement in the indicators, there was no significant growth in the average score which was 7.87%, in 15 years. Considering the history of test application, occurred in the years of 2003, 2006, 2009, 2012, 2015 and 2018, the highest historical average was registered in 2012, with 389 points. In a 15-year period, the average score of Brazilian students has not left the first level of learning. The second level has a minimum score of 420 points. According to PISA 2018 BRASIL (2020) 10% of Brazilians with the highest scores in Mathematics have reached an average of 501 points, equivalent to level three of a scale that goes up to 6 and the lowest 10% have reached an average of 277 points, staying below level 1 of learning (minimum 358). The table 1 shows the results reached by Brazilian students in the 2018 evaluation. On the scenery presented by PISA 2018 BRASIL (2020) the results of Brazilian students can be divided according to the administrative dependencies of the school's shown in table 2, where Municipal schools are highlighted for having the lowest averages.

This chapter analyzed the efficiency and effectiveness of three methods by evaluating the engagement, measuring the academic performance during this process and the preferred method for each student involved, it is important to highlight that using the preferred method by the students, during class, can work as one of the factors responsible for increasing the engagement and allowing improvements in their academic performance. This study contributes to STEM education by comparing different teaching methods and the academic performance obtained with each one of them. This research was carried out in three classrooms with 90 students with ages ranging from 14 to 15, at a Municipal public school in the city of Sao Paulo, Brazil. The three methodologies used were: Traditional class, Wolfram Alpha (digital) class and a combined class with the two previous methods. The Wolfram Alpha was the instrument used for the digital and the combined lesson. The combined classes use digital resources allied to the traditional classes. During the traditional class the tools were the blackboard and a ruler. The mathematical topics covered during the research were first and second degree polynomial functions. Due to the school's resource limitations, it wasn't possible for the students to use the digital environment individually or in small groups, in this case the teacher had to act as an intermediary while working with the digital method, to allow the students the opportunity to fully interact with the Wolfram Alpha. The interaction was made possible with the students asking for a multitude of scenarios to be put into practice with the tool so that they could see the final results.

Table 1. PISA 2018 assessment results: Percentage of Brazilians students by level of education

Learning Level	Minimum required grade n	Percentage of students %
Level 6	669	0,1
Level 5	607	0,8
Level 4	545	3,4
Level 3	482	9,3
Level 2	420	18,2
Level 1	358	27,1
Bellow Level 1	———	41

Note: BRASIL. (2020). Relatório brasil no PISA 2018. Brasília, DF: INEP/MEC

Table 2. Average of PISA 2018 assessment results: According to the school's administrative dependency

Administrative Dependency	Average of points obtained
Private	473
Federal	469
State	374
Municipal	314
Brazil	384

Note: BRASIL. (2020). Relatório brasil no PISA 2018. Brasília, DF: INEP/MEC

Benefits of Wolfram Alpha Tool to Interactive Learning Environments

The qualitative results obtained during this research showed that the students' preference for traditional classes or for combined classes was superior to the ones who preferred the classes using only technological resources. Similar results were obtained during the conduction of the quantitative research, in which it showed that the students had an inferior performance when using exclusively technological resources, when compared to other teaching methodologies studied. The results reveal that technology can complement the existing methodologies and bring newer resources to be used with the students.

The quantitative and qualitative results showed that a traditional quality class brings better teaching-learning results. Adopting complementary technologies not necessarily will make all the students perform better, but will improve the performance of the students who identify themselves better with the use of technology as a learning tool.

During this project three different teaching methodologies were compared, the traditional teaching method, a class using digital resources on the Wolfram Alpha platform and a third method combining the two previous ones, that was therefore denominated as combined. The three classrooms had classes using all three methodologies and the results showed that a class with fully digital resources is not always the best methodology to be adopted.

Students who participated in a survey conducted by the authors about using Wolfram Alpha as a way to improve engagement and learning in mathematics, which will be presented in this chapter, commented: "A traditional class already teaches a lot and the class on the computer even more and the two together are greater than the sum of their separate effects" and "Wolfram Alpha made the lesson and the examples that were used a lot easier". This kind of practice constitutes an example the interactive learning environment potential and offer an experience where the user either has its freedom to explore it or is guided by the system's path. On both scenarios the environment needs to be able to identify the learning gaps and offer a course of action to solve these issues (Bredeweg & Winkels,1998).

The Wolfram Alpha was chosen to be used during this research for its programming language where it is possible to build graphics, solve algebra and calculus problems, geometry, statistics, differential equations, and others. The Wolfram Alpha was released in 1988 with the name of Mathematica and in 2009 it received the present name.

The Wolfram Alpha has over 50,000 pages of documentation, and can be used as an introductory language to learn how to program Wolfram (2017). To Wolfram (2017), creator of this new language, while learning how to program the user needs to understand that the Wolfram is similar to the human language, but it has principles and a vocabulary that must be used in a systematic way so the correct results can be achieved.

Technology tools allied to education can be another strategy to help reduce social inequality, allowing previously excluded students (for social reasons, for example) to gain more access to knowledge (Brown et al., 2002). The studies about interactive learning environments applied to STEM education are important to comprehend what is the best line of action to be adopted with the students. The personalized teaching approach enables the students to increase the engagement and by interacting during the class it also allows them to build an even more meaningful learning process.

LITERATURE REVISION

Learning based on experimentation, contextualization, interactions and problem solving are part of constructivist pedagogical theory (Hazel, 2008). Technology empowers teachers in the creation of new education methods, with the support of visual resources and interactive medias (Huang, 2003). The application of new technologies in education is imperative for the development of alternate ways of learning, the improvement of Pedagogical techniques and increasing the involvement and interest of the students with the contents of the class, while learning (Huang, 2003).

Students have distinct ways of learning, as a result, adaptive learning environments can help, bringing them personalized support, learning processes and preferences (Bimba et. al., 2017). The authors Bimba et al. (2017) reviewed twenty different feedback systems and classified them in four groups: adaptive feedback target, adaptive feedback means, adaptive feedback goal and adaptive feedback strategy. Feedback systems are necessary in a learning environment that uses a computer-based system, because the learning process has many different characteristics.

According to Hwang and Hwang and Fu (2020) one of the future trends is a personalized guiding system applied on the educational field. The increase in researches over the years (Figure 1) exemplify the relevance of the study about new technologies and personalized learning system.

There are many tools that can be used on the creation of interactive learning environments, the gamification system is one of these options. Games can be utilized to engage students and with this engagement stimulate the training of their mathematical abilities, supporting them to accomplish a bigger number of activities completed than they would otherwise be able to do without the presence of the game, for example Brezovszky et al. (2019). On their research, Kim and Kim and Ke (2017), have proved that mathematical gamification learning environments, because of the engagement they attract, bring better results while learning when compared to non-gamified environments, especially because it is able to allow students to solve their classroom problems while involving them in different scenarios of real life.

Figure 1. The number of SLE studies in the past 50 years
Note: Gwo-Jen Hwang and Qing-Ke Fu. 2020. Advancement and research trends of smart learning environments in the mobile era. International Journal of Mobile Learning and Organization Vol. 14, No. 1, 2020, 114–129.

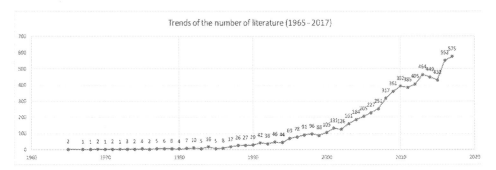

Learning mathematics by interacting with games in comparison to the traditional learning method can bring benefits to the process (Tokac et. al., 2019). The authors affirm on the research that the learning process with the games can bring positive results in different school grades and name as points to be studied: the question of the contents of the game being aligned to the school curriculum, the teacher's familiarity with a methodology based on the use of games and the quantity of time that the students must dedicate to these types of games.

Young people, considered the digital natives (Costa et. al., 2015), are responsible for changing the profile of Brazilian students, modifying the way you teach and engage these students (Ferreira et al., 2020). This profile change is connected to the way these students socialize and how they access information (Costa et al., 2015). Taking this context into consideration it is necessary for schools to start accommodating new teaching methodologies, examining the ICTs (Information and Communications Technologies) as a new approach, evaluating the cultural context where the students are inserted (Costa et al., 2015).

Viberg et. al., (2020) affirm that it is necessary for teachers to educate their students on how to use digital tools, for example, in Mathematics classes. Those authors research report that when the students are responsible of learning how to use the technological tools by themselves, they are more prone to a bigger learning curve and cannot comprehend how effective the tools are on their learning process.

A study conducted with high school students (Lin, et. al., 2020) compared the use of two methodologies (web-based and classroom-based) to be used on the teaching of classes that are part of the STEM (Science, Technology, Engineering, and Mathematics). The methodologies evaluated were the web-based Collaborative Problem-Solving Systems (wCPSS) and the classroom-based Collaborative Hands-on Learning Activities (cCHLA). After all the results were analyzed, the authors concluded that the wCPSS, with the teacher's participation as a guide, was the most effective learning method when compared to the other methods studied in this research.

The quest for a meaningful learning is necessary to overcome the mechanical learning process present at Brazil's learning system (Ferreira et al., 2020). Meaningful learning is characterized by allowing the students to learn new concepts by correlating them with other concepts already mastered and previous experiences they had. In other words the learning process must be relevant and not just involve the random memorization of concepts. New tools and methodologies must be key factors to reach those goals, among those tools are the ones that fit on the concept of digital technologies of information and communication.

The use of interactive learning environments can be applied in multiple learning approaches, including creativity teaching and innovation (Apiola et. al., 2012). Those environments have received the name of Creativity-Support Learning Environment (CSLE) and possess different pedagogical approaches, for instance the learning based in projects and in problems. Personalized systems can improve not only the academic performance, but also increase the learning motivation, improve the self-efficacy and the engagement of the students (Zhang et al., 2020). The authors employed pre-test and post-test questionnaires to determine the results in their study, and a similar course of action was applied during this research.

MATERIALS AND METHODS

The use of technologies with the intent of improving the student's learning process is predicted and advised in the Curriculum of the City of São Paulo - CCSP (Municipio, 2019). According to the Curriculum of São Paulo Municipio (2019), which is an official government guideline elaborated by the Municipal Education Secretariat of the City of São Paulo, the children and the young people were born and belong in the digital era, many times using technologies such as computers and tablets before they learn how to read and write. Therefore, the Municipal Education Secretariat suggests the use of technology as a way to promote discoveries and learning in a pleasurable way for the students, encouraging the use of it since the children's literacy stage.

This research was conducted using quantitative and qualitative data, of 90 students within the ages of 13 to 14 years old, from both sexes and that had never failed any classes in school. These students were from three classes of the ninth year of high school (9A - class one, 9B - class two e 9C - class three) in a Municipal public school, in the city of Sao Paulo, Brazil. They attended three classes, each one of them with 90 minutes of duration.

In all the classes the contents were exactly the same, following the same basic examples, but the students had the freedom to interact and request the teacher to modify some of them, in order to illustrate the different types of graphics. Throughout the time in all the classes the students were encouraged to work alongside the teacher. For instance, this type of behavior occurred mainly during the combined and the Wolfram Alpha classes.

They had never been in contact with the contents of the class and the pre-test was used to determine this. The pre-test of the first two classes is composed by 10 questions, one multiple choice question and nine short-essay questions. Every question is referring to a theoretical topic that would be taught and is available on the table 4, all the questions were distributed by difficulty level. The test taken after class to assess the knowledge of the students followed the same structure. Each question approached one of the topics taught. On the third class, due to the extent and difficulty of the topics of the theoretical content, the class was taught in five topics, as shown in table 4. To maintain the same structure throughout, the ratio of one question per taught topic was sustained in the pre-test and the assessment after class, for this reason the class three had in total five questions, all in the short-essay type.

The results of the pre-tests showed that on average 96.43% (class one), 76.18% (class two) and 90% (class three) of the students didn't have any knowledge about the contents of the class since they left blank answers for the questions they did not comprehend, or knew how to solve it. On the results of the pre-test of class two, it is possible to observe that the students accomplished better performances, that happened due to the contents assimilated during class one, which allowed some of them to make logical deductions and correctly answer a few of the questions on the pre-test of class two.

The implementation of the pre-test and the post-class test, in every one of the methodologies, offers a viewpoint to measure the difference between each one of the classes being studied in relation to the similarities and the discrepancy they had before being taught the contents of the class, and how were they performing after the class. The main goal of those tests are to have substantiated data to analyze the results by comparing all three classes accomplishments (according to each one of the three methods analyzed separately as well as altogether). The students were taken out of their comfort zone, even during the traditional class, since the classes usually had less content than what was presented during the research classes. It is also important to highlight that in none of the classes the teacher had problems related to students' behavior.

For the purpose of this research only the results of the students who participated in all of the classes and had taken all the tests on specific days were considered, for this reason from the total of 90 students initially participating, it was only considered the results of the tests of 38 students. During this research, three methodologies were used: the traditional teaching method, a fully digital class where the only instrument was the Wolfram Alpha and the combined which is comprised by the two previous methods being interchanged during the class (table 3).

The classes were taught in three consecutive Fridays and had a total length of 90 minutes. During those classes the first step was the pre-test followed by the explanation of the contents of the class. On the Monday following the classes the post-class tests were applied to determine how much of the lecture was absorbed by the students. The post-class tests were applied on September, 9th, 16th and 23rd of 2019. Those dates were chosen because the author of this research had classes with all three classrooms involved on the research. The contents taught during the classes are shown in table 4.

Table 3. Class schedule

Classes' Date	Classroom 1	Classroom 2	Classroom 3
09/06/19	Traditional	Wolfram Alpha	Combined Class
09/13/19	Combined Class	Traditional	Wolfram Alpha
09/20/19	Wolfram Alpha	Combined Class	Traditional

Table 4. Contents of the class

09/06/19 - 1st Degree Function	09/13/19 - 1st Degree Function	09/20/19 - Quadratic Functions
Function Definition	Angular Coefficient	Function Definition
E.g. Function Application	Linear Correlation Coefficient	E.g. Function Application
Dependent Variable	Constant Function	Determining the Concavity
Independent Variable	Constant Function Graph	The Vertex of a Parabola
Graph Construction	Linear Function	Signs of Functions
Roots or Zeros of a Function	Linear Function Graph	
Ascending Function	Identity Function	
Decreasing Function	Identity Function Graph	
Domain of a Function	Signs of Functions	
Image of a Function	Recognizing Functions from Graph	

RESULTS

Quantitative Results

The results of the research were organized and tabulated according to the classroom studied, the methodology used (traditional, combined and Wolfram Alpha) and the results of the tests, separated by question solved. Tables 5, 6, 7 and 8 refer to the results of class one, tables 9, 10, 11 and 12 show the results of class two and tables 13, 14, 15 and 16 display the results of Lesson three. The results were divided into four categories, did not try to solve (blank answer), missed the resolution or partially solved, grasped the concept or unraveled the problem and lastly, tried to resolve it. Did not tried to solve it indicates that the student was not feeling safe enough to leave his comfort zone and make an attempt at the problems presented. This might occur due to several factors, namely, the student had a low understanding of the class or did not retain the information to solve the problems, or they were anxious with the test and had a mental block that prevented them from applying the contents of the class. Missed the resolution or partially solved designates the student who tried to solve the problems with dedication but little assertiveness. Grasped the concept or unraveled the problem, indicates the student who aced the question or had full understanding of the concept involved in the resolution, with small execution mistakes (e.g. wrong multiplication or subtraction).

The tried to resolve it, is an index created to indicate the students who ventured out of their safe place while attempting to solve the questions, for example, they got the question right, tried to get it right or had a wrong answer. This was created to assess and compare the participation and engagement during the class, provided by each methodology.

When analyzing the results of class one, we can infer that, in relation to the students who did not try to solve the questions, (Table 5) in all of the methodologies (traditional, Wolfram Alpha and combined), the results were very similar, with an average of 30.83% (simple arithmetic mean of 30%, 28.75% and 33.75%), noting that before the class, the average of students who did not try to solve the questions was 98.39% (simple arithmetic mean of 96.43%, 98.75% and 100%).

The data that refers to the students who missed the resolution or partially solved the questions in class one (Table 6) shows by the general average that the Wolfram Alpha presented the most significant results after the student participated in the class, followed by the traditional and the combined lessons

Table 5. Students that did not try to solve the questions in the lesson 1 - 09/06/19

Question	9A – TL P-T %	9A – TL PC-T %	9B - WA P-T %	9B - WA PC-T %	9C – CC P-T %	9C – CC PC-T %
1	100	28.57	100	37.50	100	37.50
2a	100	21.43	93.75	37.50	100	62.50
2b	92.86	35.71	93.75	43.75	100	62.50
3a	100	42.86	100	43.75	100	37.50
3b	100	50	100	37.50	100	37.50
3c	92.86	50	100	37.50	100	37.50
3d	92.86	42.86	100	43.75	100	37.50
4a	92.86	14.29	100	0	100	12.50
4b	92.86	14.29	100	0	100	12.50
5	100	0	100	6.25	100	0
Average	96.43	30	98.75	28.75	100	33.75

Table 6. Students who missed the resolution or partially solved the questions in the lesson 1 - 09/06/19

Question	9A – TL P-T %	9A – TL PC-T %	9B - WA P-T %	9B - WA PC-T %	9C - CC P-T %	9C - CC PC-T %
1	0	14.29	0	12.50	0	12.50
2a	0	14.29	0	18.75	0	25
2b	7.14	28.57	0	25	0	25
3a	0	21.43	0	18.75	0	12.50
3b	0	14.29	0	18.75	0	12.50
3c	7.14	21.43	0	18.75	0	12.50
3d	7.14	28.57	0	18.75	0	12.50
4a	7.14	57.14	0	87.50	0	37.50
4b	7.14	78.57	0	81.25	0	37.50
5	0	7.14	0	43.75	0	37.50
Average	3.57	28.57	0	34.38	0	22.50

It is important to highlight, the necessity of observing the three tables 5, 6 and 7 at the same time, because they refer to the same class and assessment. For example, when we observe the results of the pre-test on question one of the table 6 and find the 0% quotient, for the correct interpretation, it should be noted that on the table 5, the

Benefits of Wolfram Alpha Tool to Interactive Learning Environments

result is 100%, that is, the entirety of the students left this question blank (without trying to solve it), consequently 0% of the students had erroneous or partially correct answers (table 6), since no one attempted to solve it. The tables were assembled to emphasize the comparative analysis between the three methodologies adopted, therefore for the data analysis of the Lesson 2 is necessary to observe the tables 9, 10 and 11 together, and the same occurs with the data of Lesson three (tables 13, 14 and 15). For example, on question one of Lesson three (table 13) the results of the post-test of the traditional Lesson were 12.5%, on the table 14 the result was 12.5%, on the table 15 the result was 75% totaling 100% (12.5% + 12.5% + 75%). The last example refers to the use of the table 16, that is comprised by the sum of the percentages of the tables 14 and 15, to represent the total percentage of the students who tried to solve the question.

The data of the students who grasped the concept or unraveled the problem (Table 7), reveals that the traditional, the Wolfram Alpha and the combined class had presented similar results, with roughly 41% (simple arithmetic mean of 41.43% and 40.64%) of the students on this category, even though the combined class stands out having the highest marker with 43.75%.

Comparing the results of the students who grasped the concept or unraveled the problem in lesson 1 (table 7) the data shows that the students who participated in the combined class had a better performance (43.78%) followed by traditional Lesson (41.43%) and Wolfram Alpha (40.63%).

Table 7. Students who grasped the concept or unraveled the problem in lesson 1

Question	9A - TL P-T %	9A - TL PC-T %	9B - WA P-T %	9B - WA PC-T %	9C - CC P-T %	9C - CC PC-T %
1	0	57.14	0	50	0	50
2a	7.14	64.29	6.25	12.50	0	12.50
2b	0	35.71	6.25	31.25	0	12.50
3a	0	35.71	0	50	0	50
3b	0	35.71	0	43.75	0	50
3c	0	28.57	0	50	0	50
3d	0	28.57	0	37.50	0	50
4a	0	28.57	0	50	0	50
4b	0	7.14	0	18,75	0	50
5	7.14	92.86	0	62.50	0	62.50
Average	1.43	41.43	1.25	40.63	0	43.75

Benefits of Wolfram Alpha Tool to Interactive Learning Environments

Observing the results that shows the students who tried to resolve it (Table 8), it becomes apparent that the average of the results obtained were very close to each other. The students who learned from the combined class were the ones with the lowest percentages with 66.25%, and the Wolfram Alpha had the highest number of attempts with 71.25%.

Table 8. Students who tried to resolve the question in lesson 1 – 09/06/19

Question	9A - TL P-T %	9A - TL PC-T %	9B - WA P-T %	9B - WA PC-T %	9C - CC P-T %	9C - CC PC-T %
1	0	71.43	0	62.50	0	62.50
2a	7.14	78.57	6.25	62.50	0	37.50
2b	7.14	64.29	6.25	56.25	0	37.50
3a	0	57.14	0	56.25	0	62.50
3b	0	50	0	62.50	0	62.50
3c	7.14	50	0	62.50	0	62.50
3d	7.14	57.14	0	56.25	0	62.50
4a	7.14	85.71	0	100	0	87.50
4b	7.14	85.71	0	100	0	87.50
5	7.14	100	0	93.75	0	100
Average	5	70	1.25	71.25	0	66.25

The data from class two shows that between the students who did not try to solve, (Table 9) the ones who learned from Wolfram Alpha had the highest number of absences with 36.21% and the combined class had the lowest with 10.32%. On the second class it is possible to observe (Table 9) that there was a reduction of 78.63% in the number of students who didn't try to solve the questions (left a blank answer), considering the average number of answers, on all the methodologies applied. During class one (Table 5), the average was 98.39% of students who left blank answers, considering all three methods. A possible explanation for this, is related to the fact of class two being a progression of class one, what might have motivated the most engaged students to try and find the logic behind the questions on the pre-test, in light of the previously acquired knowledge on 09/06/19.

Among the students who missed the resolution or partially solved the questions, in class two (Table 10) the highest percentage was from the Wolfram Alpha, with 38.89%, followed by the traditional (37.50%) and the combined (19.84%).

Table 9. Students that did not try to solve the questions – lesson 2 – 09/13/19

Question	9A - CC P-T %	9A - CC PC-T %	9B - TL P-T %	9B - TL PC-T %	9C - WA P-T %	9C - WA PC-T %
1	85.71	35.71	62.5	37.50	87.5	12.50
2	100	21.43	100	56.25	100	37.50
3a	50	0	93.75	25	87.5	62.50
3b	78.57	14.29	93.75	37.50	87.5	75
3c	78.57	7.14	100	37.50	87.5	75
3d	85.71	14.29	100	50	87.5	62.50
4a	71.43	0	56.25	6.25	75	0
4b	71.43	0	56.25	6.25	75	0
5	64.28	0	50	0	37.5	0
Average	76.18	10.32	79.16	28.47	80.55	36.11

Table 10. Students who missed the resolution or partially solved the questions in the lesson 2 - 09/13/19

Question	9A - CC P-T %	9A - CC PC-T %	9B - TL P-T %	9B - TL PC-T %	9C – WA P-T %	9C – WA PC-T %
1	14.29	35.71	37.5	50	12.5	25
2	0	0	0	6.25	0	12.50
3a	50	14.29	6.25	56.25	12.5	37.50
3b	21.43	7.14	6.25	43.75	12.5	25
3c	21.43	21.43	0	50	12.5	25
3d	14.29	7.14	0	37.50	12.5	37.50
4a	14.29	42.86	6.25	43.75	12.5	62.50
4b	7.14	42.86	12.50	43.75	12.5	62.50
5	35.71	7.14	6.25	6.25	0	50
Average	19.84	19.84	8.33	37.50	9.72	38.89

Amid the students who grasped the concept or unraveled the problem (Table 11), those who were taught following the Wolfram Alpha were the ones with the lowest markers (25%), and the combined class had the highest index (69.84%).

The data shows that in relation to those who tried to resolve, (Table 12) the students who learned from Wolfram Alpha were the ones with the lowest number of attempts (63.89%), and the combined class had the highest with 89.68%.

Benefits of Wolfram Alpha Tool to Interactive Learning Environments

Table 11. Students who grasped the concept or unraveled the problem in lesson 2

Question	9A – CC P-T %	9A – CC PC-T %	9B - TL P-T %	9B - TL PC-T %	9C – WA P-T %	9C – WA PC-T %
1	0	28.57	0	12.50	0	62.50
2	0	78.57	0	37.50	0	50
3a	0	85.71	0	18.75	0	0
3b	0	78.57	0	18.75	0	0
3c	0	71.43	0	12.50	0	0
3d	0	78.57	0	12.50	0	0
4a	0	57.14	0	50	0	25
4b	14.29	57.14	31.25	50	12.5	37.50
5	21.43	92.86	0	93.75	62.5	50
Average	3.97	69.84	3.47	34.03	8.33	25

Table 12. Students who tried to resolve the question in lesson 2 - 09/13/19

Question	9A – CC P-T %	9A – CC PC-T %	9B - TL P-T %	9B - TL PC-T %	9C – WA P-T %	9C – WA PC-T %
1	14.29	64.29	37.5	62.50	12.5	87.50
2	0	78.57	0	43.75	0	62.50
3a	50	100	6.25	75	0	37.50
3b	21.43	85.71	6.25	62.50	0	25
3c	21.43	92.86	0	62.50	0	25
3d	14.29	85.71	0	50	0	37.50
4a	28.57	100	43.75	93.75	25	100
4b	28.57	100	43.75	93.75	25	100
5	35.71	100	50	100	62.5	100
Average	23.81	89.68	20.83	71.53	13.89	63.89

The analysis of the data from class 3 for those who did not try to solve it (Table 13) shows that students who learned from Wolfram Alpha were the ones with the highest absenteeism (47.14%) after participating in the class, and the combined class had the lowest (35%).

In relation to students who missed the resolution or partially solved it (Table 14), the data indicates the Wolfram Alpha class had the highest percentage with 28.57% after the student attended the class, followed closely by the combined (25%) and the traditional class (15%).

Benefits of Wolfram Alpha Tool to Interactive Learning Environments

Table 13. Students that did not try to solve the questions in the lesson 3 - 09/20/19

Question	9A - CC		9B - TL		9C - WA	
	P-T %	PC-T %	P-T %	PC-T %	P-T %	PC-T %
1	92.86	35.71	93.75	31.25	100	12.50
2	85.72	57.14	100	56.25	100	75
3	92.86	78.57	100	50	100	75
4	85.72	35.71	68.75	18.75	87.5	37.50
5	92.86	28.57	87.5	18.75	100	25
Average	90	47.14	90	35	97.5	45

Table 14. Students who missed the resolution or partially solved the questions in the lesson 3 09/20/19

Question	9A – CC		9B - TL		9C - WA	
	P-T %	PC-T %	P-T %	PC-T %	P-T %	PC-T %
1	7.14	14.29	0	0	0	12.0
2	14.29	35.71	0	37.50	0	25
3	7.14	14.29	0	31.25	0	25
4	7.14	42.86	31.25	31.25	12.5	12.50
5	7.14	35.71	12.5	25	0	0
Average	8.57	28.57	8.75	25	2.50	15

The index showing the students who grasped the concept or unraveled the problem (Table 15) indicates that the ones who learned from Wolfram Alpha had the lowest percentage (24.29%), and the combined and traditional class were tied with both having the highest percentage at 40%.

The data referring to the students who tried to resolve it (Table 16) highlights that the students who learned from the Wolfram Alpha were the ones with the lowest number of attempts (52.86%) and the combined class had the highest (65%).

The quantitative analysis reveals that even though the research shows similar and inconclusive results, the students had the best performance with the combined class. Often than not, classes that were taught exclusively with the Wolfram Alpha methodology, performed poorly than the others. Traditional classes presented an average performance.

Table 15. Students who grasped the concept or unraveled the problem in lesson 3 - 09/20/19

Question	9A - CC		9B - TL		9C - WA	
	P-T %	PC-T %	P-T %	PC-T %	P-T %	PC-T %
1	0	50	0	68.75	0	75
2	0	7.14	0	6.25	0	0
3	0	7.14	0	18.75	0	0
4	7.14	21.43	0	50	0	50
5	0	35.71	0	56.25	0	75
Average	1.43	24.29	0	40	0	40

Table 16. Students who tried to resolve the question in lesson 3 - 09/20/19

Question	9A - CC		9B - TL		9C - WA	
	P-T %	PC-T %	P-T %	PC-T %	P-T %	PC-T %
1	7.14	64.29	6.25	68.75	0	87.50
2	14.29	42.86	0	43.75	0	25
3	7.14	21.43	0	50	0	25
4	14.29	64.29	31.25	81.25	12.5	62.50
5	7.14	71.43	12.5	81.25	0	75
Average	10	52.86	10	65	2.50	55

Qualitative Results

Of the total of the three classrooms involved in the research, only three students indicated on their questionnaire answers that they preferred the class using only the Wolfram Alpha, 20 students preferred the traditional classes and 15 students preferred the combined classes. Among the arguments used to defend the use of the traditional classes are the fact that they consider it easier to learn in this type of class and that it is easier to copy the information provided, in their notebooks. One of the students made a reasonable comment which can also be considered as a problem question for choosing these classes, is the habit or the tradition a factor that can determine the student's preference for these classes? The student's opinion is:

"Because you do not get tired so easily and it is simpler to learn because of the habit." In the comments about the combined classes, the importance that the students gave for viewing the examples using Wolfram Alpha is highlighted. The teacher, responsible for both, the classes and the research, observed during the application of the classes that the students had a macro view of the subject using Wolfram Alpha and the blackboard made it possible to unravel the details, generating a greater level of confidence and comfort for the students. On this matter, the students commented:

"A traditional class already teaches a lot and the class on the computer even more and the two together are greater than the sum of their separate effects." and "Wolfram Alpha made the lesson and the examples that were used a lot easier."

At the end of the research, the students answered the following question: "The teacher used three different ways to teach functions. Out of these three classes, which one made it easier for you to learn? Why?" The results were tabulated by room and are shown in tables 17, 18, 19 and 20. The table 18 presents the most relevant arguments presented by the students in classroom 1 about methodology preference. It is noteworthy that only students who participated in the three classes were considered for the research. The results of students who participated in one or two classes were excluded from the survey considering they didn't have enough knowledge to give an opinion about the other methodologies used. The multitude of opinions presented by the students shows that there is not only one correct way of learning, which means respecting each student's individuality is fundamental in the process of teaching and learning. Therefore, the study of new or older methodologies needs to be focused on the results of each person and not only on the group. Understanding and using the singularities of each student can bring relevant results in the long term. The following question is left for future consideration: how can a teacher promote individualized instruction for the students in a school that has an average of 30 students per class (very common scenario in public schools of Sao Paulo, Brazil).

Table 17. Students preference for each methodology

Number of Students	Classroom 1	Classroom 2	Classroom 3
Traditional Lesson	5	10	5
Lesson with Wolfram A.	3	0	0
Combined Class	6	6	3

Quanti-Qualitative Analysis

The quantitative and qualitative results obtained during the research showed the students' preference for classes in which the Wolfram Alpha tool was used allied to traditional teaching. Regarding performance, research has shown that these classes can increase students' academic performance by up to 35%.

Table 18. Most relevant arguments presented by the students in classroom 1 about methodology preference

Methodology	Reasons
Traditional Lesson	"Because all the other methods have made it harder for me to learn."
	"In my opinion, the blackboard is easier to understand."
Lesson with Wolfram Alpha	"Because I was able to be better concentrated."
Combined Class	"It was the class I learned the most."
	"I was able to see more examples on the computer."
	"Because everything I had forgotten (about Wolfram Alpha's explanation), I was able to remember during the teacher's explanation (traditional explanation)."

Table 19. Most relevant arguments presented by the students in classroom 2 about methodology preference

Methodology	Reasons
Traditional Lesson	"Because I'm used to the way the class is explained" "For me, it would be easier to stay exclusively in the classroom, because it is easier to understand the subject." "Because it is better to learn the contents of the class."
Lesson with Wolfram Alpha	------
Combined Class	"Because the teacher can show several examples with the projector." "I think the combined Class was better because it wasn't so tiresome." "Wolfram Alpha made the lesson and the examples that were used a lot easier."

Table 20. Most relevant arguments presented by the students in classroom three about methodology preference

Methodology	Reasons
Traditional Lesson	"I think it is more explanatory and we have a better understanding." "It is easier to understand."
Lesson with Wolfram Alpha	------
Combined Class	"Because the teacher showed various types of graphics on the computer and recalled the explanation in the classroom."

Conducting studies comparing the different types of methodologies is important to identify the best learning scenarios for the students. Despite the results of some researches – as Lo and Hew (2020), Zhang et al. (2020) and Brezovszky et al. (2019), indicating the use of digital elements improves the learning process of the students, the quantitative and qualitative results obtained during this research reveal that the students don't always agree that technology is key to improving their education.

The use of active methodologies, in comparison to the traditional ones, can bring new experiences while the students learn, occasionally promoting a greater engagement and enriching the learning process (Ribeiro & Passos, 2020). One of the major challenges faced by students is to identify their difficulties to determine what they should and how they should study. The development of tools with the objective of identifying learning gaps is essential to collaborate with the academic development of students. In accordance with this, one possibility is the use of technological tools such as Wolfram Alpha to carry out interactive activities in which it is possible to visualize the results of hypotheses raised by the students.

With this in mind, a study performed with 67 students of Public School with ages ranging from 14 to 17 years old, at a High School, on the State of Pernambuco, Santana et al. (2020) has indicated through the application of the three dimension Likert scale, used to measure the engagement of the students in every step of the process, that the students had a positive behavioral and emotional engagement because they were learning through active methodologies. A study carried out with Engineering students (Teixeira et al., 2020) has shown the active methodologies namely the Project Based Learning (PBL) can significantly improve the learning process of the students due to an increase of their motivation. Empirical research conducted with Software Engineer students (Serban & Vescan, 2020) has presented that a change on the methodology, to an active methodology influenced an increase in the students' grade.

Analysis of the quantitative and qualitative results and the literature review showed the importance of using active methodologies combined with new technological tools in order to improve student engagement and learning. Due to this, as a pedagogical proposal, the use of the Wolfram Alpha tool in a math class will be shown. In order to familiarize the reader with the tool, an overview of Wolfram Alpha is shown.

WOLFRAM ALPHA: DIDACTICAL APPROACHES IN THE CLASSROOM

The purpose of this topic is to explore how to work with Wolfram Alpha in the classroom with students, allowing them to develop their creativity and especially curiosity. Wolfram Alpha allows students to explore their ideas in a practical and fast way. For example, in the study of mathematical functions, the student would need to build a graph for each idea to be explored, which would present itself as a time-consuming and tiring task.

By using Wolfram Alpha the student can carry out this study in an easy, fast and intuitive way. This section will be divided into two parts. In the first part will explore functions of this tool, and in the second part will be presented a showcase script to exemplify a possible application in the classroom.

Structure and Concepts about Wolfram Alpha

Wolfram Alpha is a free tool that can be accessed online and therefore does not require the teacher/student to have a computer/cell phone/tablet with advanced configuration[1]. Wolfram Alpha has more than six thousand functions available to be used that can be accessed using the function itself or through natural language. Natural language processing is one that tries to approximate the way people write and speaks Hirschberg and Manning (2015). To use natural language, the teacher or student must write what they want in the search field, examples:

- plot a parabola
- solve 34 - 16 + 3 + 6
- is -172 smaller than 26?
- 15 - 6
- 32 + 7
- 12/4
- 20*3
- 2^3
- shape with 7 sides

The multiplication is represented by the symbol *, the letter x, that is commonly used to represent the multiplication, cannot be used to represent this operation. It is noteworthy that the multiplication of two letters (variables) is represented by a space between them. Two letters together represent a variable. Example:

- xy represents the variable xy
- x y represents the variable x being multiplied by y

Another important point to be highlighted is that in Wolfram Alpha don't use [] or {}, the user must use only the () to replace the [] and the to show the grouping levels.

When the user enters data in fractions format, the answer will be provided in fraction format, if the user provides one of the values in decimal, the result will be presented in decimal format.

Another feature available is factoring and/or expanding an expression. To use it, just put the word Factor (Figure 2) or Expand (Figure 3) in front and the expression in parentheses.

- Factor(x^2 + 6x + 9)
- Expand(x^2 + 4)^2

Figure 2. Use of the function Factor(x^2 + 6x + 9)

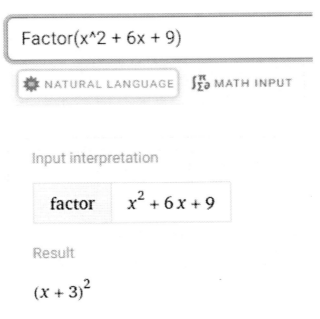

To solve an equation, the user must place the solve command (Figure 4) or roots command in front of the equation, for example:

- solve x^2 + 6 x - 6 = 0
- roots x^2 + 6 x - 6 = 0

Wolfram Alpha is a tool that allows teachers and students not only to perform calculations but also to visualize graphs, using the plot, graph or graphics command (Figure 5). Example:

Figure 3. Use of the function Expand(x^2 + 4)^2

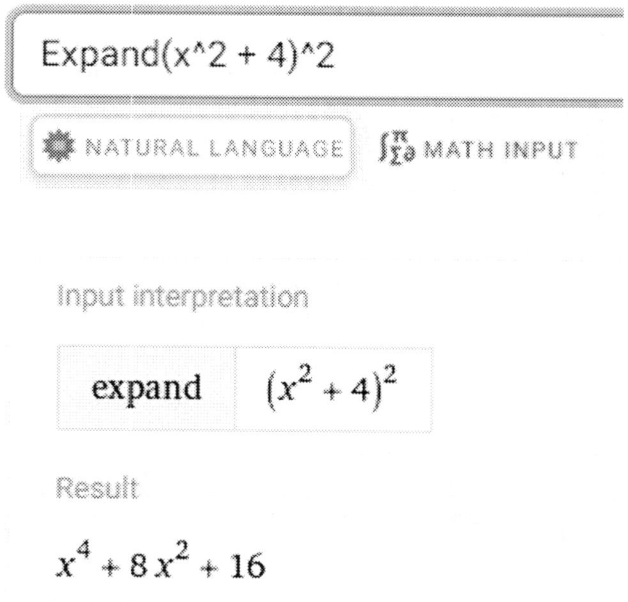
Expand(x^2 + 4)^2
NATURAL LANGUAGE
MATH INPUT
Input interpretation
expand
$(x^2 + 4)^2$
Result
$x^4 + 8x^2 + 16$

Figure 4. Use of the function solve x^2 + 6 x - 6 = 0

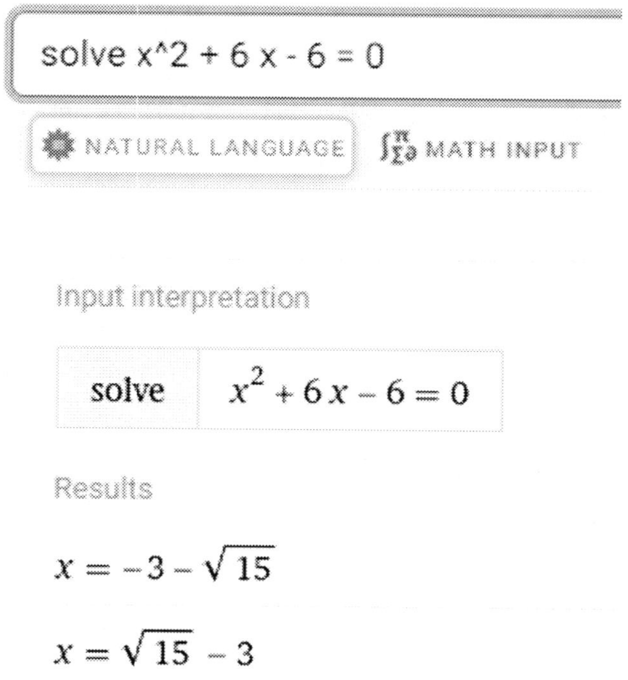
solve x^2 + 6 x - 6 = 0
NATURAL LANGUAGE
MATH INPUT
Input interpretation
solve
$x^2 + 6x - 6 = 0$
Results
$x = -3 - \sqrt{15}$
$x = \sqrt{15} - 3$

Benefits of Wolfram Alpha Tool to Interactive Learning Environments

- Plot(2x^2 + 3x -2)
- Graph(2x^2 + 3x -2)
- Graphics(2x^2 + 3x -2)

Figure 5. Use of the function Graph(2x^2 + 3 x -2, (x, -4, 3))

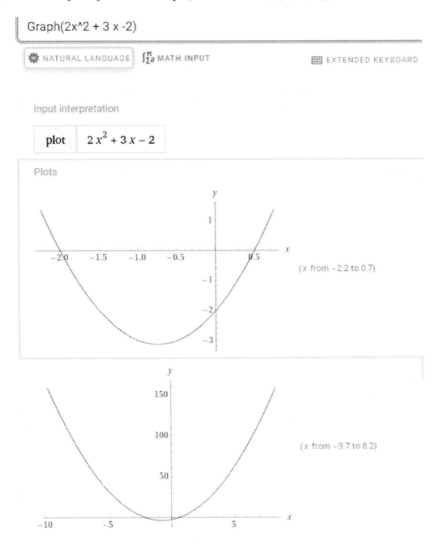

If it is of interest, the user can define the domain of the function by adding (x,min,max) to the command (Figure 6), example:

Benefits of Wolfram Alpha Tool to Interactive Learning Environments

- Plot(2x^2 + 3x -2, (x, -4, 3))
- Graph(2x^2 + 3x -2, (x, -4, 3))
- Graphis(2x^2 + 3x -2, (x, -4, 3))

Figure 6. Use of the function Graph(2x^2 + 3x -2, (x, -4, 3))

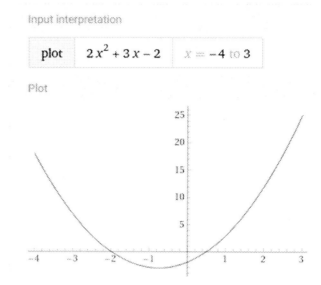

These commands can also be used in the construction of geometric figures (Figure 7):

- Plot3D[Ball[]]
- Graph3D[Ball[]]
- Graphics3D[Ball[]]

Another option to using the natural language (Figure 8) is to use the formula editor provided by Wolfram Alpha. This option is just below the search bar and is named Math Imput (Figure 9).

Benefits of Wolfram Alpha Tool to Interactive Learning Environments

Figure 7. Use of the function Graphics3D[Ball[ ]]

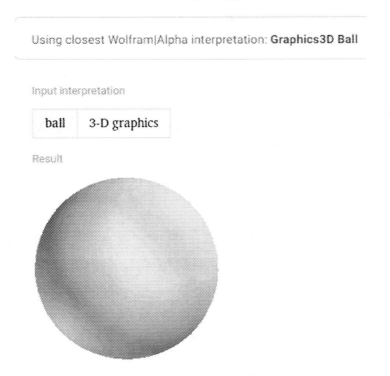

Figure 8. First page of Wolfram Alpha

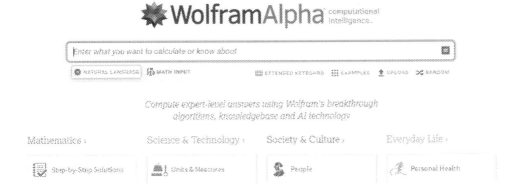

Figure 9. First page of Wolfram Alpha with Math Input select

Didactical Approaches of Wolfram Alpha

The use of Wolfram Alpha as a complementary tool to the teaching of mathematics allows not only students to understand new concepts, but mainly to explore new possibilities allowing students to stimulate creativity. With this in mind, this topic aims to give a suggestion to the teacher on how to teach the student to explore mathematical themes using this tool and developing new skills. For this example, we will use the first-degree function as a theme.

When explaining about the first-degree function, the teacher can subdivide the class into sub-themes, such as:

- Function Definition
- Dependent Variable
- Independent Variable
- Graph Construction
- Roots or Zeros of a Function
- Ascending Function
- Decreasing Function
- Domain of a Function
- Image of a Function

Benefits of Wolfram Alpha Tool to Interactive Learning Environments

There are many ways that the teacher can abort this theme, for example, he can start the explanation with a theoretical class on the definition of the function talking about the dependent and independent variables and then show examples using Wolfram Alpha or he can start the class showing some examples to instigate the curiosity of the students to later explain the definition.

One suggestion in this field is start the study by showing several graphs that represent the possibilities that exist on this topic, for example:

- Graph f(x) = 2x + 1
- Graph f(x) = - 5x
- Graph f(x) = - 5x + 1
- Graph f(x) = 10
- Graph f(x) = x
- Graph (f(x) = x/2, (x, -4, 5))
- Graph (f(x) = 2x + 1, (x, -5, 8))

After the presentation of the graphs above, the teacher will be able to teach about the angular coefficient. The teacher can opt for two different approaches. In the first approach he will be able to show several graphs by changing the angular coefficient and asking the students to observe that they are changing and making comments about. The second option, if the students have access to a device to use Wolfram Alpha, the teacher could explain how to insert de commands and guide them to discovery about the characteristics of the function. I emphasize that the teacher should guide them at first time they only change the angular coefficient.

For this demonstration, the teacher can stipulate fixed ranges for the abscissa and ordinate axis, in this way it will make it easier for the student to see the variation of the slope that will occur (Figures 10, 11 and 12). Examples:

- Graph (f(x) = x/2, (x, -5, 8), (y,-4,6))
- Graph (f(x) = 2x, (x, -5, 8), (y,-4,6))
- Graph (f(x) = 3x, (x, -5, 8), (y,-4,6))
- Graph (f(x) = 4x, (x, -5, 8), (y,-4,6))
- Graph (f(x) = -4x, (x, -5, 8), (y,-4,6))

Figure 10. Graph (f(x) = x/2, (x, -5, 8), (y,-4,6))

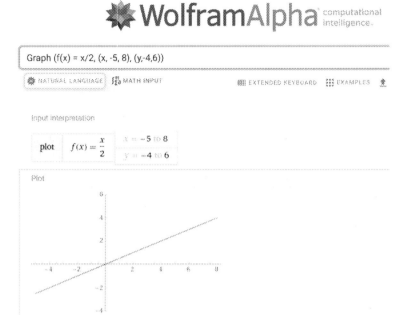

Figure 11. Graph (f(x) = 4x, (x, -5, 8), (y,-4,6))

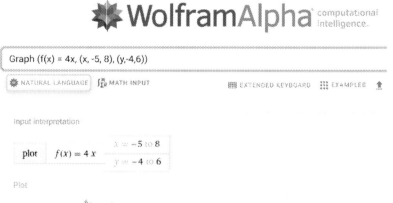

Benefits of Wolfram Alpha Tool to Interactive Learning Environments

Figure 12. Graph (f(x) = -4x, (x, -5, 8), (y,-4,6))

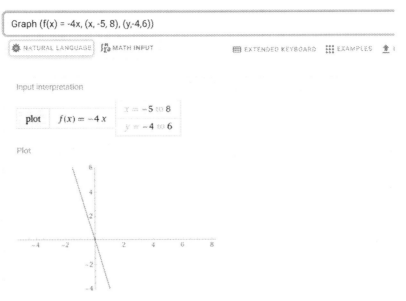

The next step is demonstrating the linear coefficient function. The teacher can use two teaching methods: show students several examples and ask them to find a pattern or teach students how to change parameters in Wolfram Alpha and allow them to discover the properties of the linear coefficient by themselves.

For this demonstration, the teacher can stipulate fixed ranges for the abscissas and ordinates axis, this way it will make it easier for the student to see what happens with the linear coefficient (Figures 13, 14 and 15). Examples:

- Graph (f(x) = x/2 + 2, (x, -5, 8), (y,-4,6))
- Graph (f(x) = 1x + 2, (x, -5, 8), (y,-4,6))
- Graph (f(x) = 4x + 6, (x, -5, 8), (y,-4,6))
- Graph (f(x) = -4x - 3, (x, -5, 8), (y,-4,6))
- Graph (f(x) = -3x - 4, (x, -5, 8), (y,-4,6))

Figure 13. Graph (f(x) = x/2 + 2, (x, -5, 8), (y,-4,6))

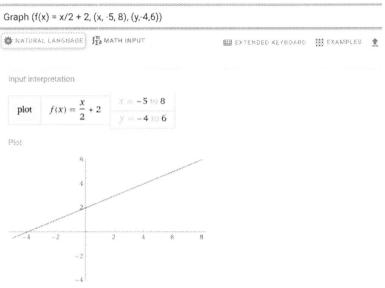

Figure 14. Graph (f(x) = 4x + 6, (x, -5, 8), (y,-4,6))

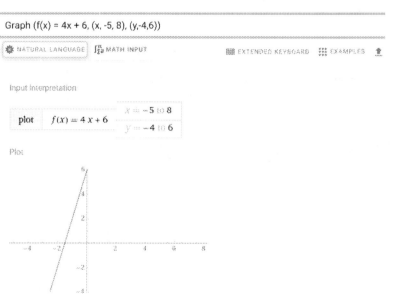

Benefits of Wolfram Alpha Tool to Interactive Learning Environments

Figure 15. Graph (f(x) = -3x - 4, (x -5, 8), (y,-4,6))

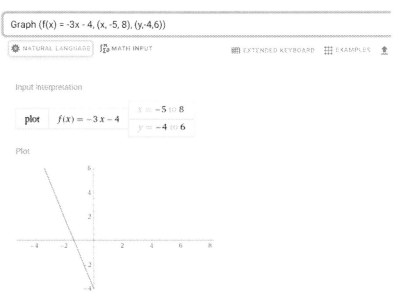

After teaching the concepts mentioned above, the teacher can redo the graphs shown to complement the explanation with topics related to increasing and decreasing functions. After this theme, one approach is work on the domain of a function and image of a function. To finish the explanation of the concepts, the teacher can use Wolfram Alpha to explain and demonstrate what the roots of a function would be (Figures 16, 17 and 18). Examples:

- Roots f(x) = x/2 + 2
- Roots f(x) = 2x + 4
- Roots f(x) = 3x + 3
- Roots f(x) = 4x + 6
- Roots f(x) = -4x - 3

After carrying out these activities in the classroom, the teacher can suggest to the students to reinforce the knowledge learned by building some graphs as homework.

Figure 16. Roots f(x) = x/2 + 2

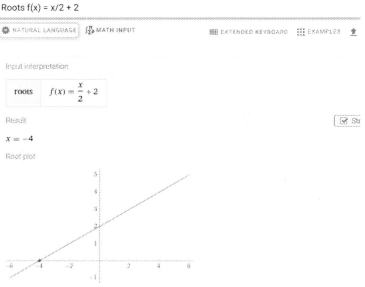

Figure 17. Roots f(x) = 3x + 3

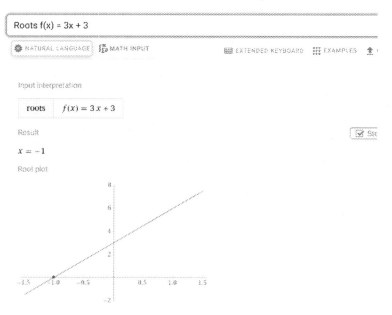

Benefits of Wolfram Alpha Tool to Interactive Learning Environments

Figure 18. Roots f(x) = -4x - 3

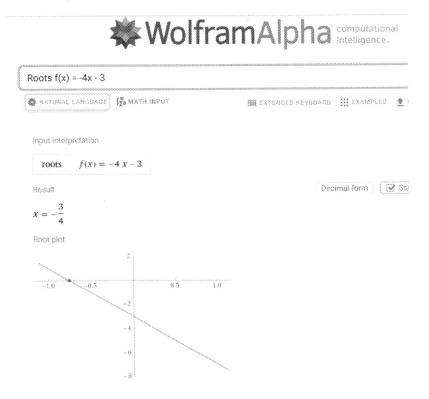

CONCLUSION AND FURTHER DIRECTIONS

According to PISA 2018 (Programme for International Student Assessment - 2018) BRASIL (2020), responsible for measuring the competences and learnings of students with 15 years old, 41% of Brazilian students are below level 1 of Mathematics learning, 27.1% have reached level 1 and 18.2% have reached level 2, the last level (level 6) was reached by 0.1% of the students who took the mathematics test. This data shows the importance of working with engagement and academic performance of Brazilian students. According to PISA 2018 BRASIL (2020) the students from municipal schools had the lower average of learning (314 points) when compared to the State schools (374 points), Federal schools (469 points) and private schools (473 points), within the students from Municipal schools the average of learning was below level 1 (minimum 358 points), due to these data the research was carried out in three classrooms with students age ranging from 14 to 15, at a Municipal public school in the city of São Paulo, Brazil. The qualitative results of the research carried out by the authors and presented in this chapter show that a remarkable quantity of students prefer the traditional classes and/or combined ones (that use traditional resources allied to the use of technology in the class), instead of classes that use technology as the main tool for learning. During the study, the students were positive that they find it easier to learn with traditional classes, mainly because they feel it's easier to register information on their notebooks. The quantitative results showed that the students had the best academic performance in classes where the applied methodology was the traditional or the combined method. The quantitative research has also shown by way of the pre-tests that the students who learned the contents of class one, by the Wolfram Alpha methodology had a lower percentage rate of attempts to solve the pre-test questions of class two when compared to the other two methodologies studied. In view of this results, this research leaves some topics for future investigations: the students' habit of learning through traditional classes might be hindering future innovations, as well as the use of new teaching methodologies could potentially bring more positive results than the use of digital resources. The overcoming of the mechanistic education with improved engagement of digital natives through meaningful learning is one of the great challenges that educators need to overcome daily in the classroom. Participating in training to update their teaching methods and adapt to new generations is fundamental for the evolution of the education STEM in schools.

For future works, is important to consider that this research had three main limitations: numbers of students, access to different school types (private, public, different parts of the city), and opportunity to study students in different grades, because of that, more studies are necessary to validate the findings. For future research directions, the authors recommend replicating this research in a larger scale, involving a greater number of public and private schools, and amplifying the diversity of students involved. It is important for future studies to consider other school grades, of high school students and is also suggested to replicate the research with middle school students. Having a customized teaching method for each student would be the best alternative, but when that is not an option it is necessary to figure out what is the ideal methodology for each group of students. This research contributes to illustrate how the use of technology can bring significant advances, even though the course of action must be adapted according to the context.

REFERENCES

Apiola, M., Lattu, M., & Pasanen, T. A. (2012). Creativity-supporting learning environment—Csle. [TOCE]. *ACM Transactions on Computing Education*, *12*(3), 1–25. doi:10.1145/2275597.2275600

Bimba, A. T., Idris, N., Al-Hunaiyyan, A., Mahmud, R. B., & Shuib, N. L. B. M. (2017). Adaptive feedback in computer-based learning environments: A review. *Adaptive Behavior*, *25*(5), 217–234. doi:10.1177/1059712317727590

BRASIL. (2020). *Relatório brasil no PISA 2018*. INEP/MEC.

Bredeweg, B., & Winkels, R. (1998). Qualitative models in interactive learning environments: An introduction. *Interactive Learning Environments*, *5*(1), 1–18. doi:10.1080/1049482980050101

Brezovszky, B., McMullen, J., Veermans, K., Hannula-Sormunen, M. M., Rodríguez-Aflecht, G., Pongsakdi, N., Laakkonen, E., & Lehtinen, E. (2019). Effects of a mathematics gamebased learning environment on primary school students' adaptive number knowledge. *Computers & Education*, *128*, 63–74. doi:10.1016/j.compedu.2018.09.011

Brown, D. J., Powell, H. M., Battersby, S., Lewis, J., Shopland, N., & Yazdanparast, M. (2002). Design guidelines for interactive multimedia learning environments to promote social inclusion. *Disability and Rehabilitation*, *24*(11-12), 587–597. doi:10.1080/09638280110111351 PMID:12182798

Costa, S. R. S., Duqueviz, B. C., & Pedroza, R. L. S. (2015). Tecnologias digitais como instrumentos mediadores da aprendizagem dos nativos digitais. *Psicologia Escolar e Educacional*, *19*(3), 603–610. doi:10.1590/2175-3539/2015/0193912

Ferreira, M., Silva Filho, O. L., Moreira, M. A., Franz, G. B., Portugal, K. O., & Nogueira, D. X. (2020). Unidade de ensino potencialmente significativa sobre óptica geométrica apoiada por vídeos, aplicativos e jogos para smartphones. *Revista Brasileira de Ensino de Física*, *42*, 42. doi:10.1590/1806-9126-rbef-2020-0057

Hazel, P. (2008). Toward a narrative pedagogy for interactive learning environments. *Interactive Learning Environments*, *16*(3), 199–213. doi:10.1080/10494820802113947

Hirschberg, J., & Manning, C. D. (2015). Advances in natural language processing. *Science*, *349*(6245), 261–266. doi:10.1126/science.aaa8685 PMID:26185244

Huang, C. (2003). Changing learning with new interactive and media-rich instruction environments: Virtual labs case study report. *Computerized Medical Imaging and Graphics*, *27*(2-3), 157–164. doi:10.1016/S0895-6111(02)00089-7 PMID:12620306

Hwang, G.-J., & Fu, Q.-K. (2020). Advancement and research trends of smart learning environments in the mobile era. *International Journal of Mobile Learning and Organization*, *14*(1), 114–129. doi:10.1504/IJMLO.2020.103911

Kim, H., & Ke, F. (2017). Effects of game-based learning in an open sim-supported virtual environment on mathematical performance. *Interactive Learning Environments*, *25*(4), 543–557. doi:10.1080/10494820.2016.1167744

Lin, K.-Y., Yu, K.-C., Hsiao, H.-S., Chang, Y.-S., & Chien, Y.-H. (2020). Effects of web-based versus classroom-based stem learning environments on the development of collaborative problem-solving skills in junior high school students. *International Journal of Technology and Design Education*, *30*(1), 21–34. doi:10.1007/s10798-018-9488-6

Lo, C. K., & Hew, K. F. (2020). A comparison of flipped learning with gamification, traditional learning, and online independent study: The effects on students' mathematics achievement and cognitive engagement. *Interactive Learning Environments*, *28*(4), 464–481. doi:10.1080/10494820.2018.1541910

Município, S. P. (2019). Secretaria municipal de educação. coordenadoria pedagógica. currículo da cidade: Ensino fundamental [ed. São Paulo: SME/COPED.]. *La Matematica*, 2.

Munoz, L., Villarreal, V., Morales, I., Gonzalez, J., & Nielsen, M. (2020). Developing an interactive environment through the teaching of mathematics with small robots. *Sensors (Basel)*, *20*(7), 1935. doi:10.3390/s20071935 PMID:32235658

Pan, Z., Zhu, J., Hu, W., Lun, H. P., & Zhou, X. (2005). Interactive learning of cg in networked virtual environments. *Computers & Graphics*, *29*(2), 273–281. doi:10.1016/j.cag.2004.12.014

Ribeiro, M. I. C., & Passos, O. M. (2020). A study on the active methodologies applied to teaching and learning process in the computing area. *IEEE Access : Practical Innovations, Open Solutions*, *8*, 219083–219097. doi:10.1109/ACCESS.2020.3036976

Santana, O. A., de Sousa, B. A., do Monte, S. R. S., de Freitas Lima, M. L., & Silva, C. F. (2020). Deep learning practice for high school student engagement in stem careers. In *2020 IEEE Global Engineering Education Conference (EDUCON)* (pp. 164–169). IEEE. 10.1109/EDUCON45650.2020.9125281

Serban, C., & Vescan, A. (2020). Towards an evaluation process around active learning based methods. In *2020 IEEE Frontiers in Education Conference (FIE)* (pp. 1–7). IEEE. 10.1109/FIE44824.2020.9273935

Teixeira, R. L. P., Silva, P. C. D., Shitsuka, R., de Araujo Brito, M. L., & Kaizer, B. M., & e Silva, P. D. C. (2020). Project based learning in engineering education in close collaboration with industry. In *2020 IEEE Global Engineering Education Conference (EDUCON)* (pp. 1945–1953). 10.1109/EDUCON45650.2020.9125341

Tokac, U., Novak, E., & Thompson, C. G. (2019). Effects of game-based learning on students' mathematics achievement: A meta-analysis. *Journal of Computer Assisted Learning*, *35*(3), 407–420. doi:10.1111/jcal.12347

Viberg, O., Gronlund, ¨. A., & Andersson, A. (2020). Integrating digital technology in math-˚ematics education: A Swedish case study. *Interactive Learning Environments*, 1–12.

Wolfram, S. (2017). *An elementary introduction to the wolfram language*. Wolfram Media, Incorporated.

Zhang, J.-H., Zou, L., Miao, J., Zhang, Y.-X., Hwang, G.-J., & Zhu, Y. (2020). An individualized intervention approach to improving university students' learning performance and interactive behaviors in a blended learning environment. *Interactive Learning Environments*, *28*(2), 231–245. doi:10.1080/10494820.2019.1636078

ENDNOTES

[1] Any device with internet access and a browser installed can use this tool that can be accessed through the website https://www.wolframalpha.com/.

Chapter 9
Smartphone and STEM

Alessio Drivet
Geogebra Institute of Turin, Italy

ABSTRACT

Covid-19 has also had a significant impact on schools, the use of distance learning has raised questions already present, in particular with respect to the meaning of tools and technologies. Leaving aside the aspects related to the use of the network and those of communication, the authors want to provide a brief overview of the fundamental issues related to the use of a smartphone for STEM teaching. A theme that sees two opposing positions (pros and cons) colliding, often unavailable for discussion and dialogue. Without taking a position, the text tackles the problem from three points of view: the hardware, the apps, and some possible activities that can be associated with the main functions activated by the students.

INTRODUCTION

The devastating COVID-19 pandemic and the consequent need to resort to Distance Learning (DAD in Italian) has forced students, teachers, and families to confront a largely unknown terrain. An educational path mediated by digital tools and the Internet requires appropriate devices, access to fast connections, and digital skills. However, it is essential to consider not only the effects that a given technology might have on the nature and quality of student learning but also the practices of teachers (Legrottaglie & Ligorio, 2014; Sinclair & Robutti, 2020).

When we ask ourselves which interdisciplinary approach to take and how to facilitate STEM learning, we should refer to the devices used, particularly smartphones. It is not trivial to say that it is an instrument considered almost an extension of the body. It is no coincidence that the term nomophobia has been coined to indicate

DOI: 10.4018/978-1-6684-5939-3.ch009

Copyright © 2024, IGI Global. Copying or distributing in print or electronic forms without written permission of IGI Global is prohibited.

the "addiction" to smartphones (Cheever, et al., 2018; Mahapatra, 2019; Wai Than & Pyae Wai Shan, 2021). There are many reflections (Crescenza, 2020; Criollo, et al., 2021; Garavaglia & Petti, 2020; Keough, 2021; Celestino, et al., 2020), research on this topic (González & Muñoz, 2020; Orben & Przybylski, 2019; Park & Kaye, 2019; Rodríguez-García, et al., 2020) and literature reviews (Busch & McCarthy, 2021; Fadda & Vivanet, 2021; Jahnke & Liebscher, 2020). Of particular significance are investigations to determine the relationship between Internet addiction, social media use disorders, and student smartphone addictions (Ramazanoglu, 2020).

Would smartphones (and tablets) be "harmful" to learning? Opinions, as often happens, are divergent. According to TIMSS (Trends in International Mathematics and Science Study), those who use mobile devices for a long time have worse results in science subjects; this seems to confirm the result of several surveys (Bravo-Sánchez, et al., 2021; Felisoni & Godoi, 2018; Lepp, et al., 2015). According to other experts, this is untrue if we focus on school performance (Kay, 2018; Abbasi, et al., 2021; Da Pra, 2021).

The prohibition or use of mobile phones depends on the same subjects involved in the education of young people: parents, teachers, and students themselves, and we must think of a pedagogy oriented to the search for guided knowledge (Cervantes-González & López, 2020).

It is, therefore, worth considering the smartphone as a teaching tool (Subramanya & Farahani, 2012). Research is particularly useful (Fowler & Stickney, 2020). The latter authors examined twenty-three applications that can be used to provide instruction with the smartphone (M-learning). They classified them into six categories: audience participation, presentation, collaboration, evaluation, news aggregators or curated content, and augmented reality.

Unfortunately, it should be emphasized that institutions have difficulty addressing these issues without falling into automatic biased approaches. Many institutions refer to numerous studies claiming that the more time a student spends on digital media, the worse his or her academic performance will be by damaging physical, emotional, mental, and social development. Many countries have taken these criticisms very seriously. In Australia, policies on the use of smartphones in the classroom may vary from school to school; some schools may allow their use for educational purposes, while others may ban them during classes. In the United Kingdom, use is generally left to the decisions of individual schools, but the percentage of those banning smartphones has risen sharply. Even in the United States, policies on smartphone use in the classroom are determined at the school district or individual school level. In China, phone use in school is often banned. In France, the use of phones in primary and middle schools has been banned since 2018. In Italy, the ban on the use of cell phones during classes has been in place since 2007. It has never been lifted even though a decalogue came out in 2017 that gave a positive interpretation of possible uses, an approach later overturned by the current Minister of Education and Merit.

There are often alternating moments of openness and moments of closure, and empirical research also presents various positions. To summarize, we could distinguish between total ban, specific restrictions, discretionary policies, and promotion of responsible use.

RESEARCH QUESTIONS

The text does not pretend to go into the merits of institutional policies but to address two issues:

1. Understand what is helpful for teachers regarding hardware and apps and from the perspective of broader teacher preparation;
2. To show some concrete examples (really tested) that can foster innovative teaching in the STEM field, especially concerning Middle and High School students. This choice stems from the fact that in Elementary School, the possession and use of smartphones is more problematic and less widespread; however, examples will also be found in the text at this school level.

To conclude the introduction, it is necessary to dwell on two fundamental aspects that should always be kept in mind, more so using tools such as those presented in the rest of the text:

1. The teacher does not convey content in a frontal lecture but guides students through experimental activities;
2. The student must formulate hypotheses, perform experiments, analyze the results, and finally come to conclusions.

We emphasize the fact that most of the literature on the subject focuses on evaluating the effectiveness of educational apps as teaching tools in STEM teaching and analyzing their impact on student learning. More simply, the text aims to introduce some elements that should form an information base for teachers, while showing how the resources could be used. For this reason, the topic is developed from three perspectives: Hardware, Applications (hereafter we will use the abbreviation app) and Activities.

HARDWARE

First, let us remember that the smartphone has sensory elements. We often use these extensions without being fully aware of them. There are several types, but a certain number of sensors can be found on all devices while others represent an added value only for certain devices. There is no complete agreement on the amount and type of sensors, but according to some, it is possible to find up to 30 "senses" on a recent, high-end smartphone. There is an extensive bibliography on the topic, but a few references with distinct points of view can help (Antar, et al., 2019; Gutiérrez, 2022; Su, et al., 2014; Zhuo, et al., 2020).

For an essential explanation of the sensors inside the smartphone, see (Liu, 2013); in the text, there is an image of some components present.

Without claiming to be exhaustive, below is a brief mention of the principal sensors. The choice is made mainly based on the activities presented below and to provide the teachers with food for thought.

Accelerometer: It is used to accurately measure the acceleration of the device (Jalal, et al., 2020); this is essential, for example, to make sure that once the smartphone is rotated, the image adapts to the position of the screen. Smartphones are equipped with three accelerometers, one for each axis. We can consider an accelerometer as a sphere to which springs that compress (or stretch) are attached. Measuring the degree to which the springs are compressed allows us to determine that there has been an acceleration in the direction in which the compressed spring is located. Many games take advantage of this tool as input; the latest implementations to support this device allow us to shake the smartphone providing a useful alternative to the classic buttons. In addition, as we will see later, some apps allow visualization of the data recorded by the sensor, allowing analysis of physical phenomena and verification of laws.

Barometer: the sensor can measure pressure and altitude using the device's built-in sensors. Since changes in atmospheric pressure normally indicate a change in weather, short-term weather changes can be monitored. The barometer can also be used in physics experiments to study the laws governing atmospheric pressure.

Brightness sensor: The smartphone uses the brightness sensor to automatically adapt the display's brightness to the ambient light and thus optimize the screen display. Data from this sensor can measure luminance. In mathematical terms, luminance is expressed as the ratio of the light intensity of the source placed in the observer's direction to the surface area perceived by the observer. Luminance is used to express the effective magnitude of a beam of light that has as its source a surface of a rather large size, taken in the direction of the observer of the light itself. A term not to be confused with illuminance, the latter expressed as the ratio of the luminous flux terminating on a surface to the area of the surface being considered.

Didactically, the brightness sensor could be used to study how light affects the growth of plants or animals.

Proximity sensor: The sensor bases the working principle on different technologies, such as emitting and receiving electromagnetic waves. The wave return makes it possible to detect the presence of an object and measure the distance at which it is located. In a school robotics project, the proximity sensor could be used to implement an obstacle avoidance system for a mobile robot. For example, the sensor detects obstacles in the robot's path and makes it change direction to avoid them.

Camera: The smartphone camera is for more than just taking photos and videos. In addition to functions such as automatically translating a text or scanning it, there are other interesting options. In elementary school, they can be used to document science experiments, collect visual data about nature, and conduct observation activities. For example, children can photograph the life cycle of a butterfly, or if they are conducting a plant growth experiment, they can take regular photos of plants to record changes over time. With a smartphone, it is possible to calculate the distance of an object from the user and its height using telemetry principles. One STEM use (Hergemöller & Laumann, 2017; Samsuar, et al., 2021) takes advantage of the ability to turn the smartphone into a microscope using lightweight accessory lenses that can fit all cell phone models. More technologically advanced microscopes on the market connect directly to a mobile device via a USB connection. At a higher cost, one can pair the smartphone with a thermal camera, measuring the radiation emitted by a body to obtain an estimate of temperature and, more importantly, fascinating colored images of the environment and bodies.

GPS: Navigation applications, such as Google Maps, have replaced many car navigators. The ability to pinpoint location and routes is based on GPS (Global Positioning System). GPS is also used by other apps to "geolocate," for example, the location of your car. Position tracking is based on exploiting radio signals generated by three satellites; the receiver, thanks to the travel time of the three signals, can calculate where it is on the planet with a little margin of error. In addition, with the signal sent by a fourth satellite, it is possible to synchronize the clock with the satellite. In this way, the smartphone becomes a satellite navigator and, in addition, allows it to be located in case of loss or theft. Of course, it is also possible to think of more educational applications, for example, in geosciences (Bursztyn, et al., 2015).

Gyroscope: It is a small rotating device that, respecting the law of conservation of angular momentum, maintains a fixed axis of rotation despite movement (Faisal, et al., 2019). With the gyroscope, one only needs to move the smartphone to shift the view within the video game or move virtual objects. As with the accelerometer, complex issues of physics and mathematics could be touched upon, but more simply, an experimental level of data collection and processing can be maintained.

Magnetometer: This sensor measures the strength and direction of a magnetic field. Using the magnetometer data, the frequency spectrum is calculated. It is used, for example, to understand the emission intensity from any device (radio, TV, PC, etc.), and, in this case, the numerical value of the emission can be significant in assessing its intensity. It allows, where present, the operation of various applications, such as a compass or metal detector. Since the smartphone magnetometer is used to measure and send information about the power and direction of the geomagnetic field on the X, Y, and Z axes to the connected device, it is possible to find extraordinary applications through the information received, such as controlling a drone.

NFC (Near Field Communication): This last tool uses technology to make two smartphones communicate quickly over a short distance. For example, we can make payments, exchange files, and connect to NFC tags. This tool could be important for cybersecurity education, for example, how NFC is used to transfer data and how attacks can exploit this technology to access sensitive data.

APP

Usually, to exploit these potentialities consciously, it is necessary to rely on apps. According to the latest 2023 data, there are 2.6 million Android apps, of which about 15 percent are for educational purposes.

Although less studied, the exciting aspect is the possibility of using more than one sensor simultaneously. For example, the simultaneous use of an accelerometer and gyroscope for mechanics problems (Monteiro & al., 2019). An interesting example in the literature is MobLeLab, a set of smartphone applications that allow the collection of scientific data. There are three types of MobLeLabs: simulators, built-in, and plug-in (Lellis-Santos & Abdulkader, 2020).

For completeness, we must distinguish between two types of apps (Bano, et al., 2018):

a) Self-developed: Researchers develop an app and then study its use for learning.
b) Third party: Teachers use a commercially developed app.

Only the second case will be examined in this text. Now, both Google Play Store and Apple App Store have many apps. For years, apps first originated on iOS (Apple's operating system), only to be ported to Android today; however, apps are developed almost immediately for both platforms. As most students own an Android smartphone, we will always refer to the applications available for this operating system.

One may wonder if one can use a smartphone to practice since the screen size may be limited compared to a computer, but the apps are designed for mobile devices and offer many features like desktop versions. Zooming and scrolling permit you to view content on the screen better.

The apps will be divided according to the principal use sector. Given the many education apps available, the choices represent only a tiny fraction of the possibilities. Obviously, this involves a subjective choice but justified by personal experience or known and easily reproduced experiments.

General App

There are specific apps and apps with general characteristics. Several are designed to create virtual classes to exchange information, documents, and notifications.

The best-known is *Google Classroom*, a platform part of Google Workspace for Education.

Seesaw has similar functions, a freemium application also available for mobile devices, which allows you to create a digital portfolio of students.

Particularly inspiring apps include the *MathCityMap* project (Barbosa & Vale, 2020; Buchholtz, 2020; Cahyono, 2018; Gurjanow, et al., 2020; Taranto, et al., 2020) and *Kahoot!* (Curto Prieto, et al., 2019; Wang & Tahir, 2020). The MathCityMap project was developed in Germany (in 2015) to encourage the school-based practice of outdoor mathematical activities. The project consists of two digital components: a web portal that allows students to build "mathematical trails" in the city with tasks based on objects observed with a mathematical eye and an application for mobile devices, which allows students to perform these trails alone or in groups, by answering proposed questions. Kahoot! is a tool typically used to check the outcome of a teaching or make competitions between participants. Users need only connect to the site, type the PIN that appears on the screen on their device, enter their name or nickname, and send the answer to a multiple-choice quiz question. They move on to the next question when the allotted time is up. Then, the correct answer appears, a histogram with the number of answers received for each option and a ranking. One can download the results to Excel for evaluation.

A similar resource is *Plickers*, particularly useful in relatively "low-tech" situations. The teacher asks a question to the class and uses their smartphone to collect the answers. Students have sheets of paper containing QR Codes that the teacher's smartphone scanner translates into answers. The app will record all the answers, which will be immediately reprocessed and available to the teacher.

Khan Academy is an online learning platform that offers video lessons, exercises, and study materials for many STEM topics, including math, science, and engineering. It is an educational app designed to teach STEM concepts at any school level.

App for Physics and Math

There are many applications in this area. We highlight some of the most popular and useful (Morales, et al., 2021; Zhelezniakov, et al., 2020).

PhET offers fun, interactive, accessible science and math simulations. Children are not superficial observers, but they interact with the simulations: they must click and drag, use sliders to change parameters and choose between distinct options. Everything has been designed for use on a PC or tablet, but one can download an app (with the payment of a small amount) to use the resources on a smartphone. Although many of the PhET simulations are designed primarily for high school students, some simulations can be adapted for elementary school students, depending on the student's level of understanding and the teacher's guidance. For example, one simulation allows students to explore the behavior of light as it passes through different materials. Another simulation allows students to explore the water cycle and how water transforms from liquid to gas and vice versa.

Phyphox can transform the smartphone into a real physics and mathematics laboratory (Pighini, 2020).

The app allows the smartphone's sensors to collect the necessary data for an experiment. One can conduct a free-fall experience using the acoustic stopwatch in the Phyphox app. The data collected from the various groups can be compared to determine the average value and introduce the error concept. In another experiment, one can determine the frequency of a pendulum using the accelerometer or measure the linear acceleration on an air track equipped with a series of magnets by exploiting field variations with the magnetometer. On the application's website, several indications exist for exploiting the device's potentialities. The relevant aspect is related to the possibility of developing non-standard skills in the search for information to develop the ability to highlight the essential properties of a particular experiment (Soboleva, et al., 2020).

Arduino Science Journal is an application that uses sensors integrated into the device to conduct experiments on the surrounding environment. For example, it allows one to measure the brightness level inside the room, use the barometer, record the movements perceived through acceleration on the different axes, or attach notes and voice notes via the microphone. To capture the data, start recording or use the snapshot function.

Among the apps that should be mentioned, there is also *Physics Toolbox Sensor Suite*, using the accelerometer, and thanks to the clear user interface, one can reproduce classic experiments such as the fall of bodies (Vogt & Kuhn, 2012) or analyze the behavior of a pendulum (Briggle, 2013).

Figure 1. Phyphox

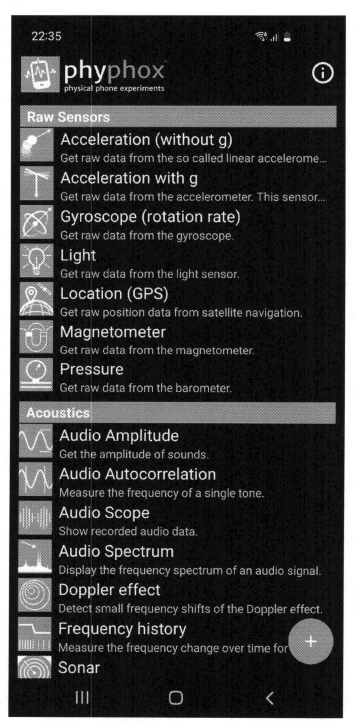

Smartphone and STEM

There are numerous apps with these characteristics, for example, *SPARKvue*, a software (for a fee after a trial period) that makes data collection, analysis, and sharing easy. The app is free, but given the small display size, it is preferable to do some practice on a PC. One of the interesting aspects of the product is that one can introduce students to coding and computer-controlled results with Blockly coding, a system that many students may have already encountered. Notoriously, Scratch is an ideal environment to introduce young people to the world of programming and, more generally, to problem-solving.

There are exciting applications if one wants to consider something that can facilitate learning mathematics.

Desmos is a graphing calculator that can create and display graphs of mathematical functions and solve problems in algebra and geometry.

In the field of geometry, it is possible to use *Geometrix*. The app instantly finds solutions to problems related to planes and solid figures. Of course, the level of use of this app must be calibrated according to the student's curriculum. For younger students, it can help them understand the characteristics of different geometric shapes and how they can calculate perimeter, area, etc. Older ones can measure themselves with more significant problems, such as answering the question: "Among all plane figures having the same perimeter, determine those having maximum area."

With *Microsoft Math Solver*, write a math problem with the virtual keyboard or use the camera to take a photo. The solver recognizes the problem immediately and helps solve it with step-by-step explanations, interactive graphs, similar problems from the web, and online video lessons. The supported problems cover a vast spectrum of mathematics: from arithmetic to algebra, from statistics to integrals.

Photomath is based on similar principles. It can produce software that can automatically "translate" the image of a written text into computational instructions. One of the advantages is that it allows seeing all the steps to arrive at the solution. To fully access the explanations, however, it is necessary to subscribe, which constitutes a limit to the full use of this resource.

In geometry, *Geometryx* is helpful; with this app, it is possible to calculate figures' most important values and parameters. The app calculates area, perimeter, segment lengths, angle measurements, etc. It also contains a useful form to understand direct and inverse formulas.

More specific is the *Probability Distributions* application, which calculates probabilities, determines percentiles, and plots the probability density function for the fundamental distributions: binomial, geometric, Poisson, normal, chi-square, etc.

Figure 2. Solution of a system with Photomath

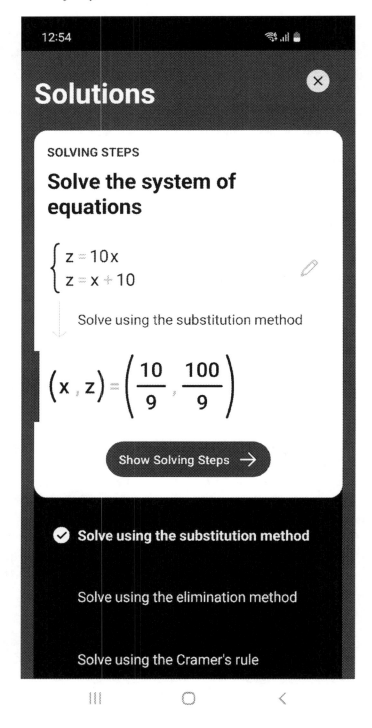

Figure 3. Example of calculating an ellipse

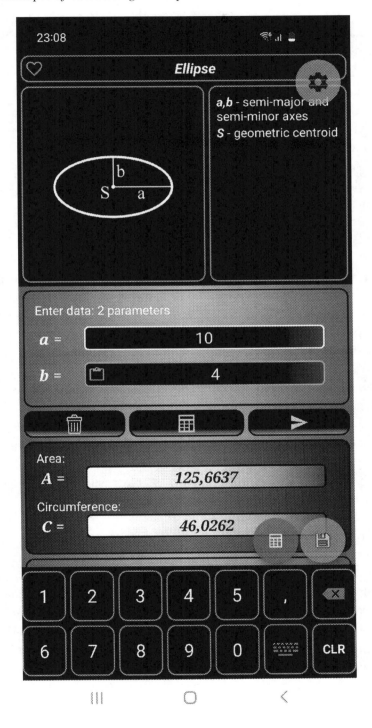

Finally, we must mention software that was born as a dynamic geometry system but whose subsequent developments have offered numerous tools for teaching activities: graphics, geometry, algebra, analysis, and statistics: *GeoGebra*. We must distinguish between several apps: GeoGebra Graphing Calculator, GeoGebra 3D Calculator, GeoGebra Geometry, and GeoGebra CAS Calculator. As the names indicate, these are apps intended for a specific field. However, it is advisable to download *GeoGebra Calculator Suite*, which incorporates all the above and, in addition, has the Probability function. For example, one can use this app to graph a function, change its parameters and see how the shape of the graph changes in real-time. As for geometry, one can work on figures, transformations, and basic geometry elements in 2D or 3D. The CAS calculator allows us to solve equations. As one can see, this is a versatile and highly effective tool.

App for Science

Changing area, *SkySafari* is a powerful pocket planetarium that puts the universe at the fingertips of the people and is easy to use. Quickly locate planets, constellations, satellites, and millions of stars and objects in the sky. Featuring rich graphics, it allows people to simulate the night sky from any part of the Earth for many years in the past or the future.

Staying in the same area, the *Solar System Scope* is a real-time model of the Solar System, the Night Sky, and Outer Space, with accurate positions of objects. One can find the online version running directly in the browser or mobile.

If one wants to range in animal and plant study, there are at least three applications to mention. *eBird*, from the Cornell Lab of Ornithology and the National Audubon Society, is the world's largest online bird-watching database. Data collected from smartphones of bird watchers worldwide and shared via the BirdLog app are made available to biologists, ornithologists, and environmental experts to track the richness and biodiversity of birds worldwide.

Another interesting app is *BirdNET*. The project uses artificial intelligence and neural networks to train computers to identify more than 3,000 of the most common species worldwide. People can record a file using their Android microphone and check if BirdNET correctly identifies the likely bird species in the recording.

Plantnet, on the other hand, is an application for collecting and identifying plants starting from a photo that is compared with the images of a botanical database. One can use PlantNet as early as elementary school as an introductory tool to learn the basic concepts of botany: what plants are and what the main parts are. Above all, during outdoor excursions, they should take photos of the plants they encounter and try to identify them later in class.

Figure 4. Plantnet

Figure 5. An example of chemical reaction

Chemistry Lab is an educational game to introduce the first elements of inorganic chemistry. This virtual lab provides more than 300 chemicals and nearly 1000 reactions.

For children aged 9-12, *Chemistry Lab* could be functional; this educational game introduces the first elements of inorganic chemistry, such as covalent bonds or balance equations.

Metal Detector measures the magnetic field with a magnetic sensor built into the smartphone. The magnetic field level (EMF) in nature is about 49μT (micro-Tesla). Any other ferromagnetic source alters the intensity of the magnetic field and, therefore, can be detected.

Magnetic Field Sensor measures the amplitude of a magnetic field using the Android phone magnetometer to measure the strength of magnetic fields. According to the developer, the EMF detector serves study purposes and is designed for electrical engineering students.

Sound level meter shows a decibel (dB) value by measuring the environmental noise. There is a limitation because the microphones of Android devices are meant for the human voice. Loud sounds (over 90 dB) cannot be recognized.

App for Robotics and Augmented Reality

A space dedicated to robotics could not be missing. From the earliest years of school, there are meaningful experiences, for example, programming Lego Mindstorms robots: students work in small groups to build and program robots. This experience combines physical construction, programming, and problem-solving. The smartphone guides the robot via voice commands in a more advanced example. In a fairly recent project (Andreotti, et al., 2021), the *MARRtino* app was created to translate voice commands into text that is then sent and can be interpreted by the program developed by the student to control the robot. It is correct to talk about a hardware and software platform to build robots simply and cost-effectively. A notable example in robotics is DuBot: an Open-Source robot for STEM and Educational Robotics (Chatzopoulos, et al., 2021).

One area on which efforts have focused is augmented reality, which is an interactive experience of a real environment where objects that reside in the real world are "augmented" by computer-generated perceptual information (Huang, et al., 2019; Padilla, et al., 2021; Yuzbasheva & Kravtsov, 2020).

Virtual reality (VR) and augmented reality (AR) help students see how abstract mathematical concepts work in a three-dimensional (3D) environment. To evaluate its potential simply and without having special equipment, download the Math VR app and print the marker proposed on the site to see the mathematical models come to life!

More generally, we can take the following quotation as the basis of the discussion: «The use of VR in education has grown dramatically in recent years due to drastic improvements in technology and low manufacturing cost. Drop-in prices have made VR more accessible to schools. The use of VR in the classroom allowed students to interact with unobservable phenomena, to take virtual trips, and increased students' motivation, engagement, and creativity. Further, using these tools allowed teachers to act as a facilitator in the classroom» (Yildirim & al., 2020, p.241).

The subdivision chosen so far is only one of many possible; one could examine the apps regarding collaboration, evaluation, and other features. For example, some of the apps presented may fall into the following areas:

- Online collaboration tools: Apps that allow students to work together on projects, communicate, and share STEM resources in real-time (Google Classroom, Seesaw).
- Formative assessment apps: Tools to create quizzes, tests, and assessment activities to measure student knowledge (Kahoot!, Plickers).
- Virtual laboratory apps: Simulations and interactive environments allow students to perform virtual experiments on scientific concepts (PhET, Chemistry Lab).
- Support teaching tools: many programs can constitute a learning tool or even help conduct specific tasks (Photomath, GeoGebra).

ACTIVITIES

Having looked at the hardware and software aspects, we want to consider some activities that could concern a smartphone owner. Reference will be made to topics that are (or could be) part of the school curricula or topics close to the wishes and behaviors of young people in this age group. The reference will always be to the use of the apps. In this case, we can limit ourselves to a few significant examples, remembering that all examples refer to activities developed in school settings.

Solving a math problem: The field is vast in that one can start from a problem suitable for elementary school to very complex types. In the first case, one might ask, "Ada has eight candies and, after eating three, gives two to Bruce. How many candies are left?" In the second case, one could ask how to deal with Zeno's paradox by asking, " Achilles runs at ten m/s, the Turtle moves at one m/s. If the Turtle has a 10 m lead, will Achilles catch up? If so, when?" Using, for example, Microsoft Math Solver or Photomath, one can write the mathematical models of the two problems on a sheet of paper and then take a picture. Appropriate comments will follow the results.

Verify the solution of geometric problems: An example would be to verify why Dido, cutting the skin of an ox into skinny strips, chose the geometrically optimal solution (between equilateral triangle, square, and semicircle) to found Carthage. Dido wanted to build a city on the sea, so she probably used the stripes to delimit a region adjacent to the coast to get a more extensive area; therefore, this element must be considered (Drivet, 2021). To explain to students that, with the same perimeter, the area of the circle is greater than that of the equilateral triangle and the square, a series of concrete examples and visual images can be used: using a ruler and compass to draw a circle with a given radius and an equilateral square or triangle with the same perimeter, using a graph to show how the area of the circle grows faster than the perimeter of an equilateral square or triangle, using mathematical formulas, etc. Taking advantage of *Geometryx*, on the other hand, is the immediate verification of which figure has the largest area at the same perimeter.

Online Games: Many kids play slots, blackjack, or roulette on their phones. A prudent position might be to direct them towards real online games more traditionally related to mathematics: riddles, logic tests, calculus tests, sudoku, skyscraper games, etc. By overcoming the teachers' reluctance for gambling, one can address questions relating to the calculus of probabilities, particularly the concept of expected value. A reference to linear functions can refer (in a less traditional but equally effective way) to the control of the loss function for some games. The material used in the BETonMATH experiment (Andrà, et al., 2018) is worth mentioning, a mathematics experience to prevent gambling abuse among secondary school students. The apps included in the project are handy for teaching purposes: *Scratch and Lose* simulate one or more "scratches" of the symbols present on the ticket of this instant lottery.

Sending an SMS: What happens when people send an SMS? People do not send a message written in letters; the text is encoded, and each letter is translated into a series of 1s and 0s via the American Standard Code for Information Interchange (ASCII). For example, 097 is the ASCII numerical representation of the character "a"; the message "test" translates into "112 114 111 118 097. At this point, it is a question of converting the characters into a binary representation: "01110000 01110010 01101111 01110110 01100001." It is an exercise that requires the knowledge of data encodings and the ability to encode alphanumeric information and recognize the distinct types of information.

It is possible to find numerous converters and apps on the net, such as *Text Converter Encoder Decoder Stylish Text*. However, this can only be a small introductory step toward fascinating topics. Think of the application of encodings to steganography, a technique that aims to hide the communication between two interlocutors (Mishra, et al., 2018; Naharuddin, et al., 2018).

Figure 6. Result of 100 scratches

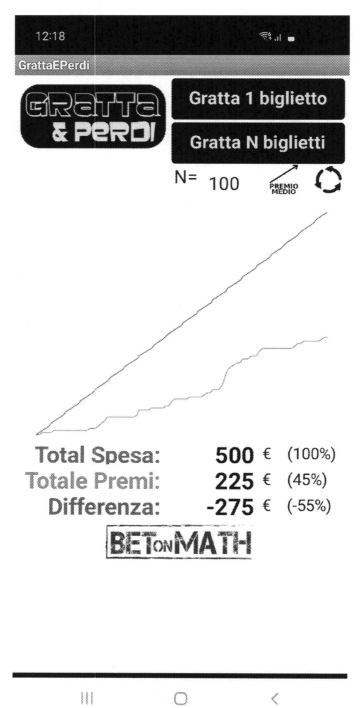

After giving space to mathematics, we can refer to another hard discipline, physics. Once again, the focus is on more than just the multiplicity of experiments that can be done with a smartphone, transforming a classroom into a laboratory. On this subject, there is immense literature focused both on the use of smartphones to simulate more classical physics experiments (Dahnuss, et al., 2021; Salinas, et al., 2019) and on the analysis of the state of research and methodological approaches (Malndonado, et al., 2022; Nuryantini, et al., 2019). This contribution presents less traditional experiences closer to students' interests and daily lives. It will then be up to the teacher to put these topics into a didactic framework.

Rotation of a salad spinner: To analyze the functioning of a salad spinner (Giusti, 2004) using the accelerometer, place the smartphone on the spinner so it is well stable. Start the centrifuge and press the "start" button on the Phyphox application to log accelerometer data. Once the centrifuge has reached the desired speed, the recording stops. Thanks to the recorded data, it will be possible to display a graph of the acceleration as a function of time. Suppose to analyze the rotation of the centrifuge. In that case, put the smartphone inside the centrifuge and use the centripetal acceleration function, which provides the angular velocity data (rad/s) and its square. Calculating the rotations per minute (multiplied by 9.55) is a good exercise. We must ask ourselves if these are enough to largely eliminate the water from the salad. Similar experiments can be done based on abundant indications in the literature (Vieyra, et al., 2015; Fahsl & Vogt, 2019; Monteiro, et al., 2022).

Time of fall of an object: The free fall experience can be conducted using the acoustic stopwatch of the Phyphox app (Leone, et al., 2022). The acoustic stopwatch starts as soon as the object is released; the time stops when it hits the ground. The data can be processed to verify the relationship between fall time and height, examine the graph, and derive regression parameters. In the second step, the t-s graph can be compared with the t-v graph, which can be obtained from the theoretical formula. A question arises: from what height can the differences between the two graphs be clearly recognized? This way, students can conduct a free-fall experience using only their mobile device and the Phyphox app without needing expensive equipment or a controlled laboratory environment.

Creating a musical ensemble with poor objects: The theme is taken from a paper (Giannelli, 2015), which presents three simple acoustic experiments conducted using a smartphone and some objects available in any kitchen. The first experiment measures the fundamental frequency of the sound emitted by a glass when one slides a wet finger along the edge and determines the different values as the water level varies. In the second case, four saucepan lids are used, the lid is struck, and the fundamental frequencies of the sounds emitted are measured. Finally, as a wind instrument, the frequency emitted by a tube of "bucatini" type pasta is determined when you close one end with your finger and blow into the other. A real "band" whose results can lead to an analysis of the direct and inverse proportionality relationships based on the frequency graphs obtained.

Widening the horizon to other disciplines, we can point out other examples.

Measuring the sound of a chemical reaction: The operation is quite simple. Just have some chemical elements available and use one of the apps already seen. Mix baking soda and vinegar (or lemon juice), then a base and an acid. The sound sensor should be able to detect the "fizzing" sound that accompanies the reaction. As the reaction unfolds, students can see the duration of the reaction from the graph and the changes recorded. It is recommended to use the "Audio Spectrum" function to measure the sound of a chemical reaction with Phyphox. The "Audio Spectrum" function provides a frequency analysis of the sound wave, showing the distribution of the different frequencies across the sound. This is useful for determining the frequency composition of the sound emitted by the chemical reaction, which can be used to distinguish different reactions or to study the relationship between the frequency composition of the sound and the chemical conditions. The "Audio Amplitude" function displays the overall sound level as a function of time, showing how the amplitude of the sound wave changes over time. It helps observe how the sound level of the chemical reaction changes over time. The "Audio Scope" function displays the waveform of the sound, showing the sound wave's shape over time, including its frequency content and amplitude. Of course, this experiment in acoustics can be accompanied by many others (Kuhn & Vogt, 2013; D'Ambrosio, 2015).

Identify pollutants: Parameters that affect water quality in the environment include multiple factors, including turbidity. Its measurement can offer valuable information on drinking water quality. Water turbidity is related to what is "clear" water. Suppose one has collected several water samples with different degrees of turbidity; using the light sensor, students can compare these samples. Of course, since the intensity of transmitted light decreases as the water column height between the light source and the cell phone sensor increases, care must be taken in setting up the experiment. Through this experiment, it is possible to see how light intensity varies as a function of the liquid present and calculate its transmittance, which is the ratio of transmitted intensity to incident intensity.

Measuring air quality: Air quality measurement apps can be used educationally to help students better understand the impact of the environment on their health and well-being. There are several apps available that can help measure air quality. For example, *IQAir* provides local data from anonymous contributors or data averages.

Smartphone and STEM

Figure 7. Data from some cities in the world

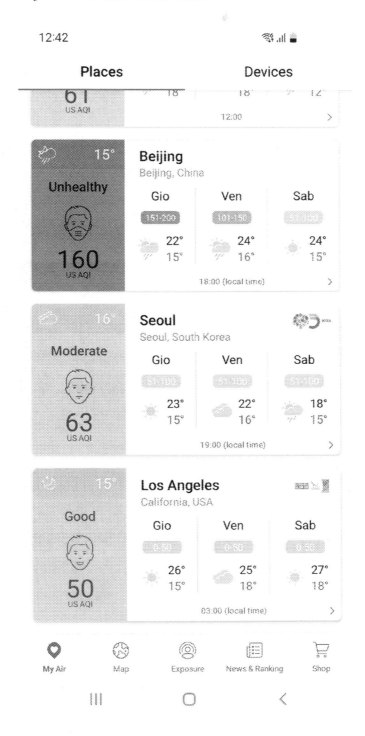

The exciting aspect is that by opening the Map option, comparisons with other large cities worldwide are possible. The local data can be viewed at home, work, and outside levels. Students can use the app to measure the air quality in their area and compare the results with other areas of the city or the world. This can help them understand how the environment affects air quality, climate, and health (Dominski, et al., 2021; Yang, et al., 2019). Alternatively, one can use *Air Quality Index* (Plaia, A., & Ruggieri, 2011), which has a different interface. The problem, which can be referred to other apps as well, is that it could be a privacy-risky app as it collects a range of information such as location, IP and stored data. However, it has excluded the presence of malware.

A tip: it is useful to compare the results with specialized websites on air quality and air pollution issues; they can provide additional information on these topics to compare with the collected data. These activities not only encouraged students to carry out environmental projects involving the assessment and improvement of air quality with the supervision of their teachers, but the use of a color scale (green represents good air, while red represents polluted air) served to introduce the interpretation of color schemes used in real-world situations, such as in graphic design, advertising, weather maps, traffic signs, etc. An interesting and recent experience on air quality, using augmented reality, conducted on a sample of children aged 7-11 years can be found in (Fernandes, et al., 2023).

Geolocation experiences: The use of GPS can facilitate many experiences. At the elementary school level, a simple goal can be set for exploration, such as finding specific landmarks in one's neighborhood; after reaching the designated point, students record its coordinates by adding geographic information. At the high school level, with the help of a " blank" map, information such as housing, roads, reliefs, and points of interest can be transferred to the map.

Let us move towards the more strictly technological sphere. An ever-growing population (including older students) is showing that they are making payments via mobile phones as an alternative to more traditional forms of payment. For example, we can analyze the status of Near Field Communication (NFC) mobile payment systems in public transport (Liébana-Cabanillas, et al., 2019) or in commercial enterprises for contactless payments. It is possible to place NFC tags that give the visitor information even in museums or places of tourist interest, so in a school trip, it is possible to collect information and suggestions for research. The problems related to the use of NFC can be stated on three levels: the first is that of the underlying technology communication, the second is related to the definition of protocols, and the third is related to security (Giese, et al., 2019). In the first case, NFC tags are small circuits in which a tiny amount of readable data is saved by approaching a device with NFC activated. As for the programming aspect, NFC Tools is an app that allows one to read and write specific tasks. To program, one must also download the NFC Tasks app.

To conclude this overview, we want to highlight two special utilities:

Mobile to PC Screen Mirroring / Sharing. The app allows users to share their Android mobile screen on a PC. It is necessary to connect both devices to the same network, open the PC browser and enter the proposed IP address. Now, it is possible to start mirroring. In a classroom equipped with an IWB, sharing what is on the smartphone will be possible.

ApowerMirror is another application that mirrors the computer's Android (or iPhone) screen. In this case, one must connect the devices to the same Wi-Fi or with a USB cable for smartphones with the Android operating system.

CONCLUSION

For obvious reasons of space, the text has just shown the tip of the iceberg of the problem. Although much has been written and spoken on the subject, and there have been several experiments, much remains to be discovered. Let us take mathematics as an example. Its history is full of tools that have allowed us to move forward, freeing ourselves from exhausting struggles on the level of calculation to concentrate on contents. Some examples are abacus, Napier's sticks, logarithmic tables, slide rules, pocket calculator, computer. The smartphone represents a different step in that it can open new horizons as an actual concentration of technology. As we have tried to demonstrate, common activities cover several fields of the STEM disciplines. The smartphone can increasingly become essential for teaching technology in higher education. The smartphone can increasingly become a key component of teaching technology in education and other tools such as iPads/tablets/Chromebooks.

Currently, numerous researchers associate M-learning with TAM, the technology acceptance model (Al-Rahmi, et al., 2021; Alsharida, et al., 2021; Gupta, et al., 2021; Hwang, et al.,2021). This is a significant field, and it is useful that further research explores this topic.

One final question: How can smartphones be used in teaching if they are banned in many schools?

REFERENCES

Abbasi, G. A., Jagaveeran, M., Goh, Y. N., & Tariq, B. (2021). The impact of type of content use on smartphone addiction and academic performance: Physical activity as moderator. *Technology in Society, 64*, 101521. doi:10.1016/j.techsoc.2020.101521

Al-Rahmi, A. M., Al-Rahmi, W. M., Alturki, U., Aldraiweesh, A., Almutairy, S., & Al-Adwan, A. S. (2021). Exploring the factors affecting mobile learning for sustainability in higher education. *Sustainability (Basel), 13*(14), 7893. doi:10.3390/su13147893

Alsharida, R., Hammood, M., & Al-Emran, M. (2021). Mobile learning adoption: A systematic review of the technology acceptance model from 2017 to 2020. [iJET]. *International Journal of Emerging Technologies in Learning, 16*(5), 147–162. doi:10.3991/ijet.v16i05.18093

Andrà, C., Verani, M., & Parolini, N. (2018). BetOnMath: Azzardo e matematica a scuola. *BetOnMath: azzardo e matematica a scuola*, 119-121.

Andreotti, M., Astone, P., Campana, D., Cartoni, A., Casaburo, F., Cavanna, F., & Tehrani, F. S. (2021). Il progetto Lab2Go per la diffusione della pratica laboratoriale nelle Scuole Secondarie di II grado. *arXiv preprint arXiv:2106.08308*.

Antar, A. D., Ahmed, M., & Ahad, M. A. R. (2019, May). Challenges in sensor-based human activity recognition and a comparative analysis of benchmark datasets: a review. In *2019 Joint 8th International Conference on Informatics, Electronics & Vision (ICIEV) and 2019 3rd International Conference on Imaging, Vision & Pattern Recognition (icIVPR)* (pp. 134-139). IEEE.

Bano, M., Zowghi, D., Kearney, M., Schuck, S., & Aubusson, P. (2018). Mobile learning for science and mathematics school education: A systematic review of empirical evidence. *Computers & Education, 121*, 30–58. doi:10.1016/j.compedu.2018.02.006

Barbosa, A., & Vale, I. (2020). Math trails through digital technology: An experience with pre-service teachers. *Research on Outdoor STEM Education in the digiTal Age, 47*.

Bravo-Sánchez, A., Morán-García, J., Abián, P., & Abián-Vicén, J. (2021). Association of the use of the mobile phone with physical fitness and academic performance: A cross-sectional study. *International Journal of Environmental Research and Public Health, 18*(3), 1042. doi:10.3390/ijerph18031042 PMID:33503943

Briggle, J. (2013). Analysis of pendulum period with an iPod touch/iPhone. *Physics Education, 48*(3), 285–288. doi:10.1088/0031-9120/48/3/285

Buchholtz, N. (2020, June). The Norwegian study math & the city on mobile learning with math trails. In *Research on Outdoor STEM Education in the digital Age. Proceedings of the ROSETA Online Conference in June 2020* (pp. 79-86). ACM. 10.37626/GA9783959871440.0.10

Bursztyn, N., Pederson, J., Shelton, B., Walker, A., & Campbell, T. (2015). Utilizing Geo-Referenced Mobile Game Technology for Universally Accessible Virtual Geology Field Trips. *International Journal of Education in Mathematics. Science and Technology*, *3*(2), 93–100.

Busch, P. A., & McCarthy, S. (2021). Antecedents and consequences of problematic smartphone use: A systematic literature review of an emerging research area. *Computers in Human Behavior*, *114*, 106414. doi:10.1016/j.chb.2020.106414

Cahyono, A. N. (2018). Learning mathematics in a mobile app-supported math trail environment. Chem: Springer International Publishing. doi:10.1007/978-3-319-93245-3

Celestino, R. & al. (2020). The cell phone in the classroom: Prohibitions, possibilities and reflections. *Revista Científica Multidisciplinar Núcleo do Conhecimento. 6*, 85-104.

Cervantes-González, E., & López, M. S. H. (2020). El móvil en las aulas de clase: ¿Se prohíbe o se incluye? *Emprennova*, *1*(1), 7–23.

Chatzopoulos, A., Kalogiannakis, M., Papadakis, S., Papoutsidakis, M., Elza, D., & Psycharis, S. (2021). DuBot: An open-source, low-cost robot for STEM and educational robotics. In Research Anthology on Usage and Development of Open Source Software (pp. 329-353). IGI Global.

Cheever, N. A., Moreno, M. A., & Rosen, L. D. (2018). When does internet and smartphone use become a problem?. *Technology and adolescent mental health*, 121-131.

Crescenza, G. (2020). Dal calamaio alla Didattica a distanza. La scuola ai tempi del COVID-19.

Criollo-C, S., Guerrero-Arias, A., Jaramillo-Alcázar, Á., & Luján-Mora, S. (2021). Mobile learning technologies for education: Benefits and pending issues. *Applied Sciences (Basel, Switzerland)*, *11*(9), 4111. doi:10.3390/app11094111

Curto Prieto, M., Orcos Palma, L., Blázquez Tobías, P. J., & León, F. J. M. (2019). Student assessment of the use of Kahoot in the learning process of science and mathematics. *Education Sciences*, *9*(1), 55. doi:10.3390/educsci9010055

D'Ambrosio, A. (2015). Esperimenti di acustica con smartphone. *Italian Journal of Educational Technology*, *23*(3), 176–180.

Da Pra, L. M. G. (2021). *Mobile learning: esempi di buona pratica basata sull'uso dello smartphone in classe.*

Dahnuss, D., Marwoto, P., Iswari, R. S., & Listiaji, P. (2021, June). Marbles and smartphone on physics laboratory: An investigation for finding coefficient of restitution. []). IOP Publishing.]. *Journal of Physics: Conference Series, 1918*(2), 022005. doi:10.1088/1742-6596/1918/2/022005

Dominski, F. H., Branco, J. H. L., Buonanno, G., Stabile, L., da Silva, M. G., & Andrade, A. (2021). Effects of air pollution on health: A mapping review of systematic reviews and meta-analyses. *Environmental Research, 201*, 111487. doi:10.1016/j.envres.2021.111487 PMID:34116013

Drivet, A. (2021). Examining an Operational Approach to Teaching Probability. IGI Global. doi:10.4018/978-1-7998-3871-5

Fadda, D., & Vivanet, G. (2021). Tecnologie digitali e didattica laboratoriale nell'educazione STEM. Evidenze scientifiche e raccomandazioni pratiche. *Collana "Quaderni dell'Osservatorio", 37*.

Fahsl, C., & Vogt, P. (2019). Determination of the radius of curves and roundabouts with a smartphone. *The Physics Teacher, 57*(8), 566–567. doi:10.1119/1.5131133

Faisal, I. A., Purboyo, T. W., & Ansori, A. S. R. (2019). A Review of accelerometer sensor and gyroscope sensor in IMU sensors on motion capture. *Journal of Engineering and Applied Sciences (Asian Research Publishing Network), 15*(3), 826–829.

Felisoni, D. D., & Godoi, A. S. (2018). Cell phone usage and academic performance: An experiment. *Computers & Education, 117*, 175–187. doi:10.1016/j.compedu.2017.10.006

Fernandes, J., Brandão, T., Almeida, S. M., & Santana, P. (2023). An educational game to teach children about air quality using augmented reality and tangible interaction with sensors. *International Journal of Environmental Research and Public Health, 20*(5), 3814. doi:10.3390/ijerph20053814 PMID:36900825

Fowler, D. C., & Stickney, L. T. (2020). Smartphone apps for use in management education. Handbook of Teaching with Technology in Management, Leadership, and Business, 263-275.

Garavaglia, A., & Petti, L. (2020). Strategie di uso dello smartphone degli studenti della scuola secondaria di secondo grado= Secondary school students' strategies for using the smartphone. *SIRD, 3*, 40–50.

Giannelli, F. (2015). Acustica in cucina. *La Fisica nella Scuola*, XLVIII, 1.

Giusti, E. (2004). La matematica in cucina. *Bollati Boringhieri*. 104-112.

González, E. B., & Muñoz, G. N. E. (2020). Implicaciones educativas del uso de dispositivos móviles en el aula: posibilidades y dificultades psicopedagógicas. *Aproximación periodística y educomunicativa al fenómeno de las redes sociales*, 571.

Gupta, Y., Khan, F. M., & Agarwal, S. (2021). Exploring Factors Influencing Mobile Learning in Higher Education-A Systematic Review. *International Journal of Interactive Mobile Technologies*, *15*(12), 140. doi:10.3991/ijim.v15i12.22503

Gurjanow, I., Zender, J., & Ludwig, M. (2020, June). MathCityMap–Popularizing mathematics around the globe with math trails and smartphone. In *Research on Outdoor STEM Education in the digital Age. Proceedings of the ROSETA Online Conference in June 2020* (pp. 103-110). ACM. 10.37626/GA9783959871440.0.13

Gutiérrez, J. D., Jiménez, A. R., Seco, F., Álvarez, F. J., Aguilera, T., Torres-Sospedra, J., & Melchor, F. (2022). GetSensorData: An extensible Android-based application for multi-sensor data registration. *SoftwareX*, *19*, 101186. doi:10.1016/j.softx.2022.101186

Hergemöller, T., & Laumann, D. (2017). Smartphone magnification attachment: Microscope or magnifying glass. *The Physics Teacher*, *55*(6), 361–364. doi:10.1119/1.4999732

Huang, K. T., Ball, C., Francis, J., Ratan, R., Boumis, J., & Fordham, J. (2019). Augmented versus virtual reality in education: An exploratory study examining science knowledge retention when using augmented reality/virtual reality mobile applications. *Cyberpsychology, Behavior, and Social Networking*, *22*(2), 105–110. doi:10.1089/cyber.2018.0150 PMID:30657334

Hwang, B. L., Chou, T. C., & Huang, C. H. (2021). Actualizing the affordance of mobile technology for mobile learning. *Journal of Educational Technology & Society*, *24*(4), 67–80.

Jahnke, I., & Liebscher, J. (2020). Three types of integrated course designs for using mobile technologies to support creativity in higher education. *Computers & Education*, *146*, 103782. doi:10.1016/j.compedu.2019.103782

Jalal, A., Quaid, M. A. K., Tahir, S. B. U. D., & Kim, K. (2020). A study of accelerometer and gyroscope measurements in physical life-log activities detection systems. *Sensors (Basel)*, *20*(22), 6670. doi:10.3390/s20226670 PMID:33233412

Kalana, M. H., Junaini, S. N., & Fauzi, A. H. (2020). Mobile augmented reality for biology learning: Review and design recommendations. *Journal of Critical Reviews*, *7*(12), 579–585.

Kay, R. (2018). Examining individual differences in the use of STEM-based mobile apps. In *EDULEARN18 Proceedings* (pp. 2069-2076). IATED. 10.21125/edulearn.2018.0577

Keough, P. D. (Ed.). (2021). *Educational Recovery for PK-12 Education During and After a Pandemic*. IGI Global. doi:10.4018/978-1-7998-6952-8

Kuhn, J., & Vogt, P. (2013). Analyzing acoustic phenomena with a smartphone microphone. *The Physics Teacher*, *51*(2), 118–119. doi:10.1119/1.4775539

Legrottaglie, S., & Ligorio, M. B. (2014). L'uso delle tecnologie a scuola: Il punto di vista dei docenti. *Italian Journal of Educational Technology*, *22*(3), 183–190.

Lellis-Santos, C., & Abdulkader, F. (2020). Smartphone-assisted experimentation as a didactic strategy to maintain practical lessons in remote education: Alternatives for physiology education during the COVID-19 pandemic. *Advances in Physiology Education*, *44*(4), 579–586. doi:10.1152/advan.00066.2020 PMID:32955344

Leone, P., Quatraro, F., & Giorgio, I. (2022). *Scienze per il Futuro, un percorso STEM in*. Atti DIDAMATICA.

Lepp, A., Barkley, J. E., & Karpinski, A. C. (2015). The relationship between cell phone use and academic performance in a sample of US college students. *SAGE Open*, *5*(1), 2158244015573169. doi:10.1177/2158244015573169

Liu, M. (2013). A study of mobile sensing using smartphones. *International Journal of Distributed Sensor Networks*, *9*(3), 272916. doi:10.1155/2013/272916

Mahapatra, S. (2019). Smartphone addiction and associated consequences: Role of loneliness and self-regulation. *Behaviour & Information Technology*, *38*(8), 833–844. doi:10.1080/0144929X.2018.1560499

Malndonado, E. A., Ramírez, P., & Avendaño, W. R. (2022). Smartphone and teamwork as a methodological tool for teaching and learning physics. [). IOP Publishing.]. *Journal of Physics: Conference Series*, *2159*(1), 012020. doi:10.1088/1742-6596/2159/1/012020

Mishra, S., Yadav, V. K., Trivedi, M. C., & Shrimali, T. (2018). Audio steganography techniques: A survey. In *Advances in Computer and Computational Sciences: Proceedings of ICCCCS 2016,* Volume 2 (pp. 581-589). Springer Singapore.

Monteiro, M., Cabeza, C., Martí, A., Vogt, P., & Kuhn, J. (2014). Angular velocity and centripetal acceleration relationship. *The Physics Teacher*, *52*(5), 312–313. Advance online publication. doi:10.1119/1.4872422

Monteiro, M., Stari, C., Cabeza, C., & Marti, A. C. (2019, August). Physics experiments using simultaneously more than one smartphone sensors. [). IOP Publishing.]. *Journal of Physics: Conference Series*, *1287*(1), 012058. doi:10.1088/1742-6596/1287/1/012058

Morales, L. G. C., Chicaiza, C. V. V., Valles, V. M. R., & Armas, J. A. C. (2021). El Software Microsoft Math Solver como recurso tecnológico para la resolución de problemas de Matemática. *Revista Conrado*, *17*(S1), 168–175.

Naharuddin, A., Wibawa, A. D., & Sumpeno, S. (2018, August). A high capacity and imperceptible text steganography using binary digit mapping on ASCII characters. In *2018 International Seminar on Intelligent Technology and Its Applications (ISITIA)* (pp. 287-292). IEEE. 10.1109/ISITIA.2018.8711087

Nuryantini, A. Y., & Yudhiantara, R. A. (2019). The Use of Mobile Application as a Media in Physics Learning. *Jurnal Penelitian dan Pembelajaran IPA, 5*(1), 72-83.

Orben, A., & Przybylski, A. K. (2019). The association between adolescent well-being and digital technology use. *Nature Human Behaviour*, *3*(2), 173–182. doi:10.1038/s41562-018-0506-1 PMID:30944443

Padilla, D. B., Martínez, A. J., Bravo, C. B., & Meneses, E. L. (2021). Didactic resources in augmented reality to improve ubiquitous learning. In *Accessibility of vulnerability Groups: from ICTS to Emotions* (pp. 25–42). Dykinson. doi:10.2307/j.ctv282jg7b.5

Park, C. S., & Kaye, B. K. (2019). Smartphone and self-extension: Functionally, anthropomorphically, and ontologically extending self via the smartphone. *Mobile Media & Communication*, *7*(2), 215–231. doi:10.1177/2050157918808327

Pighini, C. (2020). *Development and evaluation of an Android app to exploit smartphone-embedded camera and inertial sensors for monitoring of physiological parameters*. [Master's degree thesis].

Plaia, A., & Ruggieri, M. (2011). Air quality indices: A review. *Reviews in Environmental Science and Biotechnology*, *10*(2), 165–179. doi:10.1007/s11157-010-9227-2

Powell, L. M., & Karafinski, A. (2021). Awareness of volunteer computing on the grid: Content within it texts. *Issues in Information Systems*, *22*(1), 246–254.

Ramazanoglu, M. (2020). The Relationship between High School Students' Internet Addiction, Social Media Disorder, and Smartphone Addiction. *World Journal of Education*, *10*(4), 139–148. doi:10.5430/wje.v10n4p139

Rodríguez-García, A. M., Moreno-Guerrero, A. J., & Lopez Belmonte, J. (2020). Nomophobia: An individual's growing fear of being without a smartphone—a systematic literature review. *International Journal of Environmental Research and Public Health*, *17*(2), 580. doi:10.3390/ijerph17020580 PMID:31963208

Salcines-Talledo, I., González-Fernández, N., & Briones, E. (2020). The Smartphone as a pedagogic tool. Student profiles as related to its use and knowledge. [NAER Journal]. *Journal of New Approaches in Educational Research*, *9*(1), 91–109. doi:10.7821/naer.2020.1.454

Salinas, I., Monteiro, M., Martí, A. C., & Monsoriu, J. A. (2020). Analyzing the dynamics of a yo-yo using a smartphone gyroscope sensor. *The Physics Teacher*, *58*(8), 569–571. doi:10.1119/10.0002379

Samsuar, S., Artika, W., Sarong, M. A., Rahmatan, H., & Pada, A. U. T. (2021, May). Smartphone microscope based on the STEM approach as a practicum tool to improve students' scientific attitudes on Animalia. [). IOP Publishing.]. *Journal of Physics: Conference Series*, *1882*(1), 012158. doi:10.1088/1742-6596/1882/1/012158

Sinclair, N., & Robutti, O. (2020). Teaching practices in digital environments. Encyclopedia of mathematics education, 845-849.

Soboleva, E. V., Chirkina, S. E., Kalugina, O. A., Shvetsov, M. Y., Kazinets, V. A., & Pokaninova, E. B. (2020). Didactic Potential of Using Mobile Technologies in the Development of Mathematical Thinking. *Eurasia Journal of Mathematics, Science and Technology Education*, *16*(5), em1842. doi:10.29333/ejmste/118214

Su, X., Tong, H., & Ji, P. (2014). Activity recognition with smartphone sensors. *Tsinghua Science and Technology*, *19*(3), 235–249. doi:10.1109/TST.2014.6838194

Subramanya, S., & Farahani, A. (2012). Point-of-view article on: Design of a smartphone app for learning concepts in mathematics and engineering. *International Journal of Innovation Science*, *4*(3), 173–184. doi:10.1260/1757-2223.4.3.173

Taranto, E., Robutti, O., & Arzarello, F. (2020). Learning within MOOCs for mathematics teacher education. *ZDM*, 1-15.

Than, W. W., & Shan, P. W. (2021). Prevalence of Nomophobia among Undergraduate Students from Sagaing University of Education. *International Review of Social Sciences Research*, *1*(1), 54–76. doi:10.53378/346475

Vieyra, R., Vieyra, C., Jeanjacquot, P., Marti, A., & Monteiro, M. (2015). Turn your smartphone into a science laboratory. *Science Teacher (Normal, Ill.)*, *82*(9), 32. doi:10.2505/4/tst15_082_09_32

Vogt, P., & Kuhn, J. (2012). Analyzing free fall with a smartphone acceleration sensor. *The Physics Teacher*, *50*(3), 182–183. doi:10.1119/1.3685123

Wang, A. I., & Tahir, R. (2020). The effect of using Kahoot! for learning–A literature review. *Computers & Education*, *149*, 103818. doi:10.1016/j.compedu.2020.103818

Yang, Y., Ruan, Z., Wang, X., Yang, Y., Mason, T. G., Lin, H., & Tian, L. (2019). Short-term and long-term exposures to fine particulate matter constituents and health: A systematic review and meta-analysis. *Environmental Pollution*, *247*, 874–882. doi:10.1016/j.envpol.2018.12.060 PMID:30731313

Yildirim, B., Topalcengiz, E. S., Arikan, G., & Timur, S. (2020). Using virtual reality in the classroom: Reflections of STEM teachers on the use of teaching and learning tools. *Journal of Education in Science, Environment and Health*, *6*(3), 231–245. doi:10.21891/jeseh.711779

Yuzbasheva, G., & Kravtsov, H. (2020). Augmented and Virtual Reality Technologies in Teacher Retraining.

Zhelezniakov, D., Cherneha, A., Zaytsev, V., Ignatova, T., Radyvonenko, O., & Yakovchuk, O. (2020, March). Evaluating new requirements to pen-centric intelligent user interface based on end-to-end mathematical expressions recognition. In *Proceedings of the 25th International Conference on Intelligent User Interfaces* (pp. 212-220). ACM. 10.1145/3377325.3377482

Zhuo, S., Sherlock, L., Dobbie, G., Koh, Y. S., Russello, G., & Lottridge, D. (2020). Real-time smartphone activity classification using inertial sensors—Recognition of scrolling, typing, and watching videos while sitting or walking. *Sensors (Basel)*, *20*(3), 655. doi:10.3390/s20030655 PMID:31991636

ADDITIONAL READINGS

Alexandros, K., Panagiotis, L., Serafeim, T., Pavlos, T., & Athanasios, V. (2020). Possible technical problems encountered by the teacher in the incorporation of mobile phone sensors in the physics lab. *European Journal of Physics Education*, *11*(2), 5–23.

Antonietti, C., Cattaneo, A., & Amenduni, F. (2022). Can teachers' digital competence influence technology acceptance in vocational education? *Computers in Human Behavior*, *132*, 107266. doi:10.1016/j.chb.2022.107266

Breitinger, F., Tully-Doyle, R., & Hassenfeldt, C. (2020). A survey on smartphone user's security choices, awareness and education. *Computers & Security*, *88*, 101647. doi:10.1016/j.cose.2019.101647

Bulus, P. (2020). Significant of smartphone: An educational technology tool for teaching and learning. *International Journal of Innovative Science and Research Technology*, *5*(5), 1634–1638.

Clark, K. A., Welsh, K. E., Mauchline, A. L., France, D., Whalley, W. B., & Park, J. (2021). Do educators realise the value of Bring Your Own Device (BYOD) in fieldwork learning? *Journal of Geography in Higher Education*, *45*(2), 255–278. doi:10.1080/03098265.2020.1808880

Crompton, H., & Burke, D. (2018). The use of mobile learning in higher education: A systematic review. *Computers & Education*, *123*, 53–64. doi:10.1016/j.compedu.2018.04.007

Gardner, M., & Tillotson, J. W. (2019). Interpreting integrated STEM: Sustaining pedagogical innovation within a public middle school context. *International Journal of Science and Mathematics Education*, *17*(7), 1283–1300. doi:10.1007/s10763-018-9927-6

Hellesund, S. (2018). Measuring Earth's Magnetic Field Using a Smartphone Magnetometer. *arXiv preprint arXiv:1901.00857*.

Hergemöller, T., & Laumann, D. (2017). Smartphone magnification attachment: Microscope or magnifying glass. *The Physics Teacher*, *55*(6), 361–364. doi:10.1119/1.4999732

Kaimara, P., Poulimenou, S. M., Oikonomou, A., Deliyannis, I., & Plerou, A. (2019). Smartphones at schools? Yes, why not?. *European Journal of Engineering and Technology Research*, 1-6.

Kaps, A., & Stallmach, F. (2020). Tilting motion and the moment of inertia of the smartphone. *The Physics Teacher*, *58*(3), 216–217. doi:10.1119/1.5145423

Lai, C. L. (2020). Trends of mobile learning: A review of the top 100 highly cited papers. *British Journal of Educational Technology*, *51*(3), 721–742. doi:10.1111/bjet.12884

Leung, F. K. S., Stillman, G. A., Kaiser, G., & Wong, K. L. (2021). Mathematical modelling education in the cultural contexts of west and east. In *Mathematical modelling education in east and west* (pp. 3–16). Springer International Publishing. doi:10.1007/978-3-030-66996-6_1

Listiaji, P., Darmawan, M. S., Daeni, F., & Karmuji. (2020). Comparison between the use of acceleration sensor and video tracker on smartphone for spring oscillation experiment. *Physics Education, 56*(1), 013001. doi:10.1088/1361-6552/abb88b

Montag, C., Wegmann, E., Sariyska, R., Demetrovics, Z., & Brand, M. (2021). How to overcome taxonomical problems in the study of Internet use disorders and what to do with "smartphone addiction"? *Journal of Behavioral Addictions, 9*(4), 908–914. doi:10.1556/2006.8.2019.59 PMID:31668089

Mpofu, V. (2019). A theoretical framework for implementing STEM education. *Theorizing STEM Education in the 21st Century*, 109-123.

Mynbayeva, A., Sadvakassova, Z., & Akshalova, B. (2018). Pedagogy of the twenty-first century: Innovative teaching methods. *New Pedagogical Challenges in the 21st Century. Contributions of Research in Education*. IEEE.

Parmigiani, D., Traverso, A., Pennazio, V., & Olivieri, A. (2015). La ricerca di informazioni in rete: Strategie e differenze tra tablet e pc. *Italian Journal of Educational Technology, 23*(3), 148–154.

Parolin, S. O., & Pezzi, G. (2013). Smartphone-aided measurements of the speed of sound in different gaseous mixtures. *The Physics Teacher, 51*(8), 508–509. doi:10.1119/1.4824957

Pedemonte, G., & Operto, F. (2019). Roboable project: educational robotics for inclusive didactics. *Form@ re-Open Journal per la formazione in rete, 19*(1), 401-411.

rensky, M. (2009). H. sapiens digital: From digital immigrants and digital natives to digital wisdom. *Innovate: journal of online education, 5*(3).

Raharja, E. P., & Ishafit. (2021, March). Development of circular motion experiment tool using sensor smartphone for high school students. []. IOP Publishing.]. *Journal of Physics: Conference Series, 1806*(1), 012048. doi:10.1088/1742-6596/1806/1/012048

Shraim, K. (2019). Mobile Apps Criteria for Guiding STEM Teachers in Developing Mobile Learning Activities.

Sisti, D. A. (2007). How do high school students justify internet plagiarism? *Ethics & Behavior, 17*(3), 215–231. doi:10.1080/10508420701519163

Slipukhina, I., Chernetckiy, I., Kurylenko, N., Mieniailov, S., & Podlasov, S. (2021, May). Instrumental Digital Didactics of Physics Study in the Aspect of M-learning. In *Information and Communication Technologies in Education, Research, and Industrial Applications: 16th International Conference, ICTERI 2020, Kharkiv, Ukraine, October 6–10, 2020, Revised Selected Papers* (pp. 3-21). Cham: Springer International Publishing. 10.1007/978-3-030-77592-6_1

Thibaut, L., Ceuppens, S., De Loof, H., De Meester, J., Goovaerts, L., Struyf, A., Boeve-de Pauw, J., Dehaene, W., Deprez, J., De Cock, M., Hellinckx, L., Knipprath, H., Langie, G., Struyven, K., Van de Velde, D., Van Petegem, P., & Depaepe, F. (2018). Integrated STEM education: A systematic review of instructional practices in secondary education. *European Journal of STEM Education*, *3*(1), 2. doi:10.20897/ejsteme/85525

Twenge, J. M. (2017). Have smartphones destroyed a generation. *Atlantic (Boston, Mass.)*, *9*, 2017.

Wannous, J., & Horváth, P. (2021, February). Measuring the Permeability of Vacuum Using a Smartphone. In *Proceedings INNODOCT/20. International Conference on Innovation, Documentation and Education* (pp. 63-70). Editorial Universitat Politècnica de València.

Chapter 10
NSF-Funded Exploratory Study:
Lessons Learned

Eleanor Armour-Thomas
Queens College of the City University of New York, USA

ABSTRACT

In this NSF-funded exploratory study the author examined the impact of professional development on NGSS teaching of administrator-selected teachers in a large, urban, public school district in the United States. Currently, the research literature on professional development about NGSS in early grades about NGSS is sparce. Thus, the purpose of the study was to develop and implement a professional development program for Early Childhood and Elementary in-service teachers with the aim of understanding its impact on their knowledge for NGSS teaching and classroom practice. Findings from self-reports revealed improvement in teachers' knowledge for NGSS teaching particularly in the domains of lesson planning, classroom teaching, and classroom assessment. Lessons learned from the exploratory study for future professional development in professional development for NGSS teaching and learning are discussed.

DOI: 10.4018/978-1-6684-5939-3.ch010

INTRODUCTION

Two major reports, *the Framework for K-12 Science Education* (National Research Council, 2012) and the *Next Generation Science Standards: For States, By States (NGSS Lead States, 2013),* call for science teaching that is focused on the intersection of disciplinary core ideas, cross –cutting concepts and science and engineering practices. The Framework also envisions science learning as involving students' engagement with disciplinary core ideas and crosscutting concepts in the context of science and engineering practices. This shift in perspectives of teaching and learning will require models of professional development that help teachers acquire the knowledge and skills for teaching as envisioned by the Framework and NGSS. In early childhood education, the issue of high-quality science instruction is particularly challenging given the observations that many early childhood teachers are not well prepared to teach science in the early grades nor is pre-school and early childhood science education perceived as the foundation for later achievement of high-quality instruction. However, to date, the research literature is sparse on the kinds of learning experiences that support teachers in designing and implementing science integrated lessons in ways that build science literacy for early childhood learners as envisioned by NGSS. In recent years, however, models for teacher professional learning have provided some guidance for improving teacher knowledge for science teaching and learning at the elementary and early childhood level called for by the Framework. Among the design features that proven effective in prior research of professional development to enhance teacher and student learning in STEM disciplines include: targeted topics and strategies of relevance and importance to early childhood educators (Garet, 2001); provide opportunities for hands-on practice and reflections (Spillane, Reiser and Reimer, 2002); active participation and collaboration in the design and implementation of classroom activities (Penuel, Gallegar, & Moorthy, 2011); sufficient dose over a sustained period (Yoon et. al, 2007)." Gaining insights on how teacher improve knowledge and practice through professional development will provide key information about how resources should be directed to childhood programs for supporting pre- and in-service teachers to develop NGSS-based knowledge and skills for teaching.

In the proposed chapter the author will share anecdotal stories of an NSF-Funded exploratory study, *Facilitating Teachers, and Young Children's Science learning through Iterative Cycles of Professional Development.* One of the goals of that study was that teachers participating in the professional development program will gain knowledge and skills consonant with NGSS expectations for teaching.

CONTEXT OF THE STUDY

Set specifically within the context of a diverse school district in a large urban school district in the United States, the exploratory study was conducted from 2017-2018 academic year. All the schools were in a high-need school district in New York City and enrolled students from diverse backgrounds, the majority of whom were English Language learners. At the time of the study the school district offered mandatory professional development about NGSS and its alignment with New York State Science Standards and the New York City Science Scope and Sequence.

METHOD

Research Design

This chapter describes the implementation and results of a professional development as measured by self-reports and Exit Slips collected from teachers who taught in a large urban school district in New York city. Because of the exploratory nature of the study- to ascertain whether teachers [knowledge for NGSS teaching will improve after participation in a professional development program, non-experimental methods were used rather than evaluating the efficacy of a particular professional development intervention. Also, since the goal was to gain a general understanding of K-2 grade teachers' knowledge for NGSS teaching, school principals were asked to nominate teachers whom they believe were interested in participating in a professional development program about NGSS teaching and learning. All the teachers who volunteered to participate in the exploratory study had attended professional development NGSS activities sponsored by the district.

Two research questions guided the initial study: (1) Do teachers who participated in the professional development program increase their knowledge about the NGSS for teaching? (2) Do teachers who participated in the professional development program implement science lessons integrated with NGSS-based disciplinary core ideas, crosscutting concepts and engineering practices? However, only the first question will be addressed in this chapter.

Sample

A total of twenty teachers were recruited from five elementary schools in an urban school district to participate in the study. Of the total sample, eighteen were females and two were males. All of them had at least four years of teaching experiences and had participated previously in district and school level sponsored professional development related to NGSS. At the time of the study six teachers were teaching at the kindergarten level, five at first grade level, and three at the second-grade level. Two teachers were described as teaching K/ESL students and four teachers were described as science cluster teachers.

Objectives of the Professional Development Intervention Program

1. To provide teachers with a wide variety of information (e.g., research articles, artifacts, videos, concepts, principles, instructional and assessment strategies) for improving their knowledge for planning and implementing NGSS –based lessons for children in K-2 grades.
2. To provide teachers with opportunities for improving their skills in planning and implementing NGSS-based lessons for children in K-2 grades.
3. To provide teachers with opportunities for engaging in teaching practices that encourage young children in K-2 grades to show learning behaviors consonant with the NGSS.

To meet these objectives the *Facilitating Young Children's Science Learning through Iterative Cycles of Teacher Professional Development* program the research team drew from the research on professional development that showed promise for improving and learning. The design features included: (1) discipline-specific knowledge (2) pedagogical content knowledge; (3) active learning methods; (4) in-person and synchronous delivery of information; and (5) intellectual engagement of teachers in individual and collaborative participation (e.g., Guskey, 2003; Garet, Porter, Desimonie, Birman, and Yoon, 2001, and Kennedy, 2016).

The research team's *PD Theory of Action* guiding this work was that teachers will improve their knowledge and skills for NGSS-based teaching and their students will demonstrate learning behaviors consonant with NGSS when they are provided with opportunities that actively engage them individually and collaboratively to: (a) understand how disciplinary core ideas, crosscutting concepts and science and engineering practices are integrated in the early childhood curriculum; (b) understand the types of instructional and assessment strategies that promote NGSS-based teaching and learning; (c) apply their understanding of NGSS-based teaching and learning to the analysis of practices of other teachers as well as their own; and (d) gain insights about practices that enable learning behaviors in children indicative of science learning as envisioned by the *Framework* and *NGSS*.

NSF-Funded Exploratory Study

Professional Development Sessions

Teachers took part in three cycles of PD sessions, each lasting eighty minutes over three semesters (spring 2017, fall 2017 and spring 2018). The first eight PD (from March to June 2017) sessions focused on prompting the participants to reflect about what does science teaching/leaning look like and what should it look like. In doing so the principles of pedagogy, content knowledge and pedagogical content knowledge were reviewed, as well as the relationship between curriculum, instruction, and assessment in science learning. This gave the participants the opportunity to recall learning theories and pedagogies, discuss about their own practices and to connect their grade curriculum to other grades. The latter aspect was exemplified with both clips from early childhood classrooms and the NY State *Elementary Science Pupil/ Program Evaluation Test (ESPET)*. During these sessions comparison with conceptual shift between past standards and the NGSS were underlined for the participants.

In the next three sessions (September and October 2017), the participants were formally introduced to the new standards. The three dimensions were examined through guided exploration. As the participants examined the NGSS they were prompted to think about the following questions:

- What are the three major divisions that comprise the NGSS?
- How does the science content build over grade level?
- How are HOT skills integrated into the strand?
- Is it clear what students are to know and do?
- What are the six major conceptual shifts of the NGSS?
- What concepts or further concerns do you have about the standards?

Examination also focused on the six major conceptual shifts of the NGSS, the vertical and horizontal alignment of the NGSS. This was completed through three integrated activities. The three activities provided the participants with the opportunity to examine a topic (Disciplinary Core Idea) from early elementary grades through high school level, and to become familiar with the vocabulary, and recognize the conceptual change brought by the NGSS.

1. **Examining the Standards**: Participants explored one disciplinary core idea outlined in the NGSS from early elementary through high school.
2. **Understanding the NGSS Vocabulary**: **The Structure of NGSS**: In the second activity, participants reviewed the essential elements of NGSS structure (performance expectations, disciplinary core ideas, cross cutting concepts, science and engineering principles, foundation boxes, and connections boxes).

3. **NGSS Conceptual Shifts**: In the third activity, the participants were introduced to the structure of the NGSS. The purpose was to highlight the six conceptual shifts that demonstrate how NGSS are different from previous standards.
    a. Real world applications of science integrated with the three dimensions (DCI, CCC, S&E) of the NGSS
    b. Integrated approach to science, technology, and engineering K-12
    c. Coherent vertical alignment of essential DCI K-12.
    d. Deeper understanding and application of content
    e. NGSS are performance expectations not curriculum, instruction, or assessment practices
    f. NGSS correlate with the CCSS for mathematics and English- language arts
4. **Integrating the Three Dimensions**: Participants experience a model activity as they develop an understanding of the integration of the three dimensions of the NGSS.

From November 2017 to January *2018*, the PD sessions focused on helping participants' understanding of the alignment between the FOSS, the NYS Science Standards and the NYC Science Scope and Sequence. For example, the FOSS K-ESS2-1 Earth's Systems were examined along with the NYS K-Weather and Climate, and NYC first grade, unit 1 of the Scope and Sequence. Particular attention was centered on the Connection Boxes and the graphic organizers, on commonalities among the practices in science, and Mathematics. From the state standards, the participants transitioned to the city Scope and Sequence to identify the ELA/Literacy standards that can be integrated in specific science lessons. Participants were given the book: *Somewhere in the Ocean* by Jennifer Ward and T.J. Marsh to read and to identify how this book could be used to support science and ELA learning standards from the NGSS perspective. This book was chosen as it can be used in early childhood grades in multiple ways to teach science, math, and ELA. Discussion following the group activity helped the participants develop a better sense of implementation of the NGSS dimensions with the integration of ELA/Literacy. This understanding was further deepened by repeating the exercise with other books donated by the grant to the teachers to facilitate integration in their lessons

The next five sessions participants were supported in the use of novel frameworks, tools and protocols for lesson planning and analysis of video lessons. Three of those sessions consisted of asynchronous tasks that requested teachers to watch a video lesson segment on the topic of *Matter and Liquids* and then collaborate in small groups to look for and analyze NGSS Practices associated with quality science instruction in classroom settings. Participants were also asked to choose one

NSF-Funded Exploratory Study

NGSS-aligned science practice found in the video (NGSS Practice 3, 4, or 7), share a written analysis of the practice with their small group using the guidance below:

- 1. Describe your observations of the student behaviors that are associated with the science practice you selected in the table above. Note the time markers for the segments in which you observed the student behaviors that indicate the science practice (e.g., 1:35-2:22 minutes).
- 2. Identify the science core ideas, NGSS cross cutting concepts, ELA/Literacy and math concepts embedded in the practice observed. Were any aspects missing?
- 3. Where do you think this lesson falls within the science unit? Why?
- 4. Explain what you find particularly effective about what the *teacher* did in the video lesson to support students' engagement in the practice observed.
- 5. What could the teacher have done to encourage students to add more of their own ideas and prior knowledge from *outside* the classroom to their science understandings, hypotheses, questions, and inquiries/investigations?
- 6. Explain what the teacher in the video lesson could have done differently to improve student engagement in the practice observed.
- 7. What do you think were the teacher's learning goal/s and objectives for the video lesson? Do you think these outcomes were achieved? Why?

The last two PD sessions participants were asked to use an NGSS Storylines framework to plan a lesson that included Disciplinary Core Ideas (DCI, Crosscutting Concepts (CCI), Science and Engineering Practices, ELA/Literacy and Mathematics concepts. Participants were also instructed to select any lesson from a unit in their grade level from the New York City K-5 Scope and Sequence.

Storyline Phases and Components

- **The Prologue**: The context for the lesson. Where does this lesson fit in the overall unit: in the beginning, middle, or the end? What activities were performed in the lesson prior to this one? Why do you think students are ready for this lesson?
- **Act I**: *Beginning* the action of the lesson. What is your driving question/motivation? What are the set-up inquiry activities? What are the **teacher action**s and **student actions** linked to these activities? How much time will you allow for this phase?
- **Act II**: *Sustaining* the action. What is your driving question? What are the core inquiry activities? What are the **teacher actions** and **student actions** linked to these activities? How much time will you allow for this phase?

- **Act III**: *Approaching the conclusion* of the action. What is your driving question/motivation? What are the core inquiry activities? What are the **teacher actions** and **student actions** linked to these activities? How much time will you allow for this phase?

Data Collection and instrumentation

Survey

Survey data were collected using the *Teachers Knowledge about Next Generation Science Standards for Teaching* (TKNGSST) Questionnaire which was developed by members of the research team and used for this study. It was administered to nineteen participating teachers prior to and after the professional development intervention program. The TKNGSST includes twenty-one items that measure knowledge about NGSS in three domains: a) Lesson Planning (eight items), b) Classroom Teaching (10 items), and c) Classroom Assessment (three items). Each item is rated on a 5-point scale, ranging from 1 (Never) to 5 (Daily). A mean of items scores was calculated, with higher scores representing higher levels of engagement in NGSS practices. The reliability of the TKNGSST conducted during the baseline was good (internal consistency alpha = .96), with alpha being .98, .94, and .92 for Domain 1: Lesson Planning, Domain 2: Classroom Teaching, and Domain 3: Classroom Assessment, respectively. The post-intervention assessment obtained alphas of .89, .91, and .88 for the three domains of TKNGSST.

Exit Slips

Exit Slips were used after PD sessions to elicit teacher's perceptions about their professional development experiences. Members of the research team designed the questions that sought participating teachers' understanding of NGSS in general and more specifically the three dimensions for science teaching and learning: Disciplinary Core Ideas, Cross Cutting Concepts and Science & Engineering Practices. In addition, questions sought participants' understanding of how NYC Scope and Sequence connects with NGSS and NYS Science Standards and the integration of NGSS with ELA/Literacy concepts into their lesson planning, classroom practices and assessment.

Data Analysis

Research question 1 used TKNGSST survey data was "analyzed descriptively and then with one-way analyses of variance (ANOVAs) to look for change in TKNGSST after participating in a professional development program intended to improve their knowledge of NGSS for teaching. Exit Slips data were used to obtain direct reactions from participating teachers about their understanding of the three dimensions of NGSS and how to integrate them into their teaching.

FINDINGS

Teachers' Perceptions of NGSS for teaching (TKNGSST)

Pre- Professional Development (PD) Results

The baseline data of the TKNGSST indicated that our participants had low levels of knowledge about NGSS for teaching for the domains of lesson planning ($Mds = 1$) and classroom assessment ($Mds = 1$). Although participants demonstrated low levels of knowledge about NGSS for teaching related to classroom teaching, they had higher levels of knowledge in certain teaching practices. Participants reported feeling more knowledgeable on how to sequence tasks in ways that help young children engage in learning activities in order to meet the objectives of a lesson (Item 10; $Md = 5$), which types and levels of questions to ask young children in the beginning, middle and end phases of a lesson to meet the objectives of a lesson (Item 12; $Md = 5$), and how to pace the activities of a lesson to allow young children the time needed to initiate and sustain their engagement throughout the lesson (Item 16; $Md = 5$). Overall, teacher participants reported a higher level of knowledge about NGSS for teaching in the Classroom Teaching domain ($M = 3.02, SD = 1.385$) than in Lesson Planning ($M = 2.15, SD = 1.532$) and Classroom Assessment ($M = 1.89, SD = 1.449$), $t(18) = -2.839, p = .011, t(18) = 5.408$, and $p < .001$, respectively.

Post-PD Results

In contrast to baseline data, the post-PD assessment results indicated that participants had high levels of knowledge about NGSS for teaching across different domains ($Mds = 5$-6). Furthermore, the participants reported higher levels of knowledge about NGSS for teaching across the three domains (Lesson Planning, Classroom Teaching, and Classroom Assessment).

Table 1. Baseline Assessment of TKNGSST

Item	Min	Max	Range	M	Md	S.D.	25ile	50ile	75ile
Lesson Planning				2.15		1.53			2.25
1. My knowledge for designing lesson plans with the three dimensions of NGSS-based content is:	1	4	3	1.56	1.00	.984	1.00	1.00	3.00
2. My knowledge for designing NGSS lesson plans that are appropriate to young children's learning needs and strengths is:	1	6	5	2.16	1.00	1.573	1.00	1.00	4.00
3. My knowledge for designing NGSS-based lesson plans that anticipate young children's misconceptions is:	1	6	5	2.26	1.00	1.695	1.00	1.00	4.00
4. My knowledge of young children's cultural assets for designing NGSS lesson plans is:	1	5	4	2.11	1.00	1.410	1.00	1.00	3.00
5. My knowledge for designing NGSS lesson plans that are appropriate to young children's language needs and strengths is:	1	6	5	2.26	1.00	1.727	1.00	1.00	5.00
6. My knowledge for designing NGSS-based lesson plans that link learning activities, materials, and resources with learning objectives of the lesson is:	1	6	5	2.42	1.00	1.924	1.00	1.00	3.00
7. My knowledge for designing NGSS-based lesson plans that sequence learning activities in ways that help young children grow in their understanding of science is:	1	6	5	2.11	1.00	1.560	1.00	1.00	4.00
8. My knowledge for designing NGSS-based lesson plans for using materials and resources that engage young children in the beginning middle and end phases of the lesson is:	1	6	5	2.16	1.00	1.608	1.00	1.00	
Classroom Teaching				3.02		1.385			5.00
9. My knowledge of what motivational strategies to use to initiate and maintain young children's active engagement throughout the NGSS lesson is:	1	7	6	2.58	1.00	2.063	1.00	1.00	6.00
10. My knowledge of how to sequence tasks in ways that help young children engage in learning activities that are likely to enable them to meet the objectives of the lesson is:	1	7	6	4.95	5.00	1.471	4.00	5.00	4.00
11. My knowledge of how to select NGSS tasks at a level of difficulty appropriate to the learning needs and strengths of young children is:	1	7	6	2.32	1.00	1.827	1.00	1.00	

continues on following page

Table 1. Continued

Item	Min	Max	Range	M	Md	S.D.	25ile	50ile	75ile
12. My knowledge of what types and levels of questions to ask young children in the beginning, middle and end phases of the lesson to enable them to meet the objectives of the lesson is:	1	7	6	4.63	5.00	1.461	4.00	5.00	6.00
13. My knowledge of instructional strategies that help young children become aware of and use self-regulated strategies for meeting NGSS objectives of the lesson is:	1	7	6	2.32	1.00	1.827	1.00	1.00	4.00
14. My knowledge of how to use resources and materials in ways that make the NGSS tasks understandable for young children is:	1	7	6	2.16	1.00	1.708	1.00	1.00	4.00
15. My knowledge of how to select instructional arrangements that allow young children to engage in the NGSS tasks in ways that help them achieve the objectives of the lesson is:	1	7	6	2.11	1.00	1.663	1.00	1.00	3.00
16. My knowledge of how to pace the activities of the lesson to allow young children the time needed to initiate and sustain their engagement throughout the lesson is:	1	7	6	4.68	5.00	1.635	4.00	5.00	6.00
17. My knowledge of how to monitor and adjust in the NGSS lesson to ensure alignment between learning activities, resources and materials and learning objectives is:	1	7	6	2.11	1.00	1.761	1.00	1.00	3.00
18. My knowledge of how to use feedback from student responses to make changes in my Instructional and/or assessment strategies or NGSS tasks is:	1	7	6	2.37	1.00	1.921	1.00	1.00	4.00
Classroom Assessment				1.89		1.449			
19. My knowledge of how to analyze evidence of student learning related to the NGSS objectives is:	1	5	4	1.79	1.00	1.273	1.00	1.00	2.00
20. My knowledge of how to analyze evidence of students' language use and learning related to the NGSS objectives	1	7	6	1.95	1.00	1.682	1.00	1.00	2.00
21. My knowledge of how to use evidence from assessment of NGSS objectives to modify subsequent lesson planning and or classroom practice is:	1	7	6	1.95	1.00	1.682	1.00	1.00	2.00

($N = 19$)

Table 2. Post-intervention Assessment of TKNGSST

Item	Min	Max	Range	M	Md	S.D.	25ile	50ile	75ile
Lesson Planning				5.46		.583			
1. My knowledge for designing lesson plans with the three dimensions of NGSS-based content is:	3	6	3	5.00	5.00	1.000	4.50	5.00	6.00
2. My knowledge for designing NGSS lesson plans that are appropriate to young children's learning needs and strengths is:	4	7	3	5.67	6.00	.866	5.00	6.00	6.00
3. My knowledge for designing NGSS-based lesson plans that anticipate young children's misconceptions is:	3	6	3	5.22	5.00	.972	5.00	5.00	6.00
4. My knowledge of young children's cultural assets for designing NGSS lesson plans is:	3	6	3	5.22	5.00	.972	5.00	5.00	6.00
5. My knowledge for designing NGSS lesson plans that are appropriate to young children's language needs and strengths is:	5	7	2	5.78	6.00	.667	5.00	6.00	6.00
6. My knowledge for designing NGSS-based lesson plans that link learning activities, materials, and resources with learning objectives of the lesson is:	5	6	1	5.56	6.00	.527	5.00	6.00	6.00
7. My knowledge for designing NGSS-based lesson plans that sequence learning activities in ways that help young children grow in their understanding of science is:	5	6	1	5.56	6.00	.527	5.00	6.00	6.00
8. My knowledge for designing NGSS-based lesson plans for using materials and resources that engage young children in the beginning middle and end phases of the lesson is:	5	6	1	5.67	6.00	.500	5.00	6.00	6.00
Classroom Teaching				5.58		.547			
9. My knowledge of what motivational strategies to use to initiate and maintain young children's active engagement throughout the NGSS lesson is:	5	7	2	5.78	6.00	.667	5.00	6.00	6.00
10. My knowledge of how to sequence tasks in ways that help young children engage in learning activities that are likely to enable them to meet the objectives of the lesson is:	5	6	1	5.67	6.00	.500	5.00	6.00	6.00
11. My knowledge of how to select NGSS tasks at a level of difficulty appropriate to the learning needs and strengths of young children is:	5	7	2	5.56	5.00	.727	5.00	5.00	6.00

continues on following page

NSF-Funded Exploratory Study

Table 2. Continued

Item	Min	Max	Range	M	Md	S.D.	25ile	50ile	75ile
12. My knowledge of what types and levels of questions to ask young children in the beginning, middle and end phases of the lesson to enable them to meet the objectives of the lesson is:	4	7	3	5.67	6.00	.866	5.00	6.00	6.00
13. My knowledge of instructional strategies that help young children become aware of and use self-regulated strategies for meeting NGSS objectives of the lesson is:	2	7	5	5.33	6.00	1.414	5.00	6.00	6.00
14. My knowledge of how to use resources and materials in ways that make the NGSS tasks understandable for young children is:	4	6	2	5.56	6.00	.727	5.00	6.00	6.00
15. My knowledge of how to select instructional arrangements that allow young children to engage in the NGSS tasks in ways that help them achieve the objectives of the lesson is:	5	6	1	5.44	5.00	.527	5.00	5.00	6.00
16. My knowledge of how to pace the activities of the lesson to allow young children the time needed to initiate and sustain their engagement throughout the lesson is:	5	6	1	5.78	6.00	.441	5.00	6.00	6.00
17. My knowledge of how to monitor and adjust in the NGSS lesson to ensure alignment between learning activities, resources and materials and learning objectives is:	5	6	1	5.44	5.00	.527	5.00	5.00	6.00
18. My knowledge of how to use feedback from student responses to make changes in my Instructional and/or assessment strategies or NGSS tasks is:	5	6	1	5.56	6.00	.527	5.00	6.00	6.00
Classroom Assessment				5.48		.475			
19. My knowledge of how to analyze evidence of student learning related to the NGSS objectives is:	5	6	1	5.44	5.00	.527	5.00	5.00	6.00
20. My knowledge of how to analyze evidence of students' language use and learning related to the NGSS objectives	5	6	1	5.44	5.00	.527	5.00	5.00	6.00
21. My knowledge of how to use evidence from assessment of NGSS objectives to modify subsequent lesson planning and or classroom practice is:	5	6	1	5.56	6.00	.527	5.00	6.00	6.00

($N = 9$)

Table 3. Baseline and Post-intervention Comparison on TKNGSST

Domain/Item	Baseline M	Baseline S.D.	Post-Intervention M	Post-Intervention S.D.	Mean Difference d	t	df	Sig.
Lesson Planning	1.58	1.158	5.46	.582	3.88	-8.377	8	.000***
1. My knowledge for designing lesson plans with the three dimensions of NGSS-based content is:	1.33	1.000	5.00	1.000	3.67	-7.778	8	.000***
2. My knowledge for designing NGSS lesson plans that are appropriate to young children's learning needs and strengths is:	1.56	.866	5.67	.866	4.11	-9.041	8	.000***
3. My knowledge for designing NGSS-based lesson plans that anticipate young children's misconceptions is:	1.56	1.014	5.22	.972	3.66	-8.315	8	.000***
4. My knowledge of young children's cultural assets for designing NGSS lesson plans is:	1.56	1.014	5.22	.972	3.66	-8.315	8	.000***
5. My knowledge for designing NGSS lesson plans that are appropriate to young children's language needs and strengths is:	1.67	1.323	5.78	.667	4.11	-7.633	8	.000***
6. My knowledge for designing NGSS-based lesson plans that link learning activities, materials, and resources with learning objectives of the lesson is:	1.67	1.323	5.56	.527	3.89	-7.593	8	.000***
7. My knowledge for designing NGSS-based lesson plans that sequence learning activities in ways that help young children grow in their understanding of science is:	1.67	1.323	5.56	.527	3.89	-7.220	8	.000***
8. My knowledge for designing NGSS-based lesson plans for using materials and resources that engage young children in the beginning middle and end phases of the lesson is:	1.67	1.323	5.67	.500	4.00	-7.589	8	.000***
Classroom Teaching	2.46	.983	5.58	.547	3.12	-7.418	8	.000***
9. My knowledge of what motivational strategies to use to initiate and maintain young children's active engagement throughout the NGSS lesson is:	1.67	1.323	5.78	.667	4.11	-9.717	8	.000***
Table 3 (continued)								
10. My knowledge of how to sequence tasks in ways that help young children engage in learning activities that are likely to enable them to meet the objectives of the lesson is:	4.67	1.658	5.67	.500	1.00	-1.732	8	.122

continues on following page

Table 3. Continued

Domain/Item	Baseline M	Baseline S.D.	Post-Intervention M	Post-Intervention S.D.	Mean Difference d	t	df	Sig.
11. My knowledge of how to select NGSS tasks at a level of difficulty appropriate to the learning needs and strengths of young children is:	1.67	1.323	5.56	.727	3.89	-7.593	8	.000***
12. My knowledge of what types and levels of questions to ask young children in the beginning, middle and end phases of the lesson to enable them to meet the objectives of the lesson is:	4.33	1.581	5.67	.866	1.34	-1.886	8	.096
13. My knowledge of instructional strategies that help young children become aware of and use self-regulated strategies for meeting NGSS objectives of the lesson is:	1.67	1.323	5.33	1.414	3.66	-5.880	8	.000***
14. My knowledge of how to use resources and materials in ways that make the NGSS tasks understandable for young children is:	1.44	1.014	5.56	.727	4.12	-9.041	8	.000***
15. My knowledge of how to select instructional arrangements that allow young children to engage in the NGSS tasks in ways that help them achieve the objectives of the lesson is:	1.44	1.014	5.44	.527	4.00	-9.071	8	.000***
16. My knowledge of how to pace the activities of the lesson to allow young children the time needed to initiate and sustain their engagement throughout the lesson is:	4.56	1.667	5.78	.441	1.22	-2.052	8	.074
17. My knowledge of how to monitor and adjust in the NGSS lesson to ensure alignment between learning activities, resources and materials and learning objectives is:	1.44	1.014	5.44	.527	4.00	-9.798	8	-.000***
18. My knowledge of how to use feedback from student responses to make changes in my Instructional and/or assessment strategies or NGSS tasks is:	1.67	1.323	5.56	.527	3.89	-6.897	8	.000***
Classroom Assessment	1.44	1.014	5.48	.475	4.04	-9.672	8	.000***
Table 3 (continued)								
19. My knowledge of how to analyze evidence of student learning related to the NGSS objectives is:	1.44	1.014	5.44	.527	4.00	-9.798	8	.000***
20. My knowledge of how to analyze evidence of students' language use and learning related to the NGSS objectives	1.44	1.014	5.44	.527	4.00	-9.071	8	.000***
21. My knowledge of how to use evidence from assessment of NGSS objectives to modify subsequent lesson planning and or classroom practice is:	1.44	1.014	5.56	.527	4.12	-9.717	8	.000***

(N =9)

Pre- and Post-PD Comparison

Paired-sample t-tests were conducted to compare participants' baseline ratings and post-PD intervention ratings on the TKNGSST. The results as described in Table 1, showed significant improvement in all domains/items ($ps < .001$), except for items 10, 12, and 16, which obtained high ratings at baseline. The findings suggest that the professional development program was effective in significantly enhancing the participants' knowledge about NGSS teaching in the domains of lesson planning, classroom teaching, and classroom assessment. Table 1 shows the pre-post professional development comparisons of teacher knowledge about NGSS for teaching.

Post-intervention Assessment

The post-intervention assessment data of TKNGSST are presented in Table 2. In contrast to baseline data, the post-intervention assessment results indicated that our participants had important levels of knowledge about NGSS for teaching across different domains ($Mds = 5 - 6$). Furthermore, the participants reported high levels of knowledge about NGSS for teaching across different domains (Lesson Planning, Classroom Teaching, and Classroom Assessment).

Analysis of Exit Slips Professional Development

Exit Slips data were used to obtain direct reactions from participating teachers about their understanding of Disciplinary Core Ideas, crosscutting concepts, Science & Engineering Practices, ELA/Literacy and Mathematics concepts and how to integrate them into their teaching. Sample perceptions follow of participating teachers' understanding about their professional development experiences. They reported that they understood:

- How math, science and engineering concepts and practices were embedded in their current teaching and the importance of providing effective tools and vocabulary supports during constructed play.
- The ways in which they were already implementing many aspects of NGSS teaching and learning in their classrooms such as supporting children to build models, using resources for gathering data for investigations, and using STEM-related vocabulary during these activities.
- How cross-cutting concepts are integrated into different grade levels, and how to plan lessons that encourage learners to engage in NGSS practices such as recognizing patterns and engaging in arguments using evidence.

- How to plan lessons that connected science, math, and ELA/Literacy concepts and how to identify indicators of Science and Engineering Practices in a lesson.
- How to integrate concepts and skills from multiple subjects/disciplines into one science lesson and how to "spiral" and revisit curriculum throughout the year, and to "mesh" concepts from different units so that children can see how the different topics connect and affect one another.
- How to look for connections between math and science content, and how to identify where math and science concepts overlapped.
- how the choice of curriculum materials could help teachers incorporate science, ELA, and math activities into one lesson. For example, choosing science-related books for reading-aloud fostered integrated learning of science and ELA. Students could practice skills related to both ELA and science using one text
- How one activity could be designed to align with multiple NGSS Science and Engineering Practices practices and were conscious of sequencing lessons to address crosscutting concepts.
- How assessments should be designed to reflect the lesson objectives and the "driving question" of the lesson.
- How to differentiate the lesson segments so that students will better understand the lesson and how activities for a lesson should be sequenced and conducted.

DISCUSSION

The lessons learned from the exploratory study has shed important and much needed light on what is necessary to advance the professional knowledge of early childhood educators as related to creating and managing learning environments that are aligned to the Next Generation Science. Some lessons learned from this exploratory study to examine the effects of a professional development program to improve NGSS teaching among kindergarten, first and second grade teachers are discussed below.

The meaningful change in the baseline and post-professional development ratings on the *Teacher Knowledge for Next Generation of Science Standards* for *Teaching* Questionnaire suggests that the professional development program was effective in improving participating teachers' knowledge about NGSS-based teaching in the areas of lesson planning, classroom teaching and classroom assessment. This finding has added to the knowledge base about the importance of professional development in supporting teachers to implement NGSS-based teaching in early childhood classrooms even for experienced who are quite familiar with State Science Standards and with experiences in district-sponsored professional development about

NGSS. The approach of using a "Progressions" approach of a slow yet methodical approach to unpacking the Next Generation Science Standards as shown in the schedule impacted positively teacher knowledge for NGSS teaching.

Key to the vision of expressed in the Science Framework for K-12 Science Education is for teachers to help students to learn disciplinary core ideas, cross-cutting concepts in the context of science and engineering practices. In anticipation that teacher would do that with their students, PD sessions addressed such integration and was reflected in the Exit Slips responses of teachers of its importance in their teaching. It should be noted, however, that caution needs to be taken when interpreting the results of the professional develop program given the low number of participants in this exploratory study. More research is required to evaluate whether the reported positive impacts of the program are replicable and hold true on larger scales.

The positive change in teacher knowledge about NGSS teaching across different domains of lesson planning, classroom teaching, and classroom assessment suggest that the Knowledge *for NGSS-Based Teaching Questionnaire* is a useful measure for research and clinical practices in Elementary and Early Childhood teacher education programs interested in improving teacher candidates' knowledge for teaching and learning. However, as some teacher educator researchers have argued, pedagogical content knowledge may be necessary but not sufficient for enabling student learning. How teachers translate what they know about NGSS teaching into what they do to foster STEM literacy among young learners as envisioned by NGSS, is an empirical question worthy of further study.

The use of Exit Slips after each professional development session was quite a useful tool for generating information about the topics, strategies for engaging teachers, and takeaways from the experience. They were also a helpful complement to the TKNGSST for providing a nuanced understanding about how teachers were receiving the professional development intervention. Nonetheless, for a future study, a more objective observation measure will be needed to confirm or disconfirm the understandings and insights about their NGSS teaching as reported in the Exit Slips.

CONCLUSION AND DIRECTIONS FOR FUTURE RESEARCH

A few lessons were learned from an exploratory investigation of the implementation of a professional development program to improve teacher knowledge for NGSS-based teaching in a large urban district serving K- 2 children from culturally diverse backgrounds. The preliminary finding that teacher knowledge about NGSS-based teaching improved after the professional development intervention suggests useful insights for informing future research for teaching and learning as envisioned by the

NSF-Funded Exploratory Study

Science Framework for K-12 Science Education and the *Next Generation Science Standards (NGSS)*

The design features of the professional development program used in this study were consistent with those of other studies (e.g., Garet, Porter, Desimone, Birman, & Yoon, 2001; Kennedy, (2016) and should be continued in the design of a future professional development intervention for improving teacher knowledge for NGSS teaching. However, for professional development to have its full impact on NGSS teaching, future professional development research needs to also provide intellectual engagement of teachers with strategies that focus on exposing student thinking in ways necessary for promoting growth in their tri-dimensional science learning. The increase in teacher knowledge about lesson planning, classroom practice and assessment in the current study supports this proposition and suggest the inclusion of these areas for study as well. Kennedy's (2016) review of the literature on how professional development does to improve student learning provides some helpful leads for how to do so. Also, NGSS (2013, Appendix D) identified a number of strategies for supporting science learning for marginalized groups such as English language learners and low-income learners. This reference is particularly useful for a subsequent research study with an explicit focus on improving children's use of processes for learning through classroom instruction and assessment.

The encouraging finding of a change in the baseline and post-professional development ratings on the *Teacher Knowledge for Next Generation of Science Standards for Teaching Questionnaire* has added to the knowledge base about the importance of professional development in supporting teachers in the acquisition of knowledge for NGSS teaching. Some confirmation of the finding was provided from the positive comments revealed from the analysis of the Exit Slips data. These are important first steps that a future study can build upon in the development of more technically- robust measures and tools for ascertaining the effects of professional development of teacher knowledge for NGSS teaching. For example, an observation protocol should be developed to permit valid and reliable inferences about evidence that demonstrate teacher knowledge for NGSS teaching in the classroom. Furthermore, such a measure would need to be complemented with qualitative tools for analysis of teacher-student and student-student interactions to better understand how teachers apply knowledge about Disciplinary Core Ideas, Cross-Cutting Concepts and Science and Engineering Practices in actual classroom contexts and in real time.

A third lesson learned from the exploratory study is that a future study would need to consider selection criteria for recruiting participants to consent to participating in the study. First, the sample size should be big enough to ensure confidence in the results of the investigation. In the current study there was attrition among some participants who initially attended professional development sessions and who did not complete the *Knowledge for NGSS-based Teaching Questionnaire* nor the Exit

Slips. Unanticipated commitments of some participants to address school-related duties were reasons given for the uneven in participation in the current study. Second, school administrators recommended teachers in each school who taught classes across K-2 grades and so the findings could not be differentiated either by school or grade level. A future study should recruit participants in sufficient numbers to better understand how teachers at different schools and grades or within the same schools and grades experience a professional development intervention with the goal of improving their knowledge for NGSS-based teaching.

REFERENCES

Garet, M. S., Porter, A. C., Desimone, L., Birman, B. F., & Yoon, K. S. (2001). What makes professional development effective? Results from a national sample of teachers. *American Educational Research Journal*, *38*(4), 915–945. doi:10.3102/00028312038004915

Guskey, T. R. (2003). What makes professional development effective? *Phi Delta Kappan*, *84*(10), 748–750. doi:10.1177/003172170308401007

Kennedy, M. (2016). How does professional development improve teaching? *Review of Educational Research*, *86*(4), 945–980. doi:10.3102/0034654315626800

National Research Council. (2012). A framework for K-12 science education: Practices, crosscutting concepts and core ideas. Committee on Conceptual Framework for the New K-12 Science Education Standards. Board on Science Education, Division of Behavioral and Social Sciences and Education, Washington.

NGSS Lead States. (2013). *Next Generation Science Standards: For States, By States*. The National Academies Press.

Chapter 11

Integrating English Language Arts and Science:
Promising Practices for Undergraduate Elementary Teacher Licensure Candidates

Kim Brown
https://orcid.org/0000-0003-0852-8857
University of North Carolina at Asheville, USA

ABSTRACT

The theory of Pragmatism naturally gives way to the concept of integrated and hands-on teaching methodologies. Teacher training programs grounded in the liberal arts are prime spaces for pre-service elementary teachers to learn about curricular integration. Pedagogy surrounding the integration of science and English language arts is particularly pertinent for today's classrooms. This chapter provides a description of how an elementary education science methods course was revised to include teaching methods for instructing teacher licensure candidates to teach their future students using an integrated and hands-on approach. Instructor lecture outlines and lab packets which include interactive class activities, instructions for teaching essential Science content, instructions for utilizing effective English Language Arts strategies for facilitating student comprehension and concept development, and inclusion of high-quality texts from the Common Core Exemplary Text list are provided.

DOI: 10.4018/978-1-6684-5939-3.ch011

INTRODUCTION

It was the year 1897, and McKinley, a former teacher, was serving as president of the United States. Schools were beginning to teach English as a second language, and Booker T. Washington was advocating for educational changes to provide a foundation for students as lifelong learners. John Dewey had written a prolific and enduring piece centering on a personal pedagogical doctrine.

Written within this doctrine, Dewey (1897) outlined a statement of beliefs centering on five themes. The first theme is his definition of education. This definition suggests that both psychological and sociological facets characterize education. Dewey stated:

I believe that the individual who is to be educated is a social individual and that society is an organic union of individuals. If we eliminate the social factor from the child we are left only with an abstraction; if we eliminate the individual factor from society, we are left only with an inert and lifeless mass. Education, therefore, must begin with a psychological insight into the child's capacities, interests, and habits. (para. 6)

Next, Dewey defined school. Dewey's definition centers on school as a product of the student's present life, and how what occurs at school should serve as a continuation of what is occurring in the student's home life. Dewey justified this by saying:

Existing life is so complex that the child cannot be brought into contact with it without either confusion or distraction; he is either overwhelmed by multiplicity of activities which are going on, so that he loses his own power of orderly reaction, or he is so stimulated by these various activities that his powers are prematurely called into play and he becomes either unduly specialized or else disintegrated. (para. 11)

The third aspect of Dewey's philosophy defines the subject matter of education. Dewey's ideas centered on his belief that what is taught in schools should be a product of what occurs in society, and the development of students within that society. To summarize these notions, Dewey declared:

I believe, therefore, in the so-called expressive or constructive activities as the centre of correlation. I believe that this gives the standard for the place of cooking, sewing, manual training, etc., in the school. I believe that they are not special studies which are to be introduced over and above a lot of others in the way of relaxation or relief, or as additional accomplishments. I believe rather that they represent, as types, fundamental forms of social activity; and that it is possible and desirable that the child's introduction into the more formal subjects of the curriculum be through the medium of these activities. (para. 33-35)

Dewey went on to define the nature of method in education. Dewey's thoughts were that students should be active participants in their learning, and that teaching is best accomplished through the development of images for the student. Dewey also claimed, "I believe that only through the continual and sympathetic observation of childhood's interests can the adult enter into the child's life and see what it is ready for, and upon what material it could work most readily and fruitfully" (para 52) and, "I believe that the emotions are the reflex of actions. I believe that to endeavor to stimulate or arouse the emotions apart from their corresponding activities, is to introduce an unhealthy and morbid state of mind" (para. 54-55).

Finally, Dewey defined the school and social progress. Dewey's belief was that social progress and reform occur through education. Dewey asserted:

I believe it is the business of every one interested in education to insist upon the school as the primary and most effective instrument of social progress and reform in order that society may be awakened to realize what the school stands for, and aroused to the necessity of endowing the educator with sufficient equipment properly to perform his task. (para. 66)

Current educational leaders and researchers support these seminal ideas proposed by Dewey. As one such example, Darling-Hammond et al. (2020) discuss effective classroom practices as being those which:

...are grounded in the science of learning and development which supports strong, trusting relationships; collaboration in the learning process; connections to prior experience; inquiry interspersed with explicit instruction where appropriate;... support for individualized learning strategies as well as collective learning...(and) authentic, engaging tasks with real-world connections. (p. 101)

These authors' ideas mirror Dewey's themes.

Lee and Brown (2018) purport that Dewey provides a foundation for science teaching specifically. In their study of multiple science education standards used in the United States, the authors found no clear connection between teaching students how to engage in scientific inquiry as a means for helping them develop skills in informed decision-making. They underscore the importance of the fact that:

...students' decision-making in socio-scientific issues showed that students made decisions using values, but values were not explored—in John Dewey's terms, students' decisions reflected their valuing, but students did not engage in evaluation. Dewey's view that the use of scientific inquiry can improve students' value judgment provides the link between inquiry and decision-making. (p. 77)

Williams (2017) supports a return to Dewey's ideas after a seeming stray from them in modern classrooms due to the increased emphasis on standardized curricula and testing. One specific area Williams emphasizes is the integration of curricular subject areas. The author asserts that approaches such as integrated teaching help meet the needs of a diversity of students with regard to gender, ethnicity, socioeconomic status, and varying learning needs and styles.

Dewey's ideas came to be known as the educational theory of Pragmatism. This philosophy naturally gives way to the concept of integrated teaching and hands-on teaching methodologies. Many different models of integrated teaching exist, with Multidisciplinary Integration being one such example. Teacher training programs grounded in the liberal arts are prime spaces for pre-service elementary teachers to learn about curricular integration. Pedagogy surrounding the integration of Science and English Language Arts is particularly pertinent for today's classrooms. This chapter describes teaching methods for instructing elementary teacher licensure candidates on how to teach their future students using an integrated and hands-on approach. As part of this description instructor lecture outlines and lab packets which include interactive class activities, instructions for teaching essential Science content, instructions for utilizing effective English Language Arts strategies for facilitating student comprehension and concept development, and inclusion of high quality texts from the Common Core Exemplary Text list are provided. This chapter presents practical and detailed information that can be used directly in elementary science teacher education courses.

BACKGROUND

Integrated Teaching

In the third facet of Dewey's (1897) theory, where he outlined ideas concerning the subject matter of education, Dewey stated explicitly that the more formal aspects of the curriculum should be taught through what he called the constructive activities of life, such as cooking, sewing, and manual labor. Hence, out of pragmatism was borne the concept of integrated teaching. As the concepts inherent in pragmatism and integrated teaching have become entrenched in the field of education, the ideas have become more clearly defined. This clarity has provided for definitions of different types of integrated teaching, including interdisciplinary integration, transdisciplinary integration, and multidisciplinary integration (Drake & Burns, 2004).

Interdisciplinary integration involves teachers helping students explore central ideas common in different disciplines. Fuchsman (2009) described interdisciplinary integration as a process of finding the common terminology and mutual understandings between disciplines. In other words, while the different disciplines are represented in a unit of study taught through the lens of interdisciplinary integration, the common lessons among these disciplines are more important. Interdisciplinary integration is illustrated by considering a social studies unit of study on the different types of communities. Students are assigned to groups that each explore either a suburb, rural area, or city. Students are presented a rubric for their individual work contributions as well as their group's products. Groups research the characteristics of their assigned community and build a representation of this type of community in their own state using milk cartons from the cafeteria for the building structures and other art materials for the environmental factors. Groups present their research through a written product and presentation to the whole class. The concepts of research, cooperative learning, assessment, reading and writing, art, and structural design are learned as a byproduct of the social studies topic of communities that is explored.

Transdisciplinary integration, as described by Zafeirakopoulos and van der Bijl-Brouwer (2018), "…inherently involves learning how to integrate disciplines towards exploring a problem or towards developing a solution or technology. Thus, transdisciplinary innovation and transdisciplinary learning are practically interchangeable" (p. 50). These authors describe Transdisciplinarity as a way of evoking solutions to real-world problems in a universal manner.

Engaging students in project-based learning is a central idea within transdisciplinary integration. Bell (2010) stated, "Project-Based Learning (PBL) is an innovative approach to learning that teaches a multitude of strategies critical for success in the twenty-first century. Students drive their own learning through inquiry, as well as work collaboratively to research and create projects that reflect their knowledge" (p. 39). For instance, a class of students becomes interested in solving the issue of the lack of playground equipment available at their school. The teacher facilitates reading and research skills by providing students with articles to read on state guidelines and recommendations for playground composition. The teacher also provides information about health and wellness according to the curricular standards for this area. Students are provided the opportunity to do field research on the playgrounds at other schools and parks in their area. Students create a presentation, using written, oral, and visual components, for their school and school system administrators. The presentation includes information on the health benefits of the playground, the suggested equipment, a cost analysis, and suggestions for the placement on school grounds. Curriculum negotiation is another concept within transdisciplinary integration and is centered on the concept of students suggesting their own topics of interest for the teacher to develop teaching and assessments around them (Drake & Burns, 2004).

"Multidisciplinary approaches focus primarily on the disciplines. Teachers who use this approach organize standards from the disciplines around a theme" (Drake & Burns, 2004, para. 9). For instance, a teacher can teach the theme "Underground Railroad" by having students read relevant books on the lives of slaves involved in the movement, study the history surrounding the slaves' fight for freedom, explore the spiritual songs that contain codes for the freedom movement, and learn the geography relevant to the owning of slaves in the United States. The larger topic of multidisciplinary integration generally takes one of two forms: intradisciplinary or fusion. The intradisciplinary approach is taken "When teachers integrate the subdisciplines within a subject area…Integrating reading, writing, and oral communication in language arts is a common example" (Drake & Burns, 2004, para. 10). An example of the intradisciplinary approach is a classroom study of the planets as part of Earth/space science whereby students explore the presence of water on Mars as a facet of biology, the chemical composition of the planet's atmosphere, and the geologic structure of the planet's surface. Fusion involves teaching two subject areas together. As an example, when English/language Arts (ELA) are taught together with geometry, and learning activities center on using ELA skills to teach geometry, fusion has been accomplished.

Integrating English/Language Arts and Science

Integrating ELA and science can be done for a host of different reasons, and all have strong value in the elementary classroom. Iveland and Burr (2019) listed the following reasons, which are applicable to the overall classroom experience: "Reinforcing skills and content in both subjects, supporting English Language Learners and ensuring all students are engaged, and making more time for science in the classroom (particularly in elementary school) without taking time away from other subjects" (para. 5).

Burr et al. (2017) said that the integration of ELA and science strengthens students' ELA skills largely because the multifaceted skills encompassed by ELA, such as reading difficult texts; conveying tasks, including reading complex texts and formulating opinions and points of view; forming descriptions; and endorsing assertions are seemingly less complex for students when these skills are used to investigate science topics in which students are truly interested. Their assertion was that the following are realized through ELA and science integration: "Enhanced student engagement, improved ELA skills, and stronger critical thinking" (p. 2).

Pearson et al. (2010) discussed the rationale for integrating ELA and science in terms of students accessing science material while at the same time strengthening their literacy skills. The authors claimed that integration is essential for this reason, given realities in the classroom that include an increased focus on science text as opposed to scientific inquiry due to literacy teaching demands and lack of availability of high-quality science textual sources. The authors further asserted the following:

Both teachers and students could be better at reading, writing, teaching, and learning from science texts. Students struggle with the abstract concepts, with a challenging scientific lexicon and set of discourses, and with complex images, graphs, and charts. Teachers, for their part, are often not well educated in science (at the elementary level) or in scientific-specific modes of literacy instruction (at the secondary level). (para. 12)

This fact, as stated by Person, Moje, and Greenfeaf, serves as the foundation for the teaching of strategies to facilitate ELA and science integration.

By their very definitions, liberal arts institutions of higher education espouse integration concepts. Exploration of various curricular areas, making connections between distinct concepts, and expanding the mind beyond training for a particular profession are the hallmarks of a liberal arts education – and sound very similar to Dewey's (1897) pragmatist ideas. It makes perfect sense, then, that a teacher education program at a liberal arts institution would emphasize the idea of integrated teaching as a best/promising practice for the classroom. The following provides an explanation of how a portion of an elementary education science methods course was revamped to focus on the integration of science and ELA.

CONTEXT

Description of the University and Department

The university at which the science methods course is taught is the only designated undergraduate liberal arts university in the 17-campus North Carolina state university system. The university is a public state institution of higher education, classified as a Baccalaureate College of Arts and Sciences by the Carnegie classification system, and accredited by the Commission on Colleges of the Southern Association of Colleges and Schools. The university has received national recognition for its humanities and undergraduate research programs. The university founded the National Conference on Undergraduate Research more than 25 years ago, and the university emphasizes student participation in faculty-mentored research projects. Additionally, most students of the university undertake career-related internships, and are supervised by university faculty during their time working in the field. Numerous students of the university take advantage of study abroad and study away programs. Finally, many courses and programs exist on campus that engage students in service projects aimed at improving the quality of life at home and around the world, which is a major focus of the university.

The university's Department of Education has as its mission to prepare candidates for a Standard Professional I Teaching license with a liberal arts foundation. The Department of Education engages with all departments across campus in the preparation of professional educators since undergraduate candidates major in an academic area specific to their intended licensure area, along with taking additional courses necessary to earn their state teaching license. Hence, education is not a major or a minor, but is an area of concentration in addition to the academic major. This structure reflects the liberal arts model.

Because the university is a liberal arts institution, candidates take arts and sciences courses in departments across campus in which they acquire their content knowledge. Courses taken in the Department of Education are structured to build on this content knowledge in the provision of pedagogical skills. In other words, the focus of Education courses at the university is almost strictly on pedagogy. This model is supported by researchers such as Davis and Buttafuso (1994), who provide a historical perspective on the role of small liberal arts colleges and teacher preparation. Their claim is that the type of curricular cooperation that is inherent at liberal arts institutions such as the university in this study promotes the development of teachers who are knowledgeable, thoughtful, and reflective.

Structure of the Course

All kindergarten–sixth grade (K-6) licensure candidates are required to take EDUC 322 (Inquiry-Based Science Instruction, K-6). Throughout the semester, candidates enrolled in the course learn about effective science, technology, engineering, and mathematics (STEM) teaching methodologies, and how these methodologies translate to their teaching of science to future elementary students. And, while the course focuses heavily on the provision of pedagogical skills for candidates, per the liberal arts model, a great deal of science content teaching takes place. This is done to assist the numerous candidates who, even though they have taken science content courses as part of their general education course of study, still feel intimidated by and lacking in knowledge with regard to science content. To accomplish teaching all of the methods candidates need to know in one semester, in addition to content, the course is flipped. In other words, candidates access lecture material and extensive course readings outside of class, allowing for the focus during class time to be on candidate engagement in inquiry and discovery learning. Course readings primarily come from the Abruscato and DeRosa (2019) text, which includes chapters on pedagogical information and teaching strategies as well as content information elementary teachers need to know for effectively teaching concepts in the Earth, physical, and life science strands. Additional course readings include a book chapter about identifying and breaking down student misconceptions in the science classroom (National Academies of Sciences, Engineering, and Medicine, 1997); an educational brief covering concepts related to disciplinary literacy in science (Wisconsin Department of Public Instruction, 2023); an article on the benefits of using technology-based tools in the science classroom (Gonzalez, 2019); and a research article covering the teaching diverse populations, curriculum adaptation, and curriculum integration in the science classroom (Gallard, 1997).

During the first third of the course, candidates learn the basic foundations for science teaching and learning. Candidates study such topics as the national and state science education standards, the different science materials available for teaching elementary students, and the constructivist and other theories inherent in the effective teaching of science. Candidates also participate in hands-on, inquiry-based activities to learn important teaching concepts as part of the flipped course model. In one course activity, candidates participate in a multi-part lab where they build airplanes out of different papers (copy paper, newspaper, wax paper, and wrapping paper) and test their flight distances. In this one participatory experience and subsequent reflective discussion, candidates learn the theories behind science instruction, how to integrate the teaching of science content into science teaching, how to structure a lab for students, the science process skills, the scientific method, and content information related to aerodynamics and physics. A particular emphasis is placed on instructing candidates in how to teach according to the 5 Es (engagement, exploration, explanation, elaboration, and evaluation) learning cycle, which is a best practice in science teaching that is grounded in constructivism and consists of leading students through the five phases as an instructional framework. Candidates then explore the state and national science teaching standards, science kits, different text and trade books, and assessment as they prepare for participation in a service-learning project. The service-learning project involves candidates creating an event from scratch and serving as event facilitators and judges for the regional Elementary Science Olympiad, and due to this project the course is a university-designated Service-Learning Course.

The next third of the class engages candidates in learning about serving the needs of diverse students in the classroom, using technology in the curriculum, effective lesson and unit planning, classroom management, and varied science teaching strategies. Candidates practice their skills as they engage in a six-visit field experience during which they observe elementary teachers in the K-6 classroom and eventually independently teach their own inquiry-based science lesson plan. Candidates learn the best practice of science notebooking as they create their own full science notebook entries for each of their classroom visits. Candidates' classroom learning is supplemented with their participation in hands-on labs aligned with each of the science strands covered in the course and structured in an integrated manner so that effective elementary pedagogical and content teaching practices can be taught in tandem. Candidates engage in such activities as exploring constructivist theories of teaching and how to teach elementary math graphing and data analysis concepts while investigating the bubbles produced by different types of dish detergent that they create by blowing through a straw. They also dissect fruits and vegetables to explore how to erase elementary students' science misconceptions and teach health objectives, create a barometer and learn about teaching the history of the significance of the discovery of the instrument as part of the Scientific Revolution and use of the instrument in creating the first known weather maps in the 19th century, which were instrumental in the explorations taking place during the time period. In addition, candidates investigate the best design for a clay boat that can hold the most weight while learning how to create effective assessments for elementary students and teach about writing informational pieces. The physics, biology, chemistry, and environmental science concepts inherent in the labs are emphasized as a means for providing candidates with the content knowledge necessary for teaching science in their future elementary classrooms.

In the final portion of the course, candidate learning focuses on how to effectively use all of the methods learned in the course to actually teach the science content elementary students need to know. The depth and breadth of the science curriculum, as well as the limited time typically allotted an elementary teacher to teach science, allows for a rich presentation of the integrated teaching methods presented in the course. Candidates are reminded of how integration was used and demonstrated through prior course activities, and they focus on how to explicitly facilitate integrated teaching, and specifically multidisciplinary integration, with a particular emphasis on the fusion of ELA and science as a best practice in science teaching.

The Teaching of Integration Strategies

The portion of the course during which specific ELA and science integration strategies are taught is structured according to the three strands of science – Earth, physical, and life. Three course days are spent on each of the three strands, and candidates simultaneously read the associated science content chapters of the Abruscato and DeRosa (2019) text. The first and second days are dedicated to providing candidates with direct instruction on literacy teaching strategies. While the literacy strategies explored are applicable to all genres of text, a particular emphasis is placed on

Integrating English Language Arts and Science

considering the pedagogical strategies inherent in teaching using nonfiction and informational texts. Teaching using these types of texts is highlighted for two reasons. First, these are the most common types of texts candidates will use to teach science and their future students will access to learn science. Additionally, candidates in the K-6 teacher licensure program take only one Language Arts methods course, and nonfiction and informational texts are not particularly emphasized in the course due to all other genres being accentuated. As part of the literacy strategy teaching in EDUC 322, candidates explore nonfiction/informational texts from the list of Common Core Text Exemplars, which provides teachers with an index of texts to use with their students that are considered to be high quality and demonstrative of the correct level of complexity for the students' grade level. The third day is spent guiding candidates in a hands-on application of what was taught during days one and two of the particular science strand in the form of a lab that they could use in their own future elementary classrooms. Each lab activity centers on the content of the featured science strand, incorporates the literacy skills on which candidates were instructed, includes the use of the Common Core Text Exemplar text candidates explored, and uses a teaching technique on which candidates were instructed.

The Earth science segment begins on day one with providing candidates information on teaching vocabulary according to the instructor notes outline provided in Appendix 1. A particular emphasis is placed the importance of teaching vocabulary as part of science instruction, since so much of the vocabulary elementary students encounter during science learning is both new and abstract. Day two consists of teaching candidates about content area literacy according to the instructor notes outline provided in Appendix 2. As part of candidates' learning related to content area literacy, candidates are introduced to text readability and how vocabulary plays a part in this by exploring a text from the Common Core Exemplar Text list. On day three, candidates conduct the lab presented in Appendix 3. The lab leads candidates through the creation and use of a sundial, the application of vocabulary and content area literacy comprehension, and strategies explored during days one and two of the Earth science segment. After the completion of the lab, the class discusses how to facilitate a lesson with elementary students that would incorporate comprehension of the Common Core Exemplar Text presented in Appendix 2, teach the necessary vocabulary, and facilitate the completion of the sundial lab, including teaching the necessary science content.

The physical science segment begins on day one with providing candidates information on teaching pre-reading strategies according to the instructor notes outline provided in Appendix 4. This facet of literacy instruction is stressed since effective pre-reading strategies are crucial for comprehension, especially nonfiction and informational text comprehension, which are the genres students will encounter most often during science instruction. Day two consists of teaching candidates basic strategies for facilitating comprehension during reading for their future students, per the instructor notes outline provided in Appendix 5. Candidates practice developing a pre-reading and during-reading comprehension activity centering on a text from the Common

Core Exemplar Text list. On day three, candidates complete the lab presented in Appendix 6. The lab leads candidates through creating a non-Newtonian substance to explore the states of matter and through the application of the pre-reading and during-reading comprehension strategies explored during days one and two of the physical science segment. After the completion of the lab, the class discusses how to facilitate a lesson with elementary students that would incorporate pre-reading and during-reading comprehension strategies for the Common Core Exemplar Text presented in Appendix 5 and facilitate the completion of the slime-making lab, including teaching the necessary science content.

The life science segment begins on day one with teaching schema theory, per the instructor notes outline provided in Appendix 7. Ensuring that candidates know about schema theory is crucial for their science teaching, since they will be guiding their future elementary students in developing numerous new schemata as they encounter new scientific concepts. Day two consists of teaching candidates strategies for facilitating cooperative learning for their future students, per the instructor notes outline provided in Appendix 8. Candidates practice developing a cooperative learning activity centering on a text from the Common Core Exemplar Text list. On day three, candidates complete the lab presented in Appendix 9. The lab leads candidates through creating a pinhole camera to explore how the eye interprets images, and through the application of schema building and cooperative learning activities explored during days one and two of the life science segment. After the completion of the lab, the class discusses how to facilitate a lesson with elementary students that would incorporate schema building and cooperative learning strategies for the Common Core Exemplar Text presented in Appendix 8. The class then facilitates the completion of the pinhole camera lab, including teaching the necessary science content.

CONCLUSION

Dewey (1907) outlined a key underpinning of this philosophical beliefs regarding education by observing, "We do not have a series of stratified earths, one of which is mathematical, another physical, another historical, and so on. All studies grow out of relations in the one great common world" (para. 107). Dewey (1916) lamented the state of education during his time by declaring, "Only in education, never in the life of farmer, sailor, merchant, physician, or laboratory experimenter, does knowledge mean primarily a store of information aloof from doing" (p. 218). When Dewey (1897) began his work by writing his theory of education, later to become central to the concept of pragmatism, the United States was primed for the new ideas regarding education. The state of schools in the United States in Dewey's time sounds very much like the state of present-day schools. That is, the late 19th century and early 20th century, as well as the modern era, are marked by great change occurring politically, socially, and economically. Modern education leaders acknowledge that ideas such as those brought forth by Dewey should be foci of today's schools. Darling-Hammond (2021) refers to Dewey as a progressive educator, and supports Dewey's notions of the transformation of schools, "…to allow more student-centered, inquiry-driven, and community-connected approaches that nurture the whole child…(and) drawn on the sciences of learning and development…" (p. 27). Williams (2017) calls for today's classrooms to mirror Dewey's ideas by offering students opportunities to learn by doing by participating in project learning with an emphasis on curricular integration. This approach is vital, says Schiro (2012, as cited in Williams, 2017), because it "…encompasses the intellectual, social, emotional, physical, and spiritual growth of the whole child, not just academic growth" (p. 93).

Societies in both time periods call for meaningful education that mirrors the world outside of the walls of the school building and closely parallels the reality of students' lives. Curricular integration and hands-on learning are two approaches that accomplish these charges. These ideas align perfectly with best practice in teacher education, especially as part of a liberal arts program. The integration of science and ELA, specifically through multidisciplinary integration emphasizing fusion, is a perfect coupling, as it naturally allows for teacher candidates to actively explore hands-on teaching methodologies in two vital curricular areas simultaneously. Actively engaging K-6 candidates to this type of teaching and learning approach in a university methods course prepares them to teach future students according to the realities of the real world and do so in an efficient and effective manner.

REFERENCES

Abruscato, J., & DeRosa, D. A. (2019). *Teaching children science: A discovery approach* (9th ed.). Allyn and Bacon.

Allington, R. L. (2002, June 1). What I've learned about effective reading instruction: From a decade of studying exemplary elementary classroom teachers. *Phi Delta Kappan, 83*(10), 740–747. Advance online publication. doi:10.1177/003172170208301007

Anderson, J. (2012, April 14). *Edgar Dale's cone of learning*. Edu Techie. http://www.edutechie.ws/2007/10/09/cone-of-experience-media/

Area Education Agency. (2011). *Imagine, elaborate, predict, and confirm (IEPC)*. AEA. https://www.centralriversaea.org/wp-content/uploads/2017/04/iepc-checked.docx

AumSum. (2016, May 19). *Human eye* [Video]. YouTube. https://www.youtube.com/watch?v=eDIma_Ai1Rc

Bell, S. (2010). Project-based learning for the 21st century: Skills for the future. *The Clearing House: A Journal of Educational Strategies, Issues and Ideas, 83*(2), 39–43. doi:10.1080/00098650903505415

Blachowicz, C. L. Z., & Fisher, P. J. (2006). *Knowledge rating comprehension strategy*. Reading Cross Curriculum. http://readingacrosscurriculum.com/Knowledge%20Rating%20Comprehension%20Strategy.htm

Bransford, J. D., & Johnson, M. K. (1972). Contextual prerequisites for understanding: Some investigations of comprehension and recall. *Journal of Verbal Learning and Verbal Behavior, 11*(6), 717–726. doi:10.1016/S0022-5371(72)80006-9

Burr, T., Britton, T., Iveland, A., Nguyen, K., Hipps, J., & Schneider, S. (2017). *The Synergy of science and English Language Arts: Means and mutual benefits of integration*. WestEd. http://k12alliance.org/docs/Synergy-of-science-and-english-language-arts-Report2.pdf

Chen, G. (2019, March 27). *Cooperative learning*. Public School Review. https://www.publicschoolreview.com/blog/cooperative-learning

Choudhary, V. (2014, December 5). *Fun with non-Newtonian fluid - Lamar University* [Video]. YouTube. https://www.youtube.com/watch?v=RIUEZ3AhrVE

Darling-Hammond, L. (2021, Fall). What will it take to promote whole-child development, learning, and thriving at scale? Three networks offer promising models. *American Educator, 45*(3), 27.

Darling-Hammond, L., Flook, L., Cook-Harvey, C., Barron, B., & Osher, D. (2020). Implications for educational practice of the science of learning and development. *Applied Developmental Science, 24*(2), 97–140. doi:10.1080/10888691.2018.1537791

Davis, B. M., & Buttafuso, D. (1994). A case for the small liberal arts colleges and the preparation of teachers. *Journal of Teacher Education, 45*(3), 229–235. doi:10.1177/0022487194045003009

Dewey, J. (1897). My pedagogic creed. *School Journal, 54*, 77-80. http://dewey.pragmatism.org/creed.htm

Dewey, J. (1907). *The school and society.* The University of Chicago Press.

Dewey, J. (1916). *Democracy and education.* CreateSpace Independent Publishing Platform.

Drake, S. M., & Burns, R. C. (2004). *Meeting standards through integrated curriculum.* ASCD. http://www.ascd.org/publications/books/103011/chapters/What-Is-Integrated-Curriculum%C2%A2.aspx

Fuchsman, K. (2009). Rethinking integration in interdisciplinary studies. *Issues in Integrative Studies, 27*, 70–85.

Gallard, A. J. (1997). *Creating a multicultural learning environment in science classrooms.* Research Matters. https://narst.org/research-matters/multicultural-learning-environment-science-classrooms

Gonzalez, E. (2019). *The value of digital tools in science classes.* Edutopia. https://www.edutopia.org/article/value-digital-tools-science-classes

Hall, L. (2009, September). Seeing eye to eye. *National Geographic Explorer, 9*(1), 3–9.

Iveland, A., & Burr, T. (2019). Integrating science & ELA: Discoveries from the early implementer evaluators. *California Classroom Science, 31*(5). http://www.classroomscience.org/integrating-science-ela-discoveries-from-the-early-implementer-evaluators

Koscielniak, B. (2013). *About time: A first look at time and clocks.* Clarion Books.

Lee, E. H., & Brown, M. J. (2018). Connecting inquiry and values in science education: An approach based on John Dewey's philosophy. *Science & Education, 27*(1-2), 63–79. doi:10.1007/s11191-017-9952-9

My Byline Media. (2022). *Readability formulas: The Fry graph readability formula.* https://readabilityformulas.com/fry-graph-readability-formula.php

NASA.gov. (2022). *Creating a sundial and what makes day and night.* NASA. https://www.eyeonthesky.org/lessonplans/14sun_sundials.html

National Academies of Sciences, Engineering, and Medicine. (1997). *Science teaching reconsidered: A handbook.* The National Academies Press. doi:10.17226/5287

Pearson, P. D., Moje, E., & Greenleaf, C. (2010). Literacy and science: Each in the service of the other. *Science, 328*(5977), 459–463. doi:10.1126/science.1182595 PMID:20413491

Read, W. Think. (2005). *Discussion web.* https://www.readwritethink.org/files/resources/lesson_images/lesson819/graphic-organizer.pdf

Readingquest.org. (n.d.). *Story map.* Reading Quest. https://www.readingquest.org/pdf/story_map.pdf

Regents of the University of Minnesota. (2022). *Education resources for teachers: Cloze procedure.* UMN. https://dhh-resources.umn.edu/language-literacy/k-12-reading-strategies/cloze-procedure/

Science Learning Hub – Pokapū Akoranga Pūtaiao. (2012, April 5). *Pinhole cameras and eyes.* https://www.sciencelearn.org.nz/resources/58-pinhole-cameras-and-eyes

Stahl, S. A. (1999, November 1). Why innovations come and go (and mostly go): The case of whole language. *Educational Researcher, 28*(8), 13. Advance online publication. doi:10.2307/1176312

Teachnology, Inc. (n.d.). *How to study better using SQ3R. Teachnology.* https://www.teach-nology.com/teachers/lesson_plans/interdisciplinary/usingsq3r.html

TeachThought. (2022). *Reading comprehension strategies.* TechThought. https://www.teachthought.com/literacy/reading-strategies/

Technology Publishing Company. (2003). *Teacher workbooks: Graphic organizer series.* TPC. https://www.actedu.in/wp-content/uploads/2016/03/Science-Graphic-Organizers.pdf

WETA Public Broadcasting. (2022a). *Reading rockets: Anticipation guide.* WETA. https://www.readingrockets.org/strategies/anticipation_guide/

WETA Public Broadcasting. (2022b). *Reading rockets: Directed reading/thinking activity (DR-TA).* WETA. https://www.readingrockets.org/strategies/drta

WETA Public Broadcasting. (2022c). *Reading rockets: List-group-label.* WETA. https://www.readingrockets.org/strategies/list_group_label

WETA Public Broadcasting. (2022d). *Reading rockets: Semantic feature analysis.* WETA. https://www.readingrockets.org/strategies/semantic_feature_analysis

WETA Public Broadcasting. (2022e). *Reading rockets: Strategies that promote comprehension.* WETA. https://www.readingrockets.org/article/29202/

WETA Public Broadcasting. (2022f). *Word maps*. Reading rockets. https://www.readingrockets.org/strategies/word_maps

White, T. G., Graves, M. F., & Slater, W. H. (1990). Growth of reading vocabulary in diverse elementary schools: Decoding and word meaning. *Journal of Educational Psychology, 82*(2), 281–290. doi:10.1037/0022-0663.82.2.281

Williams, M. K. (2017). John Dewey in the 21st century. *Journal of Inquiry and Action in Education, 9*(1), 91–102.

Wisconsin Department of Public Instruction. (2023). *Clarifying literacy in science*. Science. https://dpi.wi.gov/science/disciplinary-literacy/types-of-literacy

Zafeirakopoulos, M., & van der Bijl-Brouwer, M. (2018). Exploring the transdisciplinary learning experiences of innovation professionals. *Technology Innovation Management Review, 8*(8), 50–59. doi:10.22215/timreview/1178

Zoehfeld, K. W., & Meisel, P. (1998). *What is the world made of? All about solids, liquids, and gases*. HarperCollins.

KEY TERMS AND DEFINITIONS

Common Core: A set of academic standards in the areas of Language Arts and Math which outline what students should know and be able to do at every grade level. To date, 41 states have adopted the Common Core standards.

English Language Arts: The teaching and learning of reading, writing, speaking, listening and viewing.

Inquiry-Based Learning: A teaching and learning technique which engages students in exploration of a topic through a careful and systematic method of asking questions and seeking explanations.

Integration: A teaching technique in which the teaching of two or more subjects are woven together as a whole.

Pedagogy: The theoretical and practical methods of how teachers teach.

Pragmatism: A philosophy in the field of Education centered on the belief that education should emphasize topics that are practical for students' lives to help them grow and develop to be better people.

STEM Education: A teaching approach which guides students in using science, technology, engineering, and/or mathematics concepts to solve problems and answer real-world questions.

APPENDIX 1

Instructor Notes Outline for Teaching Vocabulary

Have the class complete the following activity (providing the class with a handout containing the activity is the most efficient way to facilitate the activity):

You are in the $ party, and you want your party to stay in control even though the @s have a slight majority in your state. Since your party controls Congress, you get to design the shape of the voting districts for the election. Below is a map of your state indicating the geographic placement of the $ and @ voters. Draw rings around the districts to create a map dividing the 4 voting districts in your state that will enable the yellow party to win 3 out of the 4 districts (you cannot move the location of voters):

@ @ $ $ $ $ $
@ @ @ @ @ @ @
@ @ @ $ $ $ $
@ @ @ $ $ $ $
@ @ @ @ @ $ $

After drawing your map, discuss the following with a partner, and record your ideas:

What might be the effect on the green voters when they realize the yellow party has gerrymandered the district so the green party candidates can only win in a minority of the districts?

After the class finishes the activity, explain that the word gerrymander is named after Elbridge Gerry. In 1812, as the governor of Massachusetts, before he became vice president of the United States, Gerry signed a bill creating a partisan district in Boston that was such a bizarre shape it looked like a salamander. Emphasize the staying power of this word and its origin since active learning was used to teach the word. Relate this to Dale's Cone of Learning by showing the website (Anderson, 2012).

Progress with instruction according to the following outline, filling in facts and other appropriate information:

- Most important principle for vocabulary instruction: it is not enough to learn a concept, students have to see the relationship among concepts
- Often students will have background knowledge of and/or experience with a word but don't know the word at the conceptual level; hence, they can't see the relationships among other words/concepts

Integrating English Language Arts and Science

- Other times, students will have little background knowledge of or experience with a word
- Vocabulary Strategies can come either at the beginning, the middle, or at the end of the lesson
- Some facts about teaching vocabulary
  - Students get better at reading (and improve their vocabularies) by reading (Allington, 2002)
  - Students with low levels of vocabulary who are poor readers are unlikely to do the large amount of reading needed to grow their vocabularies (Stahl, 1999)
  - Vocabulary problems of children who enter school with limited vocabularies worsen over time (White et al., 1990)
- Direct Instruction
- The Dictionary/Glossary
  - Drawbacks
- Inference/Context
  - General Context
  - Non-Directive Context
  - Directive Contexts
- What Does it All Mean?
- Levels of Vocabulary Words
  - Tier 1: Basic words (dog, pencil, scary, darkness, walk – meanings don't really need to be taught)
  - Tier 2: High-frequency words that cross disciplines (committee, evaluate, argumentative, upheaval)
  - Tier 3: Specialized vocabulary (phoneme, sonnet, archipelago, isotope)
- How to Explain Words
  - Give examples of PARTICULAR circumstances in which the word might be used ("You word use the word *heave* when someone lifts something that is very heavy.")
  - Give examples in everyday language ("Someone who is *persuasive* can talk others into doing things.")
  - Identify misdirective, general, non-directive, and directive contexts
  - Identify Tier 2 words or overarching ideas that can be used to introduce/reinforce vocabulary
  - Choose most crucial words (at least three) and develop a student-friendly definition for each
  - Consider ways to reinforce students' learning with these words

Review the vocabulary instructional strategies below with the class by showing the websites:

- Semantic Feature Analysis (WETA Public Broadcasting, 2022d)
- List-Group-Label (WETA Public Broadcasting, 2022c)
- Cloze Passages (Regents of the University of Minnesota, 2022)

APPENDIX 2

Instructor Notes Outline for Teaching Content Area Literacy

Review vocabulary teaching concepts from the last class period.

Progress with instruction according to the following outline, filling in facts and other appropriate information:

- Content Literacy
    - What it means if a person is:
        - illiterate
        - functionally literate
        - aliterate
    - What it means that literacy is situational
    - What is content literacy?

Share the TeachThought (2022) website, divide the class into small groups, and have groups identify the top 5 strategies elementary students need to learn to apply to read and comprehend science informational/nonfiction texts. Have groups share and facilitate a whole class discussion on the information provided by each group.

Progress with instruction according to the following outline, filling in facts and other appropriate information:

- Explain that readability of science informational/nonfiction texts is an important consideration – lead the class in making a double-column list of the factors that make a text readable and factors that make a text difficult to read
- Explain concept density and concept clarity, and discuss how vocabulary is a factor

Introduce the Fry Readability Graph by viewing the website (My Byline Media, 2022), and have the class read Koscielniak (2013) and complete a Fry Graph on the

Integrating English Language Arts and Science

story. Have the class share results and discuss the accuracy of the Common Core Exemplar Text list showing that the Koscielniak story is on a fourth-to-fifth-grade level. Discuss the instructional implications of using this and other texts in the science classroom without checking the readability first.

APPENDIX 3

Sundial Lab Packet

Making a Sundial

(Teacher Note: Before students begin this lab, you will read aloud the text, *About Time: A First Look at Time and Clocks*. To facilitate comprehension of the text, pre-teaching of vocabulary is essential. The vocabulary that should be taught includes axis, directions [north, south, east, west], and sundial. The intent in the Explain section is for students to deduce the definition of gnomon, hour lines, dial plate, and true north, but you may find it necessary to pre-teach this vocabulary as well, considering student needs.)

Essential Question:
How can we tell the Earth is moving?

Engage:
You will be working with a partner. Decide who will be the person in charge of gathering materials and constructing the sundial, and who will be the scribe.

As you listen to the read-aloud of *About Time: A First Look at Time and Clocks*, write your answers to the following questions using knowledge you already have.

1. What causes day and night?
2. What is a sundial?

The person who is in charge of materials for this lab should collect/organize the materials listed below, as we discussed in class.

Materials:
One paper plate with a hole punched in it
A pencil
Four pieces of tape (the tape pieces have already been cut for you)
One straw
One cellphone with a compass app installed (optional)

Integrating English Language Arts and Science

Explore:
Follow the steps below to make a sundial.

1. The scribe will write the letter N anywhere on the edge of the paper plate.
2. The sundial constructor will insert one end of the straw into the paper plate's hole and tape the straw so that it can stand upright.
3. After you have listened to instructions and are outside, work with your partner to use the compass app and point yourselves to true north. The teacher will help you with this if you have trouble, or if you do not have the cellphone app.
4. The sundial constructor will orient your sundial so that the N written on your sundial is pointed true north.
5. The scribe will draw the location of the straw's shadow on the paper plate, and then write the actual time on the paper plate at the end of the shadow.
6. One partner will take the sundial with them and repeat steps 3 through 5 two more times before noon, once at exactly noon, and three times after noon today. This partner will bring the sundial back to class for the next class period.

Explain:

1. Visit the NASA.gov (2022) website (https://www.eyeonthesky.org/lessonplans/14sun_sundials.html) and read the information provided.
2. Work together as partners to decide on the definitions of the following terms. The scribe will write below your definition for each term, and the sundial constructor will then label your sundial with the terms.
   A. Gnomon
   B. Hour Lines
   C. Dial Plate
   D. True North
3. Work together as partners to explain the different drawings on your sundial that represent the straw's shadows. The scribe will write your explanation below.

Elaborate:
In the Engage section above, one of the questions you answered was, "What causes day and night?" As partners, discuss and explain how a sundial and the cause of day and night are related. The scribe will write your explanation below.

Evaluate:
As partners, decide which words go in each blank of the cloze passage below. The scribe will write your answers. After you have filled in the entire cloze passage, the sundial constructor will show your completed work to the teacher and receive

Integrating English Language Arts and Science

a sheet of paper containing the answer key to the cloze passage. Work together as partners to check your work.

The ___ fully rotates on its ___ every 24 hours. This rotation causes observable patterns such as day and ___. Although it is the Earth, and not the sun, that is moving, it appears that the sun rises in the direction of ___. As the day goes on toward the noon hour, the shadows caused by an object get ___ in length and appear on one side of the object. As the day continues to go on into the hours after noon, the shadows caused by an object get ___ in length, and switch to the other side of the object.

When we made a sundial, we used a ___ for a dial plate and a ___ for a gnomon. As the sun hit the straw, a ___ was formed that could be seen on the dial plate. By making observations of the sundial throughout a day, I drew ___ on the dial plate, which showed me that the sundial labels each hour that passes as the Earth ___ on its axis. The Earth's ___ on its ___ causes day and night, and it also caused the ___ that the straw formed on the dial plate of the ___. This is how I know the Earth is moving.

(Teacher Note - The solution to the cloze passage is as follows: Earth, axis, night, east, longer, shorter, paper plate, straw, shadow, hour lines, rotates, rotation, axis, shadows, sundial)

APPENDIX 4

Instructor Notes Outline for Teaching Pre-Reading Strategies

Show the class the Choudhary (2014) video.

Move directly into teaching the outlined points below without discussing the video, filling in facts and other appropriate information:

- Lesson Plan Focus Activity and Pre-Reading or Pre-Learning Activities
  - Activate background knowledge or schemata about topic before beginning to read
  - Help set purpose for reading
- Setting a Purpose for Reading
  - Guides the reading process the students use
  - Helps them identify strategies they can use when they read
  - Helps them identify important information to remember as they read
  - Represents the directional and motivating influences that get readers started, keeping them on course
  - Produces the vigor and potency and push to carry them through to the end
  - Represents the key element in versatility

- Versatile and Appreciative Readers
- Types of Pre-Reading Strategies
  - Demonstrations (used to display a theory, concept, or phenomenon – most often used in science, but can be done in any area)
  - Discrepant events (using something that is surprising or startling like costumes and props)
  - Visual displays (picture books and things found online can provide good visual displays)
  - Thought-provoking questions (can include essential questions, quick writes, poems, and anticipation guides)

Ask class to discuss how the video shown at the beginning of class was a pre-reading strategy. Lead the class in a discussion about the value of discrepant events as a pre-reading strategy.

Review the pre-reading instructional strategies below with the class by showing the websites:

- Directed Reading/Thinking Activity (DR-TA) (WETA Public Broadcasting, 2022b)
- IEPC Chart (Area Education Agency, 2011)
- Anticipation Guide (WETA Public Broadcasting, 2022a)

APPENDIX 5

Instructor Notes Outline for Teaching Comprehension During Reading

Progress with instruction according to the following outline, filling in facts and other appropriate information:

- Comprehension is reading
- Aspects of comprehension
  - Main Idea
  - Significant Detail (who, what, when, where, why, and how)
  - Sequencing (focus on time-order words like now, before, while, when, yet, after)
  - Making inferences (drawing conclusions based on reasoning, deriving ideas that are implied rather than directly stated)

- Critical reading (propaganda, fact/opinion, bias, word connotations, judge author's competence)
    - Cause and effect
    - Vocabulary
    - Reading rate/fluency
- Aspects of reading situation that influence comprehension
    - Purpose for reading
    - Audience
    - Importance of task to student
- Text factors influence the reading situation
    - Sentence difficulty
    - Punctuation
    - Organizational patterns and paragraph structure
    - Types of text
- Types of comprehension
    - Literal
    - Higher order
    - Critical reading
- Levels of comprehension
    - Literal
    - Interpretive level
    - Applied level

Review the comprehension during reading instructional strategies below with the class by showing the websites:

- Guided Reading Procedure (GRP) (K12reader.com, 2018)
- KWL (WETA Public Broadcasting, 2022e)
- Discussion Web (Read, Write, Think, 2005)
- Maps/Graphic Organizers (Readingquest.org, n.d.) and (Technology Publishing Company, 2003)

Have the class read Zoehfeld and Meisel's (1998) Common Core Exemplar Text. Assign small groups to develop an assignment using an effective pre-reading strategy and one of the four during-reading comprehension instructional strategy ideas above that would be used in an elementary classroom to instruct using the book. Have groups share their work with the class.

APPENDIX 6

Slime-Making Lab Packet

As the initial portion of the Engage section of the lab, the teacher shows the Choudhary (2014) video and then reads aloud the Zoehfeld and Meisel (1998) text. With no further discussion, students complete the lab.

Slime Time
Rationale:
   Students will explore matter and motion through the composition of a created substance.

Engage:
   As partners, decide who will be the scribe and who will be in charge of materials for this lab. Also, as partners, discuss the following questions. The scribe should write your exact answers to these questions in the space provided.

1. What substances do you use in your everyday life that could be classified as oils?
2. What substances do you use in your everyday life that could be classified as gels?
3. What substances do you use in your everyday life that could be classified as creams?

   The person in charge of materials should now collect a set of materials, as discussed in class.

Explore:
   As partners, you should share the responsibilities involved in making slime. On the following page, the scribe should record your observations of the substances created after the completion of steps 3, 6, 7, 9, and 11.

Step 1: Pour the entire contents of your glue bottle (4 ounces of glue) into a cup.
Step 2: Fill the empty glue bottle with warm water from the sink. Pour the water (4 ounces) into the cup containing the glue.
Step 3: Mix thoroughly, and set the water and glue solution aside.
Step 4: Measure 240 mL (1 cup) of WARM water. Pour the water into a new cup.
Step 5: Measure 5 mL (1 teaspoon) of Borax. Pour the Borax into the cup containing the warm water.

Integrating English Language Arts and Science

Step 6: Thoroughly mix the water and Borax solution until the Borax is completely dissolved.

Step 7: Pour ¾ of the water and glue solution into a Ziploc bag, and mix in 1/2 of the water and Borax solution.

Step 8: Add 2 drops of your desired color of food coloring.

Step 9: Seal the bag without letting any air remain inside, and knead the mixture.

Step 10: Pour off any excess liquid into the sink. If the slime is too sticky, add a little more water and Borax solution. If the slime is too slippery, add a little more water and glue solution. Continue to work with the mixture in this way until it reaches the consistency of slime. The slime should not stick to surfaces and should be flexible.

Step 11: Separate your slime so that each partner can have some in a bag.

Step 12: The person in charge of materials should discard any remaining water and Borax solution (but not the water and glue solution!) down the drain and throw away your trash. Both partners should clean your area using wet paper towels.

Step 13: Wash your hands thoroughly.

The scribe should record your observations (using complete sentences) of the substances created after the completion of the following steps:

3
6
7
9
11

Explain:

As partners, discuss the following questions. The scribe should record your exact answers in the space provided.

1. What happens if you pull your slime slowly?
2. What happens if you pull your slime sharply?
3. What happens if you roll your slime into a ball and drop it on a hard surface?
4. What happens when you try to flatten your slime?
5. What happens if you squeeze your slime?

Elaborate:

Imagine that you run a manufacturing company that is trying to expand its portion of the market. The company needs to investigate a variety of Slime formulations to

Integrating English Language Arts and Science

see if they can make better lubricants for machines than those currently available. What could you do to the slime to change its properties?

Evaluate:

As partners, use the Venn diagram below to show what you learned from the book read before you began the lab (*What is the World Made of? All about Solids, Liquids, and Gases*) and the slime you made. One circle should represent solids, one circle should represent liquids, and one circle should represent slime. The person in charge of materials should get a copy of the book from the table at the front of the classroom and take the lead in finding facts in the book to add to the diagram. The scribe should record your work on the diagram.

Figure 1.

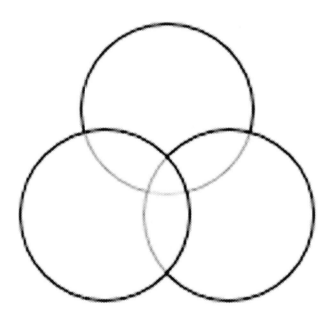

As partners, discuss the following questions. The scribe should record your answers to the questions.

1. Why did the diagram not include gasses?
2. As a result of completing the diagram, what did you learn about solids?

Integrating English Language Arts and Science

What did you learn about liquids?
What did you learn about slime?

3. What type of substance is slime?
4. What did the video you watched before completing the lab have to do with the lab?

The person in charge of materials should return the book to the table at the front of the classroom and tell the teacher you and your partner are finished with the lab. The teacher will come to you to discuss the lab and your work in the Evaluate section.

APPENDIX 7

Instructor Notes Outline for Teaching Schema Theory

Remind class of the discussions we have had regarding the importance of teaching vocabulary, attending to factors related specifically to content literacy, engaging students in pre-reading strategies, and teaching students strategies for comprehending text while engaging students in science. Tell the class we are going to focus a specific topic to ensure that students can learn the new concepts presented while learning about the associated vocabulary and reading texts related to science learning.

Progress with instructing according to the following outline, filling in facts and other appropriate information:

- The 3 levels of reading comprehension
    - independent level (90-100% comprehension)
    - instructional level (75-90%)
    - frustration level (below 75%)
- We want students to read text at their instructional level, and the texts we use to teach science should be at the independent or instructional level for students.

Provide the class with the passage at the top of the second column on page 719 of Bransford and Johnson's study (1972). After they have read the passage, ask the class to share what the passage means. (Most likely, the class will not be able to discuss the meaning of the passage.)

Show the class the image on page 718 of Bransford and Johnson's work (1972). Then, ask the class again what the passage means. Discuss the activity as a class.

Integrating English Language Arts and Science

Stress that this activity shows there must be something in a learner's consciousness to which to relate the concept for a new concept to have meaning. Describe that once the class saw the picture, they accessed the correct schema for the passage.

Progress with instruction according to the following outline, filling in facts and other appropriate information:

- Schema Theory
    - For a stimulus or new information to have meaning, there must first be something in the learner's consciousness to which it can be associated.
    - If we organize new knowledge in a personally meaningful way, then we will be able to understand and remember this knowledge.
    - We tend to see hierarchical (superordinate, coordinate, and subordinate) relationships among concepts.
- Learning occurs when learners construct their own knowledge
    - Connecting new knowledge structures to the structures of knowledge already in the mind
    - Reorganizing the knowledge structures already in the mind

Project the following list, and tell the class they have 3 minutes to learn and memorize the list, using any method they wish.

slate gold steel aluminum
bronze granite limestone silver
iron diamond platinum brass
emerald lead sapphire ruby
marble copper

Discontinue showing the list and tell the class they have 3 additional minutes to write down all they remember. Have the class discuss the activity and particularly their method for remembering the items. Share a possible solution (see the following for a suggestion).

Metals Stones
Precious Alloys Elements Precious Building
gold steel aluminum diamond slate
silver bronze lead emerald granite
platinum brass iron sapphire limestone
copper ruby marble

Integrating English Language Arts and Science

Explain that this activity shows there must be meaningful organization for learners to construct new knowledge.

Progress with instruction according to the following outline, filling in facts and other appropriate information:

- Concepts
- Entities
- Principles

Note that concepts have to be learned before entities and principles, in most cases.

Review the schema theory instructional strategies below with the class by showing the websites:

- CD Word Map (WETA Public Broadcasting, 2022f)
- Knowledge Ratings (Blachowicz & Fisher, 2006)
- SQ3R (Teachnology, Inc., n.d.)

APPENDIX 8

Instructor Notes Outline for Teaching Cooperative Learning

Explain that much of what teachers do to help students develop their schema, comprehend text and ideas, and learn new concepts is engage them in cooperative learning. Discuss that scientists work with other scientists directly and through researching the work of others, hence are constantly engaging in cooperative learning. Have the class discuss the importance of engaging students in cooperative learning in the elementary classroom.

Divide the class into small groups. Ensure that at least one member of each group has a laptop, but ideally every group member would have one. Have groups read the information (which provides the definition of, purposes for, and elements of cooperative learning, as well as descriptions of cooperative learning strategies) and watch the embedded videos (which enhance the descriptions of the cooperative learning strategies) on the Chen (2019) website. Provide groups with copies of the Hall (2009) Common Core Exemplar Text. Assign each group one of the cooperative learning strategies from Chen (2019) and have each group work cooperative to decide how they would use their assigned cooperative learning strategy to have their students comprehend the Hall (2009) text. Have each group share their ideas with the class.

APPENDIX 9

Pinhole Camera Lab Packet

Do You See What I See?
   Essential Question:
   What can you tell about how light carries images to the human eye?
   Engage:
Complete the Knowledge Rating chart below, which contains terms related to eyesight. Think about your knowledge of each term as it relates to eyesight, and write the number that explains your knowledge of the term by writing the correct number from the following ratings in the First Rating column:

1 – I do not know anything about this term.
2 – I have heard this term, but I am not sure what it means.
3 – I know the term so well that I can define it and/or use it correctly in a sentence.

Terms	First Rating	Second Rating	Third Rating	Definition
Cornea				
Refract				
Pupil				
Lens				
Retina				
Rods				
Cones				

Watch the video at https://www.youtube.com/watch?v=eDIma_Ai1Rc (AumSum, 2016). Then, do another rating of the terms in the chart using the Second Rating column.

Now begin working with your partner. Decide who will be the person in charge of gathering materials and the scribe, and who will be the person in charge of cleaning up.

Discuss the following questions as partners. The scribe should write your answers to the questions.

1. What causes a person to have to wear glasses?
2. What do you know about how light carries images to the human eye?

Integrating English Language Arts and Science

The person who is in charge of materials for this lab should collect/organize the materials listed below as we discussed in class.

Materials:
  Two pieces of black paper
  Tape
  A ruler
  A piece of plastic wrap (this has been pre-cut to the correct size)
  A piece of aluminum foil (this has been pre-cut to the correct size)
  A rubber band
  A sharp pencil
  A hand lens
  A writing pencil for each partner
  A clipboard
  Seeing Eye to Eye text
  A sheet of notebook paper for each partner
  A sheet of notebook paper for the group of four

Explore:
   Study the pinhole camera at the front of the room, which will serve as a model to help you create your camera. Working together as partners, follow the steps below to make your own pinhole camera.

1. Roll one sheet of black paper into a hollow cylinder of 30 cm in length 7 cm in diameter. Tape along the entire length of the tube to hold it together.
2. Place plastic wrap across one end of the tube you have made so that it is flat and has no wrinkles. Hold it in place with a rubber band. This forms the screen on which the image will be projected. Tape the plastic wrap all the way around the tube to hold it tight and in place. Remove the rubber band.
3. Roll the second sheet of black paper around the first tube. Be sure that it is a snug fit, but also be sure that the inside tube can slide easily within the outside tube.
4. Place the aluminium foil to form a flat surface over the end of the outside tube. Fold the side of the aluminium foil around the outside of the tube and hold it in place with a rubber band.
5. Remove the inner tube.
6. Use a sharp pencil to place a very small hole in the middle of the aluminium foil.
7. Place the inner tube back inside the outer tube by sliding the end with the plastic wrap up to the end of the outer tube with the aluminium foil.

8. Pull the inside wrap slightly away from the aluminium foil so that the hole and the screen are separated.

Explain:
   Gather your lab sheet, a writing pencil for each partner, a clipboard, a hand lens, the sharpened pencil, and your camera to take outside. Once the teacher moves the class outside, complete the steps below and record your observations after completing each step. Take turns so that both of you as partners do each step. Write your name next to your individual answer after each observation.

1. Point the end of the camera with the hole toward light and hold the open end of the camera to your eye. Make sure the sun is behind you. Ask your partner to stand about 15 feet in front of you. Look at them through the camera. Record your observations.
2. Ask your partner to again stand about 15 feet in front of you, wave their arms, and jump up and down as you look at them through the camera. Record your observations.
3. Investigate what happens to the size, brightness, and sharpness of the image when you focus on a sunny scene and do each of the following (record your observations for each):

Move the screen created by the plastic wrap further from the hole
Move the screen created by the plastic wrap closer to the hole
Place a hand lens over the hole
Make a hole that is about three time larger than your original hole
Place a hand lens over the bigger hole

Elaborate:
   Once you are back inside, the person in charge of materials should return all materials except your camera to the table at the front of the room and get copies of the *Seeing Eye to Eye* text for each partner. Read the story as individuals, and then discuss it as partners. You will then do a Think-Pair-Share activity.
   As the Think step, both you and your partner should think individually about the following questions and write your individual answers on a sheet of paper.
   As the Pair step, discuss your individual answers as partners, and decide on your final answers to each of the questions. The scribe should record your collective answers to each question below.
   As the Share step, the person in charge of materials should ask the teacher which partner group you will join and where your group of four will work, and then return to their partner. Once you and your partner are joined with your other partner group

Integrating English Language Arts and Science

at the correct work location, decide who will get a clean sheet of paper from the table at the front of the room and who will be the scribe for the small group. Both partner groups should share their responses to the questions, and the scribe should record the answers on the clean sheet of paper. Decide who will record your final small group answers on the new sheet of paper.

1. How were the images formed that you saw in the camera?
2. Why were the images upside down?
3. Why did the images become bigger but not so bright when the screen was moved further away from the hole?
4. Why did the image become brighter but blurrier when the hole was bigger?
5. How did the plastic lens cause the images to become sharply focused?
6. In what ways is this camera you made (with lens in place) similar to the human eye?
7. In what ways is the camera you made different from the human eye?

Evaluate:

On your own, without your partner or group, refer back to your Knowledge Rating Chart and do one more rating of the terms in the chart using the Third Rating column. Then, use the Definition column to write a definition for all terms you rated with a 3.

Portions of this lab are adapted from Science Learning Hub – Pokapū Akoranga Pūtaiao, 2012.

Chapter 12
Fostering Inclusivity:
Nurturing Diversity Within Elementary STEM Teacher Preparation Programs

Surjit Singha
https://orcid.org/0000-0002-5730-8677
Kristu Jayanti College (Autonomous), India

ABSTRACT

This chapter examines the profound impact of inclusivity on STEM teacher preparation programs for elementary education, emphasizing its critical role in enhancing STEM instruction. Inclusivity underscores the importance of establishing thriving learning environments encompassing abilities, race, gender, and socioeconomic status. Practical recommendations, theoretical foundations, and a current landscape analysis underscore inclusivity's critical importance when equipping educators for diverse classrooms. The conclusion emphasizes the significance of diversity in moulding culturally competent and socially conscious STEM educators. While recognizing enduring obstacles, it foresees encouraging developments in technological integration and comprehensive diversity awareness. Continuous research is critical to assessing the effectiveness of inclusivity initiatives, ascertaining their enduring consequences, and enhancing pedagogical methodologies. To advance STEM education in the future, it is imperative to prioritize evidence-based practices, adaptability, and inclusivity.

DOI: 10.4018/978-1-6684-5939-3.ch012

INTRODUCTION

In teacher preparation programs with a STEM focus, promoting inclusivity stems from recognizing that diversity is not a trivial formality but a driving force behind innovation, creativity, and comprehensive educational excellence. As we traverse the intricate terrain of modern education, it becomes progressively apparent that the preparation of elementary STEM educators entails not merely the transmission of technical expertise but also the development of an all-encompassing perspective that values diversity and actively strives to rectify inequities. In addition to demographic representation, STEM teacher preparation programs diversity encompasses recognizing and appreciating the cultural nuances, diverse experiences, and profound perspectives that students from different backgrounds contribute to the educational setting (Singer et al., 2020; Moreu et al., 2021). Through this approach, these programs have the potential to successfully dismantle obstacles, confront preconceived notions, and offer a more precise depiction of the world that awaits these prospective educators. A commitment to inclusivity in STEM education is multifaceted. The process involves developing curricula that effectively connect with students of varied backgrounds, incorporating instructional approaches that accommodate distinct learning styles, and cultivating a sense of belonging, recognition, and appreciation for each student. By combining various perspectives, academic experiences are improved, and prospective STEM educators have the cultural sensitivity to navigate an increasingly interconnected global community (Palid et al., 2023; Margot & Kettler, 2019).

Furthermore, the advocacy for inclusiveness in STEM teacher preparation programs transcends the student population, including administrators, faculty, and the wider academic community. A diverse cadre of educators enhances the educational environment through their spectrum of pedagogical approaches, research interests, and problem-solving perspectives. Promoting inclusivity among faculty members is consistent with the values emphasized in the curriculum, resulting in a mutually reinforcing impact that spans the entire educational environment (Palid et al., 2023; O'Leary et al., 2020). In the following sections of this chapter, we shall examine the concrete advantages of cultivating inclusivity in teacher preparation programs specializing in STEM. The importance of inclusivity in STEM education becomes a strategic necessity rather than a moral one, as it facilitates the development of a resilient and flexible workforce by eliminating systemic obstacles that hinder fair and equal access to these fields and enabling previously unrealized capabilities of underrepresented groups. An unwavering dedication to diversity and inclusiveness is required to transform elementary education via teacher preparation programs with a STEM focus. In doing so, we establish a foundation for a cohort of technologically savvy educators who know the subtleties of a globally interconnected, diverse, and perpetually changing society. This chapter aims to explain the complexities of promoting inclusivity in STEM education, establishing the foundation for a paradigm shift that surpasses the conventional limitations of teacher training.

The fundamental tenet of this chapter is that diversity and inclusivity are not only ethical imperatives but also essential to the efficacy and pertinence of modern education when it comes to teacher preparation programs with a STEM focus. Numerous theoretical frameworks provide support for this particular perspective. For example, critical pedagogy places significant emphasis on the capacity of education to confront and effect change regarding social inequities. Analyzing and eliminating systemic barriers that impede diverse participation in STEM fields is necessary for implementing this framework into STEM teacher preparation.

Furthermore, according to social cognitive theory, people gain knowledge by observing others; therefore, students from underrepresented backgrounds may be motivated to pursue and persevere in STEM professions through exposure to diverse role models in STEM education (Mau et al., 2020). Through an analysis of these theoretical foundations, the objective of this chapter is to present a conceptual framework that clarifies the significance of inclusivity in STEM education as a whole.

This chapter underscores the importance of promoting inclusivity in teacher preparation programs specializing in STEM fields. It distinguishes diversity from being a trivial supplement and recognizes it as an essential and foundational component that improves the effectiveness of educational endeavours. Establishing a solid theoretical framework incorporating influential concepts like critical pedagogy and social cognitive theory is necessary to support this argument. The chapter will use this theoretical lens to examine the complexities and difficulties of fostering inclusivity in STEM teacher preparation.

Moreover, the chapter probes into the present state of diversity and inclusivity in STEM teacher preparation programs, providing a thorough examination that highlights prevailing deficiencies and obstacles that demand urgent consideration. By illuminating the prevailing state of affairs, the chapter establishes the foundation for a nuanced analysis of the concrete advantages of cultivating inclusivity. This statement goes beyond the mere necessity of addressing social justice issues and effectively demonstrates how inclusivity enhances the quality and pertinence of STEM education.

Consistent with a comprehensive viewpoint, the chapter expands its scope to include pragmatic factors and offers implementable suggestions and tactics. The purpose of these insights is to provide educators, administrators, and policymakers with the essential resources required to incorporate inclusivity into STEM teacher preparation programs effortlessly. Through this approach, the chapter foresees the establishment of educational settings that not only mirror the variety of the student population but also actively cultivate an atmosphere of inclusivity.

The chapter's purview extends beyond a cursory examination of diversity statistics in STEM education. It extensively investigates the theoretical underpinnings, complexities, and obstacles associated with inclusivity. This chapter contributes substantially to the ongoing discourse on transforming elementary education via STEM teacher preparation by examining theoretical and practical aspects. In essence, it strives to present a persuasive argument favouring inclusivity as a fundamental principle critical to moulding future educators in a globalized and ever more diverse society.

THE IMPERATIVE OF INCLUSIVITY

The importance of diversity in STEM teacher preparation programs transcends societal and educational boundaries; it is a strategic necessity that transcends the simple fulfilment of quotas. Promoting diversity within these programs benefits STEM education's calibre, pertinence, and influence. The significance above is apparent in the enhanced educational atmosphere that it fosters. The contributions of educators and students, in the form of diverse perspectives, experiences, and cultural insights, improve the quality of discussions, problem-solving methodologies, and collaborative learning encounters. Exposure to various viewpoints encourages critical thinking and innovation, equipping future STEM educators with a more comprehensive and inventive mindset to confront practical obstacles (Palid et al., 2023).

Furthermore, by promoting inclusive teaching practices in STEM teacher preparation programs, aspiring educators can observe a paradigm shift in instructional approaches, prioritizing accommodating varied learning styles and backgrounds. Promoting the incorporation of various perspectives during the preparatory phase nurtures the creation of pedagogical methodologies that are attuned to the unique requirements of students stemming from diverse backgrounds, thus promoting an all-encompassing ethos in the classroom (Song et al., 2023; Salehi et al., 2021).

One additional crucial aspect is the development of global citizenship. In this regard, diverse perspectives in teacher preparation programs expose educators to various cultural norms, global issues, and scientific problem-solving methodologies. Educators who have personally encountered and embraced diversity throughout their professional development are more adept at cultivating in their pupils a sense of global citizenship, thereby equipping them to participate in a world that is interdependent and culturally heterogeneous (Akkari & Maleq, 2020; Aydın & Cinkaya, 2018).

STEM teacher preparation programs prioritizing diversity facilitate the critical approach of mitigating inequities in STEM access. These initiatives have historically been instrumental in dismantling systemic obstacles that have hindered the involvement of underrepresented communities in STEM disciplines (Song et al.,

2023). By establishing a varied cohort of STEM educators, these programs actively promote the elimination of preconceived notions, ignite enthusiasm among students of diverse backgrounds to pursue careers in STEM, and ultimately cultivate a more balanced and representative STEM workforce.

It is critical to prioritize cultural competency and social relevance in a world undergoing accelerated change. Including diverse individuals in teacher preparation programs guarantees that STEM educators possess cultural competence, which empowers them to modify STEM material in a way that connects with students of various backgrounds. Cultural competency fosters a more responsive and inclusive classroom environment, ensuring each student feels acknowledged, listened to, and appreciated (Palid et al., 2023). The fundamental importance of diversity in STEM teacher preparation programs resides in its ability to mould a forthcoming cohort of educators who possess technical expertise, social consciousness, cultural sensitivity, and the capability to confront the ever-changing obstacles of the STEM domain.

The ramifications of diversity in STEM teacher preparation programs have a significant societal impact, influencing both students and educators. The recognition and proactive promotion of diversity extend beyond the confines of the educational environment, exerting influence on the social fabric and fostering a future characterized by greater inclusivity and equity (Moreu et al., 2021; Singer et al., 2020). Incorporating diversity into STEM teacher preparation programs provides students with a profoundly transformative educational experience. In addition to gaining technical expertise, students derive advantages from engaging in dialogues with instructors and peers who contribute a wide range of viewpoints, life experiences, and cultural heritage (Palid et al., 2023). This form of exposure cultivates a more profound comprehension of the multifaceted nature of their environment, thereby encouraging tolerance, empathy, and the capacity to work together despite disparities.

Furthermore, the effects of diversity on students extend to the cultivation of essential competencies that are vital in the current global environment. Prolonged engagement with a heterogeneous group of colleagues and students improves one's capacity for effective communication, analytical reasoning, and flexibility. Proficiency in these abilities is critical for achieving academic excellence and equipping students with the necessary tools to navigate the intricacies of an interconnected global community where the value of interdisciplinary cooperation is growing (Palid et al., 2023; Song et al., 2023).

Diversity's profound societal impact on educators is also evident in STEM teacher preparation programs. Educators who have undergone diverse training are more adept at establishing inclusive learning environments that reflect the intricacies of the real world. Subsequently, this impacts subsequent cohorts of pupils by exemplifying the significance of diversity in occupational settings (Suriel & Litster, 2022).

Moreover, diversity influences educators in ways that transcend the confines of the classroom. Promoting diversity among STEM educators enhances workforce representation in these domains (Suriel & Litster, 2022). This initiative disrupts stereotypes, encourages underrepresented students to pursue STEM careers, and tackles systemic inequalities. By embracing diversity and inclusion, educators are critical to influencing societal perspectives and establishing fairer opportunities that benefit all.

Fundamentally, the ramifications of diversity incorporated into STEM teacher preparation programs transcend the boundaries of the academic establishment. It shapes a cohort of educators and learners with academic aptitude, cultural sensitivity, social consciousness, and a steadfast dedication to promoting inclusiveness in the broader social fabric. Broadly viewed, diversity in STEM teacher preparation catalyzes constructive societal change, establishing the groundwork for a future characterized by greater fairness and interdependence.

BARRIERS TO INCLUSIVITY

The endeavour to incorporate diversity into STEM programs faces numerous interconnected obstacles, all contributing to the need for more representation of people from diverse backgrounds in these disciplines. A comprehensive comprehension of these challenges' intricacies is necessary to devise efficacious approaches for advancing inclusivity in STEM. A significant obstacle pertains to the inequitable availability of high-quality education, wherein resource discrepancies and opportunities disproportionately impact students from underrepresented origins. Prejudices and preconceived notions concerning gender, race, ethnicity, and socioeconomic standing discourage individuals from pursuing careers in the STEM fields, exacerbating the problem. Another barrier to representing and supporting ambitious individuals is the need for more mentorship and visible role models from various backgrounds. Persisting systemic challenges within STEM organizations are institutional barriers, which comprise biased employment practices and a shortage of diversity in leadership areas. To address continuing disparities, it is necessary to implement explicit and inclusive policies, targeted initiatives and a dedication to diversity, equity, and inclusion. Unconscious biases that affect decision-making hurt minority groups even more, which shows how important it is to teach people about these biases and come up with ways to get rid of them. The lack of comprehensive outreach and engagement strategies hinders the interest and knowledge of underrepresented groups in STEM, highlighting the criticality of proactive initiatives and early exposure. Socioeconomic and cultural elements, including financial limitations and cultural norms, impact attitudes and decisions regarding STEM professions, necessitating interventions such as financial assistance programs and cultural competency training (Palid et al., 2023; Javier et al., 2022; Singer et al., 2020). To solve the complicated problems that keep people of different backgrounds from joining STEM fields, we must use all-encompassing methods considering educational, governmental, and social factors. It is essential to take proactive steps like targeted initiatives, policy changes, and culture transformations to create an environment encouraging and supporting young people from diverse backgrounds to do well in STEM fields.

Underrepresentation in STEM disciplines is intricately intertwined with historical, systemic, and cultural elements, which erect formidable obstacles that impede inclusiveness and equality. Discrimination and exclusion have methodically marginalized women and individuals belonging to racial and ethnic minorities throughout history, resulting in lasting consequences for their ability to obtain STEM-related educational and professional opportunities. Systemic obstacles deeply ingrained in academic and professional frameworks further compound underrepresentation. Obsessive hiring practices, restricted mentorship prospects, and unequal access to high-quality education perpetuate exclusion cycles. Furthermore, preconceived notions and societal norms influenced by cultural elements steer specific demographics away from STEM disciplines, exacerbating this disparity. The lack of prominent mentors and role models from underrepresented backgrounds contributes to a detrimental cycle of underrepresentation, which hinders individuals' ability to envision themselves succeeding in STEM professions. Unconscious biases ingrained in cultural norms influence decision-making processes in STEM, disadvantaging underrepresented groups in employment, promotion, and evaluation. There needs to be more outreach programs for people from underrepresented groups because things are already hard for them. Support systems are also not always open to the people who need them the most. It makes it harder for them to get past cultural and systemic barriers. Economic disparities present an additional barrier for individuals from lower socioeconomic origins, limiting their access to resources and opportunities. To fix this general lack of representation, we need to work hard in many areas, such as by implementing mentorship programs, policies that include everyone, campaigns that fight stereotypes, and fair and equal access to resources and education (Palid et al., 2023; Javier et al., 2022). Implementing these strategic measures is critical for removing enduring obstacles and cultivating a STEM field that is more inclusive and diverse.

STRATEGIES FOR CREATING INCLUSIVE STEM PROGRAMS

Numerous case studies and best practices illustrate effective initiatives to foster diversity in STEM programs. The following instances represent inventive methodologies and tactics that have successfully bolstered representation and inclusiveness across a range of STEM disciplines:

An immersive summer program, the Women's Technology Program (WTP) at MIT, encourages secondary school girls to pursue careers in computer science and engineering. Through exposure to female role models in STEM, practical experiences, and mentorship opportunities, WTP has substantially increased the enrollment and retention of young women in these disciplines.

The engineering department of the University of Michigan introduced a comprehensive equity initiative, emphasizing targeted recruitment and assistance for underrepresented minorities. Employing collaborations with secondary schools, community colleges, and mentorship programs, the enrollment and graduation rates of minority students in engineering have increased significantly.

Aspirations in Computing is a National Center for Women and Information Technology (NCWIT) program that rewards and acknowledges high school females for their technological and Computing accomplishments and aspirations. This initiative has effectively attracted more young women to STEM-related professions by providing a forum for mentorship, networking, and recognition.

A technology corporation, Salesforce has established comprehensive programs to promote diversity and inclusion. Their top priorities are equal compensation, diverse hiring committees, and inclusive leadership development. Salesforce's disclosure of diversity metrics and establishment of measurable objectives has evolved into an industry standard within the technology sector.

Providing research experiences in STEM disciplines, the Community College Internship Program (CCI) of Oak Ridge National Laboratory targets community college students, including those from underrepresented backgrounds. This endeavour has effectively garnered the interest of a wide-ranging cohort of individuals in STEM fields, inspiring these pupils to pursue higher education and professions in scientific inquiry.

The Computer Science Summer Institute (CSSI), organized by Google, is a three-week summer program for computer science-interested, underrepresented high school seniors. CSSI's immersive experiences, mentorship, and work environment exposure have fostered greater diversity among Google interns and full-time engineering employees.

The Academic Leadership for Women in Engineering (ALWE) Program of the Society of Women Engineers (SWE) aims to cultivate leadership abilities among female faculty members in the field of engineering. The program facilitates skill development seminars, mentorship sessions, and networking opportunities to promote and retain women in academic leadership positions.

These case studies and best practices highlight the importance of targeted initiatives, mentorship, exposure, and inclusive policies in advancing diversity in STEM. These models are of great value to institutions and organizations looking for efficient approaches to establishing environments in the STEM disciplines that are more inclusive and representative.

Implementing efficient recruitment, retention, and support strategies is critical to fostering inclusivity in STEM programs, specifically regarding attending to the distinct requirements of underrepresented communities. To augment recruitment efforts, focused outreach initiatives establish early connections with mentorship programs, community organizations, and local institutions, cultivating enthusiasm and consciousness regarding STEM prospects. Engaging in career fairs and events designed for diverse communities enhances professional exposure and fosters inclusivity. Retention mentorship programs facilitate connections between underrepresented individuals and supportive mentors, providing them with the essential guidance and insights required to navigate the complexities of STEM fields. The establishment of inclusive learning environments necessitates the incorporation of varied viewpoints into the curriculum and cultivating an environment that appreciates the contributions of every individual. Specialized workshops and professional development opportunities address underrepresented groups' unique obstacles in STEM professions. Community-building initiatives, such as affinity groups and networking events, foster a sense of inclusion and facilitate connections among underrepresented groups. Strategies to eradicate disparities should ensure all individuals have equal access to resources, including academic support services and research facilities. Scholarship programs and financial aid initiatives mitigate economic obstacles, enabling underrepresented individuals to pursue STEM education. By increasing their understanding, faculty and staff participation in cultural competency training fosters a more inclusive and supportive academic environment. It is essential to recognize and accommodate various learning styles and routes to achievement and honour individuals' distinct paths and schedules in STEM education and professional endeavours (Palid et al., 2023). Integrating these strategies dismantles barriers and establishes a flourishing, diverse, and vibrant STEM community.

Digital technologies are essential for improving inclusivity in STEM (Science, Technology, Engineering, and Mathematics) education by catering to various learning requirements, promoting collaboration, and eliminating access obstacles.

Adaptive learning platforms and educational apps are crucial in promoting diversity in STEM education. These technologies customize content to match individuals' unique learning styles and speeds, particularly benefiting students with varying skills and backgrounds. It enables them to interact with STEM materials at the most

Fostering Inclusivity

suitable level for their requirements. In addition, digital tools integrate accessibility capabilities like text-to-speech, closed captioning, and customizable font sizes. All learners, including those with disabilities, can access STEM information through these features. The internet offers a wide range of resources, such as virtual labs and simulations, that enable students to explore STEM subjects hands-on, regardless of their geographical location or the availability of costly laboratory equipment. Collaborative digital platforms, such as Google Workspace and Microsoft Teams, enable instantaneous contact and cooperation, overcoming geographical and social obstacles and promoting community among students from all backgrounds. These tools also facilitate remote learning, providing flexibility for students who encounter difficulties attending conventional lectures due to considerations such as residing in rural areas, health concerns, or work-family obligations. Coding platforms that use visual programming interfaces promote inclusivity by providing access to coding for students with a range of abilities, reducing the reliance on written language proficiency. The utilization of digital resources facilitates worldwide connectivity, enabling students to establish connections with their peers, experts, and professionals in science, technology, engineering, and mathematics (STEM). It fosters virtual collaborations and allows students to gain exposure to various perspectives within the STEM sector. Moreover, these solutions offer educators data-driven insights regarding student performance and engagement, facilitating a more focused and comprehensive teaching approach.

CULTURAL AND GLOBAL VIEWPOINTS ON INCLUSIVITY IN STEM

The international outlook on inclusivity in STEM (Science, Technology, Engineering, and Mathematics) highlights the significance of embracing cultural diversity and creating an environment that encouraging individuals from all backgrounds to feel accepted and encouraged to engage in STEM disciplines. Internationally, there is an increasing acknowledgement that various viewpoints play a crucial role in fostering innovation and addressing challenges in science, technology, engineering, and mathematics (STEM).

Cultural perspectives have a substantial impact on the formation of attitudes toward inclusiveness in the fields of science, technology, engineering, and mathematics (STEM). Certain cultures may have established gender or societal norms that impact decisions about schooling and career paths. Efforts to foster inclusivity frequently entail confronting these preconceptions and motivating people from marginalized groups to pursue STEM education and professions.

Several nations have enacted programs to tackle gender disparities in STEM disciplines, acknowledging the historical underrepresentation of women. Initiatives that offer mentorship, support networks, and educational opportunities specifically designed for girls and women play a crucial role in dismantling obstacles and promoting inclusiveness.

Furthermore, the international community acknowledges that inclusion goes beyond gender and includes race, ethnicity, socioeconomic class, and disability. Culturally sensitive approaches encompass recognizing and resolving distinct obstacles encountered by individuals from diverse cultural backgrounds, guaranteeing that STEM education and work environments are inclusive and accommodating.

Participating in international collaborations in STEM education and research enhances the global viewpoint more inclusively. Collaborations between institutions from different nations offer opportunities to interchange ideas, techniques, and exemplary approaches to advancing diversity and inclusivity. These collaborations contribute to developing a more thorough comprehension of the issues and opportunities associated with inclusion in STEM worldwide.

Various cultural viewpoints should be integrated into the curriculum to promote diversity in STEM education. It entails presenting the achievements of scientists and inventors from many origins and incorporating illustrations that resonate with pupils from various cultures. By doing this, educators can establish a learning atmosphere that is more inclusive and appreciates the vastness of global diversity.

INCLUSIVE PEDAGOGY AND CURRICULUM

Integrating inclusive teaching methodologies, curriculum development, and assessment strategies is fundamental to creating an educational setting that accommodates a wide range of requirements, adheres to the values of fairness, and enhances the overall learning experience. Inclusive teaching approaches highly value acknowledging and valuing students' varied backgrounds, learning styles, and abilities. To effectively engage students and cater to their diverse preferences, instructors may utilize various instructional strategies, including but not limited to collaborative learning, active participation, and hands-on activities. They are incorporating a range of perspectives, accents, and practical applications into STEM curricula, inclusive curriculum design endeavours to mirror and connect with the varied identities and experiences of students (Yannier et al., 2020; Somyürek, 2014; Lofstrom & Nevgi, 2006). Adaptable course structures permit investigation by individual interests, thereby fostering a sense of applicability and relevance. Inclusive assessment approaches surpass conventional methods by employing a variety of formats, including group projects and project-based evaluations, to recognize and assess distinct abilities and aptitudes. Minimizing cultural biases and ensuring transparency in assessment criteria facilitates the promotion of inclusiveness in the evaluation process. Furthermore, cultural competence in education entails instructors being conscious of and appreciative of the cultural heritage of their pupils, thereby fostering an all-encompassing learning milieu that promotes candid discourse and reciprocal regard. Implementing these inclusive strategies in concert eliminates obstacles to learning, creating an environment conducive to success and achievement for all students (Jonsson & Prins, 2019; Bearman & Ajjawi, 2018).

Cultural competence is fundamental to pedagogical practices that foster inclusive and efficient learning environments. Cultural competence in education encompasses instructors' capacity to understand, value, and harmoniously incorporate various cultural experiences, perspectives, and origins into their teaching approaches. Adopting this critical approach significantly enhances the educational experience for students of diverse cultural backgrounds. To promote cultural competence, pedagogical practices that are culturally competent integrate various case studies, perspectives, and examples into the curriculum on purpose (Nganga & Akpovo, 2020). Educators facilitate a more comprehensive comprehension of the subject matter by affirming disparate experiences and expanding the perspectives of all learners by presenting a range of voices and cultural contexts. To foster a sense of belonging among students from various cultural and religious backgrounds, Singha & Singha (2023) assert that educators must recognize the significance of faith-based education, establish safe environments for dialogues concerning faith and culture, and actively promote inclusiveness.

Furthermore, cultural competence plays a significant role in fostering an inclusive educational setting wherein students' cultural diversity is respected and treated with respect. Educators actively work to establish an environment that encourages students' appreciation, acknowledgement, and recognition of their cultural heritage, fostering a vital sense of belonging that is intrinsically linked to successful learning. Cultural competence promotes exchanging ideas, perspectives, experiences, and cultural insights among students, fostering an environment conducive to open dialogue regarding cultural differences. The interchange of thoughts and concepts mentioned above enhances the educational milieu and cultivates reciprocity and esteem among pupils from diverse cultural heritages. In addition, educators with cultural competence adapt their instructional approaches to accommodate the diverse learning styles and preferences influenced by their students' cultural heritage (Nganga & Akpovo, 2020; Puckett, 2020). As educators proactively endeavour to comprehend the cultural contexts that influence their students' learning experiences, they can customize their approaches to be more efficacious and all-encompassing. In summary, the incorporation of cultural competence into pedagogical approaches is a complex undertaking that entails the incorporation of varied viewpoints into the curriculum, the promotion of inclusive atmospheres, the facilitation of candid discussions, the modification of teaching methodologies, and the comprehension of the cultural backgrounds of students. This dedication promotes students' academic achievement and fosters the growth of a more tolerant, respectful, and globally conscious society.

MENTORSHIP AND ROLE MODELS

Considering how leaders and different role models can help prepare STEM teachers is essential. Mentors and role models of varied backgrounds are essential in an educational setting characterized by ongoing underrepresentation. Their presence is critical to cultivating an environment that is both inclusive and supportive of learning (Nkrumah & Scott, 2022; Richmond et al., 2019). Mentors and role models are indispensable individuals who provide aspiring STEM educators with inspiration, guidance, and practical insights. Their influence is significant in influencing the experiences and aspirations of these individuals. Representation in STEM teacher preparation programs is crucial because diverse role models reflect the heterogeneous demographics of students and society. Observing the achievements of individuals belonging to underrepresented groups who are also leaders in STEM disciplines conveys a significant message to those aspiring to become educators: They, too, can excel and make valuable contributions (Alemdar et al., 2022; Richmond et al., 2019).

In addition, by highlighting the accomplishments of people from various backgrounds, diverse role models dismantle preconceived notions and eradicate obstacles. Through their actions, mentors actively support the elimination of preconceived conceptions regarding the qualifications and viability of STEM professions, motivating a greater variety of aspiring educators to pursue and persevere in these domains. Mentors who possess cultural competence enhance the mentorship relationship by comprehending the distinct obstacles and prospects encountered by people of different races, ethnicities, and cultural backgrounds (Nkrumah & Scott, 2022; Richmond et al., 2019). According to Singha (2023) research, educators facilitate students' exploration of cultural identities, foster critical thinking, and enhance their proficiency in digital literacy. By being culturally competent, mentors ensure the mentorship encounter is customized and relevant to the protégé's needs. Mentorship and role modelling by individuals from underrepresented groups with comparable backgrounds transcend mere guidance; they foster a deep-seated sense of assurance and inclusion. This mentorship initiative ensures that individuals from diverse backgrounds can succeed in STEM education, promoting a more inclusive and hospitable academic setting. Mentors from various backgrounds provide valuable guidance, connections, and networks within the STEM community. Enabling underrepresented groups to gain access to resources, opportunities, and a wider professional community is of utmost importance, as it facilitates their development and progression within the industry.

In addition, including mentors from various backgrounds is crucial to rectifying implicit biases within the STEM education system. Mentors from various backgrounds create an atmosphere where people assess others based on their abilities rather than preconceived notions tied to heritage, challenging presumptions (Kricorian et al., 2020). The transformative capacity of diverse role models and mentors to inspire, guide, and empower the next generation of educators makes them crucial for STEM teacher preparation. Through their contributions, they actively cultivate an inclusive and equitable environment in STEM education, encouraging people of all backgrounds to participate, providing support, and fostering confidence in their ability to contribute significantly to the discipline.

POLICY IMPLICATIONS

The examination of policy ramifications concerning the preparation of STEM teachers highlights the complex interaction between initiatives undertaken by institutions and the government. Adopting a holistic and comprehensive approach is critical to tackle inclusivity concerns effectively. In this regard, accreditation bodies and educational organizations significantly influence the overall trajectory of STEM education. Policy formulation at the institutional level should be meticulous in promoting inclusivity in STEM teacher preparation programs. It entails the establishment of comprehensive diversity metrics and reporting systems that guarantee the visibility of the demographic makeup of students and faculty. Implementing inclusive admissions policies and prioritizing complete evaluation criteria is vital to assembling a diverse group of STEM educators.

To better prepare educators for diverse classrooms, institutions must implement curricular diversity standards incorporating culturally relevant content and inclusive teaching strategies (Salehi et al., 2021; O'Leary et al., 2020). Governmental initiatives exert considerable influence over the overall course of STEM education. Sufficient financial resources allocated to initiatives that promote inclusivity and research motivate institutions to enact efficacious measures. Governments may additionally promote diversity recruitment by incentivizing academic institutions that proactively strive to increase the diversity of their faculty and student bodies. To ensure everyone has the same and fair access to high-quality STEM education and to promote diversity at all levels, national policy frameworks should first focus on fixing systemic problems (Palid et al., 2023). Accreditation bodies and educational organizations play a crucial role in fostering inclusivity by serving as gatekeepers of program quality. Evaluating faculty, student body, and curriculum diversity is crucial in determining inclusive accreditation standards. Emphasizing inclusive teaching practices in establishing professional development standards guarantees that STEM educators possess the necessary skills and knowledge to foster inclusive and hospitable learning environments.

Moreover, these organizations possess the capacity to undertake research and advocacy, distribute optimal methodologies, carry out investigations, and champion policies that foster diversity in STEM teacher preparation. Policy implications for inclusivity in STEM teacher preparation necessitate the incorporation of the efforts of educational, governmental, institutional, and accreditation organizations in a synergistic fashion. Adopting this all-encompassing strategy is critical to fostering an encouraging and inclusive environment, enabling STEM educators to address twenty-first-century students' varied requirements adequately.

Promoting inclusivity within STEM teacher preparation programs is a critical responsibility of accreditation bodies and educational organizations. Such efforts are essential for fostering a diverse and equitable educational environment. As custodians of program quality and standards, accreditation bodies exert considerable sway over STEM teacher preparation programs to ensure that inclusiveness is a top priority. An essential way in which accreditation bodies make a valuable contribution is by formulating criteria for inclusive accreditation. The criteria above evaluate programs' efforts to promote diversity and inclusion by considering the presence of underrepresented groups among faculty and students and the inclusiveness of curricular content. Singha & Singha (2023a) argue that diversity, which encompasses differences in age, ability, religion, culture, race, ethnicity, gender, sexual orientation, and ability, is fundamental in our global context. Recognizing and embracing this wide range of perspectives and experiences is crucial for cultivating inclusive atmospheres and nurturing favourable connections in our personal and professional spheres. Furthermore, with accreditation bodies, educational institutions may establish professional development benchmarks that precede STEM educators' training in inclusive pedagogical approaches. By combining their expertise and resources, these educators are better equipped to design inclusive learning environments that cater to the varied requirements of students (Salehi et al., 2021; Moreu et al., 2021). Jones et al. (2020) validated the NextGen Scientist Survey for middle school science capital, which included expectations, experiences, task values, and familial influences. Scientific verification is required for any instrument. In addition, educational organizations and accreditation bodies promote inclusivity via advocacy and research initiatives. They conduct research to ascertain efficacious approaches, distribute optimal methodologies, and promote policies cultivating diversity in STEM teacher preparation. A critical factor in advancing diversity in STEM programs is accreditation bodies' assistance in the form of recruitment and retention tactics and recommendations. Potential recommendations could encompass support structures, mentorship programs, and outreach initiatives designed to recruit and retain members of underrepresented groups actively. Furthermore, it is imperative to cultivate partnerships with key stakeholders, including industry leaders and community organizations (Eaton, 2022). These collaborative alliances offer significant perspectives and materials, thereby augmenting the inclusiveness of STEM teacher preparation programs. The partnership between accreditation bodies and educational organizations is crucial in influencing the trajectory of STEM teacher preparation concerning inclusivity. Gender and expectations influence STEM dedication. While allowing students to enrol without prerequisites fosters equity, the persistence of gender disparities highlights the criticality of promoting inclusivity (Amin et al., 2023). Casto and Williams (2020) conducted a study that highlights significant racial and ethnic disparities in STEM secondary schools in North Carolina in comparison to the overall educational system. The study highlights a hierarchical structure within the STEM education system, uncovering discrepancies related to gender and race/ethnicity. The study supports broadening the research scope to include elementary and middle-level STEM institutions to comprehensively investigate the underlying factors contributing to these disparities. Moreover, the research implies the significance of undertaking analogous descriptive investigations on a more extensive scale, encompassing a more substantial sample of STEM high schools dispersed throughout the United States. Singha et al. (2023) examine the correlation between religious diversity and multiculturalism in education. It entails an analysis of the religious milieu and the incorporation of religious diversity into educational protocols and policies. This research investigates the importance and constraints of faith in education. The intricate relationship between religious diversity and multiculturalism reveals potential obstacles and advantages. To effectively address these challenges and seize these opportunities, it is imperative to cultivate intercultural discourse, incorporate a wide range of viewpoints into the academic curriculum, and encourage parental and community involvement. Singha & Singha (2023) investigate the influence of religious and spiritual diversity on educational practices by examining the establishment and maintenance of inclusive environments. An essential aspect of nurturing a sense of belonging among students from diverse backgrounds is the work of educators. It involves recognizing the significance of faith-based education, establishing safe environments for candid discussions regarding faith and culture, and actively promoting inclusiveness. By setting standards, encouraging professional development, getting involved in research and advocacy, giving advice on hiring and keeping teachers, and working together with stakeholders, these groups make big contributions to creating an educational environment that gives STEM teachers the skills they need to meet the needs of diverse students and fixes the problem of women not being represented enough in the field.

CASE STUDIES

Building Bridges: A Collaborative Approach to Inclusive STEM Teacher Preparation

Within an urban region, a university acknowledged the necessity of adopting a more comprehensive strategy for STEM teacher training programs targeting elementary education. The current programs failed to recruit a heterogeneous cohort of students, resulting in a lack of diversity among students and staff members. The institution decided to actively promote inclusivity and cultivate diversity in its elementary STEM teacher training programs.

The institution adopted a comprehensive strategy to tackle inclusion concerns within its STEM teacher preparation programs. The institution established a task force comprising faculty members, students, and community leaders to identify obstacles and devise measures for enhancement. The task force employed surveys and focus groups to amass current and potential students and alums's feedback. The task force used the findings to guide programmatic modifications.

The institution further partnered with nearby primary schools to build mentorship programs. The institution matched STEM teachers with varied backgrounds with potential students, enabling them to offer practical knowledge and advice. In addition, the institution proactively pursued collaborations with community organizations that advocated for STEM education among marginalized demographics.

The cooperative methodology produced favourable outcomes. There was a substantial increase in the enrollment of students from underrepresented backgrounds in STEM teacher preparation programs. The mentorship programs demonstrated success, resulting in a greater retention rate among students from varied backgrounds. Faculty and staff reported a more inclusive and supportive culture within the programs.

Consequently, through these efforts, the university received acknowledgment for its dedication to promoting inclusion in STEM education. The efficacy of their method has motivated other institutions to embrace similar strategies, generating a ripple effect in cultivating diversity within elementary STEM teacher training programs.

Cultivating Diversity: Embedding Inclusivity in the Curriculum of an Elementary STEM Teacher Preparation Program

Within a rural environment, an educational institution specializing in teacher training recognized a deficiency in the representation of diverse individuals within their programs focused on preparing elementary school teachers in science, technology, engineering, and mathematics (STEM). The curriculum, however comprehensive in terms of technical material, failed to adequately cater to the requirements and

Fostering Inclusivity

viewpoints of a heterogeneous student body. To acknowledge the significance of equipping teachers with the ability to establish meaningful connections with students from diverse backgrounds, the college embarked on a process of overhauling its curriculum and promoting inclusivity.

The college conducted a thorough evaluation of its curriculum, which included the participation of staff, students, and external experts who possess specialized knowledge in diversity and inclusion—the college organized workshops to raise faculty members' awareness of the difficulties students from underrepresented groups encounter. The curriculum underwent revision to incorporate a range of perspectives, cultural competence training, and instructional techniques that accommodated multiple learning styles.

To enhance inclusivity, the college collaborated with nearby schools catering to a wide range of student demographics. Student instructors were allowed to interact with kids from diverse backgrounds during their training. The college implemented a compulsory practicum in schools with limited resources to familiarize students with educators' difficulties in various environments.

THE LONG-TERM EFFECTS OF INCLUSIVE PRACTICES IN STEM

The enduring impacts of incorporating inclusive practices in STEM (Science, Technology, Engineering, and Mathematics) jobs are significant, fostering a more vibrant, inventive, and fair environment. As inclusivity becomes deeply ingrained in STEM areas, numerous transformative effects arise, profoundly influencing the future of these professions.

Implementing inclusive practices in STEM jobs has wide-ranging consequences that go beyond personal experiences, influencing the development of innovation and societal influence. STEM businesses foster continual innovation by embracing individuals with varied viewpoints, backgrounds, and experiences, which creates a vibrant tapestry of thinking and approach. Implementing inclusive practices leads to the formation of diverse teams which exhibit enhanced problem-solving and decision-making abilities. It fosters a culture that encourages thorough analyses and the development of practical solutions for intricate difficulties. Furthermore, the lasting effects of inclusivity also encompass a more significant presence of marginalized groups, fostering a beneficial cycle where varied experts serve as exemplars and motivating future generations to engage in STEM education and professions. The expansion of the talent pool allows for the utilization of previously unexplored potential, resulting in the inclusion of diverse talents and views that fill skill deficiencies and improve the overall capacities of STEM professionals.

Incorporating inclusive practices into a workplace environment fosters a culture characterized by respect, comprehension, and equitable opportunity. It leads to enhanced job satisfaction, elevated morale, and improved employee retention. In addition to benefiting individual careers, the impact of inclusion in STEM on society and the economy is significant. It enables a diverse and inclusive workforce to address global concerns, such as healthcare inequities and environmental issues, with a nuanced viewpoint. Implementing inclusive practices compels businesses to evaluate their policies and structures, which may result in fundamental alterations in how they recruit, promote, and provide professional development opportunities. It fosters a fairer environment for individuals seeking STEM jobs. In the end, promoting worldwide cooperation in STEM disciplines, supported by inclusive methods, provides professionals with cultural proficiency, cultivating a global mindset for addressing problems that lead to solutions with a broader influence.

FUTURE DIRECTIONS

The prospective trajectory of diversity in primary education STEM teacher preparation programs is positioned for rapid change, propelled by a growing acknowledgement of inclusivity's societal and educational implications. The expected patterns indicate a sustained commitment to cultivating inclusive and fair educational settings, specifically highlighting the pivotal role of elementary education in encouraging students to participate in STEM fields. An encouraging development is the increasing recognition that diversity comprises a wide range of identities, such as gender and ethnicity. Forthcoming endeavours will expand their reach to encompass a broader range of intersecting elements, such as socioeconomic status, abilities, and other ingredients that enrich the diversity of STEM teacher preparation programs. The integration of technology is anticipated to have a significant impact on future developments. With the continuous advancement of educational technologies, there is potential to utilize these tools to facilitate inclusive learning experiences. To address the issue of accessibility and accommodate various learning styles, virtual classrooms, immersive simulations, and online resources have the potential to bridge the divide in STEM education. Potential forthcoming challenges may involve the continuous imperative to deconstruct systemic obstacles that impede diversity in STEM disciplines. In light of evolving demographics and societal expectations, it is imperative that forthcoming programs consistently reevaluate and enhance their methodologies to address the evolving requirements of heterogeneous student populations effectively. It is still crucial to conduct research in this particular field. The effectiveness of current diversity initiatives, innovative pedagogical approaches, and the long-term effects of inclusive teacher preparation on students' academic and professional trajectories will likely be the subject of ongoing and future research. Exploring the complex interconnections among diverse identities and their influence on STEM educational experiences will be a central focus for scholars and practitioners. The prospective trajectory of diversity in primary education Preparatory programs for STEM teachers distinguish themselves by dedicating to broadening inclusivity beyond conventional limits. Anticipated drivers of positive transformations include technological integration, a comprehensive approach to diversity, and continuous research endeavours. Through confronting obstacles directly and remaining informed about developing patterns, these programs have the potential to establish a pathway towards a future in which all aspiring STEM educators possess the necessary tools to appreciate and embrace the variety of students they will motivate.

Dynamic trends, possible obstacles, and the necessity for continuous research will characterize future STEM teacher preparation programs. A significant development is the growing recognition of the need for a comprehensive understanding of diversity, which goes beyond traditional classifications to include socioeconomic status, abilities, and cultural subtleties. The convergence of technology, encompassing online platforms and virtual reality, emerges as a crucial trend, offering the potential for learning experiences that are more accessible and inclusive. A growing emphasis on intersectionality recognizes the complex identities of individuals and proposes individualized strategies to tackle obstacles stemming from race, gender, and socioeconomic standing. Nevertheless, enduring obstacles remain, most notably the imperative to surmount entrenched systemic barriers that contribute to the lack of representation in STEM fields. Ongoing challenges, including technological disparities, biased employment practices, and adapting to changing demographics, necessitate consistent and persistent efforts. Ensuring equitable access to resources and bridging the digital divide are critical considerations. For effective navigation of this intricate terrain, continuous research is essential. Critical areas for inquiry include assessing the efficacy of ongoing inclusivity initiatives, comprehending the enduring consequences for students, and honing inventive pedagogical methodologies. By incorporating evidence-based practices, embracing adaptability, and prioritizing inclusivity, STEM teacher preparation programs can actively mould a future where diversity is appreciated and crucial to the triumph of STEM education.

DISCUSSION

The discourse sheds light on the profound impact of inclusivity on STEM teacher preparation programs for elementary school students, emphasizing its critical role in determining the course of STEM education. Inclusivity is not merely an additional factor to be considered; it is a crucial component that enhances STEM education's calibre, pertinence, and influence. Recognizing the intricate aspects of diversity, including but not limited to race, gender, socioeconomic standing, and abilities, is essential in fostering atmospheres that promote the optimal development of every individual. Theoretical foundations strengthen the argument for prioritizing inclusivity in STEM teacher preparation, an exhaustive analysis of the present state of affairs, and practical suggestions. This framework serves as a guide for developing efficacious strategies and interventions. The anticipated outcome of incorporating diversity into STEM teacher preparation is developing educators with technical expertise, cultural sensitivity, and social consciousness. Acknowledging and deconstructing historical, systemic, and cultural obstacles to attain greater parity in representation across STEM fields is critical. Promising future trends in inclusivity that experts anticipate discussing include adopting technological integration, prioritizing intersectionality, and embracing holistic diversity.

Notwithstanding technological discrepancies and systemic barriers, the discourse emphasizes the criticality of continuous research to assess inclusivity initiatives. STEM teacher preparation programs play a crucial role in shaping the trajectory of STEM education, actively contributing to an environment where diversity is a prerequisite for achievement. STEM teacher preparation programs actively contribute to shaping a future where diversity is recognized and considered essential for achievement, establishing inclusivity as a dynamic entity in STEM education. It underscores the ongoing research-driven endeavours that support these efforts.

CONCLUSION

In summary, the significance of incorporating inclusivity into STEM teacher preparation programs for elementary education is profound and will continue to shape the trajectory of STEM education in the future. The preceding chapter has emphasized the critical nature of promoting diversity, not simply as a supplementary factor but as a fundamental element that enhances STEM education's calibre, pertinence, and influence. Acknowledging the complex aspects of inclusivity, which include abilities, race, gender, and socioeconomic standing, is critical for establishing environments that foster the growth and success of every individual.

Examining the current landscape, theoretical foundations, and benefits of inclusivity cooperatively strengthens the case for its fundamental importance in STEM teacher preparation. Practical recommendations provide a systematic approach to seamlessly incorporating inclusivity into these programs, guaranteeing that aspiring educators can adeptly navigate the intricacies inherent in diverse classrooms.

The importance of diversity in STEM teacher preparation programs resides in its ability to mould a forthcoming cohort of educators who possess cultural sensitivity, social consciousness, technical expertise, and readiness to confront the ever-changing obstacles of the STEM domain. It is critical to recognize and deconstruct historical, systemic, or cultural barriers to achieve greater parity in representation across STEM fields.

In anticipation of forthcoming developments, STEM teacher preparation programs are characterized by encouraging patterns, including an increased emphasis on intersectionality, technological integration, and a comprehensive comprehension of diversity. Nevertheless, persistent obstacles necessitate ongoing endeavours to surmount systemic impediments, rectify technological inequalities, and accommodate shifting demographics.

As we traverse this ever-changing terrain, continuous research assumes an essential role. Assessing the efficacy of inclusivity initiatives, ascertaining their enduring effects on students, and enhancing inventive pedagogical methodologies to mould STEM education inclusively is crucial. By incorporating principles of flexibility, fairness, and scientific verification, STEM teacher preparation programs can actively promote an environment in which diversity is fundamental to the achievement of STEM education, thereby cultivating a more equitable and inclusive society.

REFERENCES

Akkari, A., & Maleq, K. (2020). Global Citizenship Education: Recognizing diversity in a Global world. In Springer eBooks (pp. 3–13). doi:10.1007/978-3-030-44617-8_1

Alemdar, M., Cappelli, C., Gale, J., & Boice, K. L. (2022). An exploratory study of STEM teachers' mentorship networks. *International Journal of STEM Education*, *9*(1), 64. doi:10.1186/s40594-022-00383-7

Amin, S., Sanders, M. M., Kidd, A. E., & Rambo-Hernandez, K. E. (2023). How much does readiness matter? An examination of student persistence intention and engineering identity. In *2023 ASEE Annual Conference & Exposition*. https://peer.asee.org/43375

Aydın, H., & Cinkaya, M. (2018). Global citizenship education and diversity (GCEDS). *Journal for Multicultural Education*, *12*(3), 221–236. doi:10.1108/JME-05-2017-0030

Bearman, M., & Ajjawi, R. (2018). From "Seeing Through" to "Seeing with": Assessment criteria and the myths of transparency. *Frontiers in Education*, *3*, 96.. doi:10.3389/feduc.2018.00096

Casto, A. R., & Williams, J. A. (2020). Seeking proportionality in the North Carolina STEM pipeline. *High School Journal, 103*(2), 77–98. doi:10.1353/hsj.2020.0004

Eaton, S. E. (2022). New priorities for academic integrity: Equity, diversity, inclusion, decolonization and Indigenization. *International Journal for Educational Integrity, 18*(1), 10. Advance online publication. doi:10.1007/s40979-022-00105-0

Javier, D., Solis, L., Paul, M. F., Thompson, E. L., Maynard, G., Latif, Z., Stinson, K., Ahmed, T., & Vishwanatha, J. K. (2022). Implementation of an unconscious bias course for the National Research Mentoring Network. *BMC Medical Education, 22*(1), 391. doi:10.1186/s12909-022-03466-9 PMID:35597975

Jones, M. G., Ennes, M., Weedfall, D., Chesnutt, K., & Cayton, E. (2020). The development and validation of a measure of science capital, habitus, and future science interests. *Research in Science Education, 51*(6), 1549–1565. doi:10.1007/s11165-020-09916-y

Jönsson, A., & Prins, F. J. (2019). Editorial: Transparency in Assessment—Exploring the Influence of Explicit Assessment Criteria. *Frontiers in Education, 3*, 119. doi:10.3389/feduc.2018.00119

Kricorian, K., Seu, M., López, D., Ureta, E., & Equils, O. (2020). Factors influencing participation of underrepresented students in STEM fields: Matched mentors and mindsets. *International Journal of STEM Education, 7*(1), 16. doi:10.1186/s40594-020-00219-2

Löfström, E., & Nevgi, A. (2006). From strategic planning to meaningful learning: Diverse perspectives on the development of web-based teaching and learning in higher education. *British Journal of Educational Technology, 38*(2), 312–324. doi:10.1111/j.1467-8535.2006.00625.x

Margot, K. C., & Kettler, T. (2019). Teachers' perception of STEM integration and education: A systematic literature review. *International Journal of STEM Education, 6*(1), 2. doi:10.1186/s40594-018-0151-2

Mau, W., Chen, S., & Lin, C. (2020). Social cognitive factors of science, technology, engineering, and mathematics career interests. *International Journal for Educational and Vocational Guidance, 21*(1), 47–60. doi:10.1007/s10775-020-09427-2

Moreu, G., Isenberg, N., & Bräuer, M. (2021). How to promote diversity and inclusion in educational settings: Behaviour change, climate surveys, and effective Pro-Diversity initiatives. *Frontiers in Education, 6*, 668250. doi:10.3389/feduc.2021.668250

Nganga, L., & Akpovo, S. M. (2020). Culturally inclusive and contextually appropriate instructional practices: Rethinking pedagogical perspectives, practices, policies, and experiences in early childhood education programs. *Journal of Research in Childhood Education, 34*(1), 2–5. doi:10.1080/02568543.2019.1697153

Nkrumah, T., & Scott, K. A. (2022). Mentoring in STEM higher education: A synthesis of the literature to (re)present the excluded women of colour. *International Journal of STEM Education, 9*(1), 50. doi:10.1186/s40594-022-00367-7 PMID:35919282

O'Leary, E. S., Shapiro, C., Toma, S., Sayson, H. W., Levis-Fitzgerald, M., Johnson, T., & Sork, V. L. (2020). Creating inclusive classrooms by engaging STEM faculty in culturally responsive teaching workshops. *International Journal of STEM Education, 7*(1), 32. doi:10.1186/s40594-020-00230-7 PMID:32647597

Palid, O., Cashdollar, S., Deangelo, S., Chu, C., & Bates, M. S. (2023). Inclusion in practice: A systematic review of diversity-focused STEM programming in the United States. *International Journal of STEM Education, 10*(1), 2. doi:10.1186/s40594-022-00387-3

Puckett, T. (2020). The importance of developing cultural competence. In Innovations in higher education teaching and learning (pp. 7–22). doi:10.1108/S2055-364120200000028004

Richmond, G., Bartell, T. G., Floden, R. E., & Jones, N. D. (2019). How research sheds light on the pivotal role of mentors in teacher preparation. *Journal of Teacher Education, 71*(1), 6–8. doi:10.1177/0022487119887752

Salehi, S., Ballen, C. J., Trujillo, G., & Wieman, C. (2021). Inclusive instructional practices: Course design, implementation, and discourse. *Frontiers in Education, 6*, 602639. Advance online publication. doi:10.3389/feduc.2021.602639

Singer, A., Montgomery, G. M., & Schmoll, S. (2020). How to foster the formation of STEM identity: Studying diversity in an authentic learning environment. *International Journal of STEM Education, 7*(1), 57. doi:10.1186/s40594-020-00254-z

Singha, R., & Singha, S. (2023). Faith and Culture in Education: Fostering Inclusive Environments. In J. DeHart (Ed.), *The Role of Faith and Religious Diversity in Educational Practices* (pp. 149–172). IGI Global. doi:10.4018/978-1-6684-9184-3.ch007

Singha, S. (2023). Culturally Relevant Teaching in Humanities: E-Book Creation, Blogging, and Bookmaking. In D. M. Frazier (Ed.), *Teaching Humanities With Cultural Responsiveness at HBCUs and HSIs* (pp. 121–146). IGI Global. doi:10.4018/978-1-6684-9782-1.ch006

Singha, S., & Singha, R. (2023a). Understanding diversity: The power of differences. In A. M. Even & B. Christiansen (Eds.), *Enhancing Employee Engagement and Productivity in the Post-Pandemic Multigenerational Workforce* (pp. 297–313). IGI Global. doi:10.4018/978-1-6684-9172-0.ch015

Singha, S., Singha, R., & Ruben, V. M. (2023). Explorations of the Links Between Multiculturalism and Religious Diversity. In J. DeHart (Ed.), *The Role of Faith and Religious Diversity in Educational Practices* (pp. 120–148). IGI Global. doi:10.4018/978-1-6684-9184-3.ch006

Somyürek, S. (2014). An effective educational tool: Construction kits for fun and meaningful learning. *International Journal of Technology and Design Education, 25*(1), 25–41. doi:10.1007/s10798-014-9272-1

Song, Y., Martin-Hansen, L., Akerson, V. L., Buck, G. A., & Al-Balushi, S. M. (2023). STEM Teacher Education: An Overview. Palgrave studies leadership and learning in teacher education (pp. 1–15). Springer. doi:10.1007/978-3-031-27334-6_1

Suriel, R. L., & Litster, K. (2022). They expose inequities within teacher professional development and its impact on advancing equity, diversity and social justice in STEM education. In Springer eBooks (pp. 105–124). Springer. doi:10.1007/978-3-031-08150-7_6

Yannier, N., Hudson, S. E., & Koedinger, K. R. (2020). Active Learning is About More Than Hands-On: A Mixed-Reality AI System to Support STEM Education. *International Journal of Artificial Intelligence in Education, 30*(1), 74–96. doi:10.1007/s40593-020-00194-3

KEY TERMS AND DEFINITIONS

Diversity: The presence of various identities, perspectives, and backgrounds, acknowledging and valuing differences to create a prosperous and inclusive environment.

Elementary Education: The foundational stage of formal education, typically encompassing students from kindergarten through sixth grade, is crucial for laying the groundwork for academic and social development.

Equity: The fair and just distribution of resources, opportunities, and support, aiming to address and eliminate disparities among individuals and groups.

Inclusive Pedagogy: Teaching methods and approaches that embrace diversity, accommodate different learning styles, and create a supportive environment for all students to succeed.

Fostering Inclusivity

Inclusivity: Ensuring that diverse individuals are respected, valued, and actively engaged, fostering an environment where everyone feels a sense of belonging and participation.

Representation: Ensuring that all groups are adequately portrayed and included, particularly in educational settings, to provide role models and foster a sense of belonging.

STEM Teacher Preparation: Programs designed to equip educators with the knowledge, skills, and pedagogical approaches needed to teach science, technology, engineering, and mathematics (STEM) subjects.

Compilation of References

Zhuo, S., Sherlock, L., Dobbie, G., Koh, Y. S., Russello, G., & Lottridge, D. (2020). Real-time smartphone activity classification using inertial sensors—Recognition of scrolling, typing, and watching videos while sitting or walking. *Sensors (Basel)*, *20*(3), 655. doi:10.3390/s20030655 PMID:31991636

Abbasi, G. A., Jagaveeran, M., Goh, Y. N., & Tariq, B. (2021). The impact of type of content use on smartphone addiction and academic performance: Physical activity as moderator. *Technology in Society*, *64*, 101521. doi:10.1016/j.techsoc.2020.101521

Abell, S. K. (2007). Research on science teacher knowledge. In S. K. Abell & N. G. Lederman (Eds.), *Handbook of Research on Science Education* (pp. 1105–1149). Erlbaum.

Abruscato, J., & DeRosa, D. A. (2019). *Teaching children science: A discovery approach* (9th ed.). Allyn and Bacon.

Adams, A., & Laughter, J. (2012). Making space for space traders. *Multicultural Learning and Teaching*, *7*(2). doi:10.1515/2161-2412.1121

Aguirre, J. M., Zavala, M. D. R., & Katanyoutanant, T. (2012). Developing robust forms of pre-service teachers' pedagogical content knowledge through culturally responsive mathematics teaching analysis. *Mathematics Teacher Education and Development*, *14*(2), 113–136.

Akkari, A., & Maleq, K. (2020). Global Citizenship Education: Recognizing diversity in a Global world. In Springer eBooks (pp. 3–13). doi:10.1007/978-3-030-44617-8_1

Akkuş, H., & Sinem, Ü. N. E. R. (2017). The effect of microteaching on pre-service chemistry teachers' teaching experiences. *Cukurova University Faculty of Education Journal*, *46*(1), 202–230. doi:10.14812/cuefd.309459

Al Sultan, A., Henson, H. J., & Fadde, P. J. (2018). Pre-service elementary teachers' scientific literacy and self-efficacy in teaching science. *IAFOR Journal of Education*, *6*(1), 15 – 41. doi:10.22492/ije.6.1.02

Al-Balushi, S. M., Al-Harthi, A. S., & Shahat, M. A. (2022). Teacher education in Oman: Retrospectives and prospects. In: Khine, M.S. (Eds.), Handbook of research on teacher education. Springer (WOS & Scopus indexed). doi:10.1007/978-981-19-2400-2_6

Compilation of References

Al-Balushi, S. M., Martin-Hansen, L., & Song, Y. (Eds.). (2023). *Reforming Science Teacher Education Programs in the STEM Era. Palgrave Studies on Leadership and Learning in Teacher Education.* Palgrave Macmillan. doi:10.1007/978-3-031-27334-6

Alemdar, M., Cappelli, C., Gale, J., & Boice, K. L. (2022). An exploratory study of STEM teachers' mentorship networks. *International Journal of STEM Education, 9*(1), 64. doi:10.1186/s40594-022-00383-7

Allaire, F. S., & Killham, J. E. (2022). Introduction. In F. S. Allaire & J. E. Killham (Eds.), *Teaching and Learning Online: Scinece for Elementary Grade Levels* (pp. ix–ixv). Information Age Publishing.

Allaire, F. S., & Killham, J. E. (2023). Introduction. In F. S. Allaire & J. E. Killham (Eds.), *Teaching and Learning Online: Scinece for Secondary Grade Levels* (pp. ix–xv). Information Age Publishing.

Allen, D. W., & Eve, A. W. (1968). Microteaching. *Theory into Practice, 7*(5), 181–185. doi:10.1080/00405846809542153

Alliance for Excellent Education. (2013). Expanding education and workforce opportunities through digital badges. https://all4ed.org/wp-content/uploads/2013/09/DigitalBadges.pdf

Allington, R. L. (2002, June 1). What I've learned about effective reading instruction: From a decade of studying exemplary elementary classroom teachers. *Phi Delta Kappan, 83*(10), 740–747. Advance online publication. doi:10.1177/003172170208301007

Al-Rahmi, A. M., Al-Rahmi, W. M., Alturki, U., Aldraiweesh, A., Almutairy, S., & Al-Adwan, A. S. (2021). Exploring the factors affecting mobile learning for sustainability in higher education. *Sustainability (Basel), 13*(14), 7893. doi:10.3390/su13147893

Alsharida, R., Hammood, M., & Al-Emran, M. (2021). Mobile learning adoption: A systematic review of the technology acceptance model from 2017 to 2020. [iJET]. *International Journal of Emerging Technologies in Learning, 16*(5), 147–162. doi:10.3991/ijet.v16i05.18093

Ambusaidi, A. K., Shahat, M. A., & Al Musawi, A. S. (2022). Science education in Oman. In R. Huang, B. Xin, A. Tlili, F. Yang, X. Zhang, L. Zhu, & M. Jemni (Eds.), *Science education in countries along the belt & road: Future insights and new requirements* (pp. 113–127). Springer Nature Singapore. doi:10.1007/978-981-16-6955-2_8

American Association for the Advancement of Science (AAAS). (1993). *Benchmarks for scientific literacy.* AAAS.

American Association for the Advancement of Science. (1998). *Blueprints for reform: Science, mathematics, and technology education. American Association for the Advancement of Science & Project 2061.* Oxford University Press.

Amin, S., Sanders, M. M., Kidd, A. E., & Rambo-Hernandez, K. E. (2023). How much does readiness matter? An examination of student persistence intention and engineering identity. In *2023 ASEE Annual Conference & Exposition.* https://peer.asee.org/43375

Anderson, J. (2012, April 14). *Edgar Dale's cone of learning*. Edu Techie. http://www.edutechie.ws/2007/10/09/cone-of-experience-media/

Anderson, L. M., & Stillman, J. A. (2013). Student teaching's contribution to preservice teacher development: A review of research focused on the preparation of teachers for urban and high-needs contexts. *Review of Educational Research, 83*(1), 3–69. doi:10.3102/0034654312468619

Anderson, R. D. (2002). Reforming science teaching: What research says about inquiry. *Journal of Science Teacher Education, 13*(1), 1–12. doi:10.1023/A:1015171124982

Andrà, C., Verani, M., & Parolini, N. (2018). BetOnMath: Azzardo e matematica a scuola. *BetOnMath: azzardo e matematica a scuola*, 119-121.

Antar, A. D., Ahmed, M., & Ahad, M. A. R. (2019, May). Challenges in sensor-based human activity recognition and a comparative analysis of benchmark datasets: a review. In *2019 Joint 8th International Conference on Informatics, Electronics & Vision (ICIEV) and 2019 3rd International Conference on Imaging, Vision & Pattern Recognition (icIVPR)* (pp. 134-139). IEEE.

Apiola, M., Lattu, M., & Pasanen, T. A. (2012). Creativity-supporting learning environment—Csle. [TOCE]. *ACM Transactions on Computing Education, 12*(3), 1–25. doi:10.1145/2275597.2275600

Area Education Agency. (2011). *Imagine, elaborate, predict, and confirm (IEPC)*. AEA. https://www.centralriversaea.org/wp-content/uploads/2017/04/iepc-checked.docx

Aronson, B., & Laughter, J. (2016). The theory and practice of culturally relevant education: A synthesis of research across content areas. *Review of Educational Research, 86*(1), 163–206. doi:10.3102/0034654315582066

Artman, B., Danner, N., & Crow, S. R. (2020). Teacher-directed professional development: An alternative to conventional professional development. *International Journal of Self-Directed Learning, 17*(1), 39–50.

Au, K., & Jordan, C. (1981). Teaching reasoning to Hawaiian children: Finding a culturally appropriate solution. In H. Trueba, G. Guthrie, & K. Au (Eds.), *Culture and the bilingual classroom: Studies in classroom ethnography* (pp. 139–152). Newbury House.

AumSum. (2016, May 19). *Human eye* [Video]. YouTube. https://www.youtube.com/watch?v=eDIma_Ai1Rc

Avery, L. M., & Meyer, D. Z. (2012). Teaching science as science is practiced: Opportunities and limits for enhancing preservice elementary teachers' self-efficacy for science and science teaching. *School Science and Mathematics, 112*(7), 395–409. doi:10.1111/j.1949-8594.2012.00159.x

Avraamidou, L. (2019). Stories we live, identities we build: How are elementary teachers' science identities shaped by their lived experiences? *Cultural Studies of Science Education, 14*(1), 33–59. doi:10.1007/s11422-017-9855-8

Compilation of References

Aydeniz, M., & Brown, C. L. (2010). Enhancing pre-service elementary school teachers' understanding of essential science concepts through a reflective conceptual change model. *International Electronic Journal of Elementary Education, 2*(2). doi:10.1007/s10763-005-9016-5

Aydın, H., & Cinkaya, M. (2018). Global citizenship education and diversity (GCEDS). *Journal for Multicultural Education, 12*(3), 221–236. doi:10.1108/JME-05-2017-0030

Bakır, S. (2014). The effect of microteaching on the teaching skills of pre-service science teachers. *Journal of Baltic Science Education, 13*(6), 789–801. doi:10.33225/jbse/14.13.789

Bal, I. A., Alvarado–Albertorio, F., Marcelle, P., & Oaks-Garcia, C. T. (2022). Pre–service Teachers Computational Thinking (CT) and Pedagogical Growth in a Micro–credential: A Mixed Methods Study. *TechTrends, 66*(3), 468–482. doi:10.1007/s11528-022-00732-x PMID:35499060

Bandura, A. (1994). Regulative function of perceived self-efficacy. In M. G. Rumsey, C. B. Walker, & J. H. Harris (Eds.), *Personnel selection and classification* (pp. 261–271). Lawrence Erlbaum Associates, Inc. https://psycnet-apa-org.proxy006.nclive.org/record/1994-98076-013

Banilower, E., Smith, P., Malzahn, K., Plumley, C., Gordon, E., & Hayes, M. (2018). *Report of the 2018 NSSME+*. Horizon Research. https://horizon-research.com/NSSME/wp-content/uploads/2020/04/Report_of_the_2018_NSSME.pdf

Banilower, E. R., Smith, P. S., Weiss, I. R., Malzahn, K. A., & Weiss, A. M. (2013). *Report of the 2012 National Survey of Science and Mathematics Education*. Horizon Research, Inc., doi:10.1119/1.4795387

Bano, M., Zowghi, D., Kearney, M., Schuck, S., & Aubusson, P. (2018). Mobile learning for science and mathematics school education: A systematic review of empirical evidence. *Computers & Education, 121*, 30–58. doi:10.1016/j.compedu.2018.02.006

Barbosa, A., & Vale, I. (2020). Math trails through digital technology: An experience with pre-service teachers. *Research on Outdoor STEM Education in the digiTal Age, 47*.

Barbour, M. K., Siko, J., Gross, E., & Waddell, K. (2014). Virtually unprepared: Examining the preparation of K–12 online teachers. In R. Hartshorne, T. L. Heafner, & T. M. Petty (Eds.), *Teacher education programs and online learning tools* (pp. 187–208). IGI Global.

Barron, B. J., Schwartz, D. L., Vye, N. J., Moore, A., Petrosino, A., Zech, L., & Bransford, J. D. (2014). Doing with understanding: Lessons from research on problem-and project-based learning. In *Learning Through Problem Solving* (pp. 271–311). Psychology Press.

Basturk, S. (2016). Investigating the Effectiveness of Microteaching in Mathematics of Primary Pre-Service Teachers. *Journal of Education and Training Studies, 4*(5), 239–249. doi:10.11114/jets.v4i5.1509

Bay-Williams, J., & King, G. (2019). *Math fact fluency: 60+ games and assessment tools to support learning and retention*. ASCD.

Bearman, M., & Ajjawi, R. (2018). From "Seeing Through" to "Seeing with": Assessment criteria and the myths of transparency. *Frontiers in Education*, *3*, 96.. doi:10.3389/feduc.2018.00096

Beck, J., Lunsmann, C., & Garza, T. (2020). "We need to be in the classroom more": Veteran teachers' views on teacher preparation and retention. *Professional Educator*, *43*(1), 91–99.

Bekdemir, M. (2010). The pre-service teachers' mathematics anxiety related to depth of negative experiences in mathematics classroom while they were students. *Educational Studies in Mathematics*, *75*(3), 311–328. doi:10.1007/s10649-010-9260-7

Bell, P., Van Horne, K., & Cheng, B. H. (2017). Special issue: Designing learning environments for equitable disciplinary identification. *Journal of the Learning Sciences*, *26*(3), 367–375. doi:10.1080/10508406.2017.1336021

Bell, S. (2010). Project-based learning for the 21st century: Skills for the future. *The Clearing House: A Journal of Educational Strategies, Issues and Ideas*, *83*(2), 39–43. doi:10.1080/00098650903505415

Bencze, J. L. (2010). Promoting student-led science and technology projects in elementary teacher education: Entry into core pedagogical practices through technological design. *International Journal of Technology and Design Education*, *20*(1), 43–62. doi:10.1007/s10798-008-9063-7

Bhattacharyya, S., Mead, T. P., Junot, M., & Welch, A. (2013). Effectiveness of science method teaching in teacher education: A longitudinal case study. *The Electronic Journal of Science Education*, *17*(2).

Bicer, A., & Lee, Y. (2019). Effect of STEM PBL embedded informal learning on student interest in STEM majors and careers. *Journal of Mathematics Education*, *12*(1), 57–73.

Bimba, A. T., Idris, N., Al-Hunaiyyan, A., Mahmud, R. B., & Shuib, N. L. B. M. (2017). Adaptive feedback in computer-based learning environments: A review. *Adaptive Behavior*, *25*(5), 217–234. doi:10.1177/1059712317727590

Blachowicz, C. L. Z., & Fisher, P. J. (2006). *Knowledge rating comprehension strategy*. Reading Cross Curriculum. http://readingacrosscurriculum.com/Knowledge%20Rating%20Comprehension%20Strategy.htm

Black, E., Ferdig, R., & Thompson, L. A. (2021). K–12 Virtual Schooling, COVID-19, and Student Success. *JAMA Pediatrics*, *175*(2), 119–120. doi:10.1001/jamapediatrics.2020.3800 PMID:32780093

Blanchard, M., Southerland, S. A., & Granger, D. E. (2009). No silver bullet for inquiry: Making sense of teacher change following inquiry-based research experiences for teachers. *Science Education*, *93*(2), 322–360. doi:10.1002/sce.20298

Blank, R. K. (2012). *What is the impact of decline in science instructional time in elementary school?* Paper prepared for the Noyce Foundation. www.csss-science.org/downloads/NAEPElemScienceData.pdf

Compilation of References

Bleicher, R. E. (2009). Variable relationships among different science learners in elementary science-methods courses. *International Journal of Science and Mathematics Education*, *7*(2), 293–313. doi:10.1007/s10763-007-9121-8

Blickenstaff, J. C. (2005). Women and science careers: Leaky pipeline or gender filter? *Gender and Education*, *17*(4), 369–386. doi:10.1080/09540250500145072

Bock, C. (2022). Diversity, equality, and inclusion in our professions: A thin and leaky pipeline. *The Electrochemical Society Interface*, *31*(41), 41–44. doi:10.1149/2.F08221IF

Bolyard, J. J., & Moyer-Packenham, P. S. (2006, November). *The impact of virtual manipulatives on student achievement in integer addition and subtraction*. Paper presented at the annual meeting of the North American Chapter of the International Group for the Psychology of Mathematics Education, Mérida, Yucatán, Mexico.

Bolyard, J., & Moyer-Packenham, P. (2012). Making sense of integer arithmetic: The effect of using virtual manipulatives on students' representational fluency. *Journal of Computers in Mathematics and Science Teaching*, *31*(2), 93–113.

Boss, S., & Krauss, J. (2022). *Reinventing project-based learning: Your field guide to real-world projects in the digital age*. International Society for Technology in Education.

Bouck, E. C., Satsangi, R., Doughty, T. T., & Courtney, W. T. (2014). Virtual and concrete manipulatives: A comparison of approaches for solving mathematics problems for students with autism spectrum disorder. *Journal of Autism and Developmental Disorders*, *44*(1), 180–193. doi:10.1007/s10803-013-1863-2 PMID:23743958

Brady, P., & Bowd, A. (2005). Mathematics anxiety, prior experience and confidence to teach mathematics among pre-service education students. *Teachers and Teaching*, *11*(1), 37–46. doi:10.1080/1354060042000337084

Bransford, J. D., & Johnson, M. K. (1972). Contextual prerequisites for understanding: Some investigations of comprehension and recall. *Journal of Verbal Learning and Verbal Behavior*, *11*(6), 717–726. doi:10.1016/S0022-5371(72)80006-9

BRASIL. (2020). *Relatório brasil no PISA 2018*. INEP/MEC.

Bravo-Sánchez, A., Morán-García, J., Abián, P., & Abián-Vicén, J. (2021). Association of the use of the mobile phone with physical fitness and academic performance: A cross-sectional study. *International Journal of Environmental Research and Public Health*, *18*(3), 1042. doi:10.3390/ijerph18031042 PMID:33503943

Bredeweg, B., & Winkels, R. (1998). Qualitative models in interactive learning environments: An introduction. *Interactive Learning Environments*, *5*(1), 1–18. doi:10.1080/1049482980050101

Brezovszky, B., McMullen, J., Veermans, K., Hannula-Sormunen, M. M., Rodríguez-Aflecht, G., Pongsakdi, N., Laakkonen, E., & Lehtinen, E. (2019). Effects of a mathematics game-based learning environment on primary school students' adaptive number knowledge. *Computers & Education*, *128*, 63–74. doi:10.1016/j.compedu.2018.09.011

Briggle, J. (2013). Analysis of pendulum period with an iPod touch/iPhone. *Physics Education, 48*(3), 285–288. doi:10.1088/0031-9120/48/3/285

Brígido, M., Borrachero, A., Bermejo, M., & Mellado, V. (2013). Prospective primary teachers' self-efficacy and emotions in science teaching. *European Journal of Teacher Education, 36*(2), 200–217. doi:10.1080/02619768.2012.686993

Brown, A. H. (1999). Simulated classrooms and artificial students: The potential effects of new technologies on teacher education. *Journal of Research on Computing in Education, 32*(2), 307–318. doi:10.1080/08886504.1999.10782281

Brown, B. A., Boda, P., Lemmi, C., & Monroe, X. (2019). Moving culturally relevant pedagogy from theory to practice: Exploring teachers' application of culturally relevant education in science and mathematics. *Urban Education, 54*(6), 775–803. doi:10.1177/0042085918794802

Brown, D. J., Powell, H. M., Battersby, S., Lewis, J., Shopland, N., & Yazdanparast, M. (2002). Design guidelines for interactive multimedia learning environments to promote social inclusion. *Disability and Rehabilitation, 24*(11-12), 587–597. doi:10.1080/09638280110111351 PMID:12182798

Brown, J. C. (2017). A metasynthesis of the complementarity of culturally responsive and inquiry-based science education in K-12 settings: Implications for advancing equitable science teaching and learning. *Journal of Research in Science Teaching, 54*(9), 1143–1173. doi:10.1002/tea.21401

Buchholtz, N. (2020, June). The Norwegian study math & the city on mobile learning with math trails. In *Research on Outdoor STEM Education in the digital Age. Proceedings of the ROSETA Online Conference in June 2020* (pp. 79-86). ACM. 10.37626/GA9783959871440.0.10

Burr, T., Britton, T., Iveland, A., Nguyen, K., Hipps, J., & Schneider, S. (2017). *The Synergy of science and English Language Arts: Means and mutual benefits of integration.* WestEd. http://k12alliance.org/docs/Synergy-of-science-and-english-language-arts-Report2.pdf

Bursal, M. (2012). Changes in American preservice elementary teachers' efficacy beliefs and anxieties during a science methods course. *Science Education International, 23*(1), 40–55.

Bursztyn, N., Pederson, J., Shelton, B., Walker, A., & Campbell, T. (2015). Utilizing Geo-Referenced Mobile Game Technology for Universally Accessible Virtual Geology Field Trips. *International Journal of Education in Mathematics. Science and Technology, 3*(2), 93–100.

Busch, P. A., & McCarthy, S. (2021). Antecedents and consequences of problematic smartphone use: A systematic literature review of an emerging research area. *Computers in Human Behavior, 114*, 106414. doi:10.1016/j.chb.2020.106414

Bybee, R.W., Taylor, J.A., Gardner, A., Van Scotter, P. Carlson Powell, J., Westbroook, J. & Landes, N. (2006). *BSCS 5E instructional model: Origins and effectiveness.* A report prepared for the Office of Science Education, National Institutes of Health. BSCS.

Bybee, R. W. (1997). *Achieving scientific literacy: From purposes to practices.* Heinemann.

Compilation of References

Byers, A., & Mendez, F. (2016). Blended professional learning for science educators: The NSTA Learning Center. Teacher learning in the digital age: Online professional development in STEM education. In C. Dede, A. Eisenkraft, K. Frumin & A. Hartley, A. (Eds.), Teacher learning in the digital age: Online professional development in STEM education. (167-198). Harvard Education Press.

Cahyono, A. N. (2018). Learning mathematics in a mobile app-supported math trail environment. Chem: Springer International Publishing. doi:10.1007/978-3-319-93245-3

Calandra, B., Gurvitch, R., & Lund, J. (2008). An exploratory study of digital video editing as a tool for teacher preparation. *Journal of Technology and Teacher Education, 16*, 137–153.

Campbell, P. F., Nishio, M., Smith, T. M., Clark, L. M., Conant, D. L., Rust, A. H., DePiper, J. N., Frank, T. J., Griffin, M. J., & Choi, Y. (2014). The relationship between teachers' mathematical content and pedagogical knowledge, teachers' perceptions, and student achievement. *Journal for Research in Mathematics Education, 45*(4), 419–459. doi:10.5951/jresematheduc.45.4.0419

Capobianco, B. M., & Radloff, J. (2021). Elementary preservice teachers' trajectories for appropriating engineering design–based science teaching. *Research in Science Education*. Advance online publication. doi:10.1007/s11165-021-10020-y

Capraro, R. M., Capraro, M. M., Parker, D., Kulm, G., & Raulerson, T. (2005). The mathematics content knowledge role in developing preservice teachers' pedagogical content knowledge. *Journal of Research in Childhood Education, 20*(2), 102–118. doi:10.1080/02568540509594555

Capraro, R. M., & Han, S. (2014). STEM: The education frontier to meet 21st-century challenges. *Middle Grades Research Journal, 9*(3), xv.

Carlsen, W. S. (1987). Why do you ask? The effects of science teacher subject-matter knowledge on teacher questioning and classroom discourse. *Paper presented at the annual meeting of the American Educational Research Association*. ERIC Document Reproduction Service no. ED 293 181.

Cartwright, T. J., & Hallar, B. (2018). Taking risks with a growth mindset: Long-term influence of an elementary pre-service after school science practicum. *International Journal of Science Education, 40*(3), 348–370. doi:10.1080/09500693.2017.1420269

Casto, A. R., & Williams, J. A. (2020). Seeking proportionality in the North Carolina STEM pipeline. *High School Journal, 103*(2), 77–98. doi:10.1353/hsj.2020.0004

Caswell, C. J., & LaBrie, D. J. (2017). Inquiry-based learning from the learner's point of view: A teacher candidate's success story. *Journal of Humanistic Mathematics, 7*(2), 161–186. doi:10.5642/jhummath.201702.08

Cavanaugh, S. (2022). Microteaching: Theoretical Origins and Practice. *Educational Practice and Theory, 44*(1), 23–40. doi:10.7459/ept/44.1.03

Ceglie, R. (January 6-7, 2022). *Using data analytics to support school community scientific literacy: A Pilot study*. 2022 Association for Science Teacher Education Conference. Greenville, S.C.

Ceglie, R. (January, 2013). *Using science fairs to promote inquiry skills in an elementary science methods course.* Paper presented at the Association for Science Teacher Education annual international meeting, Charleston, SC.

Ceglie, R. (October 9-10, 2020). *Building inquiry skill using science fairs.* Paper presented at the Mid Atlantic Association for Science Teacher Education annual meeting, Virtual (COVID-19).

Ceglie, R. (September, 2014). *Using NSTA's Learning Center to promote content knowledge in a preservice elementary methods course.* Paper presented at the Mid Atlantic Association for Science Teacher Education annual meeting, Blowing Rock, NC.

Celestino, R. & al. (2020). The cell phone in the classroom: Prohibitions, possibilities and reflections. *Revista Científica Multidisciplinar Núcleo do Conhecimento. 6*, 85-104.

Center for Technology Implementation. (2014). *Using virtual manipulatives to teach mathematics. American Institutes for Research.* American Institutes for Research.

Cervantes, B., Hemmer, L., & Kouzekanani, K. (2015). The impact of project-based learning on minority student achievement: Implications for school redesign. *Education Leadership Review of Doctoral Research, 2*(2), 50–66.

Cervantes-González, E., & López, M. S. H. (2020). El móvil en las aulas de clase: ¿Se prohíbe o se incluye? *Emprennova, 1*(1), 7–23.

Cervato, C., & Kerton, C. (2017). Improving the science teaching self-efficacy of preservice elementary teachers: A multiyear study of a hybrid geoscience course. *Journal of College Science Teaching, 47*(2), 83–91. doi:10.2505/4/jcst17_047_02_83

Chai, C. S., Koh, J. H. L., & Tsai, C. C. (2013). A review of technological pedagogical content knowledge. *Journal of Educational Technology & Society, 16*(2), 31–51.

Chatzopoulos, A., Kalogiannakis, M., Papadakis, S., Papoutsidakis, M., Elza, D., & Psycharis, S. (2021). DuBot: An open-source, low-cost robot for STEM and educational robotics. In Research Anthology on Usage and Development of Open Source Software (pp. 329-353). IGI Global.

Cheever, N. A., Moreno, M. A., & Rosen, L. D. (2018). When does internet and smartphone use become a problem?. *Technology and adolescent mental health*, 121-131.

Chen, G. (2019, March 27). *Cooperative learning.* Public School Review. https://www.publicschoolreview.com/blog/cooperative-learning

Chen, Y. L., Huang, L. F., & Wu, P. C. (2021). Preservice preschool teachers' self-efficacy in and need for STEM education professional development: STEM pedagogical belief as a mediator. *Early Childhood Education Journal, 49*(2), 137–147. doi:10.1007/s10643-020-01055-3

Cheong, D. (2010). The effects of practice teaching sessions in second life on the change in pre-service teachers' teaching efficacy. *Computers & Education, 55*(2), 868–880. doi:10.1016/j.compedu.2010.03.018

Compilation of References

Choudhary, V. (2014, December 5). *Fun with non-Newtonian fluid - Lamar University* [Video]. YouTube. https://www.youtube.com/watch?v=RIUEZ3AhrVE

Christianakis, M. (2011). Hybrid texts: Fifth graders, rap music, and writing. *Urban Education*, *46*(5), 1131–1168. doi:10.1177/0042085911400326

Chval, K. B. (2004). Making the complexities of teaching visible for prospective teachers. *Teaching Children Mathematics*, *11*(2), 91–96. doi:10.5951/TCM.11.2.0091

Cinici, A. (2016). Pre-service Teachers' Science Teaching Self-efficacy Beliefs: The Influence of a Collaborative Peer Microteaching Program. *Mentoring & Tutoring*, *24*(3), 228–249. doi:10.1080/13611267.2016.1222812

Cisco. (2022). *Cisco Webex Meetings* [Computer software]. Cisco. https://www.webex.com/

Clausen, J. M. (2022). Learning to Fly: Development and Design of a Micro-Credentialing System for an Educator Preparation Program in the Absence of a Required Educational Technology Course. *TechTrends*, *66*(2), 276–286. https://doi-org.proxy006.nclive.org/10.1007/s11528-021-00673-x. doi:10.1007/s11528-021-00673-x PMID:34664042

Cobern, W. W., Schuster, D., Adams, B., Skjold, B. A., Mugaloglu, E. Z., Bentz, A., & Sparks, K. (2014). Pedagogy of science teaching tests: Formative assessments of science teaching orientations. *International Journal of Science Education*, *36*(3), 2265–2288. doi:10.1080/09500693.2014.918672

Cochran-Smith, M., Banks, J., Moll, L., Richert, A., Zeichner, K., LePage, P., Darling-Hammond, L., Duffy, H., & McDonald, M. (2005). Teaching Diverse Learners. In L. Darling-Hammond & J. Bransford (Eds.), *Preparing teachers for a changing world: What teachers should learn and be able to do* (pp. 232–274). Jossey-Bass.

Colclasure, B. C., Thoron, A. C., Osborne, E. W., Roberts, T. G., & Pringle, R. M. (2020). Comparing the 5E method of inquiry-based instruction and the four-stage model of direct instruction on students' content knowledge achievement in an ENR curriculum. *Journal of Agricultural Education*, *61*(3), 1–21. doi:10.5032/jae.2020.03001

Cooper, J. M., & Allen, D. W. (1970). *Microteaching: History and Present Status*. W. ERIC Clearinghouse on Teacher Education.

Costa, S. R. S., Duqueviz, B. C., & Pedroza, R. L. S. (2015). Tecnologias digitais como instrumentos mediadores da aprendizagem dos nativos digitais. *Psicologia Escolar e Educacional*, *19*(3), 603–610. doi:10.1590/2175-3539/2015/0193912

Council for the Accreditation of Educator Preparation. (n.d.a). *History of CAEP*. CAEP. https://caepnet.org/about/history

Council for the Accreditation of Educator Preparation. (n.d.b.). *Vision, mission, & goals*. CAEP. https://caepnet.org/about/vision-mission-goals

Council for the Accreditation of Educator Preparation. (n.d.c). [Elementary Teacher Preparation Standards: Updated Resources.]. *CAEP, 2018*, K-6.

Crabtree, L. M., Richardson, S. C., & Lewis, C. W. (2019). The gifted gap, STEM education, and economic immobility. *Journal of Advanced Academics, 30*(2), 203–231. doi:10.1177/1932202X19829749

Craig, T. T., & Marshall, J. (2019). Effect of project-based learning on high school students' state-mandated, standardized math and science exam performance. *Journal of Research in Science Teaching, 56*(10), 1461–1488. doi:10.1002/tea.21582

Creary, S. J., & Locke, K. (2021). To reduce the strain of overwork, learn to listen to your body. Harvard Business Review Digital Articles, 1–7. https://hbr.org/2021/11/to-reduce-the-strain-of-overwork-learn-to-listen-to-your-body

Crescenza, G. (2020). Dal calamaio alla Didattica a distanza. La scuola ai tempi del COVID-19.

Criollo-C, S., Guerrero-Arias, A., Jaramillo-Alcázar, Á., & Luján-Mora, S. (2021). Mobile learning technologies for education: Benefits and pending issues. *Applied Sciences (Basel, Switzerland), 11*(9), 4111. doi:10.3390/app11094111

Cuevas, P., Lee, O., Hart, J., & Deaktor, R. (2005). Improving science inquiry with elementary students of diverse backgrounds. *Journal of Research in Science Teaching, 42*(3), 337–357. doi:10.1002/tea.20053

Curto Prieto, M., Orcos Palma, L., Blázquez Tobías, P. J., & León, F. J. M. (2019). Student assessment of the use of Kahoot in the learning process of science and mathematics. *Education Sciences, 9*(1), 55. doi:10.3390/educsci9010055

d'Alessio, M. A. (2018). The effect of microteaching on science teaching self-efficacy beliefs in preservice elementary teachers. *Journal of Science Teacher Education, 29*(6), 441–467. doi:10.1080/1046560X.2018.1456883

D'Ambrosio, A. (2015). Esperimenti di acustica con smartphone. *Italian Journal of Educational Technology, 23*(3), 176–180.

D'Haem, J., & Griswold, P. (2017). Teacher educators' and student teachers' beliefs about preparation for working with families including those from diverse socioeconomic and cultural backgrounds. *Education and Urban Society, 49*(1), 81–109. doi:10.1177/0013124516630602

Da Pra, L. M. G. (2021). *Mobile learning: esempi di buona pratica basata sull'uso dello smartphone in classe.*

Dahnuss, D., Marwoto, P., Iswari, R. S., & Listiaji, P. (2021, June). Marbles and smartphone on physics laboratory: An investigation for finding coefficient of restitution. [). IOP Publishing.]. *Journal of Physics: Conference Series, 1918*(2), 022005. doi:10.1088/1742-6596/1918/2/022005

Dantus, S. J. (2021). *A triadic worldview? The misconception and bias of universality in Knowles' andragogy.* Commission for International Adult Education.

Compilation of References

Darling-Hammond, L. (2005). Teaching as a profession: Lessons in teacher preparation and professional development. *Phi Delta Kappan*, *87*(3), 237–240. https://journals-sagepub-com.proxy006.nclive.org/doi/pdf/10.1177/003172170508700318

Darling-Hammond, L. (2014). Strengthening clinical preparation: The holy grail of teacher education. *Peabody Journal of Education*, *89*(4), 547–561. doi:10.1080/0161956X.2014.939009

Darling-Hammond, L. (2021, Fall). What will it take to promote whole-child development, learning, and thriving at scale? Three networks offer promising models. *American Educator*, *45*(3), 27.

Darling-Hammond, L., Barron, B., Pearson, P. D., Schoenfeld, A. H., Stage, E. K., Zimmerman, T. D., Cervetti, G. N., & Tilson, J. (2008). *Powerful learning: What we know about teaching for understanding*. John Wiley & Sons, Inc.

Darling-Hammond, L., & Bransford, J. (2007). *Preparing teachers for a changing world (Report of the Committee on Teacher Education of the National Academy of Education)*. Jossey Bass.

Darling-Hammond, L., Flook, L., Cook-Harvey, C., Barron, B., & Osher, D. (2020). Implications for educational practice of the science of learning and development. *Applied Developmental Science*, *24*(2), 97–140. doi:10.1080/10888691.2018.1537791

Data U.S.A. (2022). *University of Houston-Downtown*. Data USA. https://datausa.io/profile/university/university-of-houston-downtown

Davis, B. M., & Buttafuso, D. (1994). A case for the small liberal arts colleges and the preparation of teachers. *Journal of Teacher Education*, *45*(3), 229–235. doi:10.1177/0022487194045003009

Davis, E. A. (2004). Knowledge integration in science teaching: Analyzing teachers' knowledge development. *Research in Science Education*, *34*(1), 21–53. doi:10.1023/B:RISE.0000021034.01508.b8

Davis, E. A. (2006). Preservice elementary teachers' critique of instructional materials for science. *Science Education*, *90*(2), 348–375. https://doi-org.proxy006.nclive.org/10.1002/sce.20110

de Bruïne, E. J., Willemse, T. M., D'Haem, J., Griswold, P., Vloeberghs, L., & Van Eynde, S. (2014). Preparing teacher candidates for family–school partnerships. *European Journal of Teacher Education*, *37*(4), 409–425. doi:10.1080/02619768.2014.912628

de Saxe, J. G., Bucknovitz, S., & Mahoney-Mosedale, F. (2020). The Deprofessionalization of Educators: An Intersectional Analysis of Neoliberalism and Education "Reform.". *Education and Urban Society*, *52*(1), 51–69. doi:10.1177/0013124518786398

DeHaan, R. L. (2005). The impending revolution in undergraduate science education. *Journal of Science Education and Technology*, *14*(2), 253–269. doi:10.1007/s10956-005-4425-3

Dejarnette, N. K. (2018). Implementing STEAM in the Early Childhood Classroom. European. *Journal of STEM Education: Innovations and Research*, *3*(3), 18.

Dewey, J. (1897). My pedagogic creed. *School Journal, 54*, 77-80. http://dewey.pragmatism.org/creed.htm

Dewey, J. (1907). *The school and society*. The University of Chicago Press.

Dewey, J. (1916). *Democracy and education*. CreateSpace Independent Publishing Platform.

Dewey, J. (1938). Education and democracy in the world of today. *Schools: Studies in Education, 9*(1), 96–100. doi:10.1086/665026

Diamond, B. S., Maerten-Rivera, J., Rohrer, R. E., & Lee, O. (2014). Effectiveness of a curricular and professional development intervention at improving elementary teachers' science content knowledge and student achievement outcomes: Year 1 results. *Journal of Research in Science Teaching, 51*(5), 635–658. doi:10.1002/tea.21148

Digital Learning Collaborative. (2020). *Snapshot 2020: A review of K-12 online, blended, and digital learning*. Digital Learning Collaborative. https://www.digitallearningcollab.com

Dimmick, A. (2012). Student empowerment in an environmental science classroom: Toward a framework for social justice education. *Science Education, 96*(6), 990–1012. doi:10.1002/sce.21035

Dionne, L., Reis, G., Trudel, L., Guillet, G., Kleine, L., & Hancianu, C. (2012). Students' sources of motivation for participation in science fairs: An exploratory study within the Canada-wide science fair 2008. *International Journal of Science and Mathematics Education, 10*(3), 669–693. doi:10.1007/s10763-011-9318-8

Docherty-Skippen, S. M., Karrow, D., & Ahmend, G. (2020). Doing science: Pre-service teachers' attitudes and confidence teaching elementary science and technology. *Brock Education Journal, 29*(1), 24 – 34. https://journals.library.brocku.ca/brocked

Dolenc, N. R., & Kazanis, W. H. (2020). A potential for interest driven learning to enhance the inquiry-based learning process. *Science Education, 27*(2), 121–128.

Dominski, F. H., Branco, J. H. L., Buonanno, G., Stabile, L., da Silva, M. G., & Andrade, A. (2021). Effects of air pollution on health: A mapping review of systematic reviews and meta-analyses. *Environmental Research, 201*, 111487. doi:10.1016/j.envres.2021.111487 PMID:34116013

Doran, P. (2020). What they didn't teach us: New teachers reflect on their preparation experiences. *Professional Educator, 43*(1), 59–69.

Dorph, R., Shields, P., Tiffany-Morales, J., Hartry, A., & McCaffrey, T. (2011). *High hopes-few opportunities: The status of elementary science education in California*. The Center for the Future of Teaching and Learning at WestEd.

Drake, S. M., & Burns, R. C. (2004). *Meeting standards through integrated curriculum*. ASCD. http://www.ascd.org/publications/books/103011/chapters/What-Is-Integrated-Curriculum%C2%A2.aspx

Compilation of References

Drickey, N. A. (2000). A comparison of virtual and physical manipulatives in teaching visualization and spatial reasoning to middle school mathematics students. (Doctoral dissertation, Utah State University, 2000). *Dissertation Abstracts International, 62*(02), 499A. (UMI No. 3004011).

Drivet, A. (2021). Examining an Operational Approach to Teaching Probability. IGI Global. doi:10.4018/978-1-7998-3871-5

Easterly, R. G. III, & Myers, B. E. (2011). Inquiry-based instruction for students with special needs in school based agricultural education. *Journal of Agricultural Education, 52*(2), 36–46. doi:10.5032/jae.2011.02036

Eaton, S. E. (2022). New priorities for academic integrity: Equity, diversity, inclusion, decolonization and Indigenization. *International Journal for Educational Integrity, 18*(1), 10. Advance online publication. doi:10.1007/s40979-022-00105-0

Eccles, J. S., & Wigfield, A. (2002). Motivational beliefs, values, and goals. *Annual Review of Psychology, 53*(1), 109. https://doi-org.proxy006.nclive.org/10.1146/annurev.psych.53.100901.135153

Enochs, L., & Riggs, I. (1990). Further development of an elementary science teaching efficacy belief instrument: A preservice elementary scale. *School Science and Mathematics, 90*(8), 694–706. doi:10.1111/j.1949-8594.1990.tb12048.x

Ensign, J. (2003). Including culturally relevant math in an urban school. *Educational Studies, 34*(4), 414–423.

Epstein, J. L. (2018). *School, family, and community partnerships: Preparing educators and improving schools.* Routledge.

Epstein, J. L., & Salinas, K. C. (2004). Partnering with families and communities. *Educational Leadership, 61*(8), 12–19.

Ergül, N. R., & Kargın, E. K. (2014). The effect of project based learning on students' science success. *Procedia: Social and Behavioral Sciences, 136*, 537–541. doi:10.1016/j.sbspro.2014.05.371

Eshach, H. (2007). Bridging in-school and out-of-school learning: Formal, non-formal, and informal education. *Journal of Science Education and Technology, 16*(2), 171–190. doi:10.1007/s10956-006-9027-1

Eshach, H., & Fried, M. N. (2005). Should science be taught in early childhood? *Journal of Science Education and Technology, 14*(3), 313–336. doi:10.1007/s10956-005-7198-9

Fadda, D., & Vivanet, G. (2021). Tecnologie digitali e didattica laboratoriale nell'educazione STEM. Evidenze scientifiche e raccomandazioni pratiche. *Collana "Quaderni dell'Osservatorio", 37.*

Fahsl, C., & Vogt, P. (2019). Determination of the radius of curves and roundabouts with a smartphone. *The Physics Teacher, 57*(8), 566–567. doi:10.1119/1.5131133

Faisal, I. A., Purboyo, T. W., & Ansori, A. S. R. (2019). A Review of accelerometer sensor and gyroscope sensor in IMU sensors on motion capture. *Journal of Engineering and Applied Sciences (Asian Research Publishing Network)*, *15*(3), 826–829.

Fatimah, S., Tiarina, Y., Fitrawati, F., & Mira, A. S. (2021). English teachers' and lecturers' perceptions of reflective practice through video recording at the teacher certification program. *Studies in English Language and Education*, *8*(2), 670–689. https://doi-org.proxy006.nclive.org/10.24815/siele.v8i2.18931. doi:10.24815/siele.v8i2.18931

Faulkner, S. A., & Cook, C. M. (2006). Testing vs. teaching: The perceived impact of assessment demands on middle grades instructional practices. *Research in Middle Level Education Online*, *29*(7), 1–13. https://doi-org.proxy006.nclive.org/10.1080/19404476.2006.11462030

Fayne, H. R. (2014). Preparing preservice teachers in a virtual space: A case study of a literacy methods course. *Teacher Educator*, *49*(4), 305–316. doi:10.1080/08878730.2014.934081

Felisoni, D. D., & Godoi, A. S. (2018). Cell phone usage and academic performance: An experiment. *Computers & Education*, *117*, 175–187. doi:10.1016/j.compedu.2017.10.006

Fernandes, J., Brandão, T., Almeida, S. M., & Santana, P. (2023). An educational game to teach children about air quality using augmented reality and tangible interaction with sensors. *International Journal of Environmental Research and Public Health*, *20*(5), 3814. doi:10.3390/ijerph20053814 PMID:36900825

Ferreira, M., Silva Filho, O. L., Moreira, M. A., Franz, G. B., Portugal, K. O., & Nogueira, D. X. (2020). Unidade de ensino potencialmente significativa sobre óptica geométrica apoiada por vídeos, aplicativos e jogos para smartphones. *Revista Brasileira de Ensino de Física*, *42*, 42. doi:10.1590/1806-9126-rbef-2020-0057

Finn, D. (2022). Online Learning and Universal Design: Practical Applications for Reaching Adult Learners. *COABE Journal: The Resource for Adult Education*, *11*(1), 101–109.

Flick, L. B., & Lederman, N. G. (Eds.). (2006). *Scientific inquiry and nature of science: Implications for teaching, learning, and teacher education*. Springer.

Flory, S. B. (2016). Culturally responsive pedagogy and teacher socialization. In *Teacher socialization in physical education* (pp. 178–191). Routledge.

Fonger, N. L., Stephens, A., Blanton, M., Isler, I., Knuth, E., & Gardiner, A. M. (2018). Developing a learning progression for curriculum, instruction, and student learning: An example from mathematics education. *Cognition and Instruction*, *36*(1), 30–55. doi:10.1080/07370008.2017.1392965

Fowler, D. C., & Stickney, L. T. (2020). Smartphone apps for use in management education. Handbook of Teaching with Technology in Management, Leadership, and Business, 263-275.

Compilation of References

Fox, L., Howell, S., Kazouh, A., Paul, E., & Peacock, J. (2023). *Teacher recruitment and retention trends across North Carolina and the impact of the COVID-19 pandemic*. Public School Forum of North Carolina. https://www.ncforum.org/2023/teacher-recruitment-and-retention-trends-across-north-carolina-and-the-impact-of-the-covid-19-pandemic/

Fraser, S., Beswick, K., & Crowley, S. (2019). Responding to the Demands of the STEM Education Agenda: The Experiences of Primary and Secondary Teachers from Rural, Regional and Remote Australia. *Journal of Research in STEM Education*, 5(1), 40–59. doi:10.51355/jstem.2019.62

Freeman, S., Eddy, S. L., McDonough, M., Smith, M. K., Okoroafor, N., Jordt, H., & Wenderoth, M. P. (2014). Active learning increases student performance in science, engineering, and mathematics. *Proceedings of the National Academy of Sciences of the United States of America*, 111(23), 8410–8415. doi:10.1073/pnas.1319030111 PMID:24821756

Fuchsman, K. (2009). Rethinking integration in interdisciplinary studies. *Issues in Integrative Studies*, 27, 70–85.

Gallard, A. J. (1997). *Creating a multicultural learning environment in science classrooms*. Research Matters. https://narst.org/research-matters/multicultural-learning-environment-science-classrooms

Garavaglia, A., & Petti, L. (2020). Strategie di uso dello smartphone degli studenti della scuola secondaria di secondo grado= Secondary school students' strategies for using the smartphone. *SIRD*, 3, 40–50.

Garet, M. S., Porter, A. C., Desimone, L., Birman, B. F., & Yoon, K. S. (2001). What makes professional development effective? Results from a national sample of teachers. *American Educational Research Journal*, 38(4), 915–945. doi:10.3102/00028312038004915

Garrison, D. R. (1997). Self-directed learning: Toward a comprehensive model. *Adult Education Quarterly*, 48(1), 18–33. https://doi-org.proxy006.nclive.org/10.1177/074171369704800103

Gay, G. (2002). Preparing for culturally responsive teaching. *Journal of Teacher Education*, 53(2), 106–116. doi:10.1177/0022487102053002003

Gedeborg, S. (2016). Designing social online math activities. *Mathematics Teacher*, 110(4), 272–278. doi:10.5951/mathteacher.110.4.0272

Gejda, L., & LaRocco, M. (2006). *Inquiry-based instruction in secondary science classrooms: A survey of teacher practice*. Paper presented at the 37th Annual Northeast Educational Research Association Conference, Kerhonkson, NY.

Gersten, R., Chard, D., Jayanthi, M., Baker, S., Morphy, P., & Flojo, J. (2009). *A Meta-analysis of mathematics instructional interventions for students with learning disabilities: A technical report*. Instructional Research Group.

Ghousseini, H. (2017). Rehearsals of Teaching and Opportunities to Learn Mathematical Knowledge for Teaching. *Cognition and Instruction*, 35(3), 188–211. doi:10.1080/07370008.2017.1323903

Giannelli, F. (2015). Acustica in cucina. *La Fisica nella Scuola*, XLVIII, 1.

Gibson, D., Ostashewski, N., Flintoff, K., Grant, S., & Knight, E. (2015). Digital badges in education. *Education and Information Technologies*, *20*(2), 403–410. https://doi-org.proxy006.nclive.org/10.1007/s10639-013-9291-7. doi:10.1007/s10639-013-9291-7

Giebelhaus, C. R., & Bowman, C. L. (2002). Teaching mentors: Is it worth the effort? *The Journal of Educational Research*, *95*(4), 246–254. doi:10.1080/00220670209596597

Gisev, N., Bell, J. S., & Chen, T. F. (2013). Interrater agreement and interrater reliability: Key concepts, approaches, and applications. *Research in Social & Administrative Pharmacy*, *9*(3), 330–338. doi:10.1016/j.sapharm.2012.04.004 PMID:22695215

Giusti, E. (2004). La matematica in cucina. *Bollati Boringhieri*. 104-112.

Göçer, A. (2016). Assessment of the Opinions and Practices of Student Teachers on Micro-Teaching as a Teaching Strategy. *Acta Didactica Napocensia*, *9*(2), 33–46.

Godley, A. J., & Minnici, A. (2008). Critical language pedagogy in an urban high school English class. *Urban Education*, *43*(3), 319–346. doi:10.1177/0042085907311801

Goldston, M. J., Day, J. B., Sundberg, C., & Dantzler, J. (2010). Psychometric analysis of a 5E learning cycle lesson plan assessment instrument. *International Journal of Science and Mathematics Education*, *8*(4), 633–648. doi:10.1007/s10763-009-9178-7

Gonzalez, E. (2019). *The value of digital tools in science classes*. Edutopia. https://www.edutopia.org/article/value-digital-tools-science-classes

González, E. B., & Muñoz, G. N. E. (2020). Implicaciones educativas del uso de dispositivos móviles en el aula: posibilidades y dificultades psicopedagógicas. *Aproximación periodística y educomunicativa al fenómeno de las redes sociales*, 571.

Goodnough, K., Pelech, S., & Stordy, M. (2014). Effective professional development in STEM education: The perceptions of primary/elementary teachers. *Teacher Education and Practice*, *27*(2/3), 402–423. https://www.researchgate.net/publication/281121613_Effective_Professional_Development_in_STEM_Education_The_Perceptions_of_PrimaryElementary_Teachers

Griffith, S. M., Domenech Rodríguez, M., & Anderson, A. J. (2014). Graduate ethics education: A content analysis of syllabi. *Training and Education in Professional Psychology*, *8*(4), 248–252. doi:10.1037/tep0000036

Grossman, P., Ronfeldt, M., & Cohen, J. J. (2012). *The power of setting: The role of field experience in learning to teach.*

Grossman, P. L. (1990). *The making of a teacher: Teacher knowledge and teacher education.* Teachers College Press.

Compilation of References

Gunckel, K. L., & Tolbert, S. (2018). The imperative to move toward a dimension of care in engineering education. *Journal of Research in Science Teaching*, *55*(7), 938–961. doi:10.1002/tea.21458

Gupta, Y., Khan, F. M., & Agarwal, S. (2021). Exploring Factors Influencing Mobile Learning in Higher Education-A Systematic Review. *International Journal of Interactive Mobile Technologies*, *15*(12), 140. doi:10.3991/ijim.v15i12.22503

Gurjanow, I., Zender, J., & Ludwig, M. (2020, June). MathCityMap–Popularizing mathematics around the globe with math trails and smartphone. In *Research on Outdoor STEM Education in the digital Age. Proceedings of the ROSETA Online Conference in June 2020* (pp. 103-110). ACM. 10.37626/GA9783959871440.0.13

Guskey, T. R. (2003). What makes professional development effective? *Phi Delta Kappan*, *84*(10), 748–750. doi:10.1177/003172170308401007

Gutiérrez, J. D., Jiménez, A. R., Seco, F., Álvarez, F. J., Aguilera, T., Torres-Sospedra, J., & Melchor, F. (2022). GetSensorData: An extensible Android-based application for multi-sensor data registration. *SoftwareX*, *19*, 101186. doi:10.1016/j.softx.2022.101186

Gu, X., Chen, S., Zhu, W., & Lin, L. (2015). An intervention framework designed to develop the collaborative problem-solving skills of primary school students. *Educational Technology Research and Development*, *63*(1), 143–159. doi:10.1007/s11423-014-9365-2

Gyllenpalm, J., Wickman, P., & Holmgren, S. (2010). Secondary science teachers' selective traditions and examples of inquiry-oriented approaches. *NorDiNa*, *6*(1), 44–60. doi:10.5617/nordina.269

Haefner, L., & Zembal-Saul, C. (2004). Learning by doing? Prospective elementary teachers' developing understandings of scientific inquiry and science teaching and learning. *International Journal of Science Education*, *26*(13), 1653–1674. doi:10.1080/0950069042000230709

Hall, L. (2009, September). Seeing eye to eye. *National Geographic Explorer*, *9*(1), 3–9.

Han, S., Capraro, R., & Capraro, M. M. (2015). How science, technology, engineering, and mathematics (STEM) project-based learning (PBL) affects high, middle, and low achievers differently: The impact of student factors on achievement. *International Journal of Science and Mathematics Education*, *13*(5), 1089–1113. doi:10.1007/s10763-014-9526-0

Hanuscin, D. L. (2004). A workshop approach: Instructional strategies for working within the contraints of field experiences in elementary science. *Journal of Elementary Science Education*, *16*(1), 1–8. doi:10.1007/BF03174746

Hanuscin, D. L., Lee, M. H., & Akerson, V. L. (2011). Elementary Teachers' Pedagogical Content Knowledge for Teaching the Nature of Science. *Science Education*, *95*(1), 145–167. doi:10.1002/sce.20404

Hanuscin, D. L., & Zangori, L. (2016). Developing practical knowledge of the next generation science standards in elementary science teacher education. *Journal of Science Teacher Education*, *27*(8), 799–818. doi:10.1007/s10972-016-9489-9

Hartlep, N. D., Stuchell, C. V., Whitt, N. E., & Hensley, B. O. (2021). *Critical Storytelling During the COVID-19 Pandemic* (N. D. Hartlep, C. V. Stuchell, N. E. Whitt, & B. O. Hensley, Eds.). Information Age Publishing.

Harvard-Smithsonian Center for Astrophysics (2001). *Private Universe Project in Mathematics*. Harvard.

Hazel, P. (2008). Toward a narrative pedagogy for interactive learning environments. *Interactive Learning Environments*, *16*(3), 199–213. doi:10.1080/10494820802113947

Heck, D. J., Plumley, C. L., Stylianou, D. A., Smith, A. A., & Moffett, G. (2019). Scaling up innovative learning in mathematics: Exploring the effect of different professional development approaches on teacher knowledge, beliefs, and instructional practice. *Educational Studies in Mathematics*, *102*(3), 319–342. https://doi-org.proxy006.nclive.org/10.1007/s10649-019-09895-6

Helms, A. (2018, August 2). Hundreds of NC teachers are flunking math exams. It may not be their fault. *The Charlotte Observer*. https://www.charlotteobserver.com/news/local/education/article215848065.html

Henry, H. (2018, July 10). *Research reveals boys' interest In STEM careers declining; Girls' interest unchanged*. Junior Achievement of Southern Massachusetts. https://somass.ja.org/news/blog/research-reveals-boys-interest-in-stem-careers-declining-girls-interest-unchanged

Hergemöller, T., & Laumann, D. (2017). Smartphone magnification attachment: Microscope or magnifying glass. *The Physics Teacher*, *55*(6), 361–364. doi:10.1119/1.4999732

Herrera, S. G., Holmes, M. A., & Kavimandan, S. K. (2012). Bringing theory to life: Strategies that make culturally responsive pedagogy a reality in diverse secondary classrooms. *International Journal of Multicultural Education*, *14*(3), 1–19. doi:10.18251/ijme.v14i3.608

Hirschberg, J., & Manning, C. D. (2015). Advances in natural language processing. *Science*, *349*(6245), 261–266. doi:10.1126/science.aaa8685 PMID:26185244

Holroyd, C., & Harlen, W. (1996). Primary teachers' confidence about teaching science and technology. *Research Papers in Education: Policy and Practice*, *11*(3), 323–335.

Howard, T. C. (2011). Culturally responsive pedagogy. In J. A. Banks (Ed.), *Transforming multicultural education, policy, & practice: Expanding educational opportunity* (pp. 137–163). Teachers College Press.

Hoy, W. K., & Spero, R. B. (2005). Changes in teacher efficacy during the early years of teaching: A comparison of four measures. *Teaching and Teacher Education*, *21*(4), 343–356. doi:10.1016/j.tate.2005.01.007

Compilation of References

Huang, C. (2003). Changing learning with new interactive and media-rich instruction environments: Virtual labs case study report. *Computerized Medical Imaging and Graphics*, *27*(2-3), 157–164. doi:10.1016/S0895-6111(02)00089-7 PMID:12620306

Huang, K. T., Ball, C., Francis, J., Ratan, R., Boumis, J., & Fordham, J. (2019). Augmented versus virtual reality in education: An exploratory study examining science knowledge retention when using augmented reality/virtual reality mobile applications. *Cyberpsychology, Behavior, and Social Networking*, *22*(2), 105–110. doi:10.1089/cyber.2018.0150 PMID:30657334

Hume, A., & Berry, A. (2011). Constructing CoRes - A strategy for building PCK in pre-service science teacher education. *Research in Science Education*, *41*(3), 341–355. doi:10.1007/s11165-010-9168-3

Hunt, A. W., Nipper, K. L., & Nash, L. E. (2011). Virtual vs. concrete manipulatives in mathematics teacher education: Is one type more effective than the other? *Current Issues in Middle Level Education*, *16*(2), 16.

Hurst, E. J. (2015). Digital badges: Beyond learning incentives. *Journal of Electronic Resources in Medical Libraries*, *12*(3), 182–189. https://doi-org.proxy006.nclive.org/10.1080/15424065.2015.1065661

Hurst, M. A., Polinsky, N., Haden, C. A., Levine, S. C., & Uttal, D. H. (2019). Leveraging research on informal learning to inform policy on promoting early STEM. *Social Policy Report*, *32*(3), 1–33. doi:10.1002/sop2.5

Hwang, B. L., Chou, T. C., & Huang, C. H. (2021). Actualizing the affordance of mobile technology for mobile learning. *Journal of Educational Technology & Society*, *24*(4), 67–80.

Hwang, G.-J., & Fu, Q.-K. (2020). Advancement and research trends of smart learning environments in the mobile era. *International Journal of Mobile Learning and Organization*, *14*(1), 114–129. doi:10.1504/IJMLO.2020.103911

Irvine, J. J. (1990). *Black students and school failure: Personnel, practices, and prescriptions.* Greenwood.

Iveland, A., & Burr, T. (2019). Integrating science & ELA: Discoveries from the early implementer evaluators. *California Classroom Science, 31*(5). http://www.classroomscience.org/integrating-science-ela-discoveries-from-the-early-implementer-evaluators

Jagers, R. J., Rivas-Drake, D., & Williams, B. (2019). Transformative social and emotional learning (SEL): Toward SEL in service of educational equity and excellence. *Educational Psychologist*, *54*(3), 162–184. doi:10.1080/00461520.2019.1623032

Jahnke, I., & Liebscher, J. (2020). Three types of integrated course designs for using mobile technologies to support creativity in higher education. *Computers & Education*, *146*, 103782. doi:10.1016/j.compedu.2019.103782

Jalal, A., Quaid, M. A. K., Tahir, S. B. U. D., & Kim, K. (2020). A study of accelerometer and gyroscope measurements in physical life-log activities detection systems. *Sensors (Basel)*, *20*(22), 6670. doi:10.3390/s20226670 PMID:33233412

Javeed, L. (2019). Supporting clinical practice through rehearsals. *Northwest Journal of Teaching Education*, *14*(1). https://doi.org/https://doi.org/10.15760/nwjte.2019.14.1.2

Javier, D., Solis, L., Paul, M. F., Thompson, E. L., Maynard, G., Latif, Z., Stinson, K., Ahmed, T., & Vishwanatha, J. K. (2022). Implementation of an unconscious bias course for the National Research Mentoring Network. *BMC Medical Education*, *22*(1), 391. doi:10.1186/s12909-022-03466-9 PMID:35597975

Jensen, A. R. (1969). How much can we boost IQ and scholastic achievement? *Harvard Educational Review*, *19*(1), 1–123. doi:10.17763/haer.39.1.l3u15956627424k7

Jimenez, B. A., & Besaw, J. (2020). Building early numeracy through virtual manipulatives for students with intellectual disability and autism. *Education and Training in Autism and Developmental Disabilities*, *55*(1), 28–44.

Johnson, A., Brown, J., Carlone, H., & Cuevas, A. K. (2011). Authoring identity amidst the treacherous terrain of science: A multiracial feminist examination of the journeys of three women of color in science. *Journal of Research in Science Teaching*, *48*(4), 339–366. doi:10.1002/tea.20411

Jones, M. G., Ennes, M., Weedfall, D., Chesnutt, K., & Cayton, E. (2020). The development and validation of a measure of science capital, habitus, and future science interests. *Research in Science Education*, *51*(6), 1549–1565. doi:10.1007/s11165-020-09916-y

Jones, W. M., Hope, S., & Adams, B. (2018). Teachers' perceptions of digital badges as recognition of professional development. *British Journal of Educational Technology*, *49*(3), 427–438. https://doi-org.proxy006.nclive.org/10.1111/bjet.12557

Jönsson, A., & Prins, F. J. (2019). Editorial: Transparency in Assessment—Exploring the Influence of Explicit Assessment Criteria. *Frontiers in Education*, *3*, 119. doi:10.3389/feduc.2018.00119

Jordan, N. C., Glutting, J., & Ramineni, C. (2010). The importance of number sense to mathematics achievement in first and third grades. *Learning and Individual Differences*, *20*(2), 82–88. doi:10.1016/j.lindif.2009.07.004 PMID:20401327

Kalana, M. H., Junaini, S. N., & Fauzi, A. H. (2020). Mobile augmented reality for biology learning: Review and design recommendations. *Journal of Critical Reviews*, *7*(12), 579–585.

Kang, E. J., Donovan, C., & McCarthy, M. J. (2018). Exploring elementary teachers' pedagogical content knowledge and confidence in implementing the NGSS science and engineering practices. *Journal of Science Teacher Education*, *29*(1), 9–29. doi:10.1080/1046560X.2017.1415616

Kang, R. L. (2020, July). Struggles and strengths of being preservice in a pandemic. *Educator's Update*, 2–3.

Compilation of References

Kartal, T., Ozturk, N., & Ekici, G. (2012). Developing pedagogical content knowledge in preservice science teachers through microteaching lesson study. *Procedia: Social and Behavioral Sciences*, *46*, 2753–2758. doi:10.1016/j.sbspro.2012.05.560

Kay, R. (2018). Examining individual differences in the use of STEM-based mobile apps. In *EDULEARN18 Proceedings* (pp. 2069-2076). IATED. 10.21125/edulearn.2018.0577

Kazemi, E., Ghousseini, H., Cunard, A., & Turrou, A. C. (2016). Getting inside rehearsals: Insights from teacher educators to support work on complex practice. *Journal of Teacher Education*, *67*(1), 18–31. doi:10.1177/0022487115615191

Kelley, T. R., & Knowles, J. G. (2016). A conceptual framework for integrated STEM education. *International Journal of STEM Education*, *3*(1), 1–11. doi:10.1186/s40594-016-0046-z

Kennedy, M. (2016). How does professional development improve teaching? *Review of Educational Research*, *86*(4), 945–980. doi:10.3102/0034654315626800

Keough, P. D. (Ed.). (2021). *Educational Recovery for PK-12 Education During and After a Pandemic*. IGI Global. doi:10.4018/978-1-7998-6952-8

Keys, C. W., & Bryan, L. A. (2001). Co-constructing inquiry-based science with teachers: Essential research for lasting reform. *Journal of Research in Science Teaching*, *38*(6), 631–645. doi:10.1002/tea.1023

Kim, D., & Bolger, M. (2017). Analysis of Korean Elementary Pre-Service Teachers' Changing Attitudes About Integrated STEAM Pedagogy Through Developing Lesson Plans. *International Journal of Science and Mathematics Education*, *15*(4), 587–605. doi:10.1007/s10763-015-9709-3

Kim, H., & Ke, F. (2017). Effects of game-based learning in an open sim-supported virtual environment on mathematical performance. *Interactive Learning Environments*, *25*(4), 543–557. doi:10.1080/10494820.2016.1167744

Kind, V. (2009). A conflict in your head: An exploration of trainee science teachers' subject matter knowledge development and its impact on teacher self-confidence. *International Journal of Science Education*, *31*(11), 1529–1562. doi:10.1080/09500690802226062

Kisiel, J. (2013). Introducing future teachers to science beyond the classroom. *Journal of Science Teacher Education*, *24*(1), 67–91. doi:10.1007/s10972-012-9288-x

Knowles, M. S. (1975). *Self-directed learning: A guide for learners and teachers*. Follett.

Koehler, M. J., Mishra, P., Kereluik, K., Shin, T. S., & Graham, C. R. (2014). The Technological Pedagogical Content Knowledge Framework. In J. M. Spector (Eds.), *Handbook of Research on Educational Communications and Technology* (pp. 101–111). Springer. doi:10.1007/978-1-4614-3185-5_9

Koehler, M., & Mishra, P. (2009). What is technological pedagogical content knowledge (TPACK)? *Contemporary Issues in Technology & Teacher Education*, *9*(1), 60–70.

Koh, D., & Tan, A. L. (2021). Singaporean Pre-service Teachers' Perceptions of STEM Epistemic Practices and Education. *Journal of STEM Teacher Education*, *56*(2). doi:10.30707/JSTE56.2.1649165366.257139

Kokotsaki, D., Menzies, V., & Wiggins, A. (2016). Project-based learning: A review of the literature. *Improving Schools*, *19*(3), 267–277. doi:10.1177/1365480216659733

Koscielniak, B. (2013). *About time: A first look at time and clocks*. Clarion Books.

Krall, R., Lott, K. H., & Wymer, C. L. (2009). Inservice elementary and middle school teachers' conceptions of photosynthesis and respiration. *Journal of Science Teacher Education*, *20*(1), 41–55. doi:10.1007/s10972-008-9117-4

Kricorian, K., Seu, M., López, D., Ureta, E., & Equils, O. (2020). Factors influencing participation of underrepresented students in STEM fields: Matched mentors and mindsets. *International Journal of STEM Education*, *7*(1), 16. doi:10.1186/s40594-020-00219-2

Kruse, J., Wilcox, J., Patel, N., Borzo, S., Seebach, C., & Henning, J. (2022). The Power of Practicum Support: A Quasi-experimental Investigation of Elementary Preservice Teachers' Science Instruction in A Highly Supported Field Experience. *Journal of Science Teacher Education*, *33*(4), 392–412. doi:10.1080/1046560X.2021.1949099

Kubiatko, M., & Vaculová, I. (2011). Project-based learning: Characteristic and the experiences with application in the science subjects. *Energy Education Science and Technology, Part B. Social and Educational Studies*, *3*(1), 65–74.

Kuhn, J., & Vogt, P. (2013). Analyzing acoustic phenomena with a smartphone microphone. *The Physics Teacher*, *51*(2), 118–119. doi:10.1119/1.4775539

Ladson-Billings, G. (1995). Toward a theory of culturally relevant pedagogy. *American Educational Research Journal*, *32*(3), 465–491. doi:10.3102/00028312032003465

Ladson-Billings, G. (2006). Yes, but how do we do it? Practicing culturally relevant pedagogy. In J. Landsman & C. W. Lewis (Eds.), *White teachers/diverse classrooms: A guide to building inclusive schools, promoting high expectations and eliminating racism* (pp. 29–42). Stylus Publishers.

Ladson-Billings, G. (2014). Culturally relevant pedagogy 2.0: Aka the remix. *Harvard Educational Review*, *84*(1), 74–84. doi:10.17763/haer.84.1.p2rj131485484751

Ladson-Billings, G. (2021a). *Culturally relevant pedagogy: Asking a different question*. Teachers College Press.

Ladson-Billings, G. (2021b). Does that count? How mathematics education can support justice-focused anti-racist teaching and learning. *Journal of Urban Mathematics Education*, *14*(1B, 1b), 1–5. doi:10.21423/jume-v14i1Ba444

Lampert, M., Franke, M. L., Kazemi, E., Ghousseini, H., Turrou, A. C., Beasley, H., Cunard, A., & Crowe, K. (2013). Keeping it complex: Using rehearsals to support novice teacher learning of ambitious teaching. *Journal of Teacher Education*, *64*(3), 226–243. doi:10.1177/0022487112473837

Compilation of References

Lazic, B., Knežević, J., & Maričić, S. (2021). The influence of project-based learning on student achievement in elementary mathematics education. *South African Journal of Education*, *41*(3), 1909. doi:10.15700/saje.v41n3a1909

Lee, E. H., & Brown, M. J. (2018). Connecting inquiry and values in science education: An approach based on John Dewey's philosophy. *Science & Education*, *27*(1-2), 63–79. doi:10.1007/s11191-017-9952-9

Lee, O., & Buxton, C. A. (2010). *Diversity and equity in science education: Research, policy, and practice*. Teachers College Press.

Lee, Y., Capraro, R. M., & Capraro, M. M. (2018). Mathematics teachers' subject matter knowledge and pedagogical content knowledge in problem posing. *International Electronic Journal of Mathematics Education*, *13*(2), 75–90. doi:10.12973/iejme/2698

Legrottaglie, S., & Ligorio, M. B. (2014). L'uso delle tecnologie a scuola: Il punto di vista dei docenti. *Italian Journal of Educational Technology*, *22*(3), 183–190.

Leko, M. M., & Brownell, M. T. (2011). Special education preservice teachers' appropriation of pedagogical tools for teaching reading. *Exceptional Children*, *77*(2), 229–251. doi:10.1177/001440291107700205

Lellis-Santos, C., & Abdulkader, F. (2020). Smartphone-assisted experimentation as a didactic strategy to maintain practical lessons in remote education: Alternatives for physiology education during the COVID-19 pandemic. *Advances in Physiology Education*, *44*(4), 579–586. doi:10.1152/advan.00066.2020 PMID:32955344

Leone, P., Quatraro, F., & Giorgio, I. (2022). *Scienze per il Futuro, un percorso STEM in*. Atti DIDAMATICA.

Lepp, A., Barkley, J. E., & Karpinski, A. C. (2015). The relationship between cell phone use and academic performance in a sample of US college students. *SAGE Open*, *5*(1), 2158244015573169. doi:10.1177/2158244015573169

Levitt, K. E. (2002). An analysis of elementary teachers' beliefs regarding the teaching and learning of science. *Science Education*, *86*(1), 1–22. doi:10.1002/sce.1042

Linder, S. M., & Simpson, A. (2018). Towards an understanding of early childhood mathematics education: A systematic review of the literature focusing on practicing and prospective teachers. *Contemporary Issues in Early Childhood*, *19*(3), 274–296. doi:10.1177/1463949117719553

Lin, K.-Y., Yu, K.-C., Hsiao, H.-S., Chang, Y.-S., & Chien, Y.-H. (2020). Effects of web-based versus classroom-based stem learning environments on the development of collaborative problem-solving skills in junior high school students. *International Journal of Technology and Design Education*, *30*(1), 21–34. doi:10.1007/s10798-018-9488-6

Liu, M. (2013). A study of mobile sensing using smartphones. *International Journal of Distributed Sensor Networks*, *9*(3), 272916. doi:10.1155/2013/272916

Llewellyn, D. (2002). *Inquire within: Implementing inquiry-based science standards.* Corwin Press, Inc.

Lo, C. K., & Hew, K. F. (2020). A comparison of flipped learning with gamification, traditional learning, and online independent study: The effects on students' mathematics achievement and cognitive engagement. *Interactive Learning Environments, 28*(4), 464–481. doi:10.1080/10494820.2018.1541910

Löfström, E., & Nevgi, A. (2006). From strategic planning to meaningful learning: Diverse perspectives on the development of web-based teaching and learning in higher education. *British Journal of Educational Technology, 38*(2), 312–324. doi:10.1111/j.1467-8535.2006.00625.x

Long, C. S., Harrell, P. E., Subramaniam, K., & Pope, E. (2019). Using microteaching to improve preservice elementary teachers' physical science content knowledge. *The Electronic Journal for Research in Science & Mathematics Education, 23*(4).

Lotter, C., Singer, J., & Godley, J. (2009). The influence of repeated teaching and reflection on preservice teachers' views of inquiry and nature of science. *Journal of Science Teacher Education, 20*(6), 553–582. doi:10.1007/s10972-009-9144-9

Luo, T., Hibbard, L., Franklin, T., & Moore, D. R. (2017). Preparing teacher candidates for virtual field placements via an exposure to K–12 online teaching. *Journal of Information Technology Education, 16*(1), 1–14. doi:10.28945/3626

Macias, J. (1987). The hidden curriculum of Papago teachers: American Indian strategies for mitigating cultural discontinuity in early schooling. In G. Spindler & L. Spindler (Eds.), *Interpretive ethnography at home and abroad* (pp. 363–380). Lawrence Erlbaum Associates.

Mackenzie, T. (2016). *Dive into inquiry: Amplify learning and empower student voice.* Ed Tech Team Press.

Mahapatra, S. (2019). Smartphone addiction and associated consequences: Role of loneliness and self-regulation. *Behaviour & Information Technology, 38*(8), 833–844. doi:10.1080/0144929X.2018.1560499

Maiorca, C., Roberts, T., Jackson, C., Bush, S., Delaney, A., Mohr-Schroeder, M. J., & Soledad, Y. S. (2021). Informal learning environments and impact on interest in STEM careers. *International Journal of Science and Mathematics Education, 19*(1), 45–64. doi:10.1007/s10763-019-10038-9

Malndonado, E. A., Ramírez, P., & Avendaño, W. R. (2022). Smartphone and teamwork as a methodological tool for teaching and learning physics. [). IOP Publishing.]. *Journal of Physics: Conference Series, 2159*(1), 012020. doi:10.1088/1742-6596/2159/1/012020

Marble, S. (2006). Learning to teach through lesson study. *Action in Teacher Education, 28*(3), 86–96. doi:10.1080/01626620.2006.10463422

Marble, S. (2007). Inquiring into teaching: Lesson study in elementary science methods. *Journal of Science Teacher Education, 18*(6), 935–953. doi:10.1007/s10972-007-9071-6

Compilation of References

Margot, K. C., & Kettler, T. (2019). Teachers' perception of STEM integration and education: A systematic literature review. *International Journal of STEM Education*, *6*(1), 1–16. doi:10.1186/s40594-018-0151-2

Marks, D. B. (2013). Inquiry-based learning: What's your question? *National Teacher Education Journal*, *6*(2), 21–25.

Marshall, J. C. (2013). *Succeeding with inquiry in science and math classrooms.* ASCD., doi:10.2505/9781416616085

Marshall, J. C., & Horton, R. M. (2011). The relationship of teacher-facilitated, inquiry-based instruction to student higher-order thinking. *School Science and Mathematics*, *111*(3), 93–101. doi:10.1111/j.1949-8594.2010.00066.x

Martin, L. (2010). *Relationship between teacher preparedness and inquiry-based instructional practices to students' science achievement. Evidence from TIMSS 2007* [Unpublished doctoral dissertation, Indiana University of Pennsylvania].

Martinez, A., & Christnacht, C. (2021, January 26). *Women are nearly half of U.S. workforce but only 27% of STEM workers*. United States Census Bureau. https://www.census.gov/library/stories/2021/01/women-making-gains-in-stem-occupations-but-still-underrepresented.html

Marx, R. W., & Harris, C. J. (2006). No Child Left Behind and science education: Opportunities, challenges, and risks. *The Elementary School Journal*, *106*(5), 455–466. doi:10.1086/505441

Masters, H. (2020). Using Teaching Rehearsals to Prepare Preservice Teachers for Explanation-Driven Science Instruction. *Journal of Science Teacher Education*, *31*(4), 414–434. doi:10.1080/1046560X.2020.1712047

Math Learning Center. (2022). *Pattern Shapes*. MLC. https://apps.mathlearningcenter.org/pattern-shapes/

Mau, W., Chen, S., & Lin, C. (2020). Social cognitive factors of science, technology, engineering, and mathematics career interests. *International Journal for Educational and Vocational Guidance*, *21*(1), 47–60. doi:10.1007/s10775-020-09427-2

McCall, M. (2017). Elementary Pre-Service Science Teaching Efficacy and Attitude Toward Science: Can A College Science Course Make A Difference? *The Electronic Journal of Science Education*, *21*(6).

McCarthy, J. (2019, October 23). 3 common PBL problems- and solutions. *Edutopia*. https://www.edutopia.org/article/3-common-pbl-problems-and-solutions/

McClure, E., Guernsey, L., Clements, D., Bales, S., Nichols, J., Kendall-Taylor, N., & Levine, M. (2017). Guest editorial: How to integrate STEM into early childhood education. *Science and Children*, *55*(2), 8–10. doi:10.2505/4/sc17_055_02_8

McConnell, J. (2017). A model for understanding teachers' intentions to remain in STEM education. *International Journal of STEM Education*, *4*(1), 1–21. https://doi-org.proxy006.nclive.org/10.1186/s40594-017-0061-8

McConnell, T. J., Parker, J. M., & Eberhardt, J. (2017). Assessing teachers' science content knowledge: A strategy for assessing depth of understanding. *Journal of Science Teacher Education*, *24*(4), 717–743. doi:10.1007/s10972-013-9342-3

Mehrotra, G. R., Hudson, K. D., & Self, J. M. (2017). What Are We Teaching in Diversity and Social Justice Courses? A Qualitative Content Analysis of MSW Syllabi. *Journal of Teaching in Social Work*, *37*(3), 218–233. doi:10.1080/08841233.2017.1316342

Mergler, A. G., & Tangen, D. (2010). Using microteaching to enhance teacher efficacy in pre-service teachers. *Teaching Education*, *21*(2), 199–210. doi:10.1080/10476210902998466

Merrimack College. (2022). *Merrimack College Teacher Survey*. Merrimack College. https://www.merrimack.edu/academics/education-and-social-policy/merrimack-college-teacher-survey

Meyer, D. K., Turner, J. C., & Spencer, C. A. (1997). Challenge in a mathematics classroom: Students' motivation and strategies in project-based learning. *The Elementary School Journal*, *97*(5), 501–521. doi:10.1086/461878

Mezirow, J. (1985). A critical theory of self-directed learning. *New Directions for Continuing Education*, *25*, 17–30.

Midgley, C., Anderman, E., & Hicks, L. (1995). Differences between elementary and middle school teachers and students: A goal theory approach. *The Journal of Early Adolescence*, *15*(1), 90–113. doi:10.1177/0272431695015001006

Milner, A. R., Sondergeld, T. A., Demir, A., Johnson, C. C., & Czerniak, C. M. (2011). Elementary teachers' beliefs about teaching science and classroom practice: An examination of pre/post NCLB testing in science. *Journal of Science Teacher Education*, *23*(2), 111–132. doi:10.1007/s10972-011-9230-7

Milner-Bolotin, M. (2018). Evidence-based research in STEM teacher education: From theory to practice. *Frontiers in Education*, *3*, 389767. https://doi.org/10.3389/feduc.2018.00092

Milner, R. IV. (2011). Culturally relevant pedagogy in a diverse urban classroom. *The Urban Review*, *43*(1), 66–89. doi:10.1007/s11256-009-0143-0

Ministry of Education. (2021). STEM Oman Overview of external undergraduate scholarships. *Ministry of Education Ministry of Higher Education, Research and Innovation*. MoE. https://heac.gov.om/media/doc/DE001_2021.pd

Minner, D. D., Levy, A. J., & Century, J. (2010). Inquiry-based science instruction – what is it and does it matter? Results from a research synthesis years 1984 – 2002. *Journal of Research in Science Teaching*, *47*(4), 474–496. doi:10.1002/tea.20347

Compilation of References

Mishra, S., Yadav, V. K., Trivedi, M. C., & Shrimali, T. (2018). Audio steganography techniques: A survey. In *Advances in Computer and Computational Sciences: Proceedings of ICCCCS 2016, Volume 2* (pp. 581-589). Springer Singapore.

Mishra, P., & Koehler, M. J. (2006). Technological Pedagogical Content Knowledge: A Framework for Integrating Technology in Teacher Knowledge. *Teachers College Record, 108*, 1017–1054. doi:10.1111/j.1467-9620.2006.00684.x

Mohammed, S., & Kinyo, L. (2020). Constructivist Theory as a Foundation for the Utilization of Digital Technology in the Lifelong Learning Process. *Turkish Online Journal of Distance Education, 21*(4), 90–109. doi:10.17718/tojde.803364

Molnar, A., Miron, G., Barbour, M. K., Huerta, L., Shafer, S. R., Rice, J. K., Glover, A., Browning, N., Hagle, S., & Boninger, F. (2021). *Virtual Schools in the U.S. 2021*. National Education Policy Center. https://nepc.colorado.edu/publication/virtual-schools-annual-2021

Monteiro, M., Cabeza, C., Martí, A., Vogt, P., & Kuhn, J. (2014). Angular velocity and centripetal acceleration relationship. *The Physics Teacher, 52*(5), 312–313. Advance online publication. doi:10.1119/1.4872422

Monteiro, M., Stari, C., Cabeza, C., & Marti, A. C. (2019, August). Physics experiments using simultaneously more than one smartphone sensors. []. IOP Publishing.]. *Journal of Physics: Conference Series, 1287*(1), 012058. doi:10.1088/1742-6596/1287/1/012058

Moore, T. J., Johnson, C. C., Peters-Burton, E. E., & Guzey, S. S. (2015). The need for a STEM road map. In C. C. Johnson, E. E. Peters-Burton, & T. J. Moore (Eds.), *STEM road map: a framework for integrated STEM education*. Routledge. doi:10.4324/9781315753157-1

Morales, L. G. C., Chicaiza, C. V. V., Valles, V. M. R., & Armas, J. A. C. (2021). El Software Microsoft Math Solver como recurso tecnológico para la resolución de problemas de Matemática. *Revista Conrado, 17*(S1), 168–175.

Moreu, G., Isenberg, N., & Bräuer, M. (2021). How to promote diversity and inclusion in educational settings: Behaviour change, climate surveys, and effective Pro-Diversity initiatives. *Frontiers in Education, 6*, 668250. doi:10.3389/feduc.2021.668250

Morris, D., Usher, E., & Chen, J. (2017). Reconceptualizing the sources of teaching self-efficacy: A critical review of emerging literature. *Educational Psychology Review, 29*(4), 795–833. doi:10.1007/s10648-016-9378-y

Morrison, K. A., Robbins, H. H., & Rose, D. G. (2008). Operationalizing culturally relevant pedagogy: A synthesis of classroom-based research. *Equity & Excellence in Education, 41*(4), 433–452. doi:10.1080/10665680802400006

Moyer, P. S. (2001). Are we having fun yet? How teachers use manipulatives to teach mathematics. *Educational Studies in Mathematics, 47*(2), 175–197. doi:10.1023/A:1014596316942

Município, S. P. (2019). Secretaria municipal de educação. coordenadoria pedagógica. currículo da cidade: Ensino fundamental [ed. São Paulo: SME/COPED.]. *La Matematica, 2*.

Munoz, L., Villarreal, V., Morales, I., Gonzalez, J., & Nielsen, M. (2020). Developing an interactive environment through the teaching of mathematics with small robots. *Sensors (Basel)*, *20*(7), 1935. doi:10.3390/s20071935 PMID:32235658

Murphy, T. P., & Mancini-Samuelson, G. J. (2012). Graduating STEM competent and confident teachers: The creation of a STEM certificate for elementary education majors. *Journal of College Science Teaching*, *42*(2), 18–23. https://login.proxy006.nclive.org/login?url=https://www-proquest-com.proxy006.nclive.org/scholarly-journals/graduating-stem-competent-confident-teachers/docview/1151391363/se-2

My Byline Media. (2022). *Readability formulas: The Fry graph readability formula.* https://readabilityformulas.com/fry-graph-readability-formula.php

Nadelson, L. S., Callahan, J., Pyke, P., Hay, A., Dance, M., & Pfiester, J. (2013). Teacher STEM perception and preparation: Inquiry-based STEM professional development for elementary teachers. *The Journal of Educational Research*, *106*(2), 157–168. doi:10.1080/00220671.2012.667014

Naharuddin, A., Wibawa, A. D., & Sumpeno, S. (2018, August). A high capacity and imperceptible text steganography using binary digit mapping on ASCII characters. In *2018 International Seminar on Intelligent Technology and Its Applications (ISITIA)* (pp. 287-292). IEEE. 10.1109/ISITIA.2018.8711087

NASA.gov. (2022). *Creating a sundial and what makes day and night.* NASA. https://www.eyeonthesky.org/lessonplans/14sun_sundials.html

National Academies of Sciences, Engineering, and Medicine. (1997). *Science teaching reconsidered: A handbook.* The National Academies Press. doi:10.17226/5287

National Research Council (NRC). (2012). *A framework for K-12 science education: Practices, crosscutting concepts, and core ideas.* National Academies Press. doi:10.17226/13165

National Research Council. (1996). *National Science Education Standards.* National Academy Press.

National Research Council. (2001). *Adding It Up: Helping Children Learn Mathematics.* The National Academies Press., doi:10.17226/9822

National Research Council. (2012). A framework for K-12 science education: Practices, crosscutting concepts and core ideas. Committee on Conceptual Framework for the New K-12 Science Education Standards. Board on Science Education, Division of Behavioral and Social Sciences and Education, Washington.

National Science Board (NSB). (2016). *Science and engineering indicators.* National Science Foundation.

Nazerian, T. (2020). Looking ahead: Four ways 2020 might share the future of teacher prep. *Literacy Today*, *38*(3), 26–29.

Compilation of References

Newton, D. P., & Newton, L. D. (2001). Subject content knowledge and teacher talk in the primary science classroom. *European Journal of Teacher Education*, *24*(3), 369–379. doi:10.1080/02619760220128914

Nganga, L., & Akpovo, S. M. (2020). Culturally inclusive and contextually appropriate instructional practices: Rethinking pedagogical perspectives, practices, policies, and experiences in early childhood education programs. *Journal of Research in Childhood Education*, *34*(1), 2–5. doi:10.1080/02568543.2019.1697153

NGSS Lead States. (2013). *Next Generation Science Standards: For States, By States*. The National Academies Press.

NGSS Lead States. (2013). *Next generation science standards: For states, by states*. The National Academies Press., doi:10.17226/18290

Nkrumah, T., & Scott, K. A. (2022). Mentoring in STEM higher education: A synthesis of the literature to (re)present the excluded women of colour. *International Journal of STEM Education*, *9*(1), 50. doi:10.1186/s40594-022-00367-7 PMID:35919282

North Carolina Department of Public Instruction. (2018). *North Carolina teacher evaluation process. Public Schools of North Carolina. State Board of Education*. Department of Public Instruction. https://ncchildcare.ncdhhs.gov/Portals/0/documents/pdf/2/2018_NCTeacherEvaluation_NCEES_Teacher_Manual.pdf?ver=O2SejpORRPS0nwdqgzDeNw%3d%3d

Nowicki, B. L., Sullivan-Watts, B., Shim, M. K., Young, B., & Pockalny, R. (2012). Factors influencing science content accuracy in elementary inquiry science lessons. *Research in Science Education*, *43*(3), 1135–1154. doi:10.1007/s11165-012-9303-4

Nuryantini, A. Y., & Yudhiantara, R. A. (2019). The Use of Mobile Application as a Media in Physics Learning. *Jurnal Penelitian dan Pembelajaran IPA*, *5*(1), 72-83.

O'Leary, E. S., Shapiro, C., Toma, S., Sayson, H. W., Levis-Fitzgerald, M., Johnson, T., & Sork, V. L. (2020). Creating inclusive classrooms by engaging STEM faculty in culturally responsive teaching workshops. *International Journal of STEM Education*, *7*(1), 32. doi:10.1186/s40594-020-00230-7 PMID:32647597

Orben, A., & Przybylski, A. K. (2019). The association between adolescent well-being and digital technology use. *Nature Human Behaviour*, *3*(2), 173–182. doi:10.1038/s41562-018-0506-1 PMID:30944443

Ortiz, N. A., & Ruwe, D. (2022). Black English and mathematics education: A critical look at culturally sustaining pedagogy. *Teachers College Record*, *123*(10), 185–212. doi:10.1177/01614681211058978

Ozdemir, O., & Isik, H. (2015). Effect of inquiry-based activities on prospective elementary teachers' use of science process skills and inquiry strategies. *Journal of Turkish Science Education*, *12*(1), 43–56. doi:10.12973/tused.10132a

Padilla, D. B., Martínez, A. J., Bravo, C. B., & Meneses, E. L. (2021). Didactic resources in augmented reality to improve ubiquitous learning. In *Accessibility of vulnerability Groups: from ICTS to Emotions* (pp. 25–42). Dykinson. doi:10.2307/j.ctv282jg7b.5

Palid, O., Cashdollar, S., Deangelo, S., Chu, C., & Bates, M. S. (2023). Inclusion in practice: A systematic review of diversity-focused STEM programming in the United States. *International Journal of STEM Education*, *10*(1), 2. doi:10.1186/s40594-022-00387-3

Pan, Z., Zhu, J., Hu, W., Lun, H. P., & Zhou, X. (2005). Interactive learning of cg in networked virtual environments. *Computers & Graphics*, *29*(2), 273–281. doi:10.1016/j.cag.2004.12.014

Paris, D. (2012). Culturally sustaining pedagogy: A needed change in stance, terminology, and practice. *Educational Researcher*, *41*(3), 93–97. doi:10.3102/0013189X12441244

Park, C. S., & Kaye, B. K. (2019). Smartphone and self-extension: Functionally, anthropomorphically, and ontologically extending self via the smartphone. *Mobile Media & Communication*, *7*(2), 215–231. doi:10.1177/2050157918808327

Parker, F., Bartell, T. G., & Novak, J. D. (2017). Developing culturally responsive mathematics teachers' evolving conceptions of knowing students. *Journal of Mathematics Teacher Education*, *20*, 385–407. doi:10.1007/s10857-015-9328-5

Parnell, A. (2022, February 6). You are a data person. *Inside Higher Education*. https://www.insidehighered.com/news/2022/02/07/why-everyone-higher-education-data-person

Patchen, T., & Cox-Petersen, A. (2008). Constructing cultural relevance in science: A case study of two elementary teachers. *Science Education*, *92*(6), 994–1014. doi:10.1002/sce.20282

Patrick, S. (2021). Transforming Learning through Competency-Based Education. *State Education Standard*, *21*(2), 23–29.

Pauline, R. F. (1993). Microteaching: An integral part of a science methods class. *Journal of Science Teacher Education*, *4*(1), 9–17. doi:10.1007/BF02628852

Pearson, P. D., Moje, E., & Greenleaf, C. (2010). Literacy and science: Each in the service of the other. *Science*, *328*(5977), 459–463. doi:10.1126/science.1182595 PMID:20413491

Pedaste, M., Maeots, M., Siiman, L. A., De Jong, T., Van Reisen, S. A., Kamp, E. T., Manoli, C. C., Zacharia, Z. C., & Tsourlidaki, E. (2015). Phases of inquiry-based learning: Definitions and the inquiry cycle. *Educational Research Review*, *14*, 47–61. doi:10.1016/j.edurev.2015.02.003

Pighini, C. (2020). *Development and evaluation of an Android app to exploit smartphone-embedded camera and inertial sensors for monitoring of physiological parameters.* [Master's degree thesis].

Plaia, A., & Ruggieri, M. (2011). Air quality indices: A review. *Reviews in Environmental Science and Biotechnology*, *10*(2), 165–179. doi:10.1007/s11157-010-9227-2

Plumley, C. L. (2019). *2018 NSSME+: Status of elementary school science*. Horizon Research.

Compilation of References

Powell, L. M., & Karafinski, A. (2021). Awareness of volunteer computing on the grid: Content within it texts. *Issues in Information Systems*, *22*(1), 246–254.

Powell-Moman, A. D., & Brown-Schild, V. B. (2011). The influence of a two-year professional development institute on teacher self-efficacy and use of inquiry-based instruction. *Science Educator*, *20*(2), 47–53.

Public Schools of North Carolina (2023). Report to the North Carolina General Assembly: 2021-2022 state of the teaching profession in North Carolina. https://www.google.com/url?client=internal-element-cse&cx=007953340131544038496:b3cb1hux6m4&q=https://www.dpi.nc.gov/districts-schools/districts-schools-support/district-human-capital/surveys-and-reports&sa=U&ved=2ahUKEwirqtiW0pmDAxWuFlkFHcbdBUcQFnoECAEQAQ&usg=AOvVaw3tHYhHWw5zOewmQf97KyWN

Public Schools of North Carolina. (2022). *Report to the North Carolina General Assembly 2020-2021 State of the Teaching Profession in North Carolina*. Public Schools of North Carolina. https://www.google.com/url?client=internal-element-cse&cx=007953340131544038496:b3cb1hux6m4&q=https://www.dpi.nc.gov/documents/advancedlearning/cihs/2022-ccp-cihs-annual-report/download%3Fattachment&sa=U&ved=2ahUKEwirqtiW0pmDAxWuFlkFHcbdBUcQFnoECAMQAQ&usg=AOvVaw0zX-u7iuOuSV6gPiLE5-Os

Puckett, T. (2020). The importance of developing cultural competence. In Innovations in higher education teaching and learning (pp. 7–22). doi:10.1108/S2055-364120200000028004

Ramazanoglu, M. (2020). The Relationship between High School Students' Internet Addiction, Social Media Disorder, and Smartphone Addiction. *World Journal of Education*, *10*(4), 139–148. doi:10.5430/wje.v10n4p139

Read, W. Think. (2005). *Discussion web*. https://www.readwritethink.org/files/resources/lesson_images/lesson819/graphic-organizer.pdf

Readingquest.org. (n.d.). *Story map*. Reading Quest. https://www.readingquest.org/pdf/story_map.pdf

Regents of the University of Minnesota. (2022). *Education resources for teachers: Cloze procedure*. UMN. https://dhh-resources.umn.edu/language-literacy/k-12-reading-strategies/cloze-procedure/

Reimer, K., & Moyer, P. S. (2005). Third-graders learn about fractions using virtual manipulatives: A classroom study. *Journal of Computers in Mathematics and Science Teaching*, *24*(1), 5–25.

Remesh, A. (2013). Microteaching, an efficient technique for learning effective teaching. *Journal of Research in Medical Sciences*, *18*(2), 158–163. PMID:23914219

Ribeiro, M. I. C., & Passos, O. M. (2020). A study on the active methodologies applied to teaching and learning process in the computing area. *IEEE Access : Practical Innovations, Open Solutions*, *8*, 219083–219097. doi:10.1109/ACCESS.2020.3036976

Richmond, G., Bartell, T. G., Floden, R. E., & Jones, N. D. (2019). How research sheds light on the pivotal role of mentors in teacher preparation. *Journal of Teacher Education*, *71*(1), 6–8. doi:10.1177/0022487119887752

Riegle-Crumb, C., Morton, K., Moore, C., Chimonidou, A., Labrake, C., & Kopps, S. (2015). Do inquiring minds have positive attitudes? The science education of preservice elementary teachers. *Science Education*, *99*(5)m 819 – 836. https://doi.otg/10.1002/sce.21177

Riggs, I., & Enochs, L. (1990). Toward the development of an elementary teacher's science teaching efficacy belief instrument. *Science Education*, *74*(6), 625–637. doi:10.1002/sce.3730740605

Rinke, C. R., Gladstone-Brown, W., Kinlaw, C. R., & Cappiello, J. (2016). Characterizing STEM teacher education: Affordances and constraints of explicit STEM preparation for elementary teachers. *School Science and Mathematics*, *116*(6), 300–309. doi:10.1111/ssm.12185

Rodríguez-García, A. M., Moreno-Guerrero, A. J., & Lopez Belmonte, J. (2020). Nomophobia: An individual's growing fear of being without a smartphone—a systematic literature review. *International Journal of Environmental Research and Public Health*, *17*(2), 580. doi:10.3390/ijerph17020580 PMID:31963208

Rodriguez, J. L., Jones, E. B., Pang, V. O., & Park, C. D. (2004). Promoting academic achievement and identity development among diverse high school students. *High School Journal*, *87*(3), 44–53. doi:10.1353/hsj.2004.0002

Roumell, E. A. (2019). Priming adult learners for learning transfer: Beyond content and delivery. *Adult Learning*, *30*(1), 15–22. doi:10.1177/1045159518791281

Sackes, M. (2014). How often do early childhood teachers teach science concepts? Determinants of the frequency of science teaching in kindergarten. *European Early Childhood Education Research Journal*, *22*(2), 169–184. doi:10.1080/1350293X.2012.704305

Sadler, P. M., Sonnert, G., Hazari, Z., & Tai, R. (2012). Stability and volatility of STEM career interest in high school: A gender study. *Science Education*, *96*(3), 411–427. doi:10.1002/sce.21007

Salcines-Talledo, I., González-Fernández, N., & Briones, E. (2020). The Smartphone as a pedagogic tool. Student profiles as related to its use and knowledge. [NAER Journal]. *Journal of New Approaches in Educational Research*, *9*(1), 91–109. doi:10.7821/naer.2020.1.454

Salehi, S., Ballen, C. J., Trujillo, G., & Wieman, C. (2021). Inclusive instructional practices: Course design, implementation, and discourse. *Frontiers in Education*, *6*, 602639. Advance online publication. doi:10.3389/feduc.2021.602639

Salinas, I., Monteiro, M., Martí, A. C., & Monsoriu, J. A. (2020). Analyzing the dynamics of a yo-yo using a smartphone gyroscope sensor. *The Physics Teacher*, *58*(8), 569–571. doi:10.1119/10.0002379

Compilation of References

Samsuar, S., Artika, W., Sarong, M. A., Rahmatan, H., & Pada, A. U. T. (2021, May). Smartphone microscope based on the STEM approach as a practicum tool to improve students' scientific attitudes on Animalia. []. IOP Publishing.]. *Journal of Physics: Conference Series*, *1882*(1), 012158. doi:10.1088/1742-6596/1882/1/012158

Santana, O. A., de Sousa, B. A., do Monte, S. R. S., de Freitas Lima, M. L., & Silva, C. F. (2020). Deep learning practice for high school student engagement in stem careers. In *2020 IEEE Global Engineering Education Conference (EDUCON)* (pp. 164–169). IEEE. 10.1109/EDUCON45650.2020.9125281

Santau, A. O., Maerten-Rivera, J. L., Bovis, S., & Orend, J. (2014). A mile wide or an inch deep? Improving elementary preservice teachers' science content knowledge within the context of a science methods course. *Journal of Science Teacher Education*, *25*(8), 953–976. doi:10.1007/s10972-014-9402-3

Sawchuk, S. (2016, March 30). Can "micro-credentialing" salvage teacher PD? *Education Week*, *35*(26).

Schmid, M. E., Gillian-Daniel, D. L., Kraemer, S., & Kueppers, M. (2016). Promoting student academic achievement through faculty development about inclusive teaching. *Change*, *48*(5), 16–25. doi:10.1080/00091383.2016.1227672

Schmidt, K. M., & Kelter, P. (2017). Science fairs: A qualitative study of their impact on student science inquiry learning and attitudes toward STEM. *Science Educator*, *25*(2), 126–132.

Science Learning Hub – Pokapū Akoranga Pūtaiao. (2012, April 5). *Pinhole cameras and eyes*. https://www.sciencelearn.org.nz/resources/58-pinhole-cameras-and-eyes

Semiz, K., & Ince, M. L. (2012). Preservice physical education teachers' technological pedagogical content knowledge, technology integration self-efficacy and instructional technology outcome expectations. *Australasian Journal of Educational Technology*, *28*(7). doi:10.14742/ajet.800

Serban, C., & Vescan, A. (2020). Towards an evaluation process around active learning based methods. In *2020 IEEE Frontiers in Education Conference (FIE)* (pp. 1–7). IEEE. 10.1109/FIE44824.2020.9273935

Settlage, J., Southerland, S. A., Smith, L. K., & Ceglie, R. (2009). Constructing a doubt-free teaching self: Self-efficacy, teacher identity, and science instruction within diverse settings. *Journal of Research in Science Teaching*, *46*(1), 102–125. doi:10.1002/tea.20268

Seymour, E., & Hewitt, N. M. (1997). *Talking about leaving*. Westview Press.

Seymour, E., Hunter, A. B., Harper, R. P., & Holland, D. G. (2019). *Talking about leaving revisited. Talking About Leaving Revisited: Persistence*. Relocation, and Loss in Undergraduate STEM Education. doi:10.1007/978-3-030-25304-2

Shahat, M. A., Al-Balushi, S. M., Abdullah, S., & Al-Amri, M. (2023b). *Pre- and In-service STEM Teachers' Skills in Preparing Engineering Design-based Activities: A Systematic Literature Review*. [Submitted for publication]

Shahat, M. A., & Al Amri, M. (2023). Science Teacher Preparation in Oman: Strengths and Shortcomings Related to STEM Education. In S. M. Al-Balushi, L. Martin-Hansen, & Y. Song (Eds.), *Reforming Science Teacher Education Programs in the STEM Era*. Palgrave Studies on Leadership and Learning in Teacher Education. Palgrave Macmillan. doi:10.1007/978-3-031-27334-6_10

Shahat, M. A., & Al-Balushi, S. M. (2023). The development of STEM education in the Sultanate of Oman. In *STEM Education Approaches and Challenges in the MENA Region* (pp. 56–73). IGI Global. doi:10.4018/978-1-6684-6883-8.ch003

Shahat, M. A., Al-Balushi, S. M., & Al-Amri, M. (2022). Investigating pre-service science teachers' self-efficacy beliefs for teaching science through engineering design processes. *Interdisciplinary Journal of Environmental and Science Education*, *18*(4), 2291. doi:10.21601/ijese/12121

Shahat, M. A., Al-Balushi, S. M., & Al-Amri, M. (2023a). Measuring preservice science teachers' performance on engineering design process tasks: Implications for fostering STEM education. *Arab Gulf Journal of Scientific Research*. doi:10.1108/AGJSR-12-2022-0277

Shaughnessy, M., DeFino, R., Pfaff, E., & Blunk, M. (2021). I think I made a mistake: How do prospective teachers elicit the thinking of a student who has made a mistake? *Journal of Mathematics Teacher Education*, *24*(4), 335–359. doi:10.1007/s10857-020-09461-5

Sherin, M. G., & Van Es, E. A. (2005). Using Video to Support Teachers' Ability to Notice Classroom Interactions. *Journal of Technology and Teacher Education*, *13*(3), 475–491.

Shin, M., Park, J., Grimes, R., & Bryant, D. P. (2021). Effects of using virtual manipulatives for students with disabilities: Three-level multilevel modeling for single-case data. *Exceptional Children*, *87*(4), 418437. doi:10.1177/00144029211007150

Shulman, L. (1986). Those who understand: Knowledge growth in teaching. *Educational Researcher*, *15*(1), 4–14. doi:10.2307/1175860

Shulman, L. (1987). Knowledge and teaching: Foundations of the new reform. *Harvard Educational Review*, *57*(1), 1–22. doi:10.17763/haer.57.1.j463w79r56455411

Shulman, L. S. (1986). Paradigms and research programs in the study of teaching: A contemporary perspective. In M. C. Wittrock (Ed.), *Handbook of research on teaching* (3rd ed., pp. 3–36). McMillan Publishing Company.

Sinclair, N., & Robutti, O. (2020). Teaching practices in digital environments. Encyclopedia of mathematics education, 845-849.

Sindel, K. D. (2010). *Can experiential education strategies improve elementary science teachers' perceptions of and practices in science teaching?* [Doctoral dissertation].

Singer, A., Montgomery, G. M., & Schmoll, S. (2020). How to foster the formation of STEM identity: Studying diversity in an authentic learning environment. *International Journal of STEM Education*, *7*(1), 57. doi:10.1186/s40594-020-00254-z

Compilation of References

Singha, R., & Singha, S. (2023). Faith and Culture in Education: Fostering Inclusive Environments. In J. DeHart (Ed.), *The Role of Faith and Religious Diversity in Educational Practices* (pp. 149–172). IGI Global. doi:10.4018/978-1-6684-9184-3.ch007

Singha, S. (2023). Culturally Relevant Teaching in Humanities: E-Book Creation, Blogging, and Bookmaking. In D. M. Frazier (Ed.), *Teaching Humanities With Cultural Responsiveness at HBCUs and HSIs* (pp. 121–146). IGI Global. doi:10.4018/978-1-6684-9782-1.ch006

Singha, S., & Singha, R. (2023a). Understanding diversity: The power of differences. In A. M. Even & B. Christiansen (Eds.), *Enhancing Employee Engagement and Productivity in the Post-Pandemic Multigenerational Workforce* (pp. 297–313). IGI Global. doi:10.4018/978-1-6684-9172-0.ch015

Singha, S., Singha, R., & Ruben, V. M. (2023). Explorations of the Links Between Multiculturalism and Religious Diversity. In J. DeHart (Ed.), *The Role of Faith and Religious Diversity in Educational Practices* (pp. 120–148). IGI Global. doi:10.4018/978-1-6684-9184-3.ch006

Skilbeck, M., & Connell, H. (2004). Teachers for the Future: The Changing Nature of Society and Related Issues for the Teaching Workforce. *Ministerial Council on Education, Employment, Training and Youth Affairs (NJ1)*.

Sleeter, C. E. (2008), Preparing white teachers for diverse students, in Cochran-Smith, M., FeimanNemser, S., McIntyre, D.J. and Demers, K.E. (Eds), Handbook of Research on Teacher Education: Enduring Questions in Changing Contexts. Routledge.

Sleeter, C. E. (2017). Critical race theory and the whiteness of teacher education. *Urban Education*, 52(2), 155–169. doi:10.1177/0042085916668957

Smith, M. G., & Schlaack, N. (2021). Teaching during a pandemic: Elementary candidates' experiences with engagement in distance education. *I*, 9(4), 7–22. doi:10.22492/ije.9.4.01

Soboleva, E. V., Chirkina, S. E., Kalugina, O. A., Shvetsov, M. Y., Kazinets, V. A., & Pokaninova, E. B. (2020). Didactic Potential of Using Mobile Technologies in the Development of Mathematical Thinking. *Eurasia Journal of Mathematics, Science and Technology Education*, 16(5), em1842. doi:10.29333/ejmste/118214

Soltis, L. (2016). Do mathematics courses for elementary teachers contribute to the development of mathematical knowledge needed for teaching of preservice elementary teachers? *National Teacher Education Journal*, 9(1), 71–76.

Somyürek, S. (2014). An effective educational tool: Construction kits for fun and meaningful learning. *International Journal of Technology and Design Education*, 25(1), 25–41. doi:10.1007/s10798-014-9272-1

Song, Y., Martin-Hansen, L., Akerson, V. L., Buck, G. A., & Al-Balushi, S. M. (2023). STEM Teacher Education: An Overview. Palgrave studies leadership and learning in teacher education (pp. 1–15). Springer. doi:10.1007/978-3-031-27334-6_1

Songer, N. B., Lee, H.-S., & Kam, R. (2002). Technology-rich inquiry science in urban classrooms: What are the barriers to inquiry pedagogy? *Journal of Research in Science Education*, *39*(2), 128–150. doi:10.1002/tea/10013

Spangler, D. (2019). Micro Approach, Major Impact: With Microcredentials, Educators Can Tailor Learning to Their Specific Needs. *Learning Professional*, *40*(4), 60–64.

Spronken-Smith, R., & Walker, R. (2010). Can inquiry-based learning strengthen the links between teaching and disciplinary research? *Studies in Higher Education*, *35*(6), 723–740. doi:10.1080/03075070903315502

Stahl, S. A. (1999, November 1). Why innovations come and go (and mostly go): The case of whole language. *Educational Researcher*, *28*(8), 13. Advance online publication. doi:10.2307/1176312

Steen, K., Brooks, D., & Lyon, T. (2006). The impact of virtual manipulatives on first grade geometry instruction and learning. *Journal of Computers in Mathematics and Science Teaching*, *25*(4), 373–391.

Subramanya, S., & Farahani, A. (2012). Point-of-view article on: Design of a smartphone app for learning concepts in mathematics and engineering. *International Journal of Innovation Science*, *4*(3), 173–184. doi:10.1260/1757-2223.4.3.173

Suh, J., & Moyer, P. S. (2007). Developing students' representation fluency using virtual and physical algebra balances. *Journal of Computers in Mathematics and Science Teaching*, *26*(2), 155–173.

Suh, J., Moyer, P. S., & Heo, H. (2005). Examining technology uses in the classroom: Developing fraction sense using virtual manipulative concept tutorials. *Journal of Interactive Online Learning*, *3*(4), 1–21.

Sunyoung, H. A. N., Rosli, R., Capraro, M. M., & Capraro, R. M. (2016). The effect of science, technology, engineering and mathematics (STEM) project-based learning (PBL) on students' achievement in four mathematics topics. *Journal of Turkish Science Education*, *13*(special), 3.

Suriel, R. L., & Litster, K. (2022). They expose inequities within teacher professional development and its impact on advancing equity, diversity and social justice in STEM education. In Springer eBooks (pp. 105–124). Springer. doi:10.1007/978-3-031-08150-7_6

Su, X., Tong, H., & Ji, P. (2014). Activity recognition with smartphone sensors. *Tsinghua Science and Technology*, *19*(3), 235–249. doi:10.1109/TST.2014.6838194

Swars, S. L., Daane, C. J., & Giesen, J. (2006). Mathematics anxiety and mathematics teacher efficacy: What is the relationship in elementary preservice teachers? *School Science and Mathematics*, *106*(7), 306–315. doi:10.1111/j.1949-8594.2006.tb17921.x

Sweifach, J. S. (2015). Has group work education lost its social group work essence? A content analysis of MSW course syllabi in search of mutual aid and group conflict content. *Journal of Teaching in Social Work*, *35*(3), 279–295. doi:10.1080/08841233.2015.1031928

Compilation of References

Taie, S., & Goldring, R. (2019). *Characteristics of Public and Private Elementary and Secondary Schools in the United States: Results From the 2017–18 National Teacher and Principal Survey First Look (NCES 2019-140)*. U. S. D. o. Education. https://nces.ed.gov/pubsearch/pubsinfo.asp?pubid=2019140

Tairab, H., & Al-Naqbi, A. (2017). Provision of inquiry instruction and actual level of practice as perceived by science teachers and their students. *Eurasia Journal of Mathematics, Science and Technology Education*, *14*(1). doi:10.12973/ejmste/80320

Tamim, S. R., & Grant, M. M. (2013). Definitions and uses: Case study of teachers implementing project-based learning. *The Interdisciplinary Journal of Problem-Based Learning*, *7*(2), 3. doi:10.7771/1541-5015.1323

Taranto, E., Robutti, O., & Arzarello, F. (2020). Learning within MOOCs for mathematics teacher education. *ZDM*, 1-15.

Tarman, B. (2012). Prospective Teachers' Beliefs and Perceptions about Teaching as a Profession. *Educational Sciences: Theory & Practice*, *12*(3), 1964–1973.

Tate, W. F. (1995). Returning to the root: A culturally relevant approach to mathematics pedagogy. *Theory into Practice*, *34*(3), 166–173. doi:10.1080/00405849509543676

Teachnology, Inc. (n.d.). *How to study better using SQ3R. Teachnology*. https://www.teach-nology.com/teachers/lesson_plans/interdisciplinary/usingsq3r.html

TeachThought. (2022). *Reading comprehension strategies*. TechThought. https://www.teachthought.com/literacy/reading-strategies/

Technology Publishing Company. (2003). *Teacher workbooks: Graphic organizer series*. TPC. https://www.actedu.in/wp-content/uploads/2016/03/Science-Graphic-Organizers.pdf

Teixeira, R. L. P., Silva, P. C. D., Shitsuka, R., de Araujo Brito, M. L., & Kaizer, B. M., & e Silva, P. D. C. (2020). Project based learning in engineering education in close collaboration with industry. In *2020 IEEE Global Engineering Education Conference (EDUCON)* (pp. 1945–1953). 10.1109/EDUCON45650.2020.9125341

Temel Dogan, D., & Ozgeldi, M. (2018). How do preservice mathematics teachers use virtual manipulatives to teach algebra through lesson study? *Necatibey Faculty of Education Electronic Journal of Science and Mathematics Education*, *12*(1), 152–179.

Than, W. W., & Shan, P. W. (2021). Prevalence of Nomophobia among Undergraduate Students from Sagaing University of Education. *International Review of Social Sciences Research*, *1*(1), 54–76. doi:10.53378/346475

Thorsteinson, K. (2018). Anarchy in the classroom: The efficacy of self-directed learning for critical whiteness pedagogy. Transformations. *The Journal of Inclusive Scholarship & Pedagogy*, *28*(1), 38–60. https://doi-org.proxy006.nclive.org/10.1353/tnf.2018.0003

Tippett, C. D., & Milford, T. M. (2017). Findings from a pre-kindergarten classroom: Making the case for STEM in early childhood education. *International Journal of Science and Mathematics Education*, *15*(1), 67–86. doi:10.1007/s10763-017-9812-8

Tokac, U., Novak, E., & Thompson, C. G. (2019). Effects of game-based learning on students' mathematics achievement: A meta-analysis. *Journal of Computer Assisted Learning*, *35*(3), 407–420. doi:10.1111/jcal.12347

Tooley, M., & Hood, J. (2021, January 13) *Harnessing micro-credentials for teacher growth: a model state policy guide.* Washington, DC: New America, p. 9. https://www.newamerica.org/education-policy/reports/harnessing-micro-credentials-for-teacher-growth-a-model-state-policy-guide/

Trent, M., & Gurvitch, R. (2015). Fostering Teacher Candidates' Reflective Practice through Video Editing. *Journal of Physical Education, Recreation & Dance*, *86*(5), 5, 14–20. doi:10.1080/07303084.2015.1022674

Trumper, R. (2006). Factors affecting junior high school students' interest in physics. *Journal of Science Education and Technology*, *15*(1), 47–58. https://doi-org.proxy006.nclive.org/10.1007/s10956-006-0355-6

Trygstad, P. J. (2013). *National survey of science and mathematics education: Status of elementary school science.* Horizon Research. http://www.horizon-research.com/2012ns-sme/wp-content/uploads/2013/09/2012-NS-SME-The-Status-of-Elementary-Science.pdf

Tseng, K. H., Chang, C. C., Lou, S. J., & Chen, W. P. (2013). Attitudes towards science, technology, engineering and mathematics (STEM) in a project-based learning (PjBL) environment. *International Journal of Technology and Design Education*, *23*(1), 87–102. doi:10.1007/s10798-011-9160-x

United States Department of Education. (2017). Reimagining the role of technology in education: 2017. *National education technology plan update.* US DoE. https://tech.ed.gov/files/2017/01/NETP17.pdf

Van de Walle, J. A., Karp, K. S., & Bay-Williams, J. M. (2019). *Elementary and middle school mathematics: Teaching developmentally* (10th ed.). Pearson.

VanLone, J., Pansé-Barone, C., & Long, K. (2022). Teacher preparation and the COVID-19 disruption: Understanding the impact and implications for novice teachers. *International Journal of Educational Research Open*, *3*, 100120. doi:10.1016/j.ijedro.2021.100120 PMID:35059675

Varma, T., & Hanuscin, D. L. (2008). Pre-service elementary teachers' field experiences in classrooms led by science specialists. *Journal of Science Teacher Education*, *19*(6), 593–614. doi:10.1007/s10972-008-9110-y

Viberg, O., Gronlund, Å. A., & Andersson, A. (2020). Integrating digital technology in mathematics education: A Swedish case study. *Interactive Learning Environments*, 1–12.

Vieyra, R., Vieyra, C., Jeanjacquot, P., Marti, A., & Monteiro, M. (2015). Turn your smartphone into a science laboratory. *Science Teacher (Normal, Ill.)*, *82*(9), 32. doi:10.2505/4/tst15_082_09_32

Compilation of References

Vilorio, D. (2014). STEM 101: Intro to tomorrow's jobs. *Occupational Outlook Quarterly*, 2–12. http://www.bls.gov/caree routlook/

Vogt, P., & Kuhn, J. (2012). Analyzing free fall with a smartphone acceleration sensor. *The Physics Teacher*, *50*(3), 182–183. doi:10.1119/1.3685123

Vygotsky, L. S. (1978). *Mind in society: The development of higher psychological processes*. Harvard University Press.

Walker, C. L., McGill, M. T., Buikema, A. L., & Stevens, A. M. (2008). Implementing inquiry-based learning in teaching serial dilutions. *Journal of College Science Teaching*, *37*(6), 56–61.

Wang, A. I., & Tahir, R. (2020). The effect of using Kahoot! for learning–A literature review. *Computers & Education*, *149*, 103818. doi:10.1016/j.compedu.2020.103818

Wang, P., Wu, P., Yu, K., & Lin, Y. (2015). Influence of implementing inquiry-based instruction on science learning motivation and interest: A perspective of comparison. *Procedia: Social and Behavioral Sciences*, *174*(12), 1292–1299. doi:10.1016/j.sbspro.2015.01.750

Wang, W., Schmidt-Crawford, D., & Jin, Y. (2018). Preservice teachers' TPACK development: A review of literature. *Journal of Digital Learning in Teacher Education*, *34*(4), 234–258. doi: 10.1080/21532974.2018.1498039

Watkins, J., & Mazur, E. (2013). Retaining students in science, technology, engineering, and mathematics (STEM) majors. *Journal of College Science Teaching*, *42*(5), 36–41.

Weber, R. P. (1990). Basic content analysis. Springer. doi:10.4135/9781412983488

Welder, R. M., & Champion, J. (2011). Toward an understanding of graduate preservice elementary teachers as adult learners of mathematics. *Adults Learning Mathematics*, *6*(1), 20–40.

Wendell, K. B. (2014). Design practices of preservice elementary teachers in an integrated engineering and literature experience. *Journal of Pre-College Engineering Education Research*, *4*(2), 4. doi:10.7771/2157-9288.1085

Western Governors University. (2022). *Elementary math methods: Unit 7*. Tools for Mathematics. [WGU Learning Resource, Elementary Math Methods]

West, J. D., & Bergstrom, C. T. (2021). Misinformation in and about science. *Proceedings of the National Academy of Sciences of the United States of America*, *118*(15), e1912444117. doi:10.1073/pnas.1912444117 PMID:33837146

WETA Public Broadcasting. (2022a). *Reading rockets: Anticipation guide*. WETA. https://www.readingrockets.org/strategies/anticipation_guide/

WETA Public Broadcasting. (2022b). *Reading rockets: Directed reading/thinking activity (DR-TA)*. WETA. https://www.readingrockets.org/strategies/drta

WETA Public Broadcasting. (2022c). *Reading rockets: List-group-label*. WETA. https://www.readingrockets.org/strategies/list_group_label

WETA Public Broadcasting. (2022d). *Reading rockets: Semantic feature analysis*. WETA. https://www.readingrockets.org/strategies/semantic_feature_analysis

WETA Public Broadcasting. (2022e). *Reading rockets: Strategies that promote comprehension*. WETA. https://www.readingrockets.org/article/29202/

WETA Public Broadcasting. (2022f). *Word maps*. Reading rockets. https://www.readingrockets.org/strategies/word_maps

White, T. G., Graves, M. F., & Slater, W. H. (1990). Growth of reading vocabulary in diverse elementary schools: Decoding and word meaning. *Journal of Educational Psychology, 82*(2), 281–290. doi:10.1037/0022-0663.82.2.281

Wiksten, S. (2019). Talking About Sustainability in Teacher Preparation in Finland and the United States. [NJCIE]. *Nordic Journal of Comparative and International Education, 3*(1), 69–87. doi:10.7577/njcie.3302

Williams, J. A. III, & Glass, T. S. (2019). Teacher education and multicultural courses in North Carolina. *Journal for Multicultural Education, 13*(2), 155–168. doi:10.1108/JME-05-2018-0028

Williams, J. A. III, & Lewis, C. W. (2020). Enriching their potential: Supporting Black male teacher candidates in the age of edTPA. *Peabody Journal of Education, 95*(5), 472–483. doi:10.1080/0161956X.2020.1828685

Williams, M. K. (2017). John Dewey in the 21st century. *Journal of Inquiry and Action in Education, 9*(1), 91–102.

Wisconsin Department of Public Instruction. (2023). *Clarifying literacy in science*. Science. https://dpi.wi.gov/science/disciplinary-literacy/types-of-literacy

Wolfram, S. (2017). *An elementary introduction to the wolfram language*. Wolfram Media, Incorporated.

Wong, R. S. M., Ho, F. K. W., Wong, W. H. S., Tung, K. T. S., Chow, C. B., Rao, N., Chn, K. L., & Ip, P. (2018). Parental involvement in primary school education: Its relationship with children's academic performance and psychosocial competence through engaging children with school. *Journal of Child and Family Studies, 27*(5), 1544–1555. doi:10.1007/s10826-017-1011-2

Xie, Y., & Shauman, K. A. (2003). *Women in science: Career processes and outcomes*. Harvard University Press.

Yager, R. E. (2005). Achieving the staff development model advocated in the national standards. *Science Educator, 14*, 16–24.

Yang, Y., Ruan, Z., Wang, X., Yang, Y., Mason, T. G., Lin, H., & Tian, L. (2019). Short-term and long-term exposures to fine particulate matter constituents and health: A systematic review and meta-analysis. *Environmental Pollution, 247*, 874–882. doi:10.1016/j.envpol.2018.12.060 PMID:30731313

Compilation of References

Yannier, N., Hudson, S. E., & Koedinger, K. R. (2020). Active Learning is About More Than Hands-On: A Mixed-Reality AI System to Support STEM Education. *International Journal of Artificial Intelligence in Education*, *30*(1), 74–96. doi:10.1007/s40593-020-00194-3

Yildirim, B., Topalcengiz, E. S., Arikan, G., & Timur, S. (2020). Using virtual reality in the classroom: Reflections of STEM teachers on the use of teaching and learning tools. *Journal of Education in Science, Environment and Health*, *6*(3), 231–245. doi:10.21891/jeseh.711779

Young, J. R., Ortiz, N., & Young, J. L. (2017). STEMulating interest: A meta-analysis of the effects of out-of-school time on student STEM interest. *International Journal of Education in Mathematics. Science and Technology*, *5*(1), 62–74. doi:10.18404/ijemst.61149

Yuzbasheva, G., & Kravtsov, H. (2020). Augmented and Virtual Reality Technologies in Teacher Retraining.

Zafeirakopoulos, M., & van der Bijl-Brouwer, M. (2018). Exploring the transdisciplinary learning experiences of innovation professionals. *Technology Innovation Management Review*, *8*(8), 50–59. doi:10.22215/timreview/1178

Zeichner, K. (2010). Rethinking the connections between campus courses and field experiences in college-and university-based teacher education. *Journal of Teacher Education*, *61*(1–2), 89–99. doi:10.1177/0022487109347671

Zembal-Saul, C., Blumenfeld, P., & Krajcik, J. (2000). Influence of guided cycles of planning, teaching, and reflection on prospective elementary teachers' science content representations. *Journal of Research in Science Teaching*, *37*(4), 318–339.

Zhang, J.-H., Zou, L., Miao, J., Zhang, Y.-X., Hwang, G.-J., & Zhu, Y. (2020). An individualized intervention approach to improving university students' learning performance and interactive behaviors in a blended learning environment. *Interactive Learning Environments*, *28*(2), 231–245. doi:10.1080/10494820.2019.1636078

Zhelezniakov, D., Cherneha, A., Zaytsev, V., Ignatova, T., Radyvonenko, O., & Yakovchuk, O. (2020, March). Evaluating new requirements to pen-centric intelligent user interface based on end-to-end mathematical expressions recognition. In *Proceedings of the 25th International Conference on Intelligent User Interfaces* (pp. 212-220). ACM. 10.1145/3377325.3377482

Zhou, G., Xu, J., & Martinovic, D. (2016). Developing pre-service teachers' capacity in teaching science with technology through microteaching lesson study approach. *Eurasia Journal of Mathematics, Science and Technology Education*, *13*(1), 85–103. doi:10.12973/eurasia.2017.00605a

Zoehfeld, K. W., & Meisel, P. (1998). *What is the world made of? All about solids, liquids, and gases*. HarperCollins.

About the Contributors

Emily Cayton Ph.D. is an Associate Professor in the School of Education and Human Sciences at Campbell University where she serves as the Coordinator of the Interdisciplinary Studies MEd. Program and is the Science Education specialist. Her research focuses on funding for science instructional materials and ensuring students in rural areas have access to high quality science instruction. Dr. Cayton is a former middle and high school science teacher, teaching in Wilson County Schools before pursuing her Master's and Doctorate from North Carolina State University.

Miriam Sanders is a doctoral candidate studying Curriculum and Instruction with an emphasis in Mathematics Education. Through her research she seeks to address issues of equity and diversity in mathematics education regarding mathematics intervention, culturally responsive mathematics instruction, and female students' STEM career interests.

John A. Williams III, Ph.D. is an Assistant Professor of Multicultural Education at Texas A&M University at College Station. His research focuses on developing and replicating best practices, policies, and personnel to dismantle inequitable discipline outcomes for African American students in K-12 school environments. Additionally, his research investigates how to prepare and support culturally inclusive teachers through the adaptation of multiculturalist frameworks.

***

Khalsa Hamed AL-Bahri is an Assessment officer in Ministry of Education, Oman. She is a Ph.D. student in curriculum and science education at Sultan Qaboos University. She is a STEM trainer in the Oman STEM program. She participated in multiple national conferences and published some articles nationally and internationally as a co-author.

About the Contributors

Sulaiman M. Al-Balushi is a professor of science education at Sultan Qaboos University (SQU) in Oman. He is the director of the Quality Assurance Office at Sultan Qaboos University. He served as the Dean of the College of Education (SQU) for six years (2014-2020) and was a visiting scholar at the University of Exeter (2020-2021). He contributed mainly to leading the SQU College of Education to attain international academic accreditation by NCATE in the USA in 2016. He is also a member of the Board of the Oman Academic Accreditation Authority (OAAA) and a member of different journal advisory and editorial boards. He has also been awarded various national and international university teaching, research, and reviewing awards.

Franklin S. Allaire, Ph.D. is an Associate Professor of Science Education in the Department of Urban Education at the University of Houston-Downtown where he teaches undergraduate and graduate courses in elementary and secondary science methods. His research interests focus on issues impacting the success of historically marginalized peoples in STEM-related fields and the innovative use of technologies and pedagogies in the professional development of science teachers and teacher candidates.

Elizabeth Allison received her PhD from the University of Alabama in 2015. She has served as an Assistant Professor and Instructor of elementary math and science methods, curriculum, and instruction. Prior to her time in higher education, Elizabeth was a National Board Certified Teacher with experience at the elementary and secondary levels. She publishes and presents in the areas of elementary STEM education, multiliteracies, and innovative methodology course structure and practices. She is currently the Associate Dean of National Educator Preparation for Western Governors University.

Kim Brown is an Associate Professor, the Associate Chairperson, and the Director of Accreditation and Assessment for the Department of Education at the University of North Carolina Asheville. Kim holds a doctorate in Educational Leadership, a master's degree in Curriculum and Instruction, and 9 teaching licenses. Kim teaches numerous teacher licensure courses, and her areas of expertise include Educational Assessment, Elementary Science Methods, and Elementary Literacy Methods. Kim is passionate about helping future teachers gain the skills inherent in effectively teaching a diversity of students and effective implementation of trauma-informed practices.

About the Contributors

Alessio Drivet obtained a degree at the University of Trento in 1975. Since 1976 he has been a lecturer in Mathematics, Probability and Statistics at the Commercial Institutes, retired in 2011. He has published books and articles on mathematics and computer science at various publishing houses. Since 1987 he has been engaged in contract training activities for the University of Turin and the Italian Ministry of Education. He is part of the scientific and organizational committee of DI.FI.MA and is a member of the GeoGebra Institute of Turin. He is currently working on the diffusion of mathematics among secondary school students.

Adam Hiebel spent over ten years in the K-12 institution teaching math, science, and social studies to elementary and middle school students. Adam also served as a district-wide gifted/curriculum coordinator for a large suburban school district. Adam currently teaches introduction to education and methods courses at Western Governors University. Adam received his Bachelor and Master Degrees in Education from The Ohio State University, a Master of Art in Biology Education from Western Governors University, Gifted Endorsement from the University of Cincinnati, Master of Science Degree in Psychology from Capella, Doctoral Degree in Education from Ohio University, Doctoral Degree in Psychology from CalSouthern, and Juris Doctor Degree from Purdue Global.

Amanda Kain is a dedicated educator who is passionate about demystifying mathematics and increasing conceptual knowledge. Amanda believes all students can be successful in math class when educators find ways to engage students in content and find strategies that work for them. Amanda is currently a Faculty Manager at Western Governors University with extensive experience in both math curriculum and teaching mathematics. Amanda earned her Bachelor of Arts degree from the University of Missouri – Columbia, Master of Education Degree from the University of Missouri - Saint Louis and Doctorate in Education from The University of Missouri- Kansas City.

Pollyana Notargiacomo was graduated in Pedagogy (1992) by the University of São Paulo, an institution where she also earned the title of Master (1999) and Doctor of Education (2003). In 2015 she obtained the Post Doctoral degree in Electrical Engineering by the Federal University of Uberlândia (UFU). She is currently a Professor at Mackenzie Presbyterian University, where she develops research and teaching activities at the Information and Computer College and Electrical Engineering and Computer Graduate Course. Among her areas of research, the following

About the Contributors

subjects stand out: Use of Technology in Education, Interactive Learning Environments, Learning Management Systems, Instructional Design, Education Applied to Computing, Serious Games, Culture Studies, Game Design, and Social Media. She was also awarded, with the Outstanding Paper Award in IADIS International Conference e-Society 2007.

Carol PeQueen received her BS in Mathematics from Furman University, her MS in Systems Engineering from the University of Florida, and in 2016 earned a PhD in Instructional Design from Keiser University. She has experience teaching in both K-12 and higher education environments, and has spent the last decade working in the field of teacher preparation. Carol currently serves as a senior instructor in the School of Education at Western Governors University, supporting courses in WGU's Initial Licensure Programs in Elementary Education. Her research interests include effective instructional methods in the online environment, particularly in STEM content areas, and innovative approaches to support the reimagination of teacher preparation and professional development.

Kristie Remaly received a Bachelor's Degree in Elementary and Early Childhood Education from Kutztown University, a Master's Degree in Elementary Education from University of Hawaii, and a Doctorate in Educational Leadership from the University of Phoenix. She is currently a math methods and science methods instructor at Western Governors University (WGU), where she has worked since 2017. Prior to her work with WGU, she worked in K-12 education for 20 years as an elementary school teacher and high school administrator. She served as an adjunct faculty and has supervised several student teachers. Research interests include teacher preparation as well as coaching and mentoring preservice teachers.

Megan Rzyski received her BS in Education from the University of Delaware and her MA in Mathematics Education from Western Governors University. In 2016 she was hired as a Program Mentor for Secondary Math Education at Western Governors University and is currently a senior instructor for Math and Science Methods at Western Governors University. Her research interests include effective pedagogical practices specific to math and science, distance learning, and educational technology.

Mohamed A. Shahat is an Associate Professor of science education at Sultan Qaboos University (SQU), Oman, and at Aswan University (AU), Egypt. He earned his Ph.D. in science education from the University of Duisburg-Essen, Germany. He attained a post-doctoral fellowship at the University of Duisburg-Essen. Currently, he is leading various national research projects, including STEM education at SQU.

He participated in multiple national and international conferences. He published articles in national and international journals. He published chapters in regional and global edited books. He is a member of different national and international journal editorial boards. He has also been awarded other teaching and research awards.

Surjit Singha is an academician with a broad spectrum of interests, including UN Sustainable Development Goals, Organizational Climate, Workforce Diversity, Organizational Culture, HRM, Marketing, Finance, IB, Global Business, Business, AI, Women Studies, and Cultural Studies. Currently a faculty member at Kristu Jayanti College, Dr. Surjit also serves as an Editor, reviewer, and author for prominent global publications and journals, including being on the Editorial review board of Information Resources Management Journal and a contributor to IGI Global. With over 13 years of experience in Administration, Teaching, and Research, Dr. Surjit is dedicated to imparting knowledge and guiding students in their research pursuits. As a research mentor, Dr. Surjit has nurtured young minds and fostered academic growth. Dr. Surjit has an impressive track record of over 75 publications, including articles, book chapters, and textbooks, holds two US Copyrights, and has successfully completed and published two fully funded minor research projects from Kristu Jayanti College.

Maiya A. Turner is a doctoral student in the Multicultural Education Program in the Department of Teaching, Learning, and Culture at Texas A&M University. Her research agenda centers Black educators and their retention and recruitment into the teaching profession to diversify the teacher workforce. Her experiences include serving as a High School English Language Arts teacher leader at an urban high school in Texas. Upon graduation, she hopes to train preservice teachers on the university level and continue to do the work that centers and empowers educators in education.

Jennifer Wallender received her BS in Education from Minot State University, an MS in Education Leadership from the University of Mary, and a Ph.D. in Teaching and Learning from the University of North Dakota. In 2016, she was hired and is currently a senior instructor for Math and Science Methods at Western Governors University. Her research interests include effective pedagogical practices specific to math and science, social-emotional learning, trauma-informed practices, and neurodiversity.

About the Contributors

Sandy Watson is an Associate Professor of Curriculum & Instruction at the University of Louisiana Monroe where she teaches undergraduate and graduate courses in multiculturalism and curriculum. Her research interests include science education, curriculum studies, multiculturalism and diversity, and teacher education. An educator for 26+ years, Dr. Watson has published many articles and has presented at multiple conferences across her research areas.

Erin West is a passionate advocate for children and education. She completed her doctorate in educational leadership at Appalachian State in 2022. She has served in many capacities in education, including K-12 school administration, and taught preschool, elementary, and college. Her research interests include educational policy, early care and education, curriculum, and educational leadership.

Index

5E Lesson Plan 75-76

A

academic achievement 31, 298
academic performance 59, 61, 158-159, 164, 175, 191-192, 197
acoustic stopwatch 203, 215
active modeling 132, 152
App 198, 201-203, 205, 208, 211, 215, 218-219, 271

C

Combined Class 160, 169-173
Common Core 15, 251, 254, 261-262, 267, 271, 275, 281
competency-based micro-credentials 88, 91
competency-based model 131
Conceptual Understanding 114, 130-131, 134-136, 138-139, 143, 150-152, 157
Constructivism 26, 72, 157, 259
course descriptions 25, 31, 33-40, 42
COVID-19 111-112, 118, 120, 123, 131, 136, 196
Crosscutting Concepts 140-141, 143, 157, 232-234, 237, 246
curricular integration 251, 254, 263

D

Distance Learning 196

E

education programs 5, 7, 33, 40, 59, 69-70, 73-74, 248
Educator Preparation 25-26, 28, 41, 86-88, 100, 104
Elementary Education 2-3, 5, 33, 35, 40, 60, 62, 150, 251, 257, 286-287, 289, 302, 304, 306, 310
elementary teacher candidates 112-113
Elementary Teacher Preparation 50, 124
engineering practices 29, 232-234, 237-238, 246, 248-249
English Language Arts 251, 254, 267
EPPs 25-30, 32-33, 35-36, 40-43, 86-87, 100, 104

I

Inclusive Pedagogy 296, 310
Inclusivity 53, 60, 286-291, 294-296, 299-307, 311
inquiry-based instruction 71-76
inquiry-based investigations 68, 73
Inquiry-Based Learning 58, 62, 70, 72, 74-75, 78, 133, 267
Integrated Teaching 254-255, 257, 260

J

John Dewey 252, 254

K

K–12 Education 131

L

lesson planning 8, 76, 137, 231, 236, 238-239, 246-249

M

Mathematical Representation 157
Mathematics 14-15, 25-26, 33, 35, 38-41, 50, 54-55, 57, 64, 69-70, 88, 114-115, 130-136, 138-139, 144, 147, 150-152, 157, 159, 161, 163, 184, 191, 197, 200, 203, 205, 213, 215, 219, 236-237, 246, 258, 267, 294-295, 302-303, 311
Mathematics Methods 39-40, 132-133, 151-152, 157
Methods Courses 3-5, 7, 26-30, 33-36, 39-43, 69-71, 74-75, 111, 124, 132, 137, 150-151
microteaching 111-112, 114-117, 124
M-learning 197, 219
Municipal Public School 160, 164, 191

N

NFC 201, 218-219
NGSS Standards 70

O

online learning 89, 91, 111-112, 120, 124, 132, 134, 136, 138, 202
Online pedagogy 136
Online teacher 125, 132-133, 152
online teaching 112, 120, 132, 137

P

Pedagogical Content 2-3, 6-7, 27, 40, 68-69, 117, 234-235, 248
Pedagogical Content Knowledge 2-3, 6-7, 27, 40, 68-69, 117, 234-235, 248
People of Color 25-26
practice teaching 76, 111-112, 115-117
Pragmatism 251, 254, 263, 267
preparation programs 7-10, 25-26, 51-53, 71, 86-88, 100, 104, 113-114, 117, 131-134, 136-138, 150, 152, 286-291, 298-302, 304-307
Preservice Teachers 1, 7-12, 15-16, 29, 42, 68-70, 73-74, 131-132, 137
Procedural Fluency 134, 144, 157
professional development 5-6, 32, 50, 55, 57-59, 62-65, 70-71, 86-90, 92, 94, 97, 99-104, 114, 151, 231-235, 238-239, 246-250, 289, 294, 300-301, 304
professional learning 87-93, 96-103, 105, 232
PSTs 25-26, 30-31, 35, 38-40

S

Science Content Knowledge 3, 68-71, 74, 76, 78, 113-114
Science Methods 3-4, 11, 13, 35, 39-40, 68, 70-71, 74-78, 111-112, 114-115, 117-118, 124, 251, 257
science teaching 8, 69-71, 113-115, 118-119, 124-125, 232, 235, 238, 253, 259-260, 262
Self-Directed learning 86, 88-89, 91, 93-94, 96-103, 105
Self-efficacy 2-3, 6, 8, 11-12, 52, 69, 74, 78, 101, 103, 113-114, 117, 164
standardized testing 114-115
STEM 1, 3-7, 9-16, 25-29, 31-37, 39-43, 50-65, 86-88, 91-92, 100-101, 104-105, 158-159, 162-163, 192, 196, 198, 200, 202, 211, 219, 232, 248, 258, 267, 286-290, 292-296, 298-307, 311
STEM Education 2, 50-54, 56-65, 88, 105, 158-159, 162, 267, 286-289, 294-296, 298-299, 301-307
STEM Teacher Preparation 52, 55-56, 100, 286-291, 298-302, 304-307, 311

Index

T

TAM 219
teacher education 5, 7, 28, 50-52, 55, 59, 64, 69-70, 73-74, 87, 104, 113, 143, 248, 254, 257, 263
teacher educators 40, 111-112
Teacher Preparation 7-9, 50-57, 60-61, 64, 71, 88, 90, 100, 104, 112-114, 117, 124-125, 131-138, 150-152, 258, 286-291, 298-302, 304-307, 311
Teaching Tools 198
Traditional class 160-161, 165, 172-173, 175

U

urban school district 233

V

Virtual Environments 130, 157
Virtual Manipulatives 134-136, 150-152
Virtual reality 211, 305

W

Webinars 131, 133-134, 136, 139-140, 143-144, 151-152
Wolfram Alpha 158-161, 165-167, 169-175, 177-179, 182-185, 187, 189, 192

Recommended Reference Books

IGI Global's reference books are available in three unique pricing formats:
Print Only, E-Book Only, or Print + E-Book.
Order direct through IGI Global's Online Bookstore at **www.igi-global.com** or through your preferred provider.

ISBN: 9781799897064
EISBN: 9781799897088
© 2022; 302 pp.
List Price: US$ 215

ISBN: 9781799889854
EISBN: 9781799889878
© 2022; 383 pp.
List Price: US$ 215

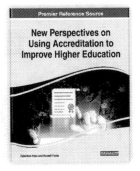

ISBN: 9781668451953
EISBN: 9781668451960
© 2022; 300 pp.
List Price: US$ 215

ISBN: 9781799852001
EISBN: 9781799852018
© 2022; 355 pp.
List Price: US$ 215

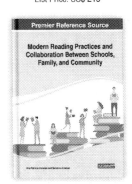

ISBN: 9781799897507
EISBN: 9781799897521
© 2022; 304 pp.
List Price: US$ 215

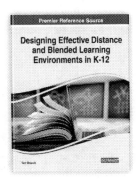

ISBN: 9781799868293
EISBN: 9781799868316
© 2022; 389 pp.
List Price: US$ 215

Do you want to stay current on the latest research trends, product announcements, news, and special offers?
Join IGI Global's mailing list to receive customized recommendations, exclusive discounts, and more.
Sign up at: **www.igi-global.com/newsletters**.

Publisher of Timely, Peer-Reviewed Inclusive Research Since 1988

www.igi-global.com   Sign up at www.igi-global.com/newsletters   facebook.com/igiglobal   twitter.com/igiglobal

Ensure Quality Research is Introduced to the Academic Community

Become an Reviewer for IGI Global Authored Book Projects

The overall success of an authored book project is dependent on quality and timely manuscript evaluations.

Applications and Inquiries may be sent to:
development@igi-global.com

Applicants must have a doctorate (or equivalent degree) as well as publishing, research, and reviewing experience. Authored Book Evaluators are appointed for one-year terms and are expected to complete at least three evaluations per term. Upon successful completion of this term, evaluators can be considered for an additional term.

If you have a colleague that may be interested in this opportunity, we encourage you to share this information with them.

Submit an Open Access Book Proposal

Have Your Work Fully & Freely Available Worldwide After Publication

Seeking the Following Book Classification Types:
Authored & Edited Monographs • Casebooks • Encyclopedias • Handbooks of Research

Gold, Platinum, & Retrospective OA Opportunities to Choose From

Easily Track Your Work in Our Advanced Manuscript Submission System With **Rapid Turnaround Times**

Double-Blind Peer Review by Notable Editorial Boards (*Committee on Publication Ethics* (COPE) Certified

Publications Adhere to All **Current OA Mandates & Compliances**

Affordable APCs *(Often 50% Lower Than the Industry Average)* Including Robust Editorial Service Provisions

Direct Connections with **Prominent Research Funders** & OA Regulatory Groups

Institution Level OA Agreements Available (Recommend or Contact Your Librarian for Details)

Join a **Diverse Community of 150,000+ Researchers Worldwide** Publishing With IGI Global

Content Spread Widely to Leading Repositories (AGOSR, ResearchGate, CORE, & More)

Retrospective Open Access Publishing

You Can Unlock Your Recently Published Work, Including Full Book & Individual Chapter Content to Enjoy All the Benefits of Open Access Publishing

Learn More

Publishing Tomorrow's Research Today
IGI Global
e-Book Collection

Including Essential Reference Books Within Three Fundamental Academic Areas

Business & Management
Scientific, Technical, & Medical (STM)
Education

- Acquisition options include Perpetual, Subscription, and Read & Publish
- No Additional Charge for Multi-User Licensing
- No Maintenance, Hosting, or Archiving Fees
- Continually Enhanced Accessibility Compliance Features (WCAG)

| Over 150,000+ Chapters | Contributions From 200,000+ Scholars Worldwide | More Than 1,000,000+ Citations | Majority of e-Books Indexed in Web of Science & Scopus | Consists of Tomorrow's Research Available Today! |

Recommended Titles from our e-Book Collection

Innovation Capabilities and Entrepreneurial Opportunities of Smart Working
ISBN: 9781799887973

Advanced Applications of Generative AI and Natural Language Processing Models
ISBN: 9798369305027

Using Influencer Marketing as a Digital Business Strategy
ISBN: 9798369305515

Human-Centered Approaches in Industry 5.0
ISBN: 9798369326473

Modeling and Monitoring Extreme Hydrometeorological Events
ISBN: 9781668487716

Data-Driven Intelligent Business Sustainability
ISBN: 9798369300497

Information Logistics for Organizational Empowerment and Effective Supply Chain Management
ISBN: 9798369301593

Data Envelopment Analysis (DEA) Methods for Maximizing Efficiency
ISBN: 9798369302552

Request More Information, or Recommend the IGI Global e-Book Collection to Your Institution's Librarian

For More Information or to Request a Free Trial, Contact IGI Global's e-Collections Team: eresources@igi-global.com | 1-866-342-6657 ext. 100 | 717-533-8845 ext. 100

Are You Ready to Publish Your Research?

IGI Global — PUBLISHER of TIMELY KNOWLEDGE

IGI Global offers book authorship and editorship opportunities across 11 subject areas, including business, computer science, education, science and engineering, social sciences, and more!

Benefits of Publishing with IGI Global:

- Free one-on-one editorial and promotional support.
- Expedited publishing timelines that can take your book from start to finish in less than one (1) year.
- Choose from a variety of formats, including Edited and Authored References, Handbooks of Research, Encyclopedias, and Research Insights.
- Utilize IGI Global's eEditorial Discovery® submission system in support of conducting the submission and double-blind peer review process.
- IGI Global maintains a strict adherence to ethical practices due in part to our full membership with the Committee on Publication Ethics (COPE).
- Indexing potential in prestigious indices such as Scopus®, Web of Science™, PsycINFO®, and ERIC – Education Resources Information Center.
- Ability to connect your ORCID iD to your IGI Global publications.
- Earn honorariums and royalties on your full book publications as well as complimentary content and exclusive discounts.

Join Your Colleagues from Prestigious Institutions, Including:

Australian National University
Massachusetts Institute of Technology
Johns Hopkins University
Harvard University
Columbia University in the City of New York

Learn More at: www.igi-global.com/publish
or by Contacting the Acquisitions Department at: acquisition@igi-global.com